THIRD EDITION

Basketball

STEPS TO SUCCESS

Hal Wissel

HUMAN KINETICS

Library of Congress Cataloging-in-Publication Data

Wissel, Hal, 1939-
Basketball : steps to success / Hal Wissel. -- 3rd ed.
p. cm.
ISBN-13: 978-1-4504-1488-3 (soft cover)
ISBN-10: 1-4504-1488-5 (soft cover)
1. Basketball--Training. 2. Basketball--Coaching. I. Title.
GV885.35.W55 2012
796.323--dc23
2011022943

ISBN-10: 1-4504-1488-5 (print)
ISBN-13: 978-1-4504-1488-3 (print)

The web addresses cited in this text were current as of July 2011, unless otherwise noted.

Managing Editor: Laura Podeschi; **Assistant Editor:** Elizabeth Evans; **Copyeditor:** Patrick Connolly; **Graphic Designer:** Keri Evans; **Graphic Artist:** Tara Welsch; **Cover Designer:** Keith Blomberg; **Photographer (cover):** © Human Kinetics; **Photographer (interior):** Chris Marion, unless otherwise noted; **Photo Asset Manager:** Laura Fitch; **Visual Production Assistant:** Joyce Brumfield; **Photo Production Manager:** Jason Allen; **Art Manager:** Kelly Hendren; **Associate Art Manager:** Alan L. Wilborn; **Illustrations:** © Human Kinetics; **Printer:** Versa Press

Human Kinetics books are available at special discounts for bulk purchase. Special editions or book excerpts can also be created to specification. For details, contact the Special Sales Manager at Human Kinetics.

Printed in the United States of America 10 9 8 7 6 5 4 3 2 1

The paper in this book is certified under a sustainable forestry program.

Human Kinetics
Website: www.HumanKinetics.com

United States: Human Kinetics
P.O. Box 5076
Champaign, IL 61825-5076
800-747-4457
e-mail: humank@hkusa.com

Canada: Human Kinetics
475 Devonshire Road Unit 100
Windsor, ON N8Y 2L5
800-465-7301 (in Canada only)
e-mail: info@hkcanada.com

Europe: Human Kinetics
107 Bradford Road
Stanningley
Leeds LS28 6AT, United Kingdom
+44 (0) 113 255 5665
e-mail: hk@hkeurope.com

Australia: Human Kinetics
57A Price Avenue
Lower Mitcham, South Australia 5062
08 8372 0999
e-mail: info@hkaustralia.com

New Zealand: Human Kinetics
P.O. Box 80
Torrens Park, South Australia 5062
0800 222 062
e-mail: info@hknewzealand.com

E5542

·dicated to
d M. Wissel
67–2000

Hal Wissel

Davı … ıo came in contact with him. … , and say good things about you.

The D … founded to continue his love for childre … pportunities that will foster their growth

David M… …outh Foundation
955 Russell Avenue
Suffield, CT 06078
www.highgoals.com

Contents

Acknowledgments

As with any project of this magnitude, many people have contributed to its successful completion. I would like to thank Human Kinetics for the opportunity to share my basketball experiences with others. Particular thanks go to Ted Miller, vice president of special acquisitions, Dr. Judy Patterson Wright, the developmental editor of the first edition, Cynthia McEntire, the developmental editor of the second edition, and Laura Podeschi, the managing editor of the third edition, whose patience, suggestions, and good humor helped me persevere through the writing. Thanks to Chris Marion, who took the photos for this new edition. Thanks also to the models in the photos, Monique Ambers, Devon Austin, Matthew Balaj, Christian Callahan, Jill Culbertson, Mychal Coleman, Harley Falasca, Stephen Frankoski, D'Andre McPhatter, Abejah McKay, Justin Nolan, Hannah Murphy, Andrea Wasik, Jabrille Williams, and Paul Wissel.

This book is based not only on my experiences as a coach, but also on my study of publications on playing and coaching basketball, attendance at numerous coaching clinics, and discussions about basketball with many coaches and players. I would like to express my sincere appreciation to Paul Ryan, my high school coach; Dr. Edward S. Steitz, my college mentor and advisor and the coach who gave me my first opportunity to coach at the college level; the inspiring coaches I have worked under, especially Hubie Brown, John Calipari, Mike Dunleavy, Frank Hamblen, Del Harris, Frank Layden, Don Nelson, and Lee Rose, who gave me opportunities to work in the National Basketball Association (NBA); my loyal and dedicated assistant coaches Wes Aldrich, Ralph Arietta, P.J. Carlesimo, Tim Cohane, Norm Gigon, Seth Hicks, Kevin McGinniss, Scott Pospichal, Joe Servon, Sam Tolkoff, Drew Tucker, and Melvin Watkins; Hank Slider, a master teacher who contributed greatly to my knowledge and understanding of shooting; and Stan Kellner, coach, author, and clinician, who stimulated my interest and research in sport psychology. Special thanks to the many dedicated players I have had the privilege of teaching and coaching and who continue to be a source of inspiration.

Last, thanks to my wife, Trudy, and our children, Steve, Scott, David, Paul, and Sharon, for listening to ideas, reading copy, and questioning methods, and especially for their love, understanding, and inspiration.

Introduction

Basketball is a team game in which you can help your team by improving your individual skills. Basketball requires integration of individual talent into unselfish team play. It requires the sound execution of fundamental skills, which, once learned, can be connected to the entire game. Basketball drills instill confidence, transfer skills to game situations, and contribute to long-term enjoyment.

CLIMBING THE STEPS TO BASKETBALL SUCCESS

Despite the size, conditioning, and talent of today's professional players, basketball success is still determined by one's ability to execute fundamental skills consistently. Fundamental skills include footwork, passing and catching, dribbling, shooting, shooting off the catch, creating your shot off the dribble, scoring in the post, and rebounding. These fundamental skills are integrated into unselfish team play, including fast break, two- and three-man plays, team offense, and team defense.

Although this book is a resource for teachers, coaches, and parents, it is primarily for the player. Players who love the game continually seek ways to improve their skills. This book focuses on the development of fundamental skills and their integration into team play through individual, small-group, and team drills. Disciplined practice of the principles described in this book will improve your skills and build your confidence.

With 12 steps total, this third edition provides a lot of new information for the player. Step 4, shooting (page 71), now includes information on shooting runners, reverse layups, and power moves, with additional drills. Three entirely new steps have also been added: step 5, shooting off the catch (page 114); step 6, creating your shot off the dribble (page 128); and step 7, scoring in the post (page 167). In today's game, more emphasis is placed on the spread offense. The international emphasis on using dribble penetration to draw defenders and then passing the ball out to other players for open three-point shots has become a trend. The National Basketball Association (NBA) rule changes that do not allow hand-checking have also contributed to this trend. The pick-and-roll and the pick-and-pop have become popular methods for gaining dribble penetration and then drawing opponents and kicking out to open shooters. Due to this trend, the new edition includes extensive coverage on executing the pick-and-roll in step 10, two- and three-man plays (page 251), and step 11, team offense (page 290), and defending the pick-and-roll in step 12, team defense (page 316).

Many young players become frustrated when they cannot shoot or handle the ball. Confidence-building offensive skills should be emphasized early because they take more time to master than skills that do not involve the ball. More advanced players improve through game competition and individual practice. Strong competition helps the advanced player improve and also reveals weaknesses to be corrected. Average players practice what they do well; exceptional players practice their weaknesses, turning them into strengths. If you have trouble shooting, learn to shoot the correct way and then practice. If you have trouble dribbling with your weak hand, practice dribbling with that hand. You will not only improve your skills, but you will increase your confidence as well.

Success depends on getting players to believe in themselves. Although confidence is greatest after success, you can develop confidence through practice. It is common to think of self-confidence in relation to natural physical talent. It is a mistake, however, to consider physical talent alone. In your playing career, you will come up against players with more physical talent. To have the confidence to defeat them, you must believe that you have worked harder and are better prepared, particularly in fundamental skills.

Each of the 12 steps in this book takes you to the next level of playing skill. The first few steps provide a solid foundation of fundamental skills and concepts. As you practice each fundamental skill, your progress will allow you to connect skills. Practicing common combinations of basketball skills will give you the experience you need to make quick, intelligent decisions on the court. You will learn to make the right moves in game situations. As you near the top of the staircase, you will become more confident in your ability to play and communicate with teammates.

Follow the same sequence with each step:

1. Read the explanation of the step, why it is important, and how to perform it.
2. Follow the photos or illustrations.
3. Review the missteps, which note common errors and corrections.
4. Perform the drills. Drills appear near the skill instructions so you can refer to the instructions easily if you have trouble with a drill.

Once you feel confident in your ability to perform the skill, have a qualified observer such as a coach, teacher, or skilled player evaluate your technique. This subjective evaluation of your skill will help you identify any weaknesses in technique before you move on to the next step.

THE SPORT OF BASKETBALL

Today, basketball is the fastest-growing sport in the world for many reasons. First, basketball is a tremendously popular spectator sport, particularly on television. The televising of NBA games worldwide and of men's and women's college games nationally has influenced many young athletes to participate in the sport. The international growth of basketball has created even more excitement and participation. Currently, over 200 countries have basketball federations.

The nature of the sport keeps people involved. Although basketball was invented to be an indoor sport, it is now played indoors and outdoors in all seasons. Almost 40 percent of play is outside in an unorganized environment.

Basketball is for everyone. Although it is an extremely youthful sport, with teenage males participating the most, it is played by both sexes of all ages and sizes and also by the physically challenged, including people in wheelchairs. Although there are advantages to being tall, there are also many opportunities for the smaller, skilled player. Participation among older players and female players is growing. More girls play interscholastic high school basketball than any other sport, and women's support groups are building networks that will continue the expansion of female participation.

Basketball competition is unique because, unlike other sports, it can be easily modified to accommodate smaller groups, different skill levels, and different kinds of players. Although most organized basketball competition consists of teams of five players, unorganized basketball competition can be played from full-court five-on-five to smaller groups of half-court three-on-three, two-on-two, or one-on-one. Growth in organized three-on-three basketball tournaments has been particularly rapid. The NBA is leading the way by sponsoring NBA Hoop It Up tournaments in more than 60 countries. Individual competition in the form of free-throw and other shooting contests sponsored by schools, clubs, and other organizations has also increased.

Finally, basketball can be played alone. All you need is a ball, a basket, a confined space (such as a driveway or playground), and your imagination to provide a competitive gamelike experience that other sports simply cannot match.

Equipment and Facilities

The circumference of a men's basketball is a maximum of 30 inches (76 cm) and a minimum of 29 1/2 inches (75 cm); a women's ball is a maximum of 29 inches (74 cm) and a minimum of 28 1/2 inches (72 cm).

The backboard measures 6 feet (1.8 m) horizontally and either 3 1/2 or 4 feet (1.1 or 1.2 m) vertically. A rectangular box measuring 24 inches (61 cm) horizontally and 18 inches (46 cm) vertically is centered on the backboard behind the ring (rim), with the top edge of its baseline level with the ring.

The basket is 18 inches (46 cm) in inside diameter and is attached to the backboard with its upper edge 10 feet (3 m) above the floor and its nearest edge 6 inches (15 cm) from the backboard.

The playing court is a rectangular surface 50 feet (15 m) by 94 feet (29 m)—usually 84 feet (26 m) for high schools. Markings designating specific areas of the court are shown in figure 1.

The free throw line is 15 feet (5 m) from the backboard. On high school courts, the three-point line is marked at 19 feet, 9 inches (5.8 m, 23 cm) from the center of the basket. On college courts, the three-point line is marked at 20 feet, 9 inches (6.1 m, 23 cm). On NBA courts, the three-point line is at 23 feet, 9 inches (7 m, 23 cm). On international courts, the three-point line is marked at 22 feet, 1.7 inches (6.7 m, 4 cm).

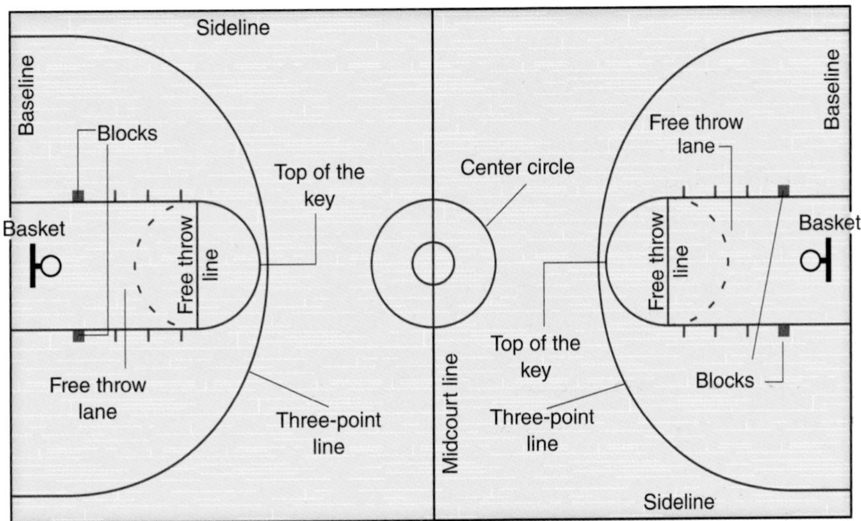

Figure 1 The basketball court.

It is likely the international three-point line will move toward the NBA distance in the next 10 years. The international three-second area has recently been reconfigured to match the NBA shape, going from a trapezoid to a rectangle.

Rules

Currently, several sets of basketball rules are in use worldwide. International rules for competition between nations are established by the Federation Interationale de Basketball (FIBA). In the United States, professional players play under the National Basketball Association (NBA) rules. College men and women play under separate sets of rules as established by the National Collegiate Athletic Association (NCAA). High schools play by rules established by the National Federation of State High School Associations (NFHS). In recent years, there has been a movement toward uniformity in rules. Differences remain, mostly in terms of length, distance, and time, rather than in substance and content. To foster children's enjoyment and development, modified rules have been devised calling for smaller basketballs, lower baskets, and scaled-down courts.

Professional games consist of four quarters of 12 minutes each. College games consist of two halves of 20 minutes each. High school games consist of four quarters of 8 minutes each. Overtime periods are used for tie games. The length of youth games is adjusted according to the age of the players.

Shot clocks vary in length for professional, international, college men's, college women's, and high school competition.

Warming Up and Cooling Down

Preparing your body for basketball practice or a game involves two phases: a five-minute warm-up to increase heart rate and basketball warm-up drills.

The first phase of preparing for strenuous basketball activity is to warm up with five minutes of offensive and defensive footwork. This will increase blood circulation and gradually prepare the body for the demands of basketball. Choose from warm-up activities such as trotting, changing pace and direction, and short sprints. Move from baseline to baseline on the court using a third of the width of the floor (lane line to lane line or lane line to sideline). Here are some offensive footwork drills described in step 1 (page 13):

- **Trotting.** Run easily from baseline to baseline and return. Do at least two round-trips.
- **Sprinting.** Sprint to the opposite free-throw line or free-throw line extended, change pace to a trot, and continue to the opposite baseline. Return in the same manner.
- **Change of pace.** Run from baseline to baseline, changing pace as you go. Return in the same manner.
- **Change of direction.** Run from baseline to baseline, changing direction as you go. Begin in an offensive stance with your left foot touching the intersection of the baseline and the lane line on your left. Run diagonally at a 45-degree angle to the lane line on your right. Make a sharp 90-degree change of direction from right to left and run diagonally to the imaginary lane line extended on your left. Make a sharp 90-degree change of direction from left to right. Continue in this manner to the opposite baseline. Return in the same manner.

Defensive footwork drills also make good warm-up drills. For each drill, start with your back to the far basket in a staggered defensive stance with one foot up, touching the baseline, and the other foot spread directly back. Here are some defense-inspired drills described in step 1 (page 26):

- **Zigzag.** Use defensive retreat steps to move back diagonally until your back foot touches the nearest sideline or lane line. Quickly drop-step with your lead foot and use retreat steps to move back diagonally until your back foot touches the nearest imaginary lane line extended or sideline. Continue changing direction at each imaginary lane line extended or sideline as you proceed to the opposite baseline. Return in the same manner.
- **Defensive attack and retreat.** Move backward using defensive attack and retreat steps until your back foot touches the half-court line. Quickly drop-step, moving the other foot back, and move backward to the baseline using attack and retreat steps until your back foot touches the baseline. Vary your attack and retreat steps as you move down the floor. Return in the same manner.
- **Reverse-run-and-turn.** Move backward using defensive attack and retreat steps. Imagine that a dribbler beats your lead foot and you must recover by using a reverse-run-and-turn. Reverse to the side of your lead foot, keeping your eyes on the imaginary dribbler, and run at least three steps before establishing a defensive position with your original lead foot up. From the baseline to the half-court line, make two reverse-run-and-turns starting with your left foot forward. From the half-court line to the opposite baseline, make two reverse-run-and-turns starting with your right foot forward. Return in the same manner.

The second phase of warming up includes basketball warm-up drills. The ballhandling warm-up described in step 2 (page 33) and the two-ball dribble drill described in step 3 (page 67) are excellent warm-up drills for the entire body. They also enhance ballhandling and dribbling skills and increase confidence. Step 4 describes several shooting warm-up drills. The hook shot warm-up (page 98) and alternate-hand hook shooting drill (page 99) are excellent for loosening the shoulders while helping develop strong- and weak-hand hook shots. The shooting warm-up drills (pages 78 to 80) help you warm up for shooting while enhancing shooting mechanics, rhythm, and confidence. The one-foot vertical jump training described in step 1 (page 17) and the toss-back passing drill (page 47) described in step 2 are also excellent basketball warm-up drills that improve skill and confidence.

At the end of basketball practice, take about five minutes to cool down. This is an excellent time to stretch because muscles are warm. Choose at least one stretch for each body part.

Key to Diagrams

Note to readers: The court diagram used throughout this book excludes many court markings so that the presentation of players' movements and passes will be as clear as possible. The college three-point line was included to serve as a distance reference point around the basket's perimeter. We hope this streamlined approach in no way hinders applications you wish to make to the NBA, college, or high school level courts.

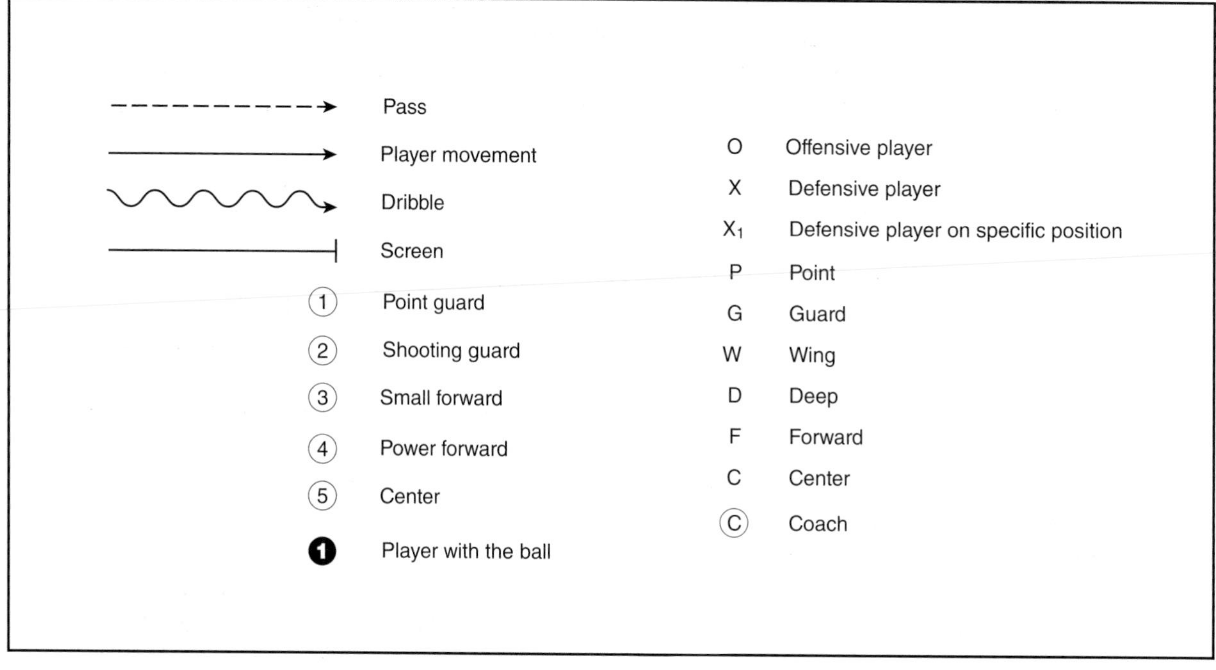

STEP 1

Footwork

Although basketball is a team game, individual execution of fundamental skills is essential for team success. Shooting, passing, dribbling, rebounding, defending, and moving both with and without the ball are the fundamental skills that you want to master. Good footwork is a prerequisite for soundly executing each of these fundamental skills.

Balance and quickness are closely related to good footwork. Being ready to start, stop, and move in any direction with balance and quickness requires good footwork. Developing good footwork lays the foundation; employing effective footwork lets you keep your body under control so that you can move with timing, deception, and quickness. Height is commonly associated with basketball success, but balance and quickness are the most important physical attributes a player can have. And although you cannot increase your height, you can improve balance and quickness through practice.

Balance means that your body is under control and in a state of readiness to make quick movements. Quickness is an asset only if you can still execute properly. Rushing or hurrying is different from being quick. If you rush, using excessive haste or performing too rapidly, you're apt to make mistakes. Rushing reflects a lack of emotional as well as physical balance or control.

Quickness refers to speed of movement when performing a skill, not just running speed. Quickness is specific to the fundamental skill being performed, such as quick movement of your feet on defense, quickly going for a rebound, or a quick release of a shot.

Good footwork is important to both offense and defense. An offensive player has the advantage of knowing what move will be made and when. Offensive footwork is used to fake the defender, get the defender off balance, move off screens, cut to the basket, avoid charging into a defender, and elude a blockout when going for an offensive rebound.

Developing good footwork is especially important when playing defense. You can try to anticipate moves, but you can never be certain what your opponent will do. Defensive success often depends on the ability to react instantly in any direction to the moves of the opponent, which requires executing defensive footwork with balance and quickness. Good footwork can force your opponent to react to you. It can also enable you to disrupt the offensive poise of your opponent, force low-percentage shots, and force turnovers. You may question just how much you can increase your natural quickness. Quickness is largely determined by genetics. But by thoroughly understanding the basic mechanics of footwork, you can definitely improve your quickness if you work at it.

Footwork is the foundation for executing each of the fundamental skills of basketball with balance and quickness. Have a trained observer—your coach, a teacher, or a skilled player—watch your offensive and defensive footwork. The observer can use the checkpoints in figures 1.1 through 1.12 to evaluate your performance and provide constructive feedback.

Some people have said that Michael Jordan was born with great natural ability and that young players cannot hope to develop his quickness and jumping ability. This type of thinking fails to consider that, although Jordan was naturally gifted, he also worked very hard to improve every facet of his game. Other naturally gifted NBA players capable of equally amazing feats simply lack Jordan's work ethic. Jordan derived sheer joy from playing and was so obsessed with winning that he constantly pushed himself to work harder in practice than anyone else. Jordan was not only regarded as the greatest player of all time, he was also regarded as the greatest practice player of all time. He can be a model for all of us trying to bring out the best in ourselves.

BALANCED STANCE

A well-balanced offensive stance enables you to move quickly, change direction, stop under control, and jump. In your offensive stance, your head is over your waist, and your back is straight. Your hands are above your waist with your elbows flexed, and your arms are kept close to your body. Your feet are at least shoulder-width apart, and your weight is evenly distributed on the balls of your feet. Your knees are flexed so that you are ready to move (figure 1.1).

Figure 1.1 **WELL-BALANCED OFFENSIVE STANCE**

Offensive stance

1. Head over waist; able to see rim and ball
2. Back straight
3. Hands above waist
4. Elbows flexed and arms close to body
5. Feet shoulder-width apart
6. Weight even on balls of feet; ready to move
7. Knees flexed

MISSTEP

Your balance is off in a forward direction.

CORRECTION

Flex your knees to get low, rather than bend at the waist, so you are ready to move backward as quickly as you can move forward.

On defense, you must be able to move quickly in any direction and change direction while maintaining balance. The prerequisite is a well-balanced stance. The defensive stance resembles the offensive stance—head over your waist, back straight, and chest out—but your feet are more than shoulder-width apart and staggered, with one foot in front of the other (figure 1.2). Having your head over your waist keeps the center of gravity over its base. Distribute your weight evenly on the balls of your feet, and flex your knees so your body is low, ready to react in any direction.

In the basic defensive stance, in which the feet are staggered one in front of the other, the front foot is called the lead foot. This stance makes it easy to move back in the direction of the back foot. Moving back requires only a short step with the back foot as you start to move. Moving back in the direction of the lead foot is much more difficult, requiring a vigorous drop step (reverse) with the lead foot while pivoting on the back foot as you start to move.

Protect your lead foot as you establish your basic defensive stance. Position your lead foot outside your opponent's body, and place your back foot in line with the middle of your opponent's body. This position protects the weakness of your lead foot and also gives the impression of an opening toward your back foot, strengthening your defensive stance.

Defensive players use three basic hand positions. In the first, one hand is kept forward on the lead-foot side to pressure the shooter, while the other hand is at the opposite side to protect against passes. In the second basic hand position, both hands are at waist level, palms up, to pressure the dribbler. This position allows you to flick at the ball with the hand that is closer to the direction in which your opponent is dribbling. In the third basic

Figure 1.2 **WELL-BALANCED DEFENSIVE STANCE**

Defensive stance

1. Head over waist
2. Back straight
3. Hands above shoulders
4. Elbows flexed
5. Wide base; weight even on balls of feet
6. Feet staggered, more than shoulder-width apart
7. Knees flexed

MISSTEP

You reach away from your body with your arm, becoming off balance in the direction of the reach.

CORRECTION

Keep your head over your waist, your hands above waist level, and your elbows flexed, with your arms close to your body.

hand position, both hands are kept above the shoulders (see figure 1.2 on page 3). This higher position forces your opponent to make lob or bounce passes that are more easily intercepted. This hand position also readies the hands to block shots, prepares you to rebound with two hands, and helps prevent reaching fouls. When both hands are above the shoulders, take care that they do not spread away from your body, causing you to lose balance. Flex your elbows to keep your arms from reaching out.

When you are guarding an opponent who has the ball, your eyes should be directed at your opponent's midsection. If the offensive player you are defending does not have the ball, one hand should point toward the offensive player, and the other should point toward the ball.

Errors in offensive and defensive stances vary with the individual. Tall players often have greater balance problems than shorter players. Typically, a tall player does not spread or flex the knees enough to keep the center of gravity low. To maintain balance in an offensive stance, spread your feet shoulder-width apart and flex your knees so you are ready to move in any direction. If you find that you do not protect your lead foot when in the defensive stance, correct this error by positioning your lead foot outside your opponent's body and aligning your back foot with the middle of your opponent's body. If you find that you are susceptible to your opponent's head and ball fakes, be sure to keep your eyes focused on your opponent's midsection, not on your opponent's head or the ball.

Footwork Drill. **STANCE**

First assume the offensive stance, and then shift your weight too far back on your heels. Next, lean too far forward, bending at the waist with your weight forward on your toes. Now correct the stance, positioning your head over your waist, moving your hands up and close to your body, distributing weight evenly on the balls of your feet, flexing your knees, and spreading your feet at least shoulder-width apart.

To Increase Difficulty

- Have a partner try to upset your balance backward by gently pushing on your shoulders.
- Have a partner try to upset your balance forward by pulling you by one of your hands.

Success Check

- Keep your head over your waist to maintain your center of gravity.
- Keep your arms close to your body.
- Stand with your knees flexed, your feet at least shoulder-width apart, and your weight on the balls of your feet.

Score Your Success

Give yourself 1 point for each element of the balanced stance that you are able to execute, for a total of 5 points:

Head over waist ___

Hands up and close to body ___

Weight evenly distributed ___

Knees flexed ___

Feet shoulder-width apart ___

Your score ___

If you increase the difficulty, give yourself 1 point each time you are able to resist your partner's attempt to upset your balance. Attempt to complete three consecutive cycles of the offensive stance without your partner pushing or pulling you off balance.

Your score ___

Footwork Drill. FOOTFIRE

Have a partner give commands. On the "Stance!" command, quickly assume an offensive stance. On the "Go!" command, move your feet up and down as quickly as you can, maintaining correct stance form for 10 seconds or until you hear the command "Stop!" Do three repetitions for 10 seconds each with 10-second rest intervals.

Success Check

- Maintain correct offensive stance form.
- Move your feet quickly.
- Aim for hitting the floor with your feet 40 to 50 times in each 10-second period.

Score Your Success

Give yourself 5 points each time you are able to hit the floor 40 to 50 times in a 10-second period, 3 points each time you hit the floor 30 to 39 times in a 10-second period, and 1 point each time you hit the floor 20 to 29 times in a 10-second period. Hitting the floor fewer than 20 times doesn't earn any points.

Times feet hit the floor, first 10-second period ___; points earned ___

Times feet hit the floor, second 10-second period ___; points earned ___

Times feet hit the floor, third 10-second period ___; points earned ___

Your score ___ (number of points earned; maximum of 15)

Footwork Drill. JUMP ROPE

Start in a balanced stance with your knees flexed and your weight on the balls of your feet. Hold the rope handles with your hands out to your sides at waist level and with your elbows close to your body. Place the rope behind your feet and swing it over your head from back to front. Jump over the rope. Add variety by skipping, jumping on one foot, crossing your arms, and jumping backward.

The best way to start a jump rope program is to jump rope for 30 seconds followed by a 30-second rest interval. Limit this program to 5 minutes, or a total of five sets. As you progress, you can jump for 60 seconds with a 30-second rest interval between sets. Once you have progressed to a 60-second set, see the score your success section to determine your mastery.

(continued)

(continued)

To Increase Difficulty

Perform a 60-second set of jumping rope followed by a 30-second rest interval.

To Decrease Difficulty

Perform a 30-second set of jumping rope followed by a 30- to 90-second rest interval.

Success Check

- Maintain a proper balanced stance.
- Keep your elbows close to your body as you swing the rope.

Score Your Success

Count your maximum number of jumps in 60 seconds.

60 jumps or more in 60 seconds = 10 points

50 to 59 jumps in 60 seconds = 8 points

40 to 49 jumps in 60 seconds = 6 points

30 to 39 jumps in 60 seconds = 4 points

20 to 29 jumps in 60 seconds = 2 points

Fewer than 20 jumps in 60 seconds = 0 points

Your score _____

OFFENSIVE FOOTWORK

Moving with and without the ball is important to individual and team offense. As an offensive player, you have an advantage over your defender in knowing what move you will make and when you will make it. Moving quickly with balance is the key. Once you develop the skills, you should be able to keep your balance while using footwork and fakes to attempt to elude the defender, who will have difficulty reacting instantly to your moves. Moving continually with and without the ball also demands superior physical conditioning. Successful players master the necessary skills and develop their physical conditioning to excel in this important part of the game.

You need to master eight basic offensive movements: change of pace, change of direction, the one-two stop and the jump stop, the front turn and the reverse turn, and the two-foot and one-foot jumps.

Change of Pace

Change of pace is a way to alter your running speed to deceive and elude the defender. Change from a fast running speed to a slower pace and then quickly change back to a fast speed without changing your basic running form.

As you run, keep your head up so you can see the rim of the basket and the ball. Take your first step with your back foot, bringing it in front of your lead foot. Run on the balls of your feet, pointing your toes in the direction you are going. Lean your upper body slightly forward and pump your arms forward in opposition to your legs, keeping your elbows flexed. Completely extend your support leg. Get your knee up and your thigh parallel to the floor as you bring it forward. To increase your speed, lengthen your stride to its maximum and increase its speed. To accelerate quickly to a faster speed, push off your back foot forcefully. You have the advantage in changing your pace because *you* decide when to change speeds. With good deception and a forceful push off your back foot, you should be at least a step quicker than your defender immediately after the change to a faster speed.

MISSTEP

You do not make a quick change from slow to fast.

CORRECTION

Push forcefully off your back foot to accelerate quickly.

Change of Direction

Change of direction underlies almost every basketball fundamental, but it is particularly important for getting open to receive a pass. An effective change of direction depends on sharply cutting from one direction to another. To execute a change of direction, step first with one foot and then step with the other foot in the opposite direction without crossing your feet. Begin with a three-quarter step rather than a full step. On your first step, flex your knee as you plant your foot firmly to stop your momentum. Turn on the ball of your foot and push off in the direction you want to go. Shift your weight and take a long step with your other foot, pointing your toes in the new direction. After the change of direction, get your lead hand up as a target to receive a pass.

Although changing direction seems like a simple move, it takes concentrated practice to execute sharply and effectively. If you find you have trouble disguising your change of direction and you slow your speed with short steps on your approach, you should use normal running form and concentrate on a two-count move: When changing from right to left, concentrate on a two-count right-left; when going from left to right, concentrate on a two-count left-right (figure 1.3).

Figure 1.3 **CHANGE OF DIRECTION**

a

b

c

First step

1. Three-quarter first step
2. Knee flexed

Second step

1. Turn on ball of foot and push off in new direction
2. Shift weight

Third step

1. Take long second step
2. Point toes in new direction
3. Keep lead hand up as target

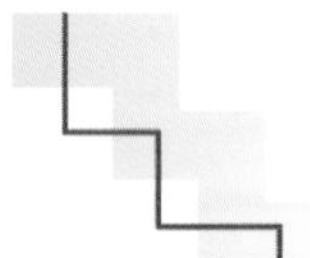

MISSTEP

You circle your turn rather than make a sharp cut.

CORRECTION

Use a three-quarter first step and flex your knee so you can pivot sharply and push off in the direction you want to go. Then shift your weight and take a long second step.

Stopping

Starting quickly is important, but so is stopping quickly. Inexperienced players often lose balance when trying to stop quickly. Learning two basic stops—the one-two stop and the jump stop—will help you stop under control.

In the one-two stop, the back foot lands first, followed by the other foot. If you execute the one-two stop as you receive a pass or on your last dribble, the foot that lands first becomes the pivot foot. The one-two stop is useful when you are running too fast to use the jump stop, when you are on the perimeter away from the basket, and especially when you are on the fast break.

Use normal running form. To execute the one-two stop (figure 1.4), first hop before the stop. This allows gravity to help slow your movement. Then lean in the opposite direction. Land on your back foot first, and then land on your lead foot. The wider your base, the more balance you will have. Flex your back knee to lower your body to a "sitting" position on the heel of your back foot. The lower you get, the better your balance. Keep your head up.

Figure 1.4 **ONE-TWO STOP**

a

b

Hop and lean back

1. Hop before stop
2. Lean in opposite direction

Land with one-two step

1. Land on back foot first
2. Land on lead foot second
3. Land with wide base
4. "Sit" on back heel
5. Keep head up

MISSTEP

You lose balance going forward, causing you to drag your pivot foot.

CORRECTION

Hop before you stop, allowing gravity to slow your forward momentum. Lean back; land first on your back foot and then on your front foot. Keep a wide base. "Sit" on the heel of your back foot. Keep your head up.

In the jump stop, both feet land simultaneously. As you catch the ball and land with a jump stop, you can use either foot as a pivot foot. The jump stop is particularly advantageous when you are moving under control without the ball, especially when you receive a pass with your back to the basket in the low-post area (within 8 feet [2.4 m] of the basket).

When executing the jump stop (figure 1.5), you should hop before the stop to allow gravity to help slow your movement, similar to the one-two stop. Lean back, then stop with both feet landing simultaneously, shoulder-width apart, with your knees flexed. Shift your weight onto the back of your feet to keep your body from moving forward.

Figure 1.5 **JUMP STOP**

a

b

Hop

1. Hop before stop
2. Keep shoulders back

Land on both feet

1. Land on both feet with feet shoulder-width apart
2. Flex knees
3. Shift weight to back of feet
4. Keep head up

MISSTEP

One foot lands before the other.

CORRECTION

Hop before you stop, lean back, and keep your feet shoulder-width apart and your knees flexed.

Offensive Footwork Drill. **ONE-TWO STOPS**

Pretend you are running on a fast break. Start in a balanced offensive stance with your feet behind the baseline. Run to the opposite baseline, making four one-two stops. Alternate the landing foot on each one-two stop. Land on your left foot for the first stop, and then land on your right foot for the next stop. Return in the same manner for a total of eight one-two stops.

Success Check

- Be sure to land with a one-two stop, coming to a complete, balanced stop.
- Maintain your balance.
- Try to execute eight successful one-two stops.

Score Your Success

8 successful one-two stops = 5 points

7 successful one-two stops = 4 points

6 successful one-two stops = 3 points

5 successful one-two stops = 2 points

4 or fewer successful one-two stops = 1 point

Your score ____

Offensive Footwork Drill. **JUMP STOPS**

Pretend you are a low-post player with your back to the basket. Start in a balanced offensive stance in front of the basket, facing the foul line. Your feet are parallel, and your hands are above your waist. Use short side steps toward the offensive right block and make a balanced jump stop outside the lane and above the block. Again using short side steps, return to a position in front of the basket and make a jump stop there. Now move to the offensive left block and make a jump stop outside the lane and above the block. Continue making jump stops, going from block to front area (in front of the basket) to block for a total of 12 jump stops.

Success Check

- Be sure to land on both feet simultaneously, coming to a complete, balanced stop.
- Maintain your balance.
- Try to execute 12 successful jump stops.

Score Your Success

12 successful jump stops = 5 points

11 successful jump stops = 4 points

10 successful jump stops = 3 points

9 successful jump stops = 2 points

8 or fewer successful jump stops = 1 point

Your score ____

Pivoting and Turning

When you have the ball, the rules allow you to take as many steps as you need in any direction with one foot while pivoting (turning) on your other foot. The foot you pivot with, or turn on, is called the pivot foot. Once you establish your pivot foot, you cannot lift it before you release the ball from your hand to dribble. When attempting a pass or shot, you may lift your pivot foot as long as you release the ball before your pivot foot hits the floor again. Once you have established your pivot foot, you cannot pivot on your other foot.

Pivoting is an essential part of many basketball skills. To pivot well, you need a balanced stance: head over waist, back straight, and knees flexed. Keep your weight on the ball of the pivot foot and do not pivot on your heel.

The two basic pivots are pivoting forward and pivoting backward. These are called the front turn, or forward pivot, and the reverse turn, or drop step. Both are important to learn. Both pivots are used to move into an advantageous position against an opponent.

For the forward pivot, or front turn, your chest leads the way. Maintain a balanced stance. Keep your weight on the ball of your pivot foot, and step forward with the nonpivot foot (figure 1.6, page 12).

In the drop step, or reverse turn, your back leads the way. Maintaining a balanced stance, keep your weight on the ball of your pivot foot, and drop your nonpivot foot back (figure 1.7, page 12).

MISSTEP

You lose balance and lift or drag your pivot foot.

CORRECTION

Keep your weight on the ball of your pivot foot as you move your nonpivot foot and maintain a balanced stance.

Figure 1.6 **FRONT TURN**

a

b

Chest leads

1. Balanced stance
2. Weight on ball of pivot foot
3. Chest leads

Forward pivot

1. Pivot on ball of foot
2. Step forward with other foot

Figure 1.7 **REVERSE TURN**

a

b

Back leads

1. Balanced stance
2. Weight on ball of pivot foot
3. Back leads

Drop step

1. Pivot on ball of foot
2. Drop other foot back

Offensive Footwork Drill.
FULL-COURT OFFENSIVE FOOTWORK

This drill allows you to practice offensive footwork such as trotting, sprinting, changing pace, and changing direction. You will use a third of the floor width from lane line to sideline as you run between baselines.

Full-court trot. Start in an offensive stance with your feet touching the baseline. Trot to the opposite baseline, emphasizing good running technique. Return in the same manner.

Full-court sprint. Start in an offensive stance with your feet touching the baseline. Sprint to the opposite free-throw line or free-throw line extended, change pace to a trot, and continue to the opposite baseline. Return in the same manner.

Full-court change of pace. Start in an offensive stance with your feet behind the baseline. Run to the opposite baseline, changing pace at least three times from sprint to trot to sprint. Return in the same manner.

Full-court change of direction. Start in an offensive stance with your left foot touching the intersection of the baseline and lane line on your left. Run diagonally at a 45-degree angle to the sideline on your right. Make a sharp 90-degree change of direction from right to left and run diagonally to the imaginary lane line extended on your left. Change direction, making a sharp 90-degree turn from left to right. Continue to change direction at each sideline and imaginary lane line as you proceed to the opposite baseline. Return in the same manner.

Success Check

- Try to complete two round-trips for each part of the drill.
- Use proper form and technique.
- Move quickly, using short, quick steps.

Score Your Success

Give yourself 5 points for completing two round-trips for each part of the drill.

Number of round-trips for the full-court trot ___; points earned ___

Number of round-trips for the full-court sprint ___; points earned ___

Number of round-trips for the full-court change of pace ___; points earned ___

Number of round-trips for the full-court change of direction ___; points earned ___

Your score ____ (out of 20)

Jumping

Everyone recognizes the importance of jumping in basketball, including the role that jumping plays in rebounding, blocking shots, and shooting. Jumping is more than gaining height. How quickly and how often you jump are more important than jumping height. Timing, balance in the air, and landing are also important components of jumping.

You want to learn two basic jumps: the two-foot jump and the one-foot jump. Use the two-foot jump (figure 1.8) when you are not on the move, when it is important to land in balance (such as in shooting a jump shot), and for jumping in succession, such as in rebounding. Start in a balanced stance—head over waist, back straight, elbows flexed, arms close to your body, and weight on the balls of your feet. Before jumping, flex your knees 60 to 90 degrees, depending on leg strength. If you can, take a short step before your takeoff. At takeoff, push quickly and forcefully off both feet, extending your ankles, knees, and hips.

The key to attaining maximum height is an explosive takeoff. The quicker and more forcefully you push against the floor, the higher you will jump. Lift both arms straight up as you jump. A smooth, fluid action without tension results in a higher jump. Land in the same spot on the balls of your feet with your knees flexed to jump again or move.

Figure 1.8 **TWO-FOOT JUMP**

a

b

Stationary start

1. Short step before takeoff
2. Head over waist; back straight
3. Elbows flexed; arms close to body
4. Weight on balls of feet
5. Knees flexed 60 to 90 degrees
6. Quick and forceful push off both feet

Two-foot jump

1. Extend ankles, knees, and hips
2. Lift both arms straight up
3. Land in same spot

The one-foot jump is for jumping on the move: shooting a layup off a drive, moving to block a shot, or moving for an offensive rebound. When you are moving, it is quicker to jump off one foot than off two feet. To jump off two feet, you have to take time to stop and prepare for the jump. One disadvantage of the one-foot jump is that it is difficult to control your body in the air and may result in a foul or even a collision with other players. In addition, after a moving one-foot jump, it is more difficult to land in balance and to change direction or make a quick second jump.

Start the one-foot jump (figure 1.9) from a run. To jump high, you must gain speed on the last three or four steps of the approach but must also be able to control that speed. The last step before the jump should be short so you can quickly dip your takeoff knee. This will change forward momentum to upward momentum.

Your takeoff knee should flex from 60 to 90 degrees, depending on leg strength. The takeoff angle should be as vertical as possible. From a balanced stance, push quickly and forcefully off your takeoff foot, extending your ankle, knee, and hip. Remember how vital takeoff explosiveness is: The quicker and more forcefully you push against the floor, the higher you will jump. Lift your opposite knee and your arms straight up as you jump. To increase your reach, you should extend your nonreaching arm downward at the top of the jump. Use a smooth, fluid action without tension, and land in balance on the balls of your feet with your knees flexed.

Figure 1.9 **ONE-FOOT JUMP**

a

b

Running start

1. Running start
2. Short step before takeoff
3. Head over waist; back straight
4. Elbows flexed; arms close to body
5. Weight on ball of takeoff foot
6. Dip takeoff knee
7. Quick, forceful push off takeoff foot

One-foot jump

1. Lift non-takeoff knee; extend ankle, knee, and hip of takeoff foot
2. Reach high, extending nonreaching arm downward
3. Land in same spot

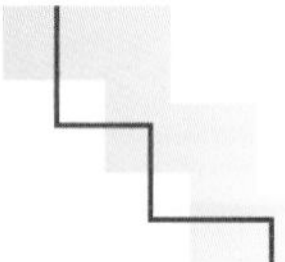

MISSTEP

You long jump rather than high jump.

CORRECTION

Shorten your last step before takeoff so you can quickly dip your takeoff knee and change forward momentum to upward momentum. On takeoff, lift your opposite knee straight up as you lift your arms. The combination of a forceful upward lift of your knee and arms increases upward momentum.

Offensive Footwork Drill. TWO-FOOT VERTICAL JUMP TEST

Chalk your fingertips, face a smooth wall, and make a mark at the height of your two-hand standing reach. Stand with your shoulders to the wall. You are allowed one step before you jump. Perform a stationary two-foot jump as high as you can, touching the wall at the top of your jump with the fingertips of your near hand. Measure the distance between the two chalk marks using a yardstick, and record the result to the nearest half inch. Do three vertical jumps, pausing for 10 seconds between each attempt.

Success Check

- Use proper form for a two-foot jump.
- Reach as high as you can.

Score Your Success

Note your inches for each trial. More than 17 inches (43 cm) is excellent and earns 5 points; 15 to 16 inches (38 to 42 cm) earns 3 points; 13 to 14 inches (33 to 37 cm) earns 1 point; fewer than 13 inches (33 cm) earns 0 points. Use your best score as your final score.

Trial 1 ___ inches; points earned ___

Trial 2 ___ inches; points earned ___

Trial 3 ___ inches; points earned ___

Your score ___ (5 points maximum)

Offensive Footwork Drill. ONE-FOOT VERTICAL JUMP TRAINING

This short drill consists of a set of 3 preliminary jumps and 5 to 10 all-out running, one-foot vertical jumps. Have a partner measure the height of your jumps at a net or backboard. The preliminary one-foot vertical jumps should be progressive in effort. On the approach, use whatever number of steps will allow for your best jumps.

For your first jump, try to touch the net or backboard about 12 inches (30 cm) below your best jumping height. On your second jump, touch about 6 inches (15 cm) above your first jump. On your third attempt, jump as high as possible. Pause 10 seconds before each jump to mentally plan for it. After the third jump, stand under the net or backboard and reach with two hands. Have your partner use a yardstick to determine the difference between your two-hand standing reach and the mark at your highest running one-foot vertical jump, recording it to the nearest half inch.

To Increase Difficulty

- Do five more jumps, trying to improve on each succeeding jump.
- If you are still improving with the fifth jump, continue until you do not touch any higher on two successive attempts.

Success Check

- Use proper technique.
- Reach as high as you can.

Score Your Success

Because this is a progressive-improvement drill, the scoring is a little different. Record your inches for each trial in the spaces provided. You want to improve with each trial, and if you do so, give yourself 5 points.

Trial 1 ___ inches

Trial 2 ___ inches

Trial 3 ___ inches

Your score _____ total inches; points earned _____

DEFENSIVE FOOTWORK

Moving your feet on defense is hard work. Success depends on desire, discipline, concentration, anticipation, and superior physical conditioning. Moving quickly with balance is the key to reacting to your opponent's moves and changing direction instantly.

To move on defense, use short, quick steps with your weight evenly distributed on the balls of your feet. Push off the foot that is farther from where you are going and step with the closer foot. Do not cross your feet. Make an exception only when your opponent moves near your lead foot. If that happens, execute a drop step to recover your defensive position. Your feet should not move closer than shoulder-width apart. Keep them as close to the floor as possible.

Flex your knees and keep your body low, your upper body erect, and your chest out. Keep your head steady. Avoid up-and-down body movements. Hopping or jumping movements are slow and put you in the air; you should be on the floor reacting to an opponent. Pressure the ball with quick flicks of whichever hand is closer to the direction your opponent is going, but do not reach or lean. Keeping your head over your waist, your arms close to your body, and your elbows flexed will help you maintain balance.

You should master these basic defensive steps or movements: the side step or slide, the attack and retreat, and the reverse or drop step. Each step starts from a defensive stance.

Side Step or Slide

Maintain a balanced defensive stance between your opponent and the basket. If your opponent moves to the side, execute a side step or slide (figure 1.10). Quickly move your feet from a staggered stance to a parallel stance. Both feet should be aligned with the direction you are going. Use short, quick steps with your weight evenly distributed on the balls of your feet. Push off the far foot and step with the foot closer to where you are going. Never cross your feet. Concentrate on keeping your balance to make quick changes of direction.

Figure 1.10 **SIDE STEP OR SLIDE**

Side step or slide

1. Push off far foot, using short, quick steps
2. Step with foot closer to where you are going
3. Lead foot continues outside opponent's body
4. Align back foot with middle of opponent's body
5. Keep feet no closer than shoulder-width apart; never cross feet
6. Keep feet close to floor
7. Keep knees flexed; no hopping or up-and-down movements
8. Keep head steady and over waist
9. Keep back straight; no leaning
10. Keep hands up
11. Keep elbows flexed and arms close to body
12. Pressure ball with quick flicking motions; do not reach

MISSTEP

You reach or lean, losing your balance.

CORRECTION

Keep your head over your waist, your hands up, your elbows flexed, and your arms close to your body.

Defensive Footwork Drill. LANE DEFENSIVE SLIDE

Start in the lane, facing the foul line, with your right foot on the lane line to your right. Use a balanced defensive stance with your feet parallel and your hands up. Using short, quick defensive side steps, move quickly to the lane line on your left, change direction, and move back to the lane line on your right. Continue as quickly as you can between the left and right lane lines.

Success Check

- Maintain correct form for a balanced defensive stance.
- Step to the side using short, quick steps.
- Keep your hands up.
- Try to touch 15 lines in 30 seconds.

Score Your Success

15 or more lines in 30 seconds = 5 points

13 or 14 lines in 30 seconds = 4 points

11 or 12 lines in 30 seconds = 3 points

9 or 10 lines in 30 seconds = 2 points

8 lines in 30 seconds = 1 point

7 lines or fewer in 30 seconds = 0 points

Your score ______

Attack and Retreat

Attacking, or moving up on your opponent, is often referred to as *closing out*. This is not an easy skill. It requires good judgment and balance. You cannot close on your opponent so fast that you lose your balance and are unable to change direction backward. Use short, quick attack steps, without crossing your feet, and protect your lead foot by positioning it slightly outside your opponent's body.

If your opponent makes a move toward the basket on the side of your back foot, you should retreat, or move back, without losing balance. You cannot retreat so fast that you lose your balance and are unable to react quickly to get closer to your opponent. As with attacking, you should use short, quick retreat steps; do not cross your feet.

Attack and retreat movements (figure 1.11) basically require the same footwork but in different directions. They both use short, quick steps, with one foot up and the other back. Keep your weight evenly distributed on the balls of your feet. Push off your back foot and step with your lead foot to attack; push off your front foot and step with your back foot to retreat. In attacking, never cross your back foot in front of your lead foot, and in retreating, never cross your lead foot in front of your back foot. For both your attack and retreat, strive for good defensive footwork.

Figure 1.11 **ATTACK AND RETREAT**

a

b

Attack

1. Push off back foot
2. Use short, quick steps, keeping feet close to floor
3. Lead foot continues outside opponent's body
4. Align back foot with middle of opponent's body
5. Keep feet no closer than shoulder-width apart; never cross feet
6. Keep knees flexed; no hopping or up-and-down movements
7. Keep head steady and over waist
8. Keep back straight; no leaning
9. Keep hands up, elbows flexed, and arms close to body
10. Pressure ball with quick flicking motions; do not reach

Retreat

1. Push off front foot
2. Use short, quick steps, keeping feet close to floor
3. Lead foot continues outside opponent's body
4. Align back foot with middle of opponent's body
5. Keep feet no closer than shoulder-width apart; never cross feet
6. Keep knees flexed; no hopping or up-and-down movements
7. Keep head steady and over waist
8. Keep back straight; no leaning
9. Keep hands up, elbows flexed, and arms close to body
10. Pressure ball with quick flicking motion; do not reach

MISSTEP: ATTACK

You hop forward with both feet parallel, preventing a quick change of direction backward.

CORRECTION

Keep your head steady and your knees flexed. Use short, quick steps. Maintain a staggered stance. Do not hop; keep your feet close to the floor.

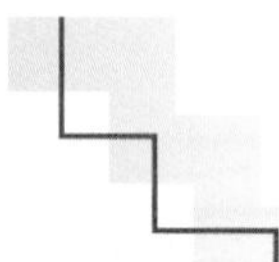

MISSTEP: RETREAT

You cross your front foot in front of your back foot, preventing a quick change of direction.

CORRECTION

Push off your front foot and step with your back foot. Do not cross your feet or bring them closer than shoulder-width apart.

Defensive Footwork Drill. LANE DEFENSIVE ATTACK AND RETREAT

Start by facing the foul line, with your right foot on the defensive right block and your left foot forward and in the lane. Use a staggered defensive stance with your left foot forward at a 45-degree angle from your right foot and with your hands up. Take short, quick attack steps with your left foot (the lead foot) forward until it touches the middle of the foul line. Quickly drop-step with your left foot. Change to retreat steps, backing up until your left foot touches the defensive left block. Immediately change direction, switching to attack steps until your right foot touches the foul line. Step back to the block as quickly as you can.

Success Check

- Maintain correct form for the defensive stance.
- Use short, quick steps.
- Execute attack steps and retreat steps using proper technique.
- Try to touch a total of 15 lines and blocks in 30 seconds.

Score Your Success

15 or more lines and blocks in 30 seconds = 5 points

13 or 14 lines and blocks in 30 seconds = 4 points

11 or 12 lines and blocks in 30 seconds = 3 points

9 or 10 lines and blocks in 30 seconds = 2 points

8 lines and blocks in 30 seconds = 1 point

7 lines and blocks or fewer in 30 seconds = 0 points

Your score ___

Reverse or Drop Step

In the basic defensive stance, the feet are staggered one foot in front of the other. The weakness of this stance is in the lead foot: It is more difficult to move back in the direction of the lead foot than in the direction of the back foot. If an opponent dribbles toward the basket past your lead foot, quickly drop-step with your lead foot while making a reverse pivot with your back foot (figure 1.12). After making the drop step, use quick retreat steps to reestablish defensive position with your lead foot forward. If you are not in position to do this, you must run and chase your opponent, then turn into position with your intended lead foot forward.

Take your drop step in the direction of your opponent's move. Keep your head up and over your waist, and keep your eyes focused on your opponent. Do not turn in the opposite direction or take your eyes off your opponent. As you perform the reverse pivot, vigorously push off your back foot in the direction of the drop step. The drop step should be straight back. The foot should move low to the floor. Do not circle or lift the lead foot high. For added momentum in the drop step, forcefully move the elbow on the side of your lead foot back close to your body.

Figure 1.12 **REVERSE OR DROP STEP**

a

b

c

Reverse pivot and drop-step

1. Perform reverse pivot on back foot
2. Drop-step straight back with lead foot, keeping foot low to floor
3. Move lead elbow back close to body

Reestablish defensive position

1. Keep eyes on opponent's midsection
2. Reestablish defensive position by using retreat steps

Reestablish lead foot

1. Use front turn to re-establish intended lead foot
2. Be ready to change direction

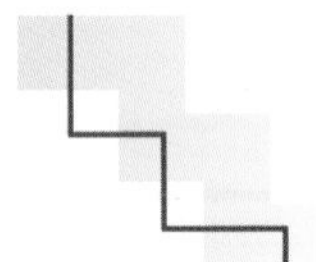

MISSTEP

You turn away from your opponent's move, losing sight of your opponent.

CORRECTION

Drop-step in the direction of your opponent's move, keeping your eyes on your opponent.

Defensive Footwork Drill. LANE DEFENSIVE ZIGZAG

Start in the lane, facing the foul line, with your right foot on the defensive right elbow (the intersection of the lane and foul lines). Stand in a staggered defensive stance with your left foot back at a 45-degree angle. Use short, quick retreat steps to move back diagonally until your left foot touches the lane line on your left, just above the block. Quickly drop-step with your right foot and use retreat steps until your right foot touches the intersection of the baseline and lane line to your right. Quickly change to an offensive stance and sprint diagonally to the defensive left elbow where you will change to a defensive stance with your left foot on the elbow. Use retreat steps until your right foot touches the lane line on your right. Drop-step with your left foot and retreat until it touches the intersection of the baseline and lane line on your left. Change to an offensive stance and sprint to the defensive right elbow. Continue a defensive zigzag from elbow to lane to the intersection of baseline and lane line, then sprint to the opposite elbow as quickly as you can.

Success Check

- Maintain proper form for both the offensive and defensive stances.
- Use short, quick steps.
- Try to touch 15 lines in 30 seconds.

Score Your Success

15 or more lines in 30 seconds = 5 points

13 or 14 lines in 30 seconds = 4 points

11 or 12 lines in 30 seconds = 3 points

9 or 10 lines in 30 seconds = 2 points

8 lines in 30 seconds = 1 point

7 lines or fewer in 30 seconds = 0 points

Your score ___

Defensive Footwork Drill. **THE WAVE**

Start in the middle of the half-court. A partner stands 20 feet (6.1 m) in front of you, randomly giving verbal commands and hand signals. On the "Defense!" command, quickly assume a defensive stance. On the "Side!" command, move quickly to the side signaled by your partner's hand. On the "Up!" command, move quickly up. On the "Back!" command, move quickly back. Your partner should also signal you to move up and back and to the other side with hand signals. Use defensive side steps for moving to the side, and use attack and retreat steps for moving up and back. Maintain a balanced defensive stance and execute good footwork with quick changes of direction.

To Increase Difficulty

- Have your partner randomly add the command "Rebound!" On this command, you should quickly execute a two-foot jump and simulate grabbing a rebound with two hands.
- Have your partner randomly add the command "Loose ball!" On this command, you should quickly assume a position with hands and feet on the floor, simulating going for a loose ball, and then get back up just as fast.
- Have your partner randomly add the command "Fast break!" On this command, you should sprint forward as you would on a fast break.

Success Check

- Use proper technique for the defensive stance and footwork.
- Use short, quick steps.
- Try to go for 30 seconds without stopping or making a mistake.

Score Your Success

30 or more seconds without a mistake = 5 points

25 to 29 seconds without a mistake = 4 points

20 to 24 seconds without a mistake = 3 points

15 to 19 seconds without a mistake = 2 points

10 to 14 seconds without a mistake = 1 point

1 to 9 seconds without a mistake = 0 points

Your score ___

Defensive Footwork Drill. FULL-COURT DEFENSIVE FOOTWORK

This drill allows you to practice defensive footwork such as the zigzag, attack and retreat, and reverse run-and-turn. In each variation, you will use a third of the floor width from lane line to sideline.

Full-court defensive zigzag. Start with your back to the far basket. Stand in a staggered defensive stance with your left foot forward and touching the intersection of the baseline and the sideline on your left; your right foot should be back at a 45-degree angle. Use defensive retreat steps to move diagonally back until your right foot touches the lane line to your right. Quickly drop-step with your left foot. Continue changing direction at each lane line and imaginary lane line extended and at each sideline as you proceed to the opposite baseline. Return in the same manner.

Full-court defensive attack and retreat. Imagine that you are guarding a dribbler. Start with your back to the far basket, standing in a balanced defensive stance with your left foot forward and touching the baseline and with your right foot spread directly back. Start moving backward using retreat steps, then move forward using attack steps, and then move backward again using retreat steps. Continue in this manner to the half-court line using defensive attack and retreat steps until your right foot touches the half-court line. Quickly drop-step, moving your left foot back. With your right foot forward, start moving backward to the baseline using retreat steps, then move forward using attack steps, and then move backward again using retreat steps. Continue in this manner until your left foot touches the baseline. Vary your attack and retreat steps, avoiding a pattern as you move down the floor. Return in the same manner.

Full-court defensive reverse run-and-turn. Imagine that a dribbler beats your lead foot and you must recover by using a reverse run-and-turn. Start in a staggered defensive stance with your back to the far basket; your left foot is forward and touching the baseline, and your right foot is spread directly back. Make an attack step and then a quick reverse run-and-turn. Reverse to the side of your lead foot, keeping your eyes on the imaginary dribbler. Run at least three steps before you turn back into position with your original foot up. From baseline to half-court line, make two reverse run-and-turns starting with an attack step with your left foot forward. From the half-court line to the opposite baseline, make two reverse run-and-turns starting with an attack step with your right foot forward. Return in the same manner.

Success Check

- Try to complete two round-trips for each part of the drill.
- Use proper form and technique.
- Move quickly, using short, quick steps.

Score Your Success

Give yourself 5 points for completing two round-trips for each part of the drill.

Number of round-trips for the full-court defensive zigzag ___; points earned ___

Number of round-trips for the full-court defensive attack and retreat ___; points earned ___

Number of round-trips for the full-court defensive reverse run-and-turn ___; points earned ___

Your score ___ (out of 15)

Offensive and Defensive Footwork Drill. FULL-COURT ONE-ON-ONE OFFENSE VERSUS DEFENSE

Work with a partner. You will play defense against your partner, who will be on offense without the ball. Your partner will attempt to use quick starts, stops, and changes of pace and direction to get a head and shoulder by you. The offensive player must stay within a third of the floor width from lane line to sideline while moving down the floor from one baseline to the other. Once your partner gets a head and shoulder by you, both of you stop. As a defender, you must stay within touching distance of the offensive player, attempting to draw an offensive foul by beating your partner to the intended spot in a set position.

Get in a defensive stance facing your partner, and touch your partner's waist to start the drill. The offensive player is awarded a point each time the offensive player gets a head and shoulder by you, and you get a point each time you draw an offensive foul. Continue the drill from whatever spot the point was gained, again starting with a defensive touch. When you reach the opposite baseline, switch roles for the return trip.

Success Check

- Use proper defensive form.
- Score more points than your partner.

Score Your Success

Give yourself 5 points if you score more points than your partner does.

Your score ___

Your partner's score ___

RATE YOUR SUCCESS

Footwork with quickness and balance is important to improved play on the court. The information and drills presented in this step will help you be ready to make that offensive move to the basket, create a turnover when you are on defense, or move out on a fast break.

In the next step, we will look at the fundamentals of passing and catching the ball. Before going to step 2, however, you should look back at how you performed the drills in this step. For each of the drills presented in this step, enter the points you earned, then add up your scores to rate your total success.

Footwork Drills

1. Stance	____ out of 5
2. Footfire	____ out of 15
3. Jump Rope	____ out of 10

Offensive Footwork Drills

1. One-Two Stops	____ out of 5
2. Jump Stops	____ out of 5
3. Full-Court Offensive Footwork	____ out of 20
4. Two-Foot Vertical Jump Test	____ out of 5
5. One-Foot Vertical Jump Training	____ out of 5

Defensive Footwork Drills

1. Lane Defensive Slide	____ out of 5
2. Lane Defensive Attack and Retreat	____ out of 5
3. Lane Defensive Zigzag	____ out of 5
4. The Wave	____ out of 5
5. Full-Court Defensive Footwork	____ out of 15

Offensive and Defensive Footwork Drill

1. Full-Court One-on-One Offense Versus Defense	____ out of 5
Total	____ **out of 110**

If you scored 60 or more points, congratulations! You have mastered the basics of this step and are ready to move on to step 2, passing and catching. If you scored fewer than 60 points, you may want to spend more time on the fundamentals covered in this step. Practice the drills again to develop mastery of the techniques and increase your scores.

STEP

2

Passing and Catching

At its best, basketball is a game in which five players move the ball as a team. Good passing and catching are the essence of team play—the skills that make basketball such a beautiful team sport.

Passing is the most neglected fundamental of the game. Players tend to not want to practice passing. Perhaps because of the attention that fans and media give to the players who score, not enough credit is given to players who make the assists. A team of good passers is a threat to the defense because any player can get the ball to any teammate at any time. Developing your ability to pass and catch makes you a better player and helps you make your teammates better.

Two basic reasons for passing are to move the ball to create good shot opportunities and to maintain possession of the ball, thereby controlling the game. Deceptive, timely, and accurate passes create scoring opportunities for your team. For players to be in position for a shot, the ball must be dribbled or passed into the scoring area. A pass travels many times faster than a dribble. Once the ball is in the scoring area, quick, accurate passes from the ball side (strong side) of the court to the weak side will open up offensive opportunities. Moving the ball keeps defenders on the go and makes them less able to give defensive help or to double-team the player with the ball.

A team that controls the ball with good passing and catching provides few opportunities for the opposition to score. Knowing when and where to pass under pressure not only provides your team with a chance to score, but also keeps your team from losing the ball through interceptions, which often result in your opponent getting easy scores.

Here are some specific uses for the pass:

- To get the ball out of a congested area, for example, after a rebound or when a player is being double-teamed
- To move the ball quickly up the court on a fast break
- To set up offensive plays
- To get the ball to an open teammate for a shot
- To move the ball around, using the pass and cut to create an opportunity for your own shot

Have a trained observer—your coach, a teacher, or a skilled player—watch you pass and catch. The observer can use the checkpoints in figures 2.1 through 2.9 to evaluate your performance and provide constructive feedback. Also, ask your coach to evaluate your decision making as a passer.

PRINCIPLES OF PASSING AND CATCHING

Understanding the principles of passing and catching improves your judgment, anticipation, timing, faking, deceptiveness, accuracy, force, and touch, all factors that affect your ability as a playmaker. These principles will help you move to a higher level of play.

See the rim. When you have the rim in view, you will be able to see the entire court in front of you, including open teammates, and whether a defender is playing you for the pass, shot, or drive.

Pass before you dribble. A pass travels many times faster than a dribble. This is particularly important during a fast break and when moving the ball against a zone.

Know your teammate's strengths and weaknesses. Recognize the position where your teammate is moving to and the next move he is likely to make. Pass the ball to your teammate when and where he can do some good.

Time lead passes. Anticipate your teammate's speed on a cut to the basket and make a well-timed lead pass, slightly ahead of your teammate, to the open area.

Use deception. Fake before you pass, but do not telegraph the pass by looking in the direction you are passing. Use your peripheral vision to see your target without looking at your receiver. Use the element of surprise.

Draw and kick. Draw your defender to you with a shot fake or dribble before passing. Do not attempt to pass against a sagging defender; a defender who is sagging will have more time and distance to react and intercept or deflect the pass.

Make passes quick and accurate. Eliminate wasted motion. Do not wind up or start the pass behind the plane of your body.

Judge the force of your pass. Pass forcefully for longer distances and use touch when you're close to the receiver.

Be sure about your pass. It is better not to pass than to risk a pass that cannot be completed. A good pass is one that is caught. Do not force a pass into a crowd or before you have an open teammate.

Pass to the side away from a closely guarded player. When your teammate is closely guarded, pass to the side away from the defender. If you receive a pass but are not in position to shoot, keep your hands above your waist, meet the pass, and catch the ball with relaxed hands, in position to make another pass.

Pass to the open shooter's far hand. When a teammate is open and in position to shoot, pass the ball to the shooter's far hand. The shooter should not have to move the hands or change body position to catch a pass that is off target. When you are open in position to shoot and you receive the pass, let the ball come to you. Jump behind the ball, catching it with your hands relaxed in block-and-tuck position, ready to shoot.

CATCHING PASSES

When you are open away from the scoring area, give the passer a good target and go to the ball to meet the pass (figure 2.1, page 32). Catch the ball with your hands soft. Keep each hand in a relaxed handshake position, forming a natural cup with your palm off the ball and your thumb and fingers relaxed and not spread. Give with the ball as you catch it, bringing your arms and hands into position in front of your chest. After receiving the pass, land with a one-two stop, see the rim and your defender, and be ready to pass upcourt.

Catching a pass when open in the scoring area is covered in step 5, shooting off the catch. Catching a pass when closely guarded in the scoring area is covered in step 6, creating your shot off the dribble. Catching a pass in the low post or at the pinch post is covered in step 7, scoring in the post.

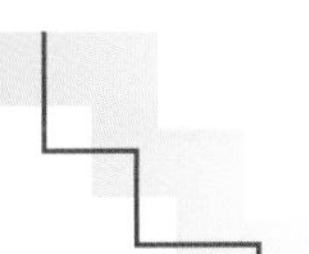

MISSTEP

You fumble the ball as you receive it.

CORRECTION

Keep your hands up. Watch the ball all the way into your hands. Keep your hands relaxed and give with the ball as you catch it.

Figure 2.1 **CATCHING A PASS**

a

Show hands

1. See ball
2. Balanced stance with feet shoulder-width apart
3. Knees flexed
4. Back straight
5. Hands up at ball distance with fingers relaxed

b

Meet ball

1. Come to meet ball
2. Make two-hand catch
3. Keep fingers relaxed
4. Give with ball on catch
5. Land with one-two stop

c

Front turn

1. Use front turn, pivoting on inside foot
2. Bring ball to front of chest with elbows out
3. See rim
4. Feet shoulder-width apart
5. Knees flexed
6. Back straight

Warm-Up Drill. **BALLHANDLING WARM-UP**

This warm-up drill consists of passing and catching the ball, moving the ball from one hand to the other. The six parts of the ballhandling drill are over your head, around your head, around your waist, around one leg, around the other leg, and figure eights through your legs.

Start in a balanced stance. Pass the ball from one hand to the other forcefully by flexing your wrists and fingers. To improve your weak hand, emphasize it through the ball. Follow through completely on each pass, pointing your fingers at your catching hand. Work for force and control, not just for quickness. On each part of the drill, pass the ball 10 times in one direction, then reverse direction and pass the ball another 10 times.

Success Check

- Attempt to go three minutes with no more than 3 errors.
- Maintain force and control.
- Follow through by pointing your fingers at your catching hand.

Score Your Success

Three minutes with 0 to 3 errors = 5 points

Three minutes with 4 to 6 errors = 3 points

Three minutes with 7 to 9 errors = 1 point

Three minutes with 10 or more errors = 0 points

Your score ___

BASIC PASSES

Basic passes include the chest pass, bounce pass, overhead pass, sidearm pass, baseball pass, behind-the-back pass, and drop pass. Practice each type of pass to make these fundamental passes automatic. Then learn to apply the correct pass for various court situations. You can practice with a partner or by yourself to develop quickness and accuracy in passing. For practicing alone, you need a ball and a flat wall or toss back. Learn decision making for passing by practicing in competitive group drills and game situations.

Chest Pass

The chest pass (figure 2.2, page 34) is the most common pass in basketball. It can be used with quickness and accuracy from most positions on the floor.

Start in a balanced stance. Hold the ball with two hands in front of your chest, keeping your elbows in. Your hands should be slightly behind the ball in a relaxed position. Locate your target without looking directly at the receiver. Look away or fake before passing. Step in the direction of your target, extending your legs, back, and arms. Force your wrists and fingers through the ball. Emphasize forcing your weak hand through the ball—the strong hand tends to dominate. The ball will go where your fingers direct it. Releasing it off the first and second fingers of both hands creates backspin and gives the ball direction. Follow through by pointing your fingers at the target with the palms facing down.

Figure 2.2 **CHEST PASS**

Ball in front of chest

1. Locate target without looking directly at receiver
2. Maintain balance
3. Keep hands slightly behind ball in relaxed handshake position
4. Keep ball in front of chest
5. Keep elbows in

Chest pass

1. Look away or fake before passing
2. Step in direction of pass
3. Extend knees, back, and arms
4. Force wrists and fingers through ball; force weak hand through ball
5. Release ball off first and second fingers
6. Follow through with arms extended, palms down, and fingers pointing to target

---

MISSTEP

Your chest pass lacks force.

CORRECTION

Start the pass with your elbows in, and force your wrists and fingers through the ball.

Bounce Pass

When a defender is between you and the target, one option is to use a bounce pass under the defender's arms. The bounce pass (figure 2.3) is effective for moving the ball to a wing on the end of a fast break or to a player cutting to the basket. Because the ball bounces off the floor, the bounce pass is a slower pass than the chest pass.

Execute the bounce pass the same as the chest pass. Pass the ball so that it bounces off the floor at a distance, allowing it to be received at about waist level. To judge the correct distance, aim for a spot two-thirds of the distance or a few feet in front of your target. Bouncing the ball too far from your target can result in a high and slow bounce that can be easily intercepted. Bouncing the ball too close to the receiver makes it too low to handle. Remember, the ball will go where the fingers direct it. Follow through by pointing your fingers at the target with the palms of your hands facing down.

Figure 2.3 **BOUNCE PASS**

a

Ball at waist level

1. Locate target without looking directly at receiver
2. Maintain balanced stance
3. Keep hands slightly behind ball in relaxed handshake position
4. Hold ball at waist level
5. Keep elbows in

b

Bounce pass

1. Look away or fake before passing
2. Aim two-thirds of distance to target
3. Step in direction of pass
4. Extend knees, back, and arms
5. Force wrists and fingers through ball; force weak hand through ball
6. Release ball off first and second fingers
7. Follow through with arms extended, palms down, and fingers pointing to target

---

MISSTEP

Your bounce pass bounces too high and slow, so it gets intercepted.

CORRECTION

Start the pass from waist level and aim the ball's bounce closer to the receiver.

Overhead Pass

Use the overhead pass (figure 2.4) when you are closely guarded and have to pass over the defender. This is also a good pass to use as an outlet pass to start a fast break against pressing defenders or as a lob to a player cutting backdoor to the basket. Like the sidearm pass discussed in the next section, the overhead pass is an option for feeding the low post.

Start in a balanced stance, holding the ball above your forehead with your elbows in and flexed about 90 degrees. Do not bring the ball behind your head; executing the pass will take longer when the ball begins behind your head, and the ball can also be stolen from behind. Step in the direction of the target, extending your legs and back to get maximum power. Quickly pass the ball, extending your arms and flexing your wrists and fingers. Release the ball off the first and second fingers (index and middle fingers) of both hands. Follow through by pointing your fingers at the target, palms down.

Figure 2.4 **OVERHEAD PASS**

a

b

Ball above forehead

1. Locate target without looking directly at receiver
2. Maintain balanced stance
3. Keep hands slightly behind ball in relaxed handshake position
4. Hold ball above forehead
5. Keep elbows in

Overhead pass

1. Look away or fake before passing
2. Step in direction of pass
3. Extend knees, back, and arms
4. Flex wrists and fingers
5. Release ball off first and second fingers
6. Follow through with arms extended, palms down, and fingers pointing to target

MISSTEP

Your overhead pass lacks force and accuracy.

CORRECTION

Make sure you are starting the pass with the ball above your forehead, not behind your head. Do not break the plane of your body with the ball. Generate force by keeping your elbows in, flexing your wrists and fingers, and extending your legs, back, and arms. Produce accuracy by pointing your fingers toward the target.

Sidearm Pass

Use the sidearm pass (figure 2.5, page 38) when you are closely guarded and have to pass around a defender. Like the overhead pass, a sidearm pass is an option for feeding the low post. Except for the position of the ball in the preparation phase, execution of the sidearm pass is similar to the overhead pass.

Start the sidearm pass by moving the ball to one side between your shoulder and hip as you step to that side. Do not bring the ball behind your body; executing the pass will take longer when the ball begins behind the body, and the ball can also be stolen. Follow through by pointing your fingers toward the target, palms to the side.

You can use two hands for the sidearm pass, as in the overhead pass, or just one hand. For a one-hand sidearm pass (figure 2.6, page 39), place your passing hand behind the ball. Keep your nonpassing hand in front of and on the ball until the point of release so you can stop and fake when needed. Practice the one-hand sidearm pass with your weak hand as well as your strong hand.

Figure 2.5 **TWO-HAND SIDEARM PASS**

a

b

Ball at side

1. Able to see target without turning to look directly at receiver
2. Balanced stance
3. Hands slightly behind ball in relaxed handshake position
4. Ball between shoulder and hip
5. Elbows in

Two-hand sidearm pass

1. Look away or fake before passing
2. Step in direction of pass
3. Extend knees, back, and arms
4. Flex wrists and fingers
5. Release ball off first and second fingers
6. Follow through with arms extended, palms to side, and fingers pointing to target

---

MISSTEP

Your sidearm pass lacks force and accuracy.

CORRECTION

Make sure you are not starting the pass with the ball behind your body. Do not break the plane of your body with the ball. Generate force by keeping your elbows in, flexing your wrists and fingers, and extending your legs, back, and arms. Produce accuracy by pointing the first and second fingers toward the target.

Figure 2.6 **ONE-HAND SIDEARM PASS**

a

Ball at side

1. Able to see target without turning to look directly at receiver
2. Balanced stance
3. Passing hand behind ball
4. Nonpassing hand in front of and on ball
5. Ball between shoulder and hip
6. Elbows in

b

One-hand sidearm pass

1. Look away or fake before passing
2. Step in direction of pass
3. Extend knees, back, and arms
4. Flex wrist and fingers
5. Keep nonpassing hand on ball until release in order to stop and fake if necessary
6. Release ball off first and second fingers
7. Follow through with passing arm fully extended, palm to side, and fingers pointing to target

Baseball Pass

For a long pass, you will often want to use the baseball pass (figure 2.7, page 40). The baseball pass can be used as an outlet pass to start a fast break, as a long lead pass to a teammate cutting toward the basket, or to inbound the ball.

Start in a balanced stance. Pivot on your back foot, turning your body to your passing-arm side. Bring the ball up to your ear with your elbow in, your passing hand behind the ball, and your balance hand in front of it, like a catcher starting to throw a baseball on a steal to second base. As you pass the ball, shift your weight from your back foot to your front foot. Extend your legs, back, and passing arm toward the target. Flex your wrist forward as you release the ball off your fingertips. Follow through by pointing your fingers at the target with the palm of your passing hand facing down. Although this is a one-hand pass, you should keep your nonpassing hand on the ball until the release so you can stop and fake if necessary.

Figure 2.7 **BASEBALL PASS**

Ball at ear

1. Able to see target without turning to look directly at receiver
2. Balanced stride
3. Body to side
4. Weight on pivot foot (back foot)
5. Hands relaxed, with passing hand behind ball and with nonpassing hand in front of it
6. Ball at ear
7. Elbow in

Baseball pass

1. Look away or fake before passing
2. Step in direction of pass
3. Extend knees, back, and arms
4. Keep two hands on ball until release
5. Flex wrist and fingers
6. Release ball off first and second fingers
7. Follow through with arm extended, palm down, and fingers pointing to target

---

MISSTEP

Your baseball pass curves.

CORRECTION

Keep your passing hand directly behind the ball—not to the side—and point your fingers at the target. The pass will go where your fingers direct it to go.

Behind-the-Back Pass

Advanced players must be able to pass behind the back. The behind-the-back pass (figure 2.8) is especially useful when a defender comes between you and a teammate on a two-on-one fast break.

Pivot on the ball of your back foot, turning your body to your passing-arm side. Using both hands, move the ball to a position behind your hip. Hold the ball with your passing hand behind the ball and with your nonpassing hand in front of the ball. Shift your weight from your back foot to your front foot as you pass the ball behind your back and toward the target. Extend your passing arm and flex your wrist and fingers, releasing the ball off your finger pads. Follow through by pointing your fingers at the target, with the palm of your passing hand up and with your passing arm contacting your back. Practice the behind-the-back pass with your weak hand as well as your strong hand.

Figure 2.8 **BEHIND-THE-BACK PASS**

a

b

Ball behind hip

1. Able to see target without turning to look directly at receiver
2. Balanced stance
3. Body to side
4. Weight on pivot foot (back foot)
5. Hands relaxed, with passing hand behind ball and with nonpassing hand in front of it
6. Ball behind hip

Behind-the-back pass

1. Look away or fake before passing
2. Step in direction of pass
3. Shift weight from back foot to front foot
4. Keep two hands on ball until release
5. Pass ball behind back
6. Extend passing arm
7. Flex wrist and fingers
8. Release ball off first and second fingers
9. Follow through with arm extended, palm up, and fingers pointing to target

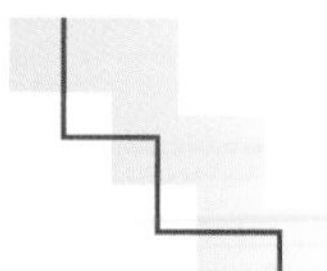

MISSTEP

Once you start the behind-the-back pass, you are unable to stop and fake.

CORRECTION

Be sure to start the pass with both hands on the ball. Do not take the nonpassing hand off the ball too soon. Use both hands to move the ball behind your hip, and keep both hands on the ball until the release.

Drop Pass

The drop pass is a good option when you are closely guarded at the high- or low-post area with your back to the basket and you want to pass the ball by your defender to a teammate cutting to the basket. The drop pass is a one-hand backward bounce pass (figure 2.9). With your back to the basket, move the ball to one side at your hip. Place your passing hand slightly on top of and behind the ball, and place your nonpassing hand under the ball. Make a drop pass (a one-hand backward bounce pass) with your passing hand. Keep two hands on the ball until the point of release so you can fake or stop the pass when needed. Follow through by pointing your fingers toward the target. Practice the one-hand drop pass with your weak hand as well as your strong hand.

Figure 2.9 **DROP PASS**

a

b

Back to basket with ball at hip

1. Back to basket
2. Balanced stance
3. Able to see target without turning to look directly at receiver
4. Ball at hip
5. Passing hand slightly on top of ball
6. Nonpassing hand under ball

Drop pass

1. Look away or fake before passing
2. Make drop pass
3. Keep two hands on ball until release
4. Follow through with fingers pointing toward target

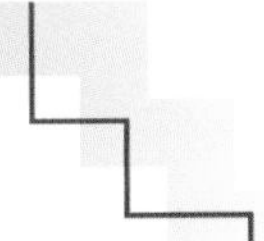

MISSTEP

Your drop pass bounces too high and slow, so it gets intercepted.

CORRECTION

Start the pass at hip level and aim the ball's bounce closer to the receiver.

Passing Drill. PARTNER PASSING

This drill helps you develop quickness, accuracy, and confidence in your passing. Choose a partner to pass and catch the ball with, executing chest, bounce, overhead, sidearm, baseball, behind-the-back, and drop passes.

For the chest, bounce, overhead, sidearm, behind-the-back, and drop passes, start in a balanced stance 15 feet (4.5 m) in front of your partner with the ball in good passing position. For the baseball pass, move back to 20 feet (6.1 m). Pass and catch the ball as quickly and accurately as you can, using a fingertip release to impart backspin and accuracy. Point your fingers in the direction of the pass, exaggerating your follow-through by leaving your arms up until the pass is caught. When you catch, make sure you are in a balanced stance with your hands up as a target, ready to move to meet each pass.

Success Check

- Use proper technique for each type of pass.
- Use proper technique for catching passes.

Score Your Success

For the chest, overhead, and sidearm passes, give yourself 5 points if you complete 40 or more passes in 30 seconds at 15 feet, 3 points if you complete 30 to 39 passes, 1 point if you complete 20 to 29 passes, and 0 points if you complete fewer than 20 passes.

Number of chest passes in 30 seconds at 15 feet ___; points earned ___

Number of overhead passes in 30 seconds at 15 feet ___; points earned ___

Number of sidearm passes in 30 seconds at 15 feet ___; points earned ___

For the bounce, behind-the-back, and drop passes, give yourself 5 points if you complete 30 or more passes in 30 seconds at 15 feet, 3 points if you complete 20 to 29 passes, 1 point if you complete 10 to 19 passes, and 0 points if you complete fewer than 10 passes.

Number of bounce passes in 30 seconds at 15 feet ___; points earned ___

Number of behind-the-back passes in 30 seconds at 15 feet ___; points earned ___

Number of drop passes in 30 seconds at 15 feet ___; points earned ___

For the baseball pass, give yourself 5 points if you complete 20 or more passes in 30 seconds at 20 feet, 3 points if you complete 15 to 19 passes, 1 point if you complete 10 to 14 passes, and 0 points if you complete fewer than 10 passes.

Number of baseball passes in 30 seconds at 20 feet ___; points earned ___

Your score ___ (points earned; maximum of 35)

Passing Drill. **PASS AND FOLLOW**

This challenging, competitive, and fun drill requires several teammates. Divide into two lines, 12 feet (3.7 m) apart. The free-throw circle or center circle can be used to help space the lines 12 feet apart. When practicing the baseball pass, move the lines to 20 feet (6.1 m) apart. The first players in each line face each other; one of them has a ball. The first player in line with the ball throws a pass to the first player in the other line, then follows the pass by running to the right behind the receiver's line. The receiver catches the ball, passes it to the next player in the first line, and follows the pass by running to the right behind the player who receives the pass (and to the end of that line). The drill continues with each player catching, passing with quickness and accuracy, and following the pass. Each type of pass is practiced for 60 seconds.

Success Check

Use proper passing form for each type of pass.

Score Your Success

For the chest and overhead passes, give yourself 5 points if you complete 100 or more passes in 60 seconds at 12 feet, 3 points if you complete 90 to 99 passes, 1 point if you complete 80 to 89 passes, and 0 points if you complete fewer than 80 passes.

Number of chest passes in 60 seconds at 12 feet ___; points earned ___

Number of overhead passes in 60 seconds at 12 feet ___; points earned ___

For the bounce, sidearm, behind-the-back, and drop passes, give yourself 5 points if you complete 60 or more passes in 60 seconds at 12 feet, 3 points if you complete 50 to 59 passes, 1 point if you complete 40 to 49 passes, and 0 points if you complete fewer than 40 passes.

Number of bounce passes in 60 seconds at 12 feet ___; points earned ___

Number of sidearm passes in 60 seconds at 12 feet ___; points earned ___

Number of behind-the-back passes in 60 seconds at 12 feet ___; points earned ___

Number of drop passes in 60 seconds at 12 feet ___; points earned ___

For the baseball pass, give yourself 5 points if you complete 40 or more passes in 60 seconds at 20 feet, 3 points if you complete 30 to 39 passes, 1 point if you complete 20 to 29 passes, and 0 points if you complete fewer than 20 passes.

Number of baseball passes in 60 seconds at 20 feet ___; points earned ___

Your score ___ (points earned; maximum of 35)

Passing Drill. **STAR PASSING**

This is another challenging, competitive, and fun drill. At least 6 players and preferably 10 players are required for the drill. Set up in a star formation in five lines of two spaced 12 feet (3.7 m) apart around the free-throw circle. The chest pass will be used in this drill. With less than 10 players, make certain to start the drill in a line with two players. The player with the ball skips passing to the line immediately to the right and passes to the first player two lines to the right. The passer then follows the pass by running to the right behind the receiver's line. The receiver then passes the ball to the first player two lines to the right and follows the pass, running to the right behind the second receiver. The drill continues with each player catching, passing with quickness and accuracy, and following the pass. Count the number of passes made in 60 seconds.

Success Check

Use proper form for the chest pass.

Score Your Success

100 or more chest passes in 60 seconds = 5 points

90 to 99 chest passes in 60 seconds = 3 points

80 to 89 chest passes in 60 seconds = 2 points

70 to 79 chest passes in 60 seconds = 1 point

Fewer than 70 chest passes in 60 seconds = 0 points

Your score ___

Passing Drill. **TOSS BACK PASSING ON THE MOVE**

Passing to a toss back and moving from side to side will help you develop quickness, accuracy, and confidence. Place the toss back in the middle of the lane. Start 12 feet (3.7 m) away from it with your outside foot touching the lane line to your left. Use the chest pass when passing and catching on the move. Starting in good passing position, pass and catch the ball as quickly and accurately as you can while moving laterally, taking short, quick side steps and not crossing your feet. Move laterally until your outside foot touches the lane line to your right. Change direction and move back to the lane line to your left, passing and catching on the move. Keep moving laterally as you pass and catch, changing direction each time you touch the line. If a toss back is not available, use a wall. Use tape to mark lines 12 feet apart to serve as lane lines.

(continued)

(continued)

To Increase Difficulty

Run laterally instead of stepping, making a one-two stop as you catch each pass.

Success Check

- Do not cross your feet when moving laterally.
- Use short, quick steps.
- Attempt to complete 20 chest passes in 30 seconds at 12 feet while moving from lane line to lane line.

Score Your Success

20 or more chest passes in 30 seconds = 5 points

18 or 19 chest passes in 30 seconds = 4 points

15 to 17 chest passes in 30 seconds = 3 points

12 to 14 chest passes in 30 seconds = 2 points

10 or 11 chest passes in 30 seconds = 1 point

Fewer than 10 chest passes in 30 seconds = 0 points

Your score ___

Passing Drill. RICOCHET PASSING

This challenging, competitive, and fun drill is performed with a partner. The objective is to develop accuracy and confidence in chest passing while also developing quickness and agility.

Stand 12 feet (3.7 m) away from and facing a toss back or wall. Your partner stands behind you. Starting in good passing position, make a chest pass as accurately as you can to the middle of the toss back and move laterally to your right, taking short, quick side steps without crossing your feet. Your partner catches the ball as it comes off the toss back and makes a chest pass before moving laterally to the right. After your partner passes, you should quickly move laterally to your left and behind your partner. Catch the ball as it comes off the toss back and make a chest pass before moving laterally to the right. After you pass, your partner quickly moves laterally to the left and behind you and catches the ball as it comes off the toss back. Continue in this manner, passing and moving laterally to your right and then to your left and behind the passer. You can modify this drill by moving laterally in the opposite direction after each pass.

Success Check

- Use proper technique for the chest pass.
- Use proper technique for catching passes.
- Do not cross your feet as you move laterally.
- Use short, quick steps.
- Attempt to complete 20 chest passes in 30 seconds at 12 feet while moving laterally.

Score Your Success

20 or more chest passes in 30 seconds = 5 points

15 to 19 chest passes in 30 seconds = 3 points

10 to 14 chest passes in 30 seconds = 1 point

Fewer than 10 chest passes in 30 seconds = 0 points

Your score ___

Passing Drill. BULL IN THE RING

This fun passing drill is done with five players on offense and one player on defense. The offensive players spread out equidistant around the free-throw circle or center circle. One offensive player has the ball. The one defender, the bull in the ring, stands in the middle of the circle. The bull tries to intercept, deflect, or touch the passes. The player with the ball may use any type of pass to any player in the circle except the closest players on either side. The passer may not hold the ball longer than two seconds. If the bull touches the ball or the passer makes a bad pass or commits a violation, the passer becomes the bull in the ring, and the defender switches to offense.

Success Check

- Use proper passing form for each type of pass.
- Do not hold the ball for more than two seconds.
- Attempt to complete five consecutive passes without a deflection, bad pass, or violation.

Score Your Success

Completing five consecutive passes or more without error = 5 points

Completing four consecutive passes without error = 3 points

Completing three consecutive passes without error = 1 point

Completing fewer than three consecutive passes without error = 0 points

Your score ___

Passing Drill. TOSS BACK PASSING

This drill consists of passing to a toss back, and it helps you develop quickness, accuracy, and confidence in your passing. A wall can be used if a toss back is not available. In this drill, you will execute the chest pass, bounce pass, overhead pass, sidearm pass, baseball pass, and behind-the-back pass. Start in a balanced stance 12 feet (3.7 m) in front of a toss back or wall (20 feet [6.1 m] for the baseball pass), holding the ball in good passing position. Pass and catch the ball as quickly and accurately as you can. The correct fingertip release will impart backspin and direct the ball straight back to you. Keep your arms up on your follow-through until the ball hits the toss back.

Success Check

- Begin in a balanced stance.
- Use proper passing technique for each type of pass.
- Follow through with each type of pass.

(continued)

(continued)

Score Your Success

For the chest, overhead, sidearm, baseball, and behind-the-back passes, give yourself 5 points if you complete 30 or more passes in 30 seconds at 12 feet (20 for the baseball pass), 3 points if you complete 25 to 29 passes, 1 point if you complete 20 to 24 passes, and 0 points if you complete fewer than 20 passes.

Number of chest passes in 30 seconds ___; points earned ___

Number of overhead passes in 30 seconds ___; points earned ___

Number of sidearm passes in 30 seconds ___; points earned ___

Number of baseball passes in 30 seconds ___; points earned ___

Number of behind-the-back passes in 30 seconds ___; points earned ___

For the bounce pass, give yourself 5 points if you complete 20 or more passes in 30 seconds at 12 feet, 3 points if you complete 15 to 19 passes, 1 point if you complete 10 to 14 passes, and 0 points if you complete fewer than 10 passes.

Number of bounce passes in 30 seconds ___; points earned ___

Your score ___ (points earned; maximum of 30)

DEVELOPING GOOD HANDS

Good hands are important when receiving a pass, rebounding a missed shot, and protecting the ball. When being evaluated by coaches or scouts, some players are assigned the negative label of having bad hands. This includes dropping, fumbling, or allowing the ball to be easily taken out of your hands. This is a label that you want to avoid. A player with the desire to develop good hands can do so by working hard at the following drills.

Developing Good Hands Drill. RAPID-FIRE OVERHEAD PASS AND CATCH

For this drill, you will pass to a toss back from a distance of only 5 feet (1.5 m). A wall can be used if a toss back is not available. This drill is excellent for developing good hands and the ability to catch the ball. The drill also helps you develop quickness, accuracy, and confidence in passing and catching using the overhead pass.

Start in a balanced stance, 5 feet in front of a toss back. Hold the ball with two hands above your forehead, with your elbows in and flexed about 90 degrees. Do not bring the ball behind your head; if you begin with the ball behind your head, it may be stolen from behind and it takes longer to execute the pass, which may allow the ball to be intercepted. Quickly extend your back and arms, and flex your wrists and fingers to get maximum power. Release the ball off the first and second fingers of each hand. Follow through by pointing your fingers at the target, palms down. Using the overhead pass, pass the ball with as much force and accuracy as you can. Catch the return off the toss back with both hands above your head.

Success Check

- Begin in a balanced stance.
- Use proper technique for overhead passing.
- Pass the ball with as much force and accuracy as you can.
- Attempt to complete as many passes and catches as you can in 30 seconds.

Score Your Success

Give yourself 5 points if you complete 60 or more passes in 30 seconds, 3 points if you complete 50 to 59 passes, 1 point if you complete 40 to 49 passes, and 0 points if you complete fewer than 40 passes.

Number of overhead passes made in 30 seconds ___; points earned ___

Developing Good Hands Drill. RAPID-FIRE ONE-HAND SIDEARM PASS AND CATCH

For this drill, you will pass to a toss back from a distance of only 5 feet (1.5 m). A wall can be used if a toss back is not available. This drill is excellent for developing good hands and the ability to catch the ball. The drill also helps you develop quickness, accuracy, and confidence in passing and catching with one hand (strong or weak hand) using the sidearm pass.

Start in a balanced stance, 5 feet in front of a toss back. Turn your body so your chest is at a right angle to the toss back. Start with the ball in your strong hand; your weak hand is down at your side (you will use only one hand throughout this entire drill). Using a sidearm pass with your strong hand, pass the ball with as much force and accuracy as you can. Catch the return off the toss back with only your strong hand. Count the number of sidearm passes made with your strong hand in 30 seconds. Next, perform the same action with your weak hand.

Success Check

- Begin in a balanced stance with your body at a right angle to the toss back.
- Use a one-hand sidearm technique for passing and catching.
- Pass the ball with as much force and accuracy as you can.
- Attempt to complete as many passes and catches as you can in 30 seconds.

Score Your Success

Give yourself 5 points if you complete 50 or more passes in 30 seconds, 3 points if you complete 40 to 49 passes, 1 point if you complete 30 to 39 passes, and 0 points if you complete fewer than 30 passes.

Number of sidearm passes made with strong hand in 30 seconds ___; points earned ___

Number of sidearm passes made with weak hand in 30 seconds ___; points earned ___

Your score ___ (points earned; maximum of 10)

Developing Good Hands Drill. **RAPID-FIRE ONE-HAND BEHIND-THE-BACK PASS AND CATCH**

For this drill, you will pass to a toss back from a distance of only 5 feet (1.5 m). A wall can be used if a toss back is not available. The drill helps you develop quickness, accuracy, and confidence in passing and catching with one hand (strong or weak hand) using the behind-the-back pass. This is a more challenging drill for developing good hands than the previous drill.

Start in a balanced stance, 5 feet in front of a toss back. Turn your body so your chest is at a right angle to the toss back. Start with the ball in your strong hand; your weak hand is down at your side (you will use only one hand throughout this entire drill). Using a behind-the-back pass with your strong hand, pass the ball with as much force and accuracy as you can. Catch the return off the toss back with only your strong hand. Count the number of behind-the-back passes made with your strong hand in 30 seconds. Next, perform the behind-the-back pass with your weak hand.

Success Check

- Begin in a balanced stance with your body at a right angle to the toss back.
- Use a one-hand behind-the-back technique for passing and catching.
- Pass the ball with as much force and accuracy as you can.
- Attempt to complete as many passes and catches as you can in 30 seconds.

Score Your Success

Give yourself 5 points if you complete 40 or more passes in 30 seconds, 3 points if you complete 30 to 39 passes, 1 point if you complete 20 to 29 passes, and 0 points if you complete fewer than 20 passes.

Number of behind-the-back passes made with strong hand in 30 seconds ___; points earned ___

Number of behind-the-back passes made with weak hand in 30 seconds ___; points earned ___

Your score ___ (points earned; maximum of 10)

Developing Good Hands Drill.
DROP PASS, PIVOT, AND CATCH

For this drill, you will pass to a wall from a distance of only 5 feet (1.5 m). This drill is excellent for developing good hands and the ability to react to and catch quick passes. The drill also helps you develop quickness, accuracy, and confidence in your passing using the one-hand drop pass (with your strong or weak hand).

Start in a balanced stance 5 feet from a wall with your back to the wall (use a toss back if a wall is not available). Start with the ball in both hands at your right side at hip level. Your right hand should face the wall, and your nonpassing hand should be used to balance the ball. Make a drop pass to the wall with your right hand. Pass the ball with as much force and accuracy as you can. Perform a front pivot on your right foot to your right side and react quickly to catch the ball with two hands as it quickly returns off the wall. Now perform a reverse pivot on the same foot so your back is again toward the wall. Next, make a drop pass to the wall with your left hand, passing the ball with as much force and accuracy as you can. Perform a front pivot on your left foot to your left side and react quickly to catch the ball with two hands as it quickly returns off the wall. Perform a reverse pivot on the same foot so your back is again toward the wall. Continue performing the drill, alternating right- and left-handed drop passes.

Success Check

- Begin in a balanced stance with your back to the wall.
- Use proper technique for the drop pass.
- Pass the ball with as much force and accuracy as you can.
- Use a proper front pivot and reverse pivot.
- Attempt to complete as many passes and catches as you can in 30 seconds.

Score Your Success

Give yourself 5 points if you complete 40 or more passes in 30 seconds, 3 points if you complete 30 to 39 passes, 1 point if you complete 20 to 29 passes, and 0 points if you complete fewer than 20 passes.

Number of drop passes made in 30 seconds ___; points earned ___

RATE YOUR SUCCESS

Good passing and catching techniques are vital for team players who want to help their teams perform. In this step, we have covered the proper way to make various passes and the correct form for catching the pass. In the next step, we will look at fundamentals of dribbling the ball. Before going to step 3, however, look back at how you performed the drills in this step. For each of the drills in this step, enter the points you earned, then add up your scores to rate your total success.

Warm-Up Drill

	Drill	Points
1.	Ballhandling Warm-Up	____ out of 5

Passing Drills

	Drill	Points
1.	Partner Passing	____ out of 35
2.	Pass and Follow	____ out of 35
3.	Star Passing	____ out of 5
4.	Toss Back Passing on the Move	____ out of 5
5.	Ricochet Passing	____ out of 5
6.	Bull in the Ring	____ out of 5
7.	Toss Back Passing	____ out of 30

Developing Good Hands Drills

	Drill	Points
1.	Rapid-Fire Overhead Pass and Catch	____ out of 5
2.	Rapid-Fire One-Hand Sidearm Pass and Catch	____ out of 10
3.	Rapid-Fire One-Hand Behind-the-Back Pass and Catch	____ out of 10
4.	Drop Pass, Pivot, and Catch	____ out of 5

Total ____ **out of 155**

If you scored 80 or more points, congratulations! You have mastered the basics of this step and are ready to move on to step 3, dribbling. If you scored fewer than 80 points, you may want to spend more time on the fundamentals covered in this step. Practice the drills again to develop mastery of the techniques and increase your scores.

STEP

3

Dribbling

Dribbling is an integral part of basketball and is vital to individual and team play. Like passing, dribbling is a way of moving the ball. To maintain possession of the ball while you move, you have to dribble.

At the start of the dribble, the ball must leave your hand before you lift your pivot foot from the floor. While dribbling, you may not touch the ball with both hands simultaneously or allow it to come to rest in your hand.

The ability to dribble with your weak hand as well as your strong hand is a key to advancing your level of play. If you only dribble well with your strong hand, you can be overplayed to that side and be made virtually ineffective. To protect the ball while dribbling, keep your body between your defender and the ball. In other words, when you drive to your weak-hand side (to your left if you are right-handed), you dribble with the weak (left) hand to protect the ball with your body.

Dribbling allows you to move the ball by yourself. By dribbling, you can advance the ball up the court and evade pressure by defenders. Every team needs at least one skilled dribbler who can advance the ball up the court on a fast break and protect it against defensive pressure.

SPECIFIC USES FOR THE DRIBBLE

Here are some specific uses for the dribble:

- To move the ball out of a congested area when passing to a teammate is impossible, such as after a rebound or when being double-teamed
- To advance the ball up the court when no receivers are open, especially against pressure defenses
- To move the ball up the court on a fast break when teammates are not open in position to score
- To penetrate the defense for a drive to the basket
- To draw a defender to you in order to create an opening for a teammate

- To set up offensive plays
- To improve your position or angle before passing to a teammate
- To create your own shot

Dribbling is the most misused fundamental of the game. You need to understand when and when not to dribble. A pass travels many times faster than a dribble, so before you dribble, look to pass to open teammates. If you dribble too much, your teammates will tend to stop moving, making the defense's job easier. Excessive dribbling can destroy teamwork and morale. Learn to minimize the use of the dribble. Dribbling should have a purpose—it should take you somewhere. Do not waste it.

Don't get into the bad habit of bouncing the ball automatically the moment you receive it. By dribbling unnecessarily, you may miss the opportunity to pass to an open teammate, or you may stop your dribble before you have an open teammate. When you immediately dribble the ball once or twice and then pick it up, you have made it easier for your defender to apply pressure against your shot. This also makes it easier for your opponent to defend against the pass, because you are no longer a threat to drive. Once you start to dribble, remember not to stop until you have an open teammate to receive your pass.

To be an effective playmaker, you must become skilled at dribbling with either hand. Strive to reach the point where you feel that the ball is an extension of your hand. Keep your head up to see the entire court, and make the right decision at the right time. How well you dribble—your control, timing, deceptiveness, and quickness—largely determines your progress as a playmaker.

Have a trained observer—your coach, a teacher, or a skilled player—watch your dribbling skills. The observer can use the checklists in figures 3.1 through 3.10 to evaluate your performance and provide corrective feedback. Also, ask your coach to evaluate your decisions in using the dribble.

The basic dribble moves to learn include the control dribble, speed dribble, footfire dribble, change-of-pace dribble, retreat dribble, crossover dribble, inside-out dribble, reverse dribble, and behind-the-back dribble. Work to make your dribbling skills automatic so you can devote your full attention to the various situations taking place on the court. Learn how quickly you can dribble while maintaining control. In practice, strive to improve your ability, but in games, know your limitations. Dribbling is a skill that you can practice by yourself. All you need is a ball, a level spot, and an eagerness to improve.

Dribbling Drill. DRIBBLE WARM-UP

The dribble warm-up helps you develop your ability and confidence in dribbling with either the strong or weak hand. The drill's five parts are crossover, figure eight, one knee, sitting, and lying down.

Crossover. From a balanced stance, change the ball from one hand to the other, dribbling it below knee level and no wider than your knees. Keep your nondribbling hand up to protect the ball. Also change the position of your feet and body to protect the ball. Alternating from right to left and from left to right, complete 20 repetitions (10 with each hand).

Figure eight. Dribble the ball in a figure eight from back to front through your legs and around your legs. Change from one hand to the other after the ball goes through your legs. After 10 repetitions, change direction and dribble the ball in a figure eight from front to back through your legs and around your legs for 10 more repetitions.

One knee. Dribble the ball as you kneel on one knee. Starting in front of your knee, dribble around to one side and under your front knee. Change hands and dribble behind your back leg. Again change from one hand to the other and continue to the starting point in front of your knee. Dribble in a figure eight for 10 repetitions in one direction, then reverse and dribble in a figure eight for 10 repetitions in the opposite direction.

Sitting. Continue dribbling as you sit down. Dribble for 10 repetitions on one side while sitting. Raise your legs, dribble the ball under them to the other side, and dribble on that side for 10 repetitions.

Lying down. Continue dribbling as you lie on your back. While lying down, dribble for 10 repetitions on one side. Sit up, raise your legs, dribble the ball under them to the other side, lie down again, and dribble on the other side for 10 repetitions.

Success Check

- Dribble with confidence.
- Work your weak hand as much as your strong hand.
- Attempt to complete 10 repetitions without error in each direction for each part of the drill.

Score Your Success

For each part of the drill, record how many dribbles you complete to each side without error. Give yourself 5 points for completing 10 repetitions without error to each side.

	Right	Left	Points
Crossover	___	___	___
Figure eight	___	___	___
One knee	___	___	___
Sitting	___	___	___
Lying down	___	___	___
Your score			___

CONTROL DRIBBLE

Use the control dribble (figure 3.1) when you are closely guarded and must keep the ball protected and under control. A well-balanced stance, which is basic to the control dribble, makes you a triple threat to shoot, pass, or drive. It allows you to move quickly, change direction, change pace, and stop under control while protecting the ball. Learn to dribble without looking at the ball. Keep your head up and keep the rim of the basket in view. This will allow you to see the entire court, open teammates, and defenders.

Keep your head over your waist and keep your back straight. Your feet should be at least shoulder-width apart, your weight evenly distributed on the balls of your feet, and your knees flexed. Be prepared to move. Keep the elbow of your dribbling hand close to your body. Your dribbling hand should be in a relaxed position with the thumb relaxed and the fingers spread comfortably. Dribble the ball off your finger pads with fingertip control, flexing your wrist and fingers to impart force on the ball. Do not pump your arm. Dribble the ball no higher than knee level and keep it close to your body. Keep your nondribbling hand in a protective position close to the ball. Position your body between your defender and the ball.

Figure 3.1 **CONTROL DRIBBLE**

Control dribble

1. Keep head up and see rim
2. Dribble
3. Make sure ball leaves hand before pivot foot leaves floor
4. Dribble ball off finger pads using strong wrist and finger flexion
5. Protect ball with body and nondribbling hand

MISSTEP

You look at the ball when dribbling.

CORRECTION

Keep your head up and see the rim.

SPEED DRIBBLE

The speed dribble (figure 3.2) is useful when you are not closely guarded, when you must move the ball quickly up the open floor, and when you have a quick drive to the basket. For speed dribbling, use a high dribble at waist level, keep your head up, and keep the rim of the basket in view. This will allow you to see the entire court, open teammates, and defenders.

Start by throwing the ball out several feet and running after it. Remember, the ball must leave your hand before you lift your pivot foot. Push the successive dribbles out at waist level, flexing your wrist and fingers to put force on the ball. Dribble the ball off your finger pads with fingertip control.

Figure 3.2 **SPEED DRIBBLE**

Speed dribble

1. Keep head up and see rim
2. Throw ball out several feet and run after it
3. Push dribble forward at waist level
4. Make sure ball leaves hand before pivot foot leaves floor
5. Dribble ball off finger pads using strong wrist and finger flexion
6. Protect ball with body and nondribbling hand

MISSTEP

You take too many dribbles.

CORRECTION

Push each dribble out at waist level and run after the ball, keeping the number of dribbles to a minimum.

Speed dribbling is important, but so is stopping quickly with balance. After dribbling at full speed, inexperienced players often lose balance and control as they try to stop quickly. The one-two stop (figure 3.3) can prevent you from dragging your pivot foot and traveling when you stop after speed dribbling. This is especially important on a fast break.

In the one-two stop, your back foot lands first, followed by your other foot. When the one-two stop is executed on your last dribble, the foot that lands first becomes your pivot foot. Hopping before executing the one-two stop allows gravity to help slow your momentum. Lean in the opposite direction and land with a wide base. The wider your base, the more stable you will become. Flex your back knee to lower your body to a "sitting" position on the heel of your back foot. The lower you get, the more you will be in balance. Keep your head up.

Figure 3.3 **ONE-TWO STOP AFTER SPEED DRIBBLE**

a

b

Hop and lean back

1. Hop before stop
2. Lean back
3. Catch ball off last dribble

One-two stop

1. Land first on back foot
2. Land second on lead foot
3. Land with wide base
4. Keep head up and see rim

MISSTEP

You lose balance forward, causing you to drag your pivot foot.

CORRECTION

Hop before you stop, allowing gravity to slow your momentum. Lean back and land first on your back foot, then on your front foot. Maintain a wide base for stability. "Sit" on the heel of your back foot. Keep your head up.

FOOTFIRE DRIBBLE

As you approach a defender in the open court, you can use the footfire dribble (figure 3.4) to stop moving while keeping the dribble alive. The footfire dribble enables you to gain balance and see or read the defender's positioning. This is especially useful at the end of a fast break. You will be a triple threat to shoot, pass, or drive as you dribble.

To execute the footfire dribble, quickly change from a speed dribble to a control dribble, coming to a stop while keeping the dribble alive. Dribble in place, facing the basket with feet shoulder-width apart. Move your feet up and down as rapidly and as close to the floor as you can, as if they are on a hot surface. This rapid footfire movement helps you gain complete balance while also temporarily freezing your defender. The effectiveness of the footfire dribble comes from gaining complete balance and control, reading the defender's position, and faking before you make your next move to shoot, pass, or drive.

Figure 3.4 **FOOTFIRE DRIBBLE**

a

b

c

Speed dribble

1. Keep head up and see rim
2. Speed dribble at waist level

Footfire dribble

1. Change from speed dribble to control dribble and continue dribbling
2. Move feet up and down rapidly (footfire)

Head up

1. Keep head up and see rim
2. Become triple threat to shoot, pass, or drive
3. Head fake before next move

MISSTEP

You are unstable during the footfire dribble.

CORRECTION

Emphasize complete balance and control with your feet shoulder-width apart and your knees flexed.

CHANGE-OF-PACE DRIBBLE

The change-of-pace dribble (figure 3.5) is useful for deceiving and eluding a defender. To execute the change-of-pace dribble, change your dribble method from control to speed and quickly back to control. The effectiveness of your change of pace depends on your deceptiveness and quickness. Push the dribble out to change quickly from a slower to a faster speed. In changing your pace, you have the advantage because *you* decide when to change speeds. With good deception and a forceful push of the dribble to quickly increase speed, you should be at least a step ahead of your defender just after changing pace from control dribble to speed dribble.

Figure 3.5 **CHANGE-OF-PACE DRIBBLE**

Control to speed dribble

1. Keep head up and see rim
2. Change to speed dribble at waist level
3. Push dribble out and run after it

Speed to control dribble

1. Keep head up and see rim
2. Change to control dribble at knee level
3. Protect ball with body and nondribbling hand

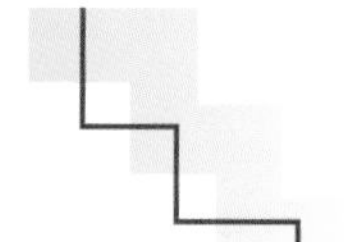

MISSTEP

You do not control the dribble when changing from speed dribble to control dribble.

CORRECTION

Widen your base and flex your knees to gain balance. Dribble the ball at knee level or lower.

RETREAT DRIBBLE

The retreat dribble is used to avoid trouble caused by defensive pressure. The retreat dribble is often used before using a crossover and speed dribble to elude a trap set by two defenders. Retreating with the dribble allows you to create space between you and the defenders, putting you in position to make a crossover and speed dribble to get by the trap.

To execute the retreat dribble (figure 3.6), use short, quick retreat steps while dribbling backward. As you retreat, protect the ball and maintain a balanced stance. Make a controlled change-of-direction dribble and explode past the defenders with a speed dribble. Keep your head up and see the rim so you can see and pass to open teammates.

Figure 3.6 **RETREAT DRIBBLE (TO SPEED DRIBBLE)**

a

b

Retreat dribble

1. Keep head up and see rim
2. Change to retreat dribble with ball at knee level
3. Use short, quick retreat steps
4. Protect ball with body and nondribbling hand

Speed dribble

1. Keep head up and see rim
2. Change to speed dribble with ball at waist level
3. Push dribble out and run after it

MISSTEP

You have trouble retreating quickly.

CORRECTION

Do not lean forward; maintain your balance, and use short, quick retreat steps.

CROSSOVER DRIBBLE

The crossover dribble is important when you are in the open court on a fast break, when you need to get open on a drive to the basket, or when you need to create an opening for your shot. The effectiveness of your crossover dribble is based on how sharply you change your dribble from one direction to another. You can make the crossover dribble when using a control dribble or when dribbling at full speed. To execute a crossover dribble when closely guarded (figure 3.7), cross the ball in front of you at a backward angle, switching the dribble from one hand to the other. Making the crossover at a backward angle helps prevent your defender from deflecting or stealing the ball. Dribble the ball close to you at knee level or lower with a control dribble. To execute a crossover dribble when you are dribbling at full speed, dribble the ball at waist level and cross the ball in front of you at a forward angle. When you make the crossover dribble, get your nondribbling hand up and change your lead foot and body position for protection.

Figure 3.7 **CROSSOVER DRIBBLE (OFF CONTROL DRIBBLE)**

a

b

Control dribble

1. Keep head up and rim in view
2. Control dribble at knee level
3. Protect ball with body and nondribbling hand

Crossover dribble

1. Cross ball in front at backward angle, switching hands
2. Dribble close to body
3. Protect ball with body and nondribbling hand

MISSTEP

You dribble the ball too high or too wide when changing direction.

CORRECTION

Dribble at knee level and close to your body.

INSIDE-OUT DRIBBLE

The inside-out dribble is a fake crossover dribble off a control or footfire dribble. This deceptive dribble can be used to get open on a drive to the basket or for a shot. When executing the inside-out dribble (figure 3.8), start by using a head fake to the opposite side and at the same time moving your hand and the ball in as though you will be making a crossover dribble. Instead of releasing the ball and dribbling it in front of you to your other hand, rotate your hand over the ball and dribble it outside your base back to the side from which you started. Dribble close to your body at knee level. Protect the ball with your body and nondribbling hand.

Figure 3.8 **INSIDE-OUT DRIBBLE (FAKE CROSSOVER)**

a

b

Fake crossover

1. Keep head up and see rim
2. Use head fake to opposite direction
3. Fake crossing ball in front
4. Quickly rotate hand over ball and then push ball back to same side with inside-out motion

Dribble ball back

1. Dribble ball back to same side outside base
2. Control dribble at knee level
3. Protect ball with body and nondribbling hand

MISSTEP

Your inside-out dribble is not deceptive.

CORRECTION

Make a head fake in the opposite direction.

REVERSE DRIBBLE

The reverse dribble keeps your body between the ball and the defender for protection as you change direction. The disadvantage, however, is that you temporarily take your eyes off other defenders who may attempt a blind-sided steal of the ball. The reverse dribble is best used as an offensive move to counter a strong defensive overplay to your dribbling side. It enables you to create your own shot in the opposite direction.

The reverse dribble (figure 3.9) is a two-dribble move. Start by dribbling backward, and then pivot backward on your opposite foot while turning your shoulders back toward your dribbling-hand side. Bring your back foot forward as you pull a second dribble forward, close to your body, using the same hand. After completing the reverse-dribble move, change hands for your next dribble.

Figure 3.9 **REVERSE DRIBBLE**

a

Dribble ball back

1. Keep head up and see rim
2. Dribble ball back behind body
3. Protect ball with body and non-dribbling hand

b

Reverse pivot

1. Reverse pivot on front foot
2. Step through with back foot
3. Pull second dribble forward

c

Change hands

1. Change hands
2. Control dribble at knee level
3. Protect ball with body and non-dribbling hand

MISSTEP

You change hands on your dribble as you reverse, causing you to dribble too wide.

CORRECTION

First dribble backward. As you reverse pivot, emphasize pulling the ball forward and close to your body using your same hand.

Dribbling Drill.
KNOCK THE BALL OUT OF THE CIRCLE

This drill helps you develop the ability to dribble with your head up and to protect the ball against pressure. Select another player as an opponent. You each have a basketball. Dribble within either the free-throw circle or the center circle. Each of you tries to deflect the other's basketball outside the circle.

To Increase Difficulty

- Require both participants to dribble with their weak hand only.
- Allow more contact than normal to work on dribbling under severe defensive pressure.

Success Check

- Keep your head up.
- Protect the ball with your body and your nondribbling hand.
- Be aware of your partner's movements.

Score Your Success

You score 1 point each time you knock your opponent's ball out of the circle. Play until someone scores 5 points.

Your score ____

BEHIND-THE-BACK DRIBBLE

The behind-the-back dribble keeps your body between the ball and the defender for protection as you change direction. This dribble is best used on the open floor when a defensive player in front is overplaying you to your dribbling side. Although developing the behind-the-back dribble takes more practice than other dribble moves, it is well worth the effort. Compared to the crossover dribble, the behind-the-back dribble allows you to keep your body between the ball and a defender. Compared to the reverse dribble, it allows you to change direction without taking your eyes off the rim or other defenders. The behind-the-back dribble is much quicker than the reverse dribble and almost as quick as the crossover dribble.

Like the reverse dribble, the behind-the-back dribble (figure 3.10, page 66) is a two-dribble move. Again, dribble backward. Move your pelvis forward as you pull a second dribble behind your back, close to your body, in a forward direction to your other hand. After your second dribble, change hands. Use your body and nondribbling hand for protection.

Figure 3.10 **BEHIND-THE-BACK DRIBBLE**

a

b

c

First dribble behind body

1. Keep head up and see rim
2. Dribble ball behind body
3. Protect ball with body and non-dribbling hand

Pull second dribble behind back

1. Move pelvis forward
2. Pull second dribble behind back and then forward

Switch hands

1. Switch hands
2. Control dribble at knee level

MISSTEP

You dribble too wide.

CORRECTION

Emphasize pulling the ball forward and close to your body on the second dribble, using the same hand.

Dribbling Drill. TWO-BALL DRIBBLE

Dribbling two balls is fun and will help you develop dribbling ability and confidence with both hands. This drill has six parts: together, alternate one up and one down, crossover, inside out, through the legs, and side pull forward and back. Each part includes dribbling two balls simultaneously. If a ball gets away, keep dribbling the other while you recover the stray ball.

Together. Dribble two basketballs below knee level simultaneously.

Alternate one up and one down. Dribble two basketballs simultaneously so that one ball is up while the other is down.

Crossover. Switch the balls from one hand to the other by crossing them back and forth in front of you, keeping them low and close to your body. Mix up how you switch the balls rather than executing each crossover with the same hand going in front.

Inside out. An inside-out dribble is a fake change of direction. While dribbling two balls, start one ball inside, then rotate your hand over the ball to dribble it outside your base on the same side. Perform the inside-out dribble alternating hands and then with both hands simultaneously.

Through the legs. Dribble one ball through the legs, then dribble the other ball through the legs. Next, dribble both balls through the legs, first dribbling both balls back to front and then dribbling both balls front to back.

Side pull forward and back. Start by dribbling two balls, one on each side of your body. Then dribble them backward and forward by flexing your wrists and fingers in an action that is similar to pushing the balls back and forth.

Success Check

- Work both hands.
- Try to complete 20 dribbles without error for each part of the drill.

Score Your Success

For each part of the drill, record how many dribbles you complete without error. If you complete 20 or more dribbles, give yourself 5 points. If you complete 15 to 19 dribbles, give yourself 3 points. If you complete 10 to 14 dribbles, give yourself 1 point. If you complete fewer than 10 dribbles, give yourself 0 points.

Number of together dribbles ___; points earned ___

Number of alternate one-up and one-down dribbles ___; points earned ___

Number of crossover dribbles ___; points earned ___

Number of inside-out dribbles with right hand ___; points earned ___

Number of inside-out dribbles with left hand ___; points earned ___

Number of inside-out dribbles with both hands ___; points earned ___

Number of through-the-leg dribbles with right hand ___; points earned ___

Number of through-the-leg dribbles with left hand ___; points earned ___

Number of through-the-leg dribbles with both hands ___; points earned ___

Number of side pull forward and back dribbles ___; points earned ___

Your score ___ (points earned; maximum score of 50)

Dribbling Drill. MOVING TWO-BALL DRIBBLE

After dribbling two balls in a stationary position, you can now move on to the challenge of dribbling two balls while moving. This drill will help you improve your weak- and strong-hand dribbling ability and thus your confidence. This drill also has six parts: zigzag, attack and retreat, stop and go, change of pace, reverse, and fake reverse.

Zigzag. Dribble two balls up the court in a zigzag manner (dribbling diagonally to one side and then the other). Change direction by crossing both balls in front.

Attack and retreat. Dribble two balls up the court using an attack and retreat (dribbling forward and then back without crossing your feet). Alternate the lead foot each time you attack and retreat.

Stop and go. Dribble two balls up the court using a stop-and-go dribble. Speed dribble by pushing both balls forward. Stop sharply, with your body under full control, and keep dribbling as you stop.

Change of pace. Dribble two balls up the court while changing pace (speed to control and control to speed). Use imagination to add deception, accelerating at various speeds.

Reverse. Dribble two balls while zigzagging up the court, changing direction by using a reverse pivot. Dribble both balls back to one side, then reverse pivot on your lead foot while pulling both balls close to where your body was before your reverse pivot.

Fake reverse. Dribble two balls while zigzagging up the court. Before changing direction, use a fake reverse by dribbling both balls back to one side and turning your head and shoulders back. Then quickly turn your head and shoulders forward as you dribble both balls forward again.

Success Check

- Dribble with confidence.
- Work both hands.
- For the zigzag and attack and retreat, attempt to complete two full-court trips with no more than one error on each trip.
- For the stop and go, change of pace, reverse, and fake reverse, attempt to complete two full-court trips with no more than three errors on each trip.

Score Your Success

For the zigzag and attack and retreat, give yourself 5 points if you complete two full-court trips with no more than one error on each trip. For the stop and go, change of pace, reverse, and fake reverse, give yourself 5 points if you complete two full-court trips with no more than three errors on each trip.

	Number of full-court trips	Number of errors	Points
Zigzag	___	___	___
Attack and retreat	___	___	___
Stop and go	___	___	___
Change of pace	___	___	___
Reverse	___	___	___
Fake reverse	___	___	___
Your score			___

Dribbling Drill. DRIBBLE CONES

Set up five cones: one at the baseline, one halfway between the baseline and half-court, one at half-court, one halfway between half-court and the opposite baseline, and one at the opposite baseline. The drill has three parts: crossover dribble, behind-the-back dribble, and retreat dribble and crossover. Dribble at full speed during each part of the drill.

Crossover dribble. Start at the baseline cone. Dribble at full speed with your strong hand. After passing the second cone, make a crossover dribble and switch the ball to your weak hand. Speed dribble with your weak hand until you pass the next cone. Make a crossover dribble back to your strong hand. Continue in this manner to the opposite baseline. Turn and dribble back to the original cone, making a crossover dribble and switching hands as you pass each cone.

Behind-the-back dribble. This part of the drill is executed the same way except that you make a full-speed behind-the-back dribble after you pass each cone.

Retreat dribble and crossover. Speed dribble to the first cone. Execute a retreat dribble, taking at least three dribbles back. Perform a crossover dribble, and then resume the speed dribble to the next cone. Continue in this manner to the opposite baseline and back.

Success Check

- Dribble with speed and confidence.
- For the crossover dribble, attempt to pass 10 cones in 30 seconds.
- For the behind-the-back dribble, attempt to pass 8 cones in 30 seconds.
- For the retreat dribble and crossover, attempt to pass 6 cones in 30 seconds.

(continued)

(continued)

Score Your Success

For the crossover dribble, give yourself 5 points if you pass 10 cones in 30 seconds, 3 points if you pass 8 or 9 cones, 1 point if you pass 6 or 7 cones, and 0 points if you pass fewer than 6 cones. For the behind-the-back dribble, give yourself 5 points if you pass 8 cones in 30 seconds, 3 points if you pass 7 cones, 1 point if you pass 6 cones, and 0 points if you pass fewer than 6 cones. For the retreat dribble and crossover, give yourself 5 points if you pass 6 cones in 30 seconds, 3 points if you pass 5 cones, 1 point if you pass 4 cones, and 0 points if you pass fewer than 4 cones.

Number of cones passed using crossover dribble ___; points earned ___

Number of cones passed using behind-the-back dribble ___; points earned ___

Number of cones passed using retreat dribble and crossover ___; points earned ___

Your score ___ (points earned; maximum of 15)

RATE YOUR SUCCESS

If you can dribble the ball with confidence and control, you will have many options as you move the ball around the court. You will be able to move to create better passing lanes, outmaneuver the defense, and control the pace of play.

In the next step, we will look at the fundamentals of shooting the ball. Before going to step 4, however, look back at how you performed the drills in this step. For each of the drills presented in this step, enter the points you earned, then add up your scores to rate your total success.

Dribbling Drills

1. Dribble Warm-Up	____ out of 25
2. Knock the Ball Out of the Circle	____ out of 5
3. Two-Ball Dribble	____ out of 50
4. Moving Two-Ball Dribble	____ out of 30
5. Dribble Cones	____ out of 15
Total	____ **out of 125**

If you scored 65 or more points, congratulations! You have mastered the basics of this step and are ready to move on to step 4, shooting. If you scored fewer than 65 points, you may want to spend more time on the fundamentals covered in this step. Practice the drills again to develop mastery of the techniques and increase your scores.

STEP

4

Shooting

Shooting is the most important skill in basketball. The fundamental skills of passing, dribbling, defense, and rebounding may enable you to get a high-percentage shot, but you must still be able to make the shot. A large part of shooting is mental attitude. In addition to shooting skill, you must have confidence in yourself to shoot well. The integration of the mental and mechanical aspects of shooting fosters shooting success.

When you have an accurate shot, you force your defender to play you tight and to become vulnerable to a fake, allowing you to pass and drive as well as shoot. If you lack an accurate shot, a defender can play back in anticipation of a drive or pass; the defender is then less susceptible to your fake. When you do not have the ball, your defender can play farther off you and be in better position to give defensive help to a teammate guarding another player. To be successful, a team must have players who can make the outside shot.

A great shooter is often called a *pure shooter* because of his smooth, free-flowing shot or soft touch. Some players think that a pure shooter is naturally gifted—born that way. This is a misconception. Great shooters are made, not born.

A pure shooter such as hall of famer and two-time NBA Most Valuable Player Steve Nash, who can drive hard around an opponent and then effortlessly pull up for a soft jump shot, may appear to have been born a shooter. His thoughts are not on the mechanics of the shot, but rather on the position and movement of teammates and defenders. A pure shooter considers faking the shot, delivering a pass, driving for the basket, or reversing direction to pull the ball out and reset the offense. For Nash and other great shooters, the skill is automatic. Like other talented people, pure shooters perform their skills to a maximum level without conscious thought. Each was a beginner at one time, however, and each developed into a pure shooter through dedicated practice.

Shooting is a skill you can practice by yourself. Once you understand correct mechanics, all you need is a ball, a basket, and an eagerness to improve. But it is also helpful to practice shooting under game conditions, including the pressure situations that occur late in a game. Practice with a partner providing the defensive pressure of an opponent. Remember that through practice you will develop shooting skill and confidence. You can also benefit from having a trained observer such as a coach, a teacher, or a skilled player watch you shoot and provide corrective feedback. However, most of your shooting practice will occur when a coach or teacher is not present; therefore, you must learn to analyze your shot's reaction on the rim in order to reinforce successful execution or identify shooting errors and their possible causes.

SHOOTING CONFIDENCE

Believe in yourself. You want to have confidence in your ability to make the shot every time you shoot. Confident shooters control their thoughts, feelings, and shooting skill. Basketball is a mental as well as physical game. Developing the mental aspect is a key to enhancing shooting as well as performance in all fundamentals.

One way to improve your confidence is to realize that the basket is big. It is so large that over three and a half balls can fit in the rim. This surprises most players. You can get on a ladder and fit three balls side by side over the rim and still have enough space to fit and turn your hand between each ball. Realizing that the basket is this big should give you a psychological boost.

Another way to boost your confidence is to keep your follow-through straight up until the ball reaches the rim. Not only is this mechanically correct, but more important, you will look and act like a shooter.

You want to believe that each time you shoot, the ball will go in. Good shooters stay confident even when they hit a cold streak and miss a few shots. After a missed shot, mentally correct the miss and visualize a good shot. Repeating positive affirmation statements such as "I'm a shooter," "All net," or "Count it!" to yourself can promote confident thoughts about you and your ability to shoot. You can also boost your confidence by reminding yourself of past successes.

Being able to shoot under pressure distinguishes great shooters from good shooters. You want to take the shot not only when your team is ahead, but also when the pressure is on. The direct correlation between shooting confidence and shooting success is the most consistent factor in great shooters.

POSITIVE SELF-TALK

As important as confidence is, accurate shooting requires more than positive thinking; it also requires shooting skill. Neither mental confidence nor mechanics alone is enough. Success results from integration of the mental and mechanical aspects of shooting.

When you think, you are in a sense talking to yourself. That talk can be either positive or negative. A technique called *positive self-talk* can help you integrate the mental and mechanical aspects of shooting, hastening the improvement of your shot. Positive self-talk involves using key words to enhance performance.

Select words that reinforce correct mechanics, establish rhythm, and build confidence. The key words should be positive, concise (preferably one syllable), and personalized. A positive word that you associate with a successful shot is called an *anchor* word. Select your own personal anchor word that allows you to visualize your shot going in, such as *yes, net, whoosh, swish, in,* or *through.*

Words that key the correct mechanics of your shot are called *trigger* words. Here are some examples of trigger words:

- *High!* Start your shot high and avoid lowering the ball.
- *Straight!* Make your shooting hand go straight to the basket.
- *Front!* Trigger the position of the shooting hand facing the rim.

- *Point!* Trigger the correct release of the ball off the pads of your index finger.
- *Up!* Key a high arc.
- *Through!* Key any part of your follow-through, including shoulders, arm, wrist, and fingers.
- *Head in!* Trigger the follow-through of your head and shoulders toward the basket and eliminate leaning back or stepping back.
- *Legs!* Trigger the use of your legs.
- *Down and up!* Key the down-and-up action of your legs that provides rhythm and force for your shot.

Identify two words that trigger the correct mechanics and one anchor word to reinforce shooting success. Sometimes a word can be both a trigger and an anchor word. For example, *through* can be used as a trigger word that keys the follow-through of your shoulders, arm, wrist, and fingers; *through* can also be an anchor word for the ball going through the basket.

Say your words in rhythm, from the time your shooting motion starts with your legs until you release the ball off your index finger. For example, if *legs* and *through* are your trigger words and *yes* is your anchor word, you would say the following in rhythm with your shot: "Legs-through-yes!" It works better if you say your words aloud rather than to yourself.

Saying your personalized key words in an even rhythm establishes the rhythm of your shot and enhances your mechanics and confidence. Devote time to mental as well as physical practice. Relax and mentally practice saying your key words in the rhythm of your shot as you visualize shooting and seeing the ball go in the basket.

Your goal is to reduce conscious thought and promote automatic execution of your shot. Trigger words help make the mechanics of your shot automatic, and an anchor word, which reinforces a successful shot, helps build your confidence. As your shooting improves, one trigger word may suffice. Eventually, an anchor word may be all you need to trigger the automatic action of your shot.

SHOOTING RHYTHM

Skills should be smooth, free flowing, and rhythmical. This is especially true in shooting. Mechanics are important, but you want to have good mechanics without being mechanical. Your shot should be smooth and rhythmical rather than mechanical. All parts of your shot should flow together in a sequential rhythm.

Rhythm and range come from a down-and-up motion of your legs. Start with your knees slightly flexed. Saying the key words *down and up!* from the start of your shot until the release of the ball will trigger the down-and-up action of your legs, providing rhythm and range for your shot. Your legs and shooting arm work together. As your legs go up, your arm goes up. As your legs reach full extension, your back, shoulders, and shooting arm extend in a smooth, continuous upward direction. Use the down-and-up motion of your legs for rhythm, rather than lowering the ball for rhythm.

EVALUATING YOUR SHOT

Learn to shoot correctly and then practice intelligently each day. Develop an understanding of your own shot. You can always benefit from having an instructor or coach watch you shoot. Most of your practice, however, occurs when a coach is not present. Personal feedback (information about your performance) can help you determine what adjustments to make. Three basic sources of performance feedback are observing the reaction of your shot on the rim, internally feeling your shot, and using video analysis of your shooting form.

Analyzing a shot's reaction on the rim can reinforce successful execution or reveal most shooting errors and their possible causes. For example, the ball goes where your shooting arm, hand, and finger direct it. If you miss to the right (or left), your shooting arm, hand, and finger are pointing in that direction. Perhaps your body faces in the direction of the miss rather than being square to the basket, or your elbow is out, causing your follow-through to go to the right.

If you see that the ball hits the right of the rim and rolls off to the left, you know that you shot the ball with sidespin. In general, sidespin is caused by your shooting hand starting on the side of the ball and then rotating behind it. If you overrotate your shooting hand, the ball will hit the right side of the rim with sidespin and roll left. If you underrotate, the ball will hit the left side of the rim and roll right. Sidespin is also caused by the ball sliding off your ring finger rather than your shooting finger.

Your sense of feel also yields clues. You might feel your shooting hand rotate to the right or feel the ball come off your ring finger instead of your shooting finger. Both mistakes will give the ball sidespin. An excellent method for developing feel is to shoot free throws with your eyes closed. Have a partner rebound and tell you whether the shot was successful. After a miss, your partner should tell you the specific direction of the miss and the reaction of the ball on the rim. By analyzing your shot, you can detect and correct errors before they become bad habits.

SHOOTING MECHANICS

Most players shoot seven basic shots: the one-hand set shot, the free throw, the jump shot, the three-point shot, the hook shot, the layup, and the runner. These shots all share certain basic mechanics, including sight, balance, hand position, elbow-in alignment, rhythmical shooting motion, and follow-through. The best way to develop your shot is to concentrate on only one or two mechanics at a time.

Sight. Focus your eyes on the basket, aiming just over the front of the rim for all shots except bank shots. Use a bank shot when you are at a 45-degree angle to the backboard. A 45-degree angle falls within the distance between the box and the middle hash mark on the lane line. The distance for the bank angle—called the *45-degree funnel*—widens as you move out. When shooting a bank shot, aim for the top near corner of the box on the backboard.

Sight your target as soon as possible and keep your eyes focused on the target until the ball reaches the goal. Your eyes should never follow the flight of the ball or your defender's hand. Concentrating on the target helps eliminate distractions such as shouting, towel waving, an opponent's hand, or even a hard foul.

Balance. Balance leads to power and rhythmic control of your shot. Your base, or foot position, is the foundation of your balance, and keeping your head over your feet (base) controls your balance.

Spread your feet comfortably to shoulder width and point your toes straight ahead. Pointing your toes straight aligns your knees, hips, and shoulders with the basket. The foot on the side of your shooting hand (right foot for a right-handed shot) is forward. The toe of your back foot is aligned with the heel of the foot on your shooting side (toe-to-heel relationship).

Flex your legs at the knees. This gives crucial power to your shot. Beginning and fatigued players often fail to flex their knees. To compensate for the lack of power from not using their legs, they tend to throw the ball from behind the head or shove the ball from the hip. Both of these actions produce errors.

Your head should be over your waist and feet. Your head controls your balance and should be slightly forward, with your shoulders and upper body inclining forward toward the basket. Your shoulders should be relaxed.

Hand position. Hand position is the most misunderstood part of shooting. You want to make sure that you start and finish your shot with your shooting hand facing the basket (behind the ball). Placing the nonshooting hand (also called the balance hand) under the ball for balance is also important. This position, with the shooting hand facing the basket (behind the ball) and the nonshooting hand under the ball, is called the *block-and-tuck*. It leaves your shooting hand free to shoot the ball, rather than having to balance *and* shoot the ball.

Place your hands fairly close together. Relax both hands and spread the fingers comfortably. Keep the thumb of your shooting hand relaxed and not spread apart; this helps you avoid tension in your hand and forearm. A relaxed hand position (like a handshake) forms a natural cup, enabling the ball to contact the pads of your fingers and not your palm. Place your nonshooting hand slightly under the ball. The weight of the ball balances on at least two fingers: the ring finger and the little finger. The arm of your nonshooting hand should be in a comfortable position, with the elbow pointing slightly back and to the side. Your shooting hand is set behind the ball, facing the basket, with your index finger directly at the ball's midpoint. The ball is released off the pads of your index finger. On a free throw, you have time to align your index finger with the valve or another marking at the midpoint of the ball. Developing fingertip control and touch leads to a soft, accurate shot.

Elbow-in alignment. Hold the ball comfortably in front of and above your shooting shoulder between your ear and shoulder. Keep your shooting elbow in. When your shooting elbow is in, the ball is aligned with the basket. Some players do not have the flexibility to place the shooting hand behind the ball with the hand facing the front of the basket while keeping the elbow in. If this is the case, you should first place the shooting hand behind the ball, facing the front of the basket, and then move the elbow in as far as your flexibility allows.

Rhythmical shooting motion. Shooting involves synchronizing the extension of your legs, back, shoulders, and shooting arm and the flexion of your wrist and fingers. Shoot the ball with a smooth, free-flowing, and rhythmical lifting motion.

The initial force and rhythm for your shot come from a down-and-up motion of your legs. Start with your knees slightly flexed. Bend your knees and then fully extend them in a down-and-up motion. Saying the key words *down and up!* from the start of your shot until the release of the ball will trigger the down-and-up action of your legs, providing rhythm and range for your shot. Your legs and shooting arm work together. As your legs go up, your arm goes up. As your legs reach full extension, your back, shoulders, and shooting arm extend in a smooth, continuous upward direction. Be sure to keep the ball high with your shooting hand facing the basket. Use the down-and-up motion of your legs for rhythm, rather than lowering the ball for rhythm. Keeping the ball high fosters a quick release and also provides less chance for error.

As your arm goes up, the ball is tipped back from your nonshooting hand to your shooting hand. A good guide is to tip the ball back only until there is a wrinkle in the skin between your wrist and forearm. This angle provides a quick release and consistent follow-through. Direct your arm, wrist, and fingers straight toward the basket at a 45- to 60-degree angle, extending your shooting arm completely at the elbow. The final force and control of your shot come from flexing your wrist and fingers forward toward a spot just over the front of the rim. Release the ball off the pads of your index finger with soft fingertip touch to impart backspin on the ball and soften the shot. Keep your nonshooting hand on the ball until the point of release.

The amount of force you impart to the ball depends on the range of the shot. For short distances, the arm, wrist, and fingers provide most of the force. Long-range outside shots require the down-and-up motion of your legs with more force from your legs, back, and shoulders, and a complete follow-through.

Follow-through. After releasing the ball off the pads of your index finger, keep your arm up and fully extended with your index finger pointing straight to the target just over the front of the rim. The palm of your shooting hand should face slightly forward and down, and the palm of your balance hand should face slightly up. Keep your eyes on your target. Exaggerate your follow-through. Hold your arm up in a complete follow-through position until the ball reaches the basket, then react to the rebound or get into defensive position. Holding your follow-through until the ball reaches the basket is not only good mechanics, but it also makes you look and act like a shooter and increases your confidence.

Understanding Your Shot and Becoming Your Own Best Coach

Becoming a better shooter takes self-discipline, hard work, and correct practice. Most of the time you will be practicing alone without a coach to help you. Learning to understand your own shot and become your own best coach will help you practice correctly and improve. Here are some tips to help you do this:

Have confidence in yourself. Always start with what you are doing well.

Ask yourself, "When I am shooting well, what am I doing?" There is no wrong answer to this question. It simply gives an indication of your confidence level and what you know about your own shot. If you respond with the answer "I just shoot," this may indicate that you have confidence and that you are not overthinking when you shoot. If your answer is "When I'm shooting well, my hand is going straight toward the basket," then you have an idea of what you want to do when shooting.

Tell yourself, "I want to shoot with confidence and rhythm. I want to focus on the one mechanic that helps my shot the most. I want to learn to coach myself." Select two or three one-syllable key words that you associate with what you want to do.

Keep it simple. Too much thinking causes paralysis by analysis. Shooting should be smooth, free flowing, and rhythmical. Your key words are short, concise, and positive. Say your words with confidence and rhythm from the start of your shot to the release of the ball.

Be positive. Eliminate thinking about the shot or shots that you missed. Negative thinking distracts you. It makes you tense. It causes you to lose your confidence. When you miss a shot, immediately correct it with a positive key word that you associate with making the shot. Visualize a good shot and always act as if you have made it. Act like a shooter!

Strive to keep your confidence level high. Keep reminding yourself that you can and will achieve your goals. Motivate yourself to consistently do what it takes to reach your goals. Commit to daily, specific, measurable goal setting and correct practice. Commitment fosters confidence. Never think for one moment that you will have anything less than success. Constantly tell yourself, "I am a shooter!"

Be enthusiastic, energized, and tenacious to inspire yourself to reach new heights. This will also inspire your team.

Above all, make it enjoyable! You become a better player when you have high spirits, a bright smile, and a sense of humor.

Shooting Drill. STRONG-HAND SHOOTING WARM-UP

Shooting close to the basket as a warm-up helps you develop confidence, correct form, and rhythm. One-hand shooting, using either the strong hand or the weak hand, is an excellent way to develop your ability to start and complete a shot with your shooting hand facing the front of the rim. This helps eliminate side rotation. It also fosters the technique of lifting the ball to the basket rather than throwing the ball. This drill is particularly beneficial if your nonshooting hand tends to interfere with your shot (for example, if you thumb the ball with your nonshooting hand). The drill allows you to focus on having the shooting hand in the correct position facing the front of the rim. Keep your shooting elbow in. When your shooting elbow is in, the ball is aligned with the basket. Some players do not have the flexibility to keep the shooting hand facing the front of the rim while keeping the elbow in. If this is the case, first face your shooting hand toward the front of the rim, then move the elbow in as far as your flexibility allows.

Start in a balanced stance about 9 feet (2.7 m) in front of the backboard with your shooting hand facing the front of the rim while keeping your elbow in as far as your flexibility allows. Your shooting hand is above your shoulder between your ear and shoulder. Be sure to use your nonshooting hand to place the ball in your shooting hand. Do not reach for the ball with your shooting hand, because reaching results in the natural tendency to place your shooting hand on the side of the ball and may cause you to put sidespin on the ball when you shoot. Once the ball is placed in your shooting hand, lower your nonshooting hand to your side. Balance the ball in your shooting hand with your index finger at the ball's midpoint. Check that your forearm is at a right angle to the floor. This position helps you lift the ball to the basket rather than throw it.

Use your personalized key words in rhythm with your shot and when you are correcting your shot. If you tend to bring the ball back and throw it rather than lift it to the basket, emphasize the key word *front!* If your shot misses to your strong-hand side of the rim because your elbow is out, consider using the key word *in!* Shoot, leaving your arm up on the follow-through until the ball hits the floor. The correct hand position—the shooting hand behind the ball and facing the front—and the release off the pads of your index finger will impart backspin, causing the ball to bounce back to you.

If you miss, get feedback from the feel of your shot and the reaction of the ball on the rim. Emphasize the key word that you feel will produce a successful shot. For example, if your shot was short and you felt that the miss came from not using your legs, emphasize the word *legs!* If the shot was short because of an incomplete follow-through, emphasize the word *through!* If the shot was short because of a slow rhythm, quicken the down-and-up movement of your legs as you say the key words *down and up!* with a quicker rhythm. If your shot was long, shoot with a higher arc using the word *up!* If your shot missed to the side, correct the shot using the key word *straight!* After correcting your shot with a key word, visualize a successful shot with good form, again saying your key words.

Record the number of strong-hand shots made out of 10 attempts. When you make 5 consecutive shots, you can increase the distance by taking a giant step back.

To Increase Difficulty

- After making 5 consecutive shots from 9 feet, take a giant step back to increase the distance to 12 feet (3.7 m).
- After making 5 consecutive shots from 12 feet, take a giant step back to the foul line (15 feet [4.6 m] from the backboard).

Success Check

- Use your nonshooting hand to place the ball in your shooting hand. Do not reach for the ball.
- Use your key words in rhythm.
- Analyze the shot by the reaction of the ball on the rim and by the feel of the shot.
- Use correct shooting mechanics.
- Successfully complete 5 consecutive shots from each distance.

Score Your Success

Give yourself 1 point for each shot made. Attempt to make 5 consecutive shots from each distance.

Consecutive shots made from 9 feet ___

Consecutive shots made from 12 feet ___

Consecutive shots made from 15 feet ___

Your score ___ (15 points maximum)

Shooting Drill. WEAK-HAND SHOOTING WARM-UP

One-hand shooting using the weak hand is an excellent way to develop your ability to shoot weak-hand shots, particularly weak-hand layups. Perform the drill in the same way as the strong-hand shooting warm-up, but use your weak hand. When using your weak hand, you may have a tendency to shove the ball and miss toward the opposite side of the rim. Emphasize the down-and-up movement of your legs, which will help your range and ability to lift the ball straight to the basket. Consider using the key words *down and up!* Record the number of weak-hand shots made out of 10 attempts. Your goal is to make 5 consecutive shots. After making 5 consecutive shots from 9 feet (2.7 m), increase the distance to 12 feet (3.7 m). After making 5 consecutive shots from 12 feet, move back to the foul line (15 feet [4.6 m] from the backboard).

Success Check

- Use your nonshooting hand to place the ball in your shooting hand. Do not reach for the ball.
- Use your key words in rhythm.
- Analyze the shot by the reaction of the ball on the rim and by the feel of the shot.
- Use correct shooting mechanics.
- Successfully complete 5 consecutive shots from each distance.

(continued)

(continued)

Score Your Success

Give yourself 1 point for each shot made. Attempt to make 5 consecutive shots from each distance.

Consecutive shots made from 9 feet ___

Consecutive shots made from 12 feet ___

Consecutive shots made from 15 feet ___

Your score ___ (15 points maximum)

Shooting Drill. THREE-FINGER DRILL

You will use only three fingers in this drill—the little finger and ring finger of your nonshooting hand to balance the ball and the index finger of your shooting hand to shoot the ball. This drill enables you to focus on shooting the ball off the pads of your index finger with a soft touch. Start about 9 feet (2.7 m) from the basket with your shooting hand facing the front of the rim while keeping your elbow in as far as your flexibility allows. Place your shooting hand above your shoulder between your ear and shoulder. Check that your shooting forearm is at a right angle to the floor. This position helps you lift the ball to the basket rather than throw it. Balance the ball with your nonshooting hand under the ball. Keep the elbow of your nonshooting hand out. Bring the ball to your shooting hand. Now balance the ball using only the little and ring fingers of your nonshooting hand. The other fingers of your nonshooting hand should be off the ball. Place the pads of the index finger of your shooting hand behind the ball at the ball's midpoint. Lift the ball to the basket and release the ball off the pads of your index finger with a soft touch, emphasizing the key word *point!* Follow through by fully extending your shooting arm and pointing your index finger over the front of the rim.

Success Check

- Repeat your key words in rhythm with your shot.
- Balance the ball with the little finger and ring finger of your weak hand under the ball.
- Place the pads of your index finger behind the ball and facing the front.

Score Your Success

Give yourself 1 point for each shot made. Attempt to make 10 consecutive shots using only three fingers.

Consecutive shots made using only three fingers ___

Your score ___ (10 points maximum)

ONE-HAND SET SHOT

An inside jump shot involves jumping and then shooting the ball at the top of your jump. The arm, wrist, and fingers supply most of the force. On a one-hand set shot (figure 4.1, page 82), you lift the ball simultaneously with the upward extension of your legs, back, and shoulders.

If your shot is short, this usually indicates that you are not using your legs, you are not following through, or you are using a slow or uneven rhythm. Use neural feedback—feeling—to determine whether you need more force from your legs, a more consistent follow-through (keeping your arm up until the ball reaches the basket), or a quicker or more evenly paced rhythm.

If your shot is long, this usually indicates that your shooting arm is extending on too flat a trajectory (less than 45 degrees), your shoulders are leaning back, or your hands are too far apart on the ball, preventing you from lifting it. Move your shoulders to a relaxed forward position, move your hands closer together, or raise your shooting arm higher to put a higher arc on your shot. Follow through with your head in to avoid leaning back or stepping back. Extend your arm completely for every shot.

If your right-handed shot hits the left side of the rim, you are not squaring up to face the basket, or you are starting with the ball on your right hip or too far to your right, shoving the ball from right to left as you shoot. Shoving the ball is the result of not using the down-and-up action of your legs for power. Square your body to the basket, setting the ball on the shooting side of your head between your ear and shoulder, with your elbow in. Make your shooting arm, wrist, and fingers go straight through to the basket.

If your shot lacks range, control, and consistency—or if you miss short, long, or to either side—you probably lower the ball, bring it behind your head or shoulder, or throw the ball to the basket with an inconsistent follow-through. These errors result from not using your legs for power. Start your shot with the ball high in front of your ear and shoulder. Emphasize force from your legs, and complete the follow-through by keeping your arm up until the ball reaches the basket.

When a shot hits the rim and circles out or skims from front to back and out, rather than hitting the rim and dropping in, this might mean that you are starting your shot with your shooting hand on the side of the ball and rotating the hand behind the ball as you shoot. It could also mean that you are releasing the ball off your ring finger instead of your shooting finger. Another possible cause is thumbing the ball—pushing the ball with the thumb of your nonshooting hand. These mistakes give the ball sidespin instead of backspin. Start your shot with your hands in block-and-tuck position—your shooting hand behind the ball and your balance hand under the ball. Release the ball off your index finger. If your mechanics appear to be correct but the shot lacks control and the ball hits hard on the rim, you probably rest the ball on your palm. Relax the thumb of your shooting hand, and set the ball on your finger pads with your palm off the ball. Then you can release the ball off your index finger with backspin, control, and a soft touch.

Figure 4.1 **ONE-HAND SET SHOT**

a

Shooting hand high and in front

1. Eyes on target
2. Feet shoulder-width apart and toes straight
3. Knees slightly flexed
4. Shoulders relaxed
5. Nonshooting hand under ball; shooting hand facing front of rim
6. Elbow in
7. Ball high between ear and shoulder

b

Lower knees

1. Look at target
2. Lower knees before shot

c

Shoot one-hand set shot

1. Knees and arms go up together
2. Extend legs, back, shoulders, and elbow
3. Flex wrist and fingers forward
4. Release ball off pads of index finger
5. Keep nonshooting hand on ball until release
6. Follow through with arm extended, index finger pointing to target until ball goes through net

---

MISSTEP

Your mechanics appear to be correct, but you still miss the basket.

CORRECTION

Have someone watch your eyes as you shoot. You probably do not focus your eyes on the target. Concentrate on the target, not on the ball's flight, until the ball reaches the basket.

FREE THROW

Successful free-throw shooting requires confidence, a routine, relaxation, rhythm, and concentration. Relaxation, rhythm, and a routine contribute to concentration and confidence.

Confidence. Think positively. You always shoot from the same place on the line. No one is guarding you. The basket is big; over three and a half balls can fit in the rim. Using affirmation statements can promote confident thoughts about yourself and your ability to shoot. For example, you can say to yourself, "I am a shooter," or you can remind yourself of past successes. Visualizing a successful shot before shooting can also increase confidence. In addition, acting like a shooter before and after shooting will lead to confidence. Part of acting like a shooter is to exaggerate your follow-through by keeping your shooting arm up until the ball reaches the basket. With confidence—and sound mechanics—you cannot miss.

Routine. Develop a sound routine for the free throw. A routine helps you relax, focus, and shoot with rhythm. Most important, using a routine will enhance your confidence. Your routine may include using visualization to practice your free throw mentally. You may want to physically simulate your free-throw stroke as a part of your routine—many great free-throw shooters do this, such as NBA players Steve Nash and Ray Allen. Your routine may include dribbling a set number of times, checking pre-shot mechanics, and taking a deep breath to relax. There is no single routine that works for everyone. You want to select a routine that works for you. Once you adopt a sound routine, you should stay with it. Don't copy fads or repeatedly change your routine.

Most players use the one-hand shot for a free throw (figure 4.2, page 85), taking the time to control each of the basic mechanics: sight, balance, hand position, elbow-in alignment, rhythmical shooting motion, and follow-through. Here is a sample routine that you can adjust to fit you. Stand a few feet behind the free-throw line until the official hands you the ball. You will stay more relaxed there. If you hear negative remarks from the crowd or you recognize your own negative thoughts, interrupt them with the word *stop*. Take a deep breath and let go of the negative thoughts as you exhale. Replace them with a positive statement of affirmation such as "I'm a shooter," "Nothing but net," or "Count it!"

Once you receive the ball, position your feet, making certain to line up the ball (not your head) with the middle of the basket. Use the small indentation (nail) mark in the floor at the exact middle of the free-throw line that marks the free-throw circle. Set your shooting foot slightly outside this mark, lining up the ball with the middle of the basket.

Set up in a balanced stance. Some players bounce the ball a certain number of times to help them relax. When you bounce the ball, keep your shooting hand on top. This helps ensure that you will have your shooting hand facing the basket when you set the ball high in position to shoot. Use a relaxed hand position, and line up your index finger with the valve on the ball. Next, check your elbow-in alignment.

Relaxation. Learn to relax when shooting free throws. You have more time to think when shooting free throws than when shooting other shots. Trying too hard may cause undue physical or emotional tension. Use deep breathing to relax your mind and body. For a free throw, you should particularly relax your shoulders; take a deep breath and let your shoulders drop and loosen. Do the same for your arms, hands, and fingers. Learn to relax other parts of your body. Controlling your breathing and relaxing your muscles are especially useful in a free-throw routine. Make sure that taking a deep breath to relax is part of your routine.

Rhythm. Start your shot high and use the down-and-up motion of your legs for rhythm rather than lowering the ball for rhythm. The down-and-up motion of your legs provides momentum for your shot and is particularly helpful when shooting late in the game when your legs are tired. By starting the ball high and using your legs for rhythm, you will lessen the chance for error that can come with lowering the ball. Exaggerate your follow-through, keeping your eyes on the target and your shooting arm up until the ball reaches the basket. Shooting a free throw is different than shooting from the field because you have time to think. Thinking can cause a slower rhythm, along with the tendency for your free throw to be short.

Shoot the free throw with a smooth, free-flowing rhythm. Using personalized key words can help you establish a smooth, sequential rhythm. Say your words in the rhythm of your shot. For example, if your trigger words are *legs* and *through* and your anchor word is *yes,* put them together—*legs-through-yes!*—in rhythm with your shot, from the start of your shot until the ball is released. Using personalized key words this way establishes your rhythm, enhances your mechanics, and builds confidence.

Concentration. The last and most important step before initiating the free-throw motion is to eliminate all distractions and focus on the target just over the front of the rim. Keep from being distracted by the crowd or your own negative thoughts. When you hear a negative statement or recognize your own negative thoughts, eliminate the negatives with the word *stop,* and use positive affirmations. Confidence and concentration go together. Concentrate on shooting a successful shot, and let go of any previous shots that missed or any thoughts of what you might do wrong. Stay in the present. Visualize shooting a successful free throw while you emphasize your anchor word: *Yes! Net! In! Through!* Most of all, enjoy the moment. Keep your focus on the target as you shoot. See it, shoot it, count it!

Figure 4.2 **FREE THROW**

Free-throw routine

1. Shooting foot slightly outside mark
2. Balanced stance with knees slightly flexed
3. Nonshooting hand under ball; shooting hand facing basket with thumb relaxed
4. Elbow in
5. Ball between ear and shoulder
6. Shoulders relaxed
7. Concentrate on target just over front of rim

Say key words in rhythm

1. Say key words in rhythm
2. Lower knees before shot

Shoot free throw

1. Knees and arms go up together
2. Extend legs, back, shoulders, and elbow
3. Flex wrist and fingers forward
4. Release ball off pads of index finger
5. Keep nonshooting hand on ball until release
6. Shoot with confidence and rhythm
7. Follow through with arm extended, index finger pointing to target, and arm up until ball goes through net

---

MISSTEP

You feel tense before and during your free throw.

CORRECTION

Use deep breathing to relax your mind and body. Breathe in deeply and exhale fully. Relax your shoulders, letting them drop and loosen. Do the same for your arms, hands, and fingers. Learn to relax other parts of your body as necessary.

Free-Throw Drill. DAILY PRACTICE

Shoot a set number of free throws each day. Practice sets of 10 free throws after other drills. Because a player rarely shoots more than 2 free throws in a row during a game, when you are doing this drill, you should never take more than 2 successive free throws without moving off the line.

Practice under pressure. Use your imagination, and compete against yourself. For example, imagine that time is out and that making the free throw will win the game. Record the number of free throws you make out of every 100 attempts, and constantly challenge your own record. Do the same with consecutive free throws.

Be confident. Use positive affirmation statements before you go to the line, and visualize a successful shot just before shooting. Having a routine will help you build confidence for free throws. Use deep breathing and muscle relaxation techniques. The final step before shooting is to eliminate all distractions and focus on the basket. Say your personalized key words in rhythm from the start of your free throw to the release of the ball. If you miss, visualize a successful free throw with good form, again saying your key words.

Success Check

- Use your routine and say your key words before shooting a free throw.
- Be confident in your ability to make each free throw.
- Visualize a successful shot before shooting the ball.

Score Your Success

Shoot 100 free throws. Give yourself 1 point for each free throw made. Record your score. Also record the highest number of consecutive free throws. Challenge your record every time you perform the drill.

Number of free throws made out of 100 ____

Your score ___ (100 maximum)

Consecutive free throws made ___

Free-Throw Drill. EYES CLOSED

Research has shown that a combination of free-throw practice with eyes closed and free-throw practice with eyes open improves shooting more than free-throw practice with eyes open alone. Shooting with your eyes closed removes vision as your dominant sense, heightening your other senses, particularly kinesthetic sense (feel of body movement) and touch.

Visualize a successful shot and focus on the basket immediately before closing your eyes. Shoot a free throw with your eyes closed. Have a partner rebound the ball and give you feedback on each shot, including the reaction of the ball on the rim. Use this feedback and your kinesthetic and tactile senses to adjust your shot as necessary. Complete 20 free-throw attempts. Your partner should help you keep track of how many shots you make out of 20 and how many consecutive shots you make.

Success Check

- Use correct form for the free throw.
- Rely on your kinesthetic and tactile senses rather than on your eyes.
- Use your key words and visualization to help you make each shot.

Score Your Success

Shoot 20 free-throw attempts with your eyes closed. Give yourself 1 point for each free throw made. Record your score. Also record the highest number of consecutive free throws. Challenge your record every time you perform the drill.

Number of free throws made out of 20 ____

Your score ___ (20 maximum)

Number of consecutive free throws made ___

JUMP SHOT

A jump shot (figure 4.3, page 88) is similar to a one-hand set shot except for two basic adjustments. In a jump shot, you align the ball higher and shoot after jumping, rather than shoot with the simultaneous extension of your legs. Because you jump first and then shoot, your upper body, arm, wrist, and fingers must generate more force.

Align the ball between your ear and shoulder, but raise the ball, sighting the target below rather than above the ball, as you would in a one-hand set shot. Place your forearm at a right angle to the floor. Jump straight up off both feet, fully extending your ankles, knees, back, and shoulders. Do not float forward, backward, or to the side.

How high you jump depends on the range of the shot. On an inside jump shot, when you are closely guarded, your legs should generate enough force to jump higher than the defender. You shoot at the top of your jump; therefore, your arm, wrist, and fingers provide most of the force. You may feel as though you are hanging in the air as you release the ball.

On most long-range outside jump shots, you have more time; therefore, you don't need to jump higher than your defender. You will be able to use more force from your legs for shooting the ball rather than for gaining height on the jump. You will feel that you are shooting the ball *as* you jump rather than at the top of your jump. Strive for a balanced jump that enables you to shoot without straining. Balance and control are more important than gaining maximum height on your jump. Smooth rhythm and a complete follow-through are also important components of long-range jump shooting. Land in balance in the same spot as your takeoff.

Figure 4.3 **JUMP SHOT**

a

b

c

Shooting hand high and in front

1. Feet shoulder-width apart, toes straight
2. Knees slightly flexed
3. Shoulders relaxed
4. Elbow in
5. Ball high between ear and shoulder
6. Nonshooting hand under ball; shooting hand facing front of rim

Lower knees

1. Look at target
2. Lower knees before shot

Shoot jump shot

1. Knees and arms go up together
2. Extend legs, back, shoulders, and elbow
3. Flex wrist and fingers forward
4. Release ball off pads of index finger
5. Keep nonshooting hand on ball until release
6. Follow through with arm extended, index finger pointing to target until ball goes through net

---

MISSTEP

You lower the ball for rhythm, which lengthens the shooting stroke, creating more room for error. This makes the shot easier to block.

CORRECTION

Keep the ball high and use the down-and-up action of your legs for rhythm; do not lower the ball.

Jump Shot Drill. JUMP SHOT WARM-UP

The objective of this drill is to help you develop confidence, form, rhythm, and range for making jump shots. Start in a balanced stance about 9 feet (2.7 m) in front of the basket. Perform jump shots from that distance, using correct form for each shot. For a jump shot, the ball is held higher than for a one-hand set shot. The height of your jump depends on the range. When close to the basket, you should release the ball at the top of your jump; your arm, wrist, and fingers should provide most of the force. On long-range outside jump shots, you don't need to jump as high, allowing you to use more force from your legs for the shot. Strive for a balanced jump so you can follow through until the ball hits the floor. Say your three personalized key words in rhythm from the start of your shot to the release of the ball.

To Increase Difficulty

- After making five consecutive shots from 9 feet, move back to 12 feet (3.7 m).
- After making five consecutive shots from 12 feet, move back to the foul line (15 feet [4.6 m] from the backboard).
- After making five consecutive shots from 15 feet, move back again. Continue to move back until you are unable to make five consecutive jump shots.

Success Check

- Say your key words in rhythm with your shot.
- Jump the correct height for the shot, depending on your range.
- Use proper mechanics for the jump shot.
- Attempt to make five consecutive jump shots at each distance.

Score Your Success

Record the number of shots made at each distance. Give yourself 5 points each time you successfully complete five consecutive jump shots.

Consecutive jump shots made at 9 feet ___; points earned ___

Consecutive jump shots made at 12 feet ___; points earned ___

Consecutive jump shots made at 15 feet ___; points earned ___

Consecutive jump shots made at 18 feet ___; points earned ___

Consecutive jump shots made at 21 feet (top of free-throw circle) ___; points earned ___

Consecutive jump shots made at 24 feet (NBA three-point line) ___; points earned ___

Your score ___ (30 points maximum)

Jump Shot Drill. BANK JUMP SHOT WARM-UP

The bank jump shot warm-up is the same as the regular jump shot warm-up except that you shoot from a 45-degree angle on each side of the basket. Start in a balanced stance at a 45-degree angle to the backboard, within the distance between the block and the middle hash mark on the lane. The distance of the bank angle, which widens as you move out, is called the *45-degree funnel.* For bank shots, aim for the top near corner of the box on the backboard, saying your key words in rhythm from the start of your shot to the release of the ball. Shoot from both the right and left sides of the basket.

To Increase Difficulty

- After making five consecutive bank jump shots from 9 feet (2.7 m) on both the right and left sides of the basket, move back to 12 feet (3.7 m).
- After making five consecutive bank jump shots from 12 feet on both the right and left sides of the basket, move back to 15 feet (4.6 m).
- After making five consecutive bank jump shots from 15 feet on both the right and left sides of the basket, move back to 18 feet (5.5 m).

Success Check

- Say your key words in rhythm with the shot.
- Use correct mechanics for the bank jump shot.
- Successfully complete five bank jump shots from each side and each distance.

Score Your Success

Record the number of bank jump shots you make on each side and at each distance. Give yourself 5 points each time you successfully complete five consecutive bank jump shots.

Consecutive bank jump shots at 9 feet, right side ___; points earned ___

Consecutive bank jump shots at 9 feet, left side ___; points earned ___

Consecutive bank jump shots at 12 feet, right side ___; points earned ___

Consecutive bank jump shots at 12 feet, left side ___; points earned ___

Consecutive bank jump shots at 15 feet, right side ___; points earned ___

Consecutive bank jump shots at 15 feet, left side ___; points earned ___

Consecutive bank jump shots at 18 feet, right side ___; points earned ___

Consecutive bank jump shots at 18 feet, left side ___; points earned ___

Your score ___ (40 points maximum)

THREE-POINT SHOT

For a three-point shot (figure 4.4, page 92), you should set up far enough behind the line to avoid concern about stepping on the line and to focus your sight on the basket. Do not look down at the line and lose sight of your target. Use a balanced jump shot, shooting the ball without straining as you jump.

The longer the shot, the more important correct mechanics, sequence, and rhythm become. On three-point shots, you usually have time and do not need much height on your jump. You can use more force from your legs and can generate additional force by stepping into the shot. You can also benefit from the sequential buildup of force from your back and shoulders. On this shot, you should feel as if you are shooting the ball as you jump, rather than at the top of your jump (as when outjumping your defender on a closely guarded inside shot).

Strive for a balanced jump that enables you to shoot without straining. Balance and control are more important than maximum height. Smooth rhythm and a complete follow-through enhance long-range jump shooting, and as with all jump shots, on three-point shots, you should land in balance in the same spot as your takeoff.

Successful three-point shooters excel by mastering the following: a smooth, even rhythm; the sequential use of the legs, back, and shoulders; correct mechanics, such as hand position and elbow-in alignment; and a complete follow-through.

MISSTEP

Your shot is short.

CORRECTION

When a three-point shot is short, this usually indicates that (1) you do not use your legs, back, and shoulders; (2) you do not follow through; or (3) you have a slow or uneven rhythm. Determine through feel which element is the problem. Emphasize generating force from your legs, back, and shoulders. Complete the follow-through by keeping your arm up until the ball reaches the basket. Increase the speed of your rhythm, or pace it more evenly.

Figure 4.4 **THREE-POINT SHOT**

Hands and feet ready

1. Positioned behind three-point line
2. Feet shoulder-width apart, toes straight
3. Knees flexed
4. Elbow in
5. Ball high between ear and shoulder
6. Shoulders relaxed
7. Nonshooting hand under ball; shooting hand facing basket with thumb relaxed
8. Step into shot, if necessary

Shoot with confidence and rhythm

1. Jump without straining, shooting on way up
2. Shoot with confidence and rhythm
3. Generate sequential power from legs, back, and shoulders
4. Extend elbow
5. Flex wrist and fingers forward
6. Release ball off index finger
7. Keep nonshooting hand on ball until release
8. Execute follow-through

Three-Point Shot Drill.
SHOOTING FROM A CHAIR

Shooting from a chair is the single best lead-up drill for developing your ability to shoot both three-point shots and free throws. The objectives of shooting from a chair include the following:

1. To develop confidence in three-point shooting and free-throw shooting
2. To foster consistency in lifting the ball to the basket and holding the follow-through until the ball reaches the net
3. To learn to focus on correcting a specific error

Center yourself both mentally and physically. Learn to physically center yourself when sitting in the chair. When you are physically centered, you are in a state of readiness; your muscles relax, and you breathe a little deeper and more slowly than usual. Being physically centered also involves balancing your weight evenly for the skill you will be performing, which is particularly helpful for gaining power. When you are physically centered, it helps you become mentally centered. When you are centered, you are more alert, focused, and confident. Centering allows you to raise your center of gravity and transfer force from your back to your shoulders in order to generate full power for the shot.

Visualize a successful shot with good form before you shoot. Visualization is the technique of seeing a mental picture of a successful shot in your mind. Visualization just before you shoot can produce a more free-flowing, smooth rhythm and increase confidence.

Work for the sequential buildup of force from your back, shoulders, arm, wrist, and fingers as you shoot. Use feedback from the feel of the shot and its distance, direction, and reaction on the rim.

Correct a shooting error by using personalized key words. Say the words with confidence and rhythm from the start of your shot to the release of the ball. Here are some examples of errors and suggested key words for correcting them:

1. Correct a shot that is short by emphasizing the key word *through!* This triggers you to keep your follow-through straight up until the ball reaches the net.
2. Correct a shot that is long by emphasizing the key word *up!* This triggers you to lift your shooting hand up higher to put more arc on your shot.
3. Correct the error of bringing the ball back or leaning back and throwing the ball (rather than lifting it to the basket) by using the key word *front!* This triggers you to ensure that your head, shoulders, and shooting hand go to the rim.
4. Correct misses to your weak-hand side of the rim—caused by lowering and shoving the ball—by using the key words *high!* and *straight!* These key words trigger you to set the ball high and shoot straight.

(continued)

(continued)

5. Correct misses to your strong-hand side of the rim—caused by your elbow being out—by using the key word *in!* This triggers you to keep your elbow in.
6. Correct the error of rotating the shooting hand sideward (causing sidespin) by using the key word *straight!* This triggers you to start with your shooting hand facing straight at the basket and to make sure your hand goes straight during the follow-through.
7. Correct the error of lowering the ball or swiveling the ball to your opposite hip by using the key words *high!* and *straight!* These key words trigger you to set the ball high and shoot straight.

Set the chair 9 feet (2.7 m) from the basket (two giant steps in front of the free-throw line). Sit on the front edge of the chair with your shoulders facing forward, your feet aligned with the legs of the chair, and your toes straight.

Start with your shooting hand facing the front of the rim while keeping your elbow in as far as your flexibility allows. Your shooting hand is above your shoulder between your ear and shoulder. *Important note:* Use your nonshooting hand to place the ball in your shooting hand. Avoid reaching for the ball with your shooting hand. The index finger of your shooting hand should be at the ball's midpoint. Check that your forearm is at a right angle to the floor. This position helps you lift the ball to the basket rather than lower it or throw it.

To Increase Difficulty

- After making five consecutive shots from 9 feet, move the chair back until you are 12 feet (3.7 m) from the basket.
- After making five consecutive shots from 12 feet, move the chair back until you are 15 feet (4.6 m) from the basket (free-throw distance).
- After making five consecutive shots from 15 feet, move the chair back until you are 18 feet (5.5 m) from the basket.
- After making five consecutive shots from 18 feet, move the chair back until you are 21 feet (6.4 m) from the basket (top of circle).

Success Check

- Use proper form.
- Say your key words in rhythm with the shot.
- Attempt to make five consecutive shots at each distance.

Score Your Success

Record the number of consecutive shots you make at each distance. You earn 5 points each time you make five consecutive shots.

Consecutive shots made at 9 feet ___; points earned ___

Consecutive shots made at 12 feet ___; points earned ___

Consecutive shots made at 15 feet ___; points earned ___

Consecutive shots made at 18 feet ___; points earned ___

Consecutive shots made at 21 feet ___; points earned ___

Your score ___ (25 points maximum)

Three-Point Shot Drill. AROUND THE WORLD

This drill helps you develop the ability to shoot three-point shots against the pressure of a clock. You will shoot three-point shots from five spots: left corner, left wing, top, right wing, and right corner (around the world). You must make two consecutive three-point shots from one spot before moving to the next spot. Your goal is to make two consecutive three-point shots from each spot in a total of 2 minutes.

Choose a teammate to rebound and pass to you. Start with a ball at the left corner. You must make two three-pointers in a row before moving to the left wing and so on.

To Increase Difficulty

- After making two consecutive shots from each spot within a time limit of 2 minutes, reduce the time limit to 90 seconds.
- Increase the number to three consecutive shots from each spot within a time limit of 2 minutes.
- After making three consecutive shots from each spot within a time limit of 2 minutes, reduce the time limit to 90 seconds.

Success Check

- Use proper technique for the three-point shot.
- Say your key words with confidence and in rhythm from the start of your shot to the release.
- Attempt to make two consecutive three-point shots at each spot in a total of 2 minutes.

Score Your Success

You have a time limit of 2 minutes. You must make two consecutive shots from each of the five spots. You must make two in a row before moving to the next spot. You earn 2 points each time you make two consecutive shots.

Consecutive shots made at left corner ___; points earned ___

Consecutive shots made at left wing ___; points earned ___

Consecutive shots made at top ___; points earned ___

Consecutive shots made at right wing ___; points earned ___

Consecutive shots made at right corner ___; points earned ___

Your score ___ (10 points maximum)

HOOK SHOT

The advantage of the hook shot (figure 4.5) is that it is difficult to block, even for taller opponents. The hook shot is generally limited to an area close to the basket, a range of 10 to 12 feet (3 to 3.7 m). By learning to shoot the hook shot with either hand, you will greatly increase your effectiveness in the lane. When well executed, the hook forces an opponent to overplay you, and a fake hook can create an opening in the opposite direction for a power move, drive, or pass. Contrary to popular belief, the hook shot is not difficult to learn. With practice, you will be able to use your weak hand as well as your strong hand for shooting the hook shot.

Start in a balanced stance with your back to the basket, your feet spread shoulder-width apart, and your knees flexed. Sight your target by looking over your shoulder in the direction you will turn to shoot. Within a 45-degree angle of the backboard (above the block and below the middle hash mark on the lane line), accuracy is aided by using the backboard to soften the shot. When banking the shot, aim for the top near corner of the backboard. If you aren't at a 45-degree angle, aim just over the rim.

In most instances, you will make a ball fake in the opposite direction of your intended shot. After your fake, move your shooting hand under and your nonshooting hand behind and slightly on top of the ball. This is called the *hook shot position.* Flex the elbow of your shooting arm and position it at your hip, keeping the ball in direct alignment with your shooting shoulder.

Use the foot opposite your shooting side to step away from the defender. As you step, hold the ball back and protect it with your head and shoulders, rather than lead with the ball. As you step, pivot in, turning your body toward the basket. Lift the knee on your shooting side and jump off your pivot foot.

Shoot by lifting the ball to the basket with a hook motion as you extend your shooting arm in an ear-to-ear direction. Flex your wrist and fingers toward the target and release the ball off your index finger, keeping the balance hand on the ball until the release. Land in balance, ready to rebound any missed shot with two hands and score using a power move. A missed hook shot should be thought of as a pass to yourself. A defender attempting to block your hook shot will not be in position to box out and prevent you from getting the rebound.

If you put side rotation on the ball, the shot will hit the rim and, rather than pull in, will circle out or skim from front to back and out. If you start with your hands on the sides of the ball and rotate them to the side as you shoot, or if you release the ball off your ring finger instead of your index finger, you will put side rotation on the ball. Both mistakes produce sidespin instead of backspin. Start in hook shot position, with your shooting elbow aligned with your hip. Place your shooting hand under the ball, and place your balance hand slightly behind and on top of the ball. Release the ball off your index finger to get backspin, and the ball will pull in if it hits the rim.

If your right-handed shot hits the right side of the rim, you are bringing your arm in front of your head on the follow-through. If your right-handed shot hits the left side of the rim, you are bringing your arm behind your head on the follow-through. To correct either problem, start by holding the ball in hook shot position, with your shooting elbow aligned with your hip. This allows you to extend your arm with an ear-to-ear motion straight to the basket.

If your shot is consistently short or long, you probably have incomplete and inconsistent elbow extension. Extend your arm completely on every shot.

Figure 4.5 **HOOK SHOT**

a

b

Shooting hand under ball

1. Back to basket
2. Feet shoulder-width apart
3. Knees flexed
4. Shoulders relaxed
5. Shooting hand under ball; nonshooting hand behind ball
6. Elbow at hip
7. Ball back, protected by head and shoulders

Step and shoot hook shot

1. Step and pivot in
2. Lift ball in ear-to-ear direction
3. Extend elbow
4. Flex wrist and fingers
5. Release ball off index finger
6. Keep balance hand on ball until release
7. Land in balance, ready to rebound

MISSTEP

You lose protection and control of the ball as you shoot.

CORRECTION

You are taking your balance hand off the ball too soon. Keep your balance hand on the ball until the release.

Hook Shot Drill. **HOOK SHOT WARM-UP**

In this drill, you will shoot hook shots with both your strong and weak hands. Start with your head under the front of the rim, facing the sideline in a balanced stance. Hold the ball in hook shot position with your shooting elbow at your side, your shooting hand under the ball, and your balance hand slightly behind and on top of the ball. Shoot the hook shot by lifting the ball to the basket in an ear-to-ear motion, keeping your balance hand on the ball until the release. Use two hands to catch the ball as it comes through the basket or to rebound on a missed shot. Treat a missed shot as a pass to yourself.

Success Check

- Shoot with confidence.
- Use correct mechanics.
- Attempt to make five consecutive hook shots with each hand.

Score Your Success

Record the number of consecutive hook shots made with each hand. Give yourself 5 points each time you make five consecutive hook shots.

Consecutive hook shots made with strong hand ___; points earned ___

Consecutive hook shots made with weak hand ___; points earned ___

Your score ___ (10 points maximum)

Hook Shot Drill. **HOOK SHOT WARM-UP WITH CROSSOVER STEP**

After you can make five consecutive warm-up hook shots with each hand, move to the hook shot with a crossover step. Start with your head under the front of the rim. Face the sideline while holding the ball in hook shot position. Using your inside foot (foot closest to the basket), make a crossover step toward the foul line and shoot a hook shot. Pivot toward the basket on the crossover step and lift your shooting side knee as you shoot.

Success Check

- Use your key words as you make the shot.
- Use correct hook shot mechanics.
- Try to make five consecutive hook shots with each hand.

Score Your Success

Record the number of consecutive hook shots with a crossover step made with each hand. Give yourself 5 points each time you make five consecutive hook shots.

Consecutive hook shots with crossover step made with strong hand ___; points earned ___

Consecutive hook shots with crossover step made with weak hand ___; points earned ___

Your score ___ (10 points maximum)

Hook Shot Drill.
ALTERNATE-HAND HOOK SHOOTING (MIKAN DRILL)

In this drill, you will alternate shooting right-handed and left-handed bank hook shots using a crossover step. For the first shot, use your right hand. Start under the rim, facing the right sideline. Hold the ball in hook shot position with your right hand under the ball. Using your left foot (foot closest to the basket), make a crossover step at a 45-degree angle away from the backboard. Pivot toward the basket on the step and lift your right knee as you shoot a right-handed bank hook shot, aiming for the high near corner of the box on the backboard. Catch the ball with two hands after either a made shot or a rebound. Now face the offensive left sideline. Hold the ball in hook shot position with your left hand under the ball. Using your right foot (foot closest to the basket), make a crossover step at a 45-degree angle away from the backboard. Pivot and shoot a left-handed bank hook shot, catching the ball with two hands. Continue the drill, alternating between right-handed and left-handed hook shots.

Success Check

- Use both hands to catch the ball after a made shot or to rebound a missed shot.
- Try to make 10 consecutive alternate-hand hook shots while using the crossover step.

Score Your Success

Record the number of consecutive alternate-hand hook shots made. Give yourself 10 points when you make 10 consecutive hook shots.

Consecutive alternate-hand hook shots made ___; points earned ___

Your score ___ (10 points maximum)

LAYUP

The layup shot (figure 4.6, page 100) is used near the basket after a cut or drive. To jump high on a layup, you must have speed on the last three or four steps of your cut or drive, but you must also control your speed. Step with your opposite foot. The step before your layup should be short so you can quickly dip your takeoff knee in order to change forward momentum to upward momentum. Lift your shooting-side knee and the ball straight up as you jump, bringing the ball between your ear and shoulder. When shooting the layup, do not swivel the ball to the side, allowing it to be blocked or stolen. If your shooting hand rotates to the side, it will put sidespin on the ball, causing the ball to roll off the rim. Lift the ball straight up as you shoot; your shooting hand should be directly behind the ball to give it backspin, causing it to pull into the basket. Aim the ball high above the top near corner of the box on the backboard so it will drop into the basket. This way, even if you are fouled, the ball will still have a chance of going in. Keep your nonshooting hand on the ball until the release for protection and balance. Shoot the ball off your index finger with a soft touch. Jump and land in the same spot as your takeoff. Be ready to rebound the ball with two hands in case the shot is missed.

Figure 4.6 **LAYUP**

a

b

Dribble pickup

1. When outside hand (hand away from defender) is right hand, prepare to shoot right-handed layup
2. Take short step with inside foot before last dribble
3. Dip takeoff (inside) knee
4. Pick up ball at shooting-side knee
5. Shooting (outside) hand on top; nonshooting hand under ball
6. Eyes on target
7. Aim high above top near corner of box on backboard

Shoot layup

1. Raise ball straight up to shoot with shooting hand facing target
2. Jump straight up, pushing off takeoff foot
3. Protect ball with nonshooting hand until release
4. Shoot layup high above top near corner of box on backboard
5. Land in balance at spot of takeoff, ready to rebound

MISSTEP

You miss the shot because you float forward.

CORRECTION

Pick the ball up at your shooting-side knee in order to change forward momentum to upward momentum.

Layup Drill. **ONE-DRIBBLE LAYUP**

This drill leads up to shooting layups off the dribble using both the strong and weak hands. First, practice with your strong hand. Start in a balanced stance at the middle hash mark on the lane on your strong side. Use your strong-side foot as a pivot foot; this foot should be forward, and your weak-side foot should be back. Take a short step with your weak-side foot and dribble with your strong hand. Pick up the ball at your strong-side knee with your balance hand under the ball and your shooting hand behind it in block-and-tuck position. Jump straight up and shoot a strong-hand layup high above the box on the backboard. Land in balance and catch the ball with two hands whether you make the shot or have to get a rebound.

Next, practice the same way with your weak hand. Your weak-side foot should be forward, and your strong-side foot should be back. Take a short step with your strong-side foot and dribble with your weak hand. Pick up the ball at your weak-side knee, and shoot a weak-hand layup.

Success Check

- Pick up the ball with your balance hand under the ball and your shooting hand on top of the ball.
- Use correct layup technique.
- Try to make five consecutive one-dribble layups with each hand.

Score Your Success

Record the number of one-dribble layups you make with each hand. Give yourself 5 points each time you make five consecutive one-dribble layups.

Consecutive one-dribble layups made with strong hand ___; points earned ___

Consecutive one-dribble layups made with weak hand ___; points earned ___

Your score ___ (10 points maximum)

Layup Drill. SPEED DRIBBLE LAYUP

This challenging layup drill combines the use of strong- and weak-hand speed and reverse dribbles. The drill consists of alternately driving from each elbow (the intersection of the foul line and lane line) and shooting layups with your right hand when dribbling right and with your left hand when dribbling left.

Start at the right elbow in a balanced stance with your left foot forward and your right foot back. Drive to the basket using a speed dribble with your right hand and shoot a right-handed layup. Catch the ball with two hands and speed dribble out to the left elbow, using your right (outside) hand. Place your left foot on the elbow and reverse dribble, pulling the ball back toward the basket with your right hand.

Drive to the basket using a speed dribble with your left hand and shoot a left-handed layup. Catch the ball with two hands and speed dribble to the right elbow, using your left (outside) hand. Place your right foot on the elbow and reverse dribble, pulling the ball back toward the basket with your left hand. Continue the drill for 30 seconds, alternately driving and shooting layups on each side of the basket.

Success Check

- Use good layup technique.
- Catch the ball with both hands.

Score Your Success

Record the number of layups you make in 30 seconds. Give yourself 1 point for each layup made. Eight or more layups in 30 seconds is excellent, six or seven layups is good, and five or fewer requires more practice. A quick, great layup shooter might make nine.

Layups made in 30 seconds ___

Your score ___ (8 points maximum)

Layup Drill. SPEED DRIBBLE LAYUP VERSUS CHASER

This drill develops your ability to speed dribble and make a driving layup while protecting the ball against a pursuing defensive player. Select another player as your opponent. Start at half-court on your strong-hand side, facing the sideline. Your opponent, who will be the defensive chaser, will start one step behind you. Your opponent's lead foot will be touching your back foot.

The drill starts when you initiate a drive to the basket using a speed dribble. The chaser should provide as much defensive pressure as possible, trying to deflect your dribble or pressure your shot. Use the dribble to evade the defender and shoot the layup. Switch offensive and defensive roles with your partner after each shot attempt. Each player makes five shot attempts.

To Increase Difficulty

Start on your weak-hand side and dribble with your weak hand.

Success Check

- Use proper layup technique.
- Use good footwork and dribble technique to move around the defender.
- Protect the ball with your nonshooting hand and arm.

Score Your Success

Each successful shot counts as 1 point. Try to score more points than your partner. Give yourself 10 points if you score more than your partner.

Your score ___

REVERSE LAYUP

The reverse layup shot (figure 4.7, page 104) is used under the basket after a cut or drive. The difference between a regular layup and a reverse layup is that the reverse layup is shot with your shooting hand under the ball. To jump high on a reverse layup, you must have speed on the last three or four steps of your cut or drive, but you must also control your speed on your last step before shooting.

From a position under the basket, face the sideline, place your shooting hand under the ball, and place your nonshooting hand slightly on top of and behind the ball. Take a short step at a 45-degree angle away from the backboard with your nonshooting-side foot. The step before your reverse layup should be short so you can quickly dip your takeoff knee in order to change forward momentum to upward momentum. Pivot to the middle of the lane on your nonshooting-side foot, and at the same time, turn your head and shoulders to the middle. Lift your shooting-side knee and the ball straight up as you jump, bringing the ball between your ear and shoulder. Aim high above the top near corner of the box on the backboard. This way, even if you are fouled, the ball will still have a chance of going in. Lift the ball straight up as you shoot, keeping your shooting hand directly under the ball to give it backspin. When shooting the reverse layup, do not swivel the ball to the side, allowing it to be blocked or stolen. If your shooting hand rotates to the side, it will put sidespin on the ball, causing the ball to roll off the rim. Release the ball off your index finger with a soft touch. Keep your nonshooting hand on the ball until the release. Otherwise, you will lose protection and control of the ball as you shoot. Jump and land in the same spot as your takeoff. Be ready to rebound the ball with two hands in case the shot is missed.

Figure 4.7 **REVERSE LAYUP**

a

b

Dribble pickup

1. Start under basket, facing sideline
2. Take short step with nonshooting foot at 45-degree angle away from backboard
3. Dip nonshooting-side knee
4. Shooting hand under ball; nonshooting hand behind ball
5. Shooting-side elbow at hip
6. Eyes on target
7. Aim high above top near corner of box on backboard

Shoot reverse layup

1. Pivot to middle on nonshooting-side foot
2. Turn head and shoulders toward middle of lane
3. Focus eyes on target
4. Lift shooting-side knee
5. Jump straight up, pushing off takeoff foot
6. Lift ball to basket with shooting hand under ball
7. Keep nonshooting hand on ball until release
8. Release ball off pads of index finger with backspin
9. Land in balance at spot of takeoff

MISSTEP

When you shoot the reverse layup, the ball rolls off the rim because of sidespin.

CORRECTION

You are rotating your shooting hand sideward, putting sidespin on the ball. Keep your shooting hand directly under the ball and lift the ball straight up to give it backspin.

Reverse Layup Drill. ONE-DRIBBLE REVERSE LAYUP

This drill leads up to shooting reverse layups off the dribble using both the right and left hands. First, practice with your right hand. Start in a balanced stance under the basket while facing the offensive left sideline. Take a short step with your left foot toward the sideline. Take one dribble with your right hand and pick the ball up with your right hand under the ball. Shoot a right-handed reverse layup. Be ready to rebound the ball with two hands in case the shot is missed. Repeat.

Next, practice the same way with your left hand. Start in a balanced stance under the basket while facing the offensive right sideline. Take a short step with your right foot toward the sideline. Take one dribble with your left hand and pick the ball up with your left hand under the ball. Shoot a left-handed reverse layup. Be ready to rebound the ball with two hands in case the shot is missed. Repeat.

Success Check

- Pick up the ball with your shooting hand under the ball.
- Use correct technique for the reverse layup.
- Try to make five consecutive one-dribble reverse layups with each hand.

Score Your Success

Record the number of one-dribble reverse layups you make with each hand. Give yourself 5 points each time you make five consecutive one-dribble reverse layups.

Consecutive one-dribble reverse layups made with strong hand ___; points earned ___

Consecutive one-dribble reverse layups made with weak hand ___; points earned ___

Your score ___ (10 points maximum)

Reverse Layup Drill. SPEED DRIBBLE REVERSE LAYUP

This challenging reverse layup drill combines the use of strong- and weak-hand speed and reverse dribbles. The drill consists of alternately driving from each elbow (the intersection of the foul line and lane line) and shooting reverse layups with your right hand when dribbling right and with your left hand when dribbling left.

Start at the right elbow in a balanced stance with your left foot forward and your right foot back. Drive right to a spot under the basket using a speed dribble with your outside (right) hand and shoot a right-handed reverse layup. Catch the ball with two hands and speed dribble out to the left elbow with your outside (right) hand. Place your inside (left) foot on the elbow and reverse dribble, pulling the ball back toward the basket with your outside (right) hand.

Drive left to a spot under the basket using a speed dribble with your outside (left) hand and shoot a left-handed reverse layup. Catch the ball with two hands and speed dribble to the right elbow, using your outside (left) hand. Place your inside (right) foot on the elbow and reverse dribble, pulling the ball back toward the basket with your outside (left) hand. Continue the drill for 30 seconds, alternately driving and shooting reverse layups on each side of the basket.

Success Check

- Use proper technique for the reverse layup.
- Catch the ball with both hands.

Score Your Success

Record the number of reverse layups you make in 30 seconds. Give yourself 1 point for each reverse layup made. Eight or more layups in 30 seconds is excellent, six or seven layups is good, and five or fewer requires more practice.

Layups made in 30 seconds ___

Your score ___ (8 points maximum)

RUNNER

The runner (figure 4.8), or extended layup shot, is used away from the basket when a quick shot is needed off a cut or drive. The runner is shot the same way as the layup except the takeoff position is farther from the basket. This shot is often used when you have driven or cut by your defender and are being picked up by a taller opponent who is looking to block your shot. The runner enables you to get the shot off quicker than a jump shot, and it is therefore less likely to be blocked by a shot blocker.

Control your speed after a cut or dribble. The step before your takeoff should be short so you can quickly dip your takeoff knee in order to change forward momentum to upward momentum. Pick the ball up with your shooting hand on top of the ball in front of your shooting-side knee. Lift your shooting-side knee and the ball straight up. Avoid swiveling the ball to the side, which can cause the ball to be stolen or can put sidespin on the shot. Shoot the ball with a soft touch over the reach of a shot blocker. Keep your balance hand on the ball until the release for protection. Land in balance.

Follow through by keeping your arm up and fully extended at the elbow and keeping your index finger pointing straight at the target over the front of the rim. When you shoot the ball outside the lane, be ready to get back on defense. When you shoot the ball inside the lane, be ready to rebound the ball.

Figure 4.8 **RUNNER (EXTENDED LAYUP)**

a

b

Dip knee

1. Take short step
2. Dip knee on takeoff
3. Shoulders relaxed
4. Nonshooting hand under ball; shooting hand on top of ball
5. Elbow in
6. Raise ball between ear and shoulder

Shoot runner

1. Lift shooting-side knee
2. Jump straight up, extending leg, back, and shoulders
3. Extend elbow
4. Point index finger to target
5. Keep balance hand on ball until release
6. Follow through until ball reaches target
7. Land at spot of takeoff

MISSTEP

Your shot misses long or to the side because you float forward or sideward.

CORRECTION

Make the step before your takeoff short so you can quickly dip your takeoff knee and change forward or sideward momentum to upward momentum.

Runner Drill.
ONE-DRIBBLE RUNNER (EXTENDED LAYUP)

This drill leads up to shooting runners off the dribble with both the strong and weak hands. Start with your strong hand. Stand in a balanced stance 9 feet (2.7 m) in front of the basket. Your strong-side foot (the pivot foot) should be forward, and your weak-side foot should be back. The drill action is similar to the one-dribble layup. Dribble with your strong hand. Take a short step with your weak-side foot and pick up the ball at your strong-side knee; you should pick up the ball with your balance hand under the ball and your shooting hand on top of the ball. Jump straight up and shoot a strong-hand runner. Land in balance, ready to rebound or get back on defense.

Practice the same way with your weak hand. Your weak-side foot should be forward, and your strong-side foot should be back. Dribble with your weak hand. Set up with your strong-side foot and pick up the ball at your weak-side knee. Jump straight up and shoot a weak-hand runner. Land in balance, ready to rebound or get back on defense.

To Increase Difficulty

- After making five consecutive one-dribble runners from 9 feet, move back to a spot 12 feet (3.7 m) in front of the basket.
- After making five consecutive one-dribble runners from 12 feet, move back to a spot 15 feet (4.6 m) in front of the basket.

Success Check

- Pick up the ball with your balance hand under and your shooting hand on top of the ball.
- Use correct technique for the runner.
- Make five consecutive one-dribble runners with each hand at each distance.

Score Your Success

Record the number of consecutive one-dribble runners you make at each distance and to each side. Give yourself 5 points each time you are able to make five consecutive one-dribble runners.

Consecutive one-dribble runners from 9 feet, strong hand ___; points earned ___

Consecutive one-dribble runners from 9 feet, weak hand ___; points earned ___

Consecutive one-dribble runners from 12 feet, strong hand ___; points earned ___

Consecutive one-dribble runners from 12 feet, weak hand ___; points earned ___

Consecutive one-dribble runners from 15 feet, strong hand ___; points earned ___

Consecutive one-dribble runners from 15 feet, weak hand ___; points earned ___

Your score ___ (30 points maximum)

POWER MOVE

The power move (figure 4.9, page 110) is a strong way to score when you are close to the basket and guarded by one or more defenders. This move is most often used after you get an offensive rebound, but it may also be used on a drive to the basket. Hold the ball high with two hands in a protected position in front of your forehead; your elbows should be out. Keep your shoulders parallel with the backboard. A defender might be behind you or to the side of you. Step with your inside foot (foot closest to the defender) toward the defender in order to create space for your power move. Make a strong shot fake. Step in with the same foot used to step back. Make a second shot fake if necessary. Move the ball to the side of your forehead away from the defender. Aim the ball high above the box. Jump off both feet. Shoot the ball with two hands. Keep your shoulders parallel with the backboard, and do not open up on the shot. Expect to be fouled. Be strong and make the shot even if fouled. Land in balance, ready to rebound a possible miss with two hands. Go up again with as many power moves as it takes to score.

MISSTEP

You lower the ball, and the ball is stolen or your shot is blocked.

CORRECTION

Hold the ball with two hands. Keep the ball protected high in front of your forehead with your elbows out and your shoulders parallel with the backboard. Make one or two shot fakes to get the defender or defenders to straighten their legs, then go up strong with the power move.

Figure 4.9 **POWER MOVE**

a

Ball in protected position

1. Ball held with two hands
2. Ball in front of forehead
3. Elbows out
4. Shoulders parallel with backboard

b

Step toward defender and shot fake

1. Step toward defender
2. Make strong shot fake

c

Step in and shot fake

1. Step in with same foot
2. Make second shot fake if necessary
3. Move ball to side of forehead away from defender with elbows out
4. Shoulders parallel with backboard

d

Make power move

1. Aim ball high above box on backboard
2. Jump off both feet
3. Shoot ball with two hands
4. Expect to be fouled and still make shot
5. Land in balance, ready to rebound

Power Move Drill. SHOT FAKE POWER MOVE

Start in a balanced stance close to the basket and at one side of the rim. Hold the ball high with two hands in a protected position in front of your forehead with your elbows out. Keep your shoulders parallel with the backboard. Step with your inside foot toward an imaginary defender. Make a strong shot fake. Step in with the same foot used to step toward the defender. Make a second shot fake. Move the ball to the side of your forehead away from the imaginary defender. Make a power move. Land in balance, ready to rebound a possible miss with two hands. Go up again with as many power moves as it takes to score. Repeat, then move to the other side of the rim.

To Increase Difficulty

Add two defenders, one on each side of you. The defenders should have their hands straight up and should give some resistance to your power move by lightly bumping your arms or body.

Success Check

- Hold the ball high with two hands in a protected position.
- Make the shot fake look like a shot.
- Shoot the ball high on the backboard.

Score Your Success

Record the number of successful power moves made out of five attempts from each side of the rim. Try to make five consecutive power moves on each side.

Number of power moves made on right side of rim ___; points earned ___

Number of power moves made on left side of rim ___; points earned ___

Your score ___ (10 points maximum)

RATE YOUR SUCCESS

The only way to score is by putting the ball in the basket. Developing the ability to shoot various types of shots will help make you an offensive threat from every area on the floor.

In the next step, we will look at shooting off the catch. Before going to step 5, however, look back at how you performed the drills in this step. For each of the drills presented, enter the points you earned, then add up your scores to rate your total success.

Shooting Drills

1. Strong-Hand Shooting Warm-Up ____ out of 15
2. Weak-Hand Shooting Warm-Up ____ out of 15
3. Three-Finger Drill ____ out of 10

Free-Throw Drills

1. Daily Practice ____ out of 100
2. Eyes Closed ____ out of 20

Jump Shot Drills

1. Jump Shot Warm-Up ____ out of 30
2. Bank Jump Shot Warm-Up ____ out of 40

Three-Point Shot Drills

1. Shooting From a Chair ____ out of 25
2. Around the World ____ out of 10

Hook Shot Drills

1. Hook Shot Warm-Up ____ out of 10
2. Hook Shot Warm-Up With Crossover Step ____ out of 10
3. Alternate-Hand Hook Shooting (Mikan Drill) ____ out of 10

Layup Drills

1. One-Dribble Layup ____ out of 10
2. Speed Dribble Layup ____ out of 8
3. Speed Dribble Layup Versus Chaser ____ out of 10

Reverse Layup Drills

1. One-Dribble Reverse Layup ____ out of 10
2. Speed Dribble Reverse Layup ____ out of 8

Runner Drill

1. One-Dribble Runner (Extended Layup) ____ out of 30

Power Move Drill

1. Shot Fake Power Move ____ out of 10

Total ____ **out of 381**

If you scored 200 or more points, congratulations! You have mastered the basics of this step and are ready to move on to step 5, shooting off the catch. If you scored fewer than 200 points, you may want to spend more time on the fundamentals covered in this step. Practice the drills again to develop mastery of the techniques and increase your scores.

STEP 5

Shooting off the Catch

Most shots in basketball are open shots (end of fast break, draw-and-kick, ball passed out of trap, ball rotated versus zone or help defense, cutting off screen, pick-and-pop, and long rebound are examples). On open shots, you should face the basket and catch and shoot in one motion. The best pass is one that enables you to catch the ball within your shooting range and in position to shoot. Your shooting range is the distance within which you can consistently make the outside shot. If you are open to shoot the ball within your shooting range, give the passer a good target with your hands up and in shooting position. As the pass is thrown, jump behind the ball, facing the basket in position to shoot. Let the ball come to your hands; do not reach for the ball.

SHOOTING OFF THE CATCH WITH A QUICK RELEASE

To shoot with a quick release, you want to have your hands and feet ready. Give the passer a good target with your hands up above your shoulders in shooting position; your knees should be slightly flexed. Good passes make good shots. A good pass is one that hits the receiver's target and enables the receiver to catch the ball in position to shoot with a quick release.

Jump behind the ball on passes that are slightly off target. When you are not able to catch the ball with your hands and feet ready to shoot in rhythm, use a shot fake before your shot. The shot fake gives you time to adjust your hands and feet and establish a shooting rhythm. Only use a step and turn when closely guarded.

Catch the ball with your hands in a relaxed position, giving with the ball as it is caught. Use the block-and-tuck method to catch the ball. Be in shooting position with your shooting hand facing the basket (behind the ball) and your nonshooting hand under the ball. Do not catch the ball with your hands on the sides of the ball, rotating them into position, because when rushed you'll put sidespin on the ball. The passer should aim for your far hand, which will block the pass.

Lower your knees just before the catch, and extend upward on the catch in a quick, rhythmical down-and-up motion. Make sure you keep the ball high, with the shooting hand facing the basket. Create rhythm by using the down-and-up motion of your legs rather than by lowering the ball. Keeping the ball high fosters a quick release and also decreases the chance for error.

Use key words to help you learn correct mechanics, establish rhythm, and build confidence. Use one to three one-syllable words in rhythm. Key words should be positive, concise, and personal. Say the words aloud in rhythm from the start of your shot until the release of the ball. Emphasize the last word for confidence. As described in step 4 (page 72), words that key the correct mechanics of your shot are called trigger words or cue words. Examples of trigger words for a quick release and rhythmical leg action are *down and up!* (to trigger the down-and-up action of your legs for rhythm and range) or *up and in!* (to start your shot high and avoid lowering the ball).

SHOOTING OFF THE CATCH ON A PASS FROM IN FRONT

When you receive a pass from in front (inside out), you should catch the ball by blocking it with your nonshooting (far) hand; your shooting hand should be behind the ball and facing the front of the basket. Reset your nonshooting hand under the ball. Your knees lower just before the catch, and your knees and shooting hand go up on the catch, enabling you to shoot in rhythm with a quick release (figure 5.1, page 116).

MISSTEP

You receive a pass but have a slow release because you lower the ball before shooting it.

CORRECTION

Catch the ball in position to shoot, keeping the ball high. Catch and shoot the ball in one smooth motion. Lower your knees just before the catch and extend upward on the catch in a quick, rhythmical down-and-up motion.

Figure 5.1 **SHOOTING OFF THE CATCH ON A PASS FROM IN FRONT**

a

Shooting hand in front

1. Face basket so you can see passer and basket
2. Feet shoulder-width apart and toes straight
3. Knees slightly flexed
4. Hands high between ear and shoulder
5. Shooting hand faces basket; nonshooting hand faces slightly up

b

Catch and shoot in rhythm

1. Jump behind ball in position to shoot
2. Keep arms in; do not reach
3. Block ball with shooting hand
4. Tuck nonshooting hand under ball
5. Knees lower just before catch and extend on shot

Shooting off the Catch Drill. CATCH AND SHOOT OFF PASS FROM IN FRONT (INSIDE OUT)

In this drill, you will shoot from five outside spots—the wings and corners on each side and the top. Start at the top, directly in front of the basket. Face the basket in position to catch and shoot within your shooting range. A partner stands at the inside low-post area with a ball. Your partner begins the drill by making a chest pass to your shooting hand. If the pass is off target, jump behind the ball. Let the ball come to you; never reach for the ball. Catch the ball by blocking it with your shooting hand and tucking your nonshooting hand under the ball. Your knees lower just before the catch, and your knees and shooting hand go up on the catch, enabling you to shoot in rhythm with a quick release. After each shot attempt, your partner goes for a two-hand rebound and passes the ball back out to you. Take five shots and then switch positions with your partner. After you both shoot from the top, you and your partner move to one of the other positions. Each of you takes five shots at each position.

To Increase Difficulty

Shoot from behind the three-point line.

Success Check

- Use your key words, and use correct form.
- Catch and shoot in one smooth motion.

Score Your Success

Record the number of shots you make from each position on the court. Give yourself 1 point for each shot you make out of five attempts.

Made shots from top ___; points earned ___

Made shots from right wing ___; points earned ___

Made shots from left wing ___; points earned ___

Made shots from right corner ___; points earned ___

Made shots from left corner ___; points earned ___

Your score ___ (25 points maximum)

SHOOTING OFF THE CATCH ON A PASS FROM THE STRONG-HAND SIDE

When you receive a pass from your strong-hand side, catch the ball by blocking it with your nonshooting (far) hand; your shooting hand should be behind the ball and facing the front of the basket. Reset your nonshooting hand under the ball. Your knees lower just before the catch, and your knees and shooting hand go up on the catch, enabling you to shoot in rhythm with a quick release (figure 5.2).

Figure 5.2 **SHOOTING OFF THE CATCH ON A PASS FROM THE STRONG-HAND SIDE**

a

b

Shooting hand in front

1. Face basket; see passer and basket
2. Feet shoulder-width apart
3. Knees flexed
4. Hands high between ear and shoulder
5. Nonshooting hand faces passer; shooting hand faces basket

Block ball with nonshooting hand

1. Jump behind ball
2. Lower knees before catch
3. Keep arms in; do not reach
4. Block ball with nonshooting hand
5. Place shooting hand behind ball
6. Reset nonshooting hand under ball

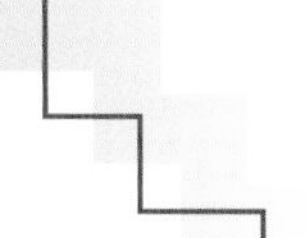

MISSTEP

When you receive a pass from the side, you face the passer and reach for the ball, slowing your release.

CORRECTION

Face the basket, turn your head to see the pass, and let the ball come to you. Jump behind the ball, and catch and shoot in one motion.

Shooting off the Catch Drill. CATCH AND SHOOT OFF PASS FROM STRONG-HAND SIDE

In this drill, you will shoot from three outside spots on your weak-hand side of the court—the elbow, the wing, and the corner. Start at the elbow on your weak-hand side. Set up within your shooting range. Face the basket with your hands and feet in position to catch and shoot with a quick release. A partner stands at the elbow on your strong-hand side with a ball. Your partner begins the drill by making a chest pass to your far (nonshooting) hand. If the pass is off target, jump behind the ball. Let the ball come to you; never reach for the ball. Catch the ball by blocking it with your nonshooting hand; your shooting hand should be behind the ball and facing the front of the basket. Reset your nonshooting hand under the ball. Your knees lower just before the catch, and your knees and shooting hand go up on the catch, enabling you to shoot in rhythm with a quick release. After each shot attempt, your partner goes for a two-hand rebound, dribbles back out to the elbow on your strong-hand side, and passes the ball back out to you. Take five shots and then switch positions with your partner. After you both shoot from the elbow on the weak-hand side, you and your partner will shoot from the wing on the weak-hand side. After you both shoot from the wing, you and your partner will shoot from the corner on the weak-hand side. When passing to the wing and corner from the elbow on the strong-hand side, use an overhead pass. You and your partner both take five shots at each position.

To Increase Difficulty

Shoot from behind the three-point line.

Success Check

- Use your key words, and use correct form.
- Catch and shoot in one motion.

Score Your Success

Record the number of shots you make from each position on the court. Give yourself 1 point for each shot you make out of five attempts.

Made shots from elbow on weak-hand side ___; points earned ___

Made shots from wing on weak-hand side ___; points earned ___

Made shots from corner on weak-hand side ___; points earned ___

Your score ___ (15 points maximum)

SHOOTING OFF THE CATCH ON A PASS FROM THE WEAK-HAND SIDE

If a pass comes from your weak-hand side, block the ball with your shooting (far) hand, and tuck your nonshooting hand under the ball. Then take your shooting hand off the ball and reset it behind the ball, facing the target. Your knees lower just before the catch, and your knees and shooting hand go up on the catch, enabling you to shoot in rhythm with a quick release (figure 5.3).

Figure 5.3 **SHOOTING OFF THE CATCH ON A PASS FROM THE WEAK-HAND SIDE**

a

Shooting hand faces passer

1. Face basket; see passer and basket
2. Feet shoulder-width apart
3. Knees flexed
4. Hands high between ear and shoulder
5. Shooting hand faces passer; nonshooting hand faces up

b

Block ball with shooting hand

1. Jump behind ball in position to shoot
2. Lower knees before catch
3. Keep arms in; do not reach
4. Block ball with shooting hand

c

Reset shooting hand

1. Tuck nonshooting hand under ball
2. Take shooting hand off ball and reset it behind ball, facing target

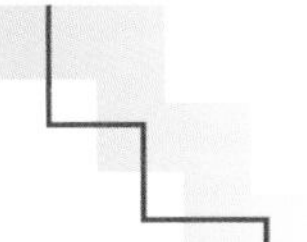

MISSTEP

You catch the ball with your hands on the sides and rotate the ball into position, causing sidespin.

CORRECTION

Your shooting hand should always be behind the ball and facing the target before you shoot. When you receive a pass from your weak-hand side, your shooting hand is your far hand. After catching the ball, take your shooting hand off the ball and reset it behind the ball for the shot.

Shooting off the Catch Drill. **CATCH AND SHOOT OFF PASS FROM WEAK-HAND SIDE**

In this drill, you will shoot from three outside spots on your strong-hand side of the court—the elbow, the wing, and the corner. Start at the elbow on your strong-hand side. Set up within your shooting range. Face the basket with your hands and feet in position to catch and shoot with a quick release. A partner stands at the elbow on your weak-hand side with a ball. Your partner begins the drill by making a chest pass to your far (shooting) hand. Let the ball come to you; never reach for the ball. Catch the ball by blocking it with your shooting hand and having your nonshooting hand under the ball. Reset your shooting hand behind the ball, facing the front of the basket, and shoot in one motion. Your knees lower just before the catch, and your knees and shooting hand go up on the catch, enabling you to shoot in rhythm with a quick release. After each shot attempt, your partner goes for a two-hand rebound, dribbles back out to the elbow on your weak-hand side, and passes the ball back out to you. Take five shots and then switch positions with your partner. After you both shoot from the elbow on the strong-hand side, you and your partner will shoot from the wing on the strong-hand side. After you both shoot from the wing, you and your partner will shoot from the corner on the strong-hand side. When passing to the wing and corner from the elbow on the weak-hand side, use an overhead pass. You and your partner both take five shots at each position.

To Increase Difficulty

Shoot from behind the three-point line.

Success Check

- Use your key words, and use correct form.
- Catch and shoot in one motion.

Score Your Success

Record the number of shots you make from each position on the court. Give yourself 1 point for each shot you make out of five attempts.

Made shots from elbow on strong-hand side ___; points earned ___

Made shots from wing on strong-hand side ___; points earned ___

Made shots from corner on strong-hand side ___; points earned ___

Your score ___ (15 points maximum)

Shooting off the Catch Drill. CATCH AND SHOOT OFF TOSS TO ELBOW

One objective of this drill is to develop your ability to catch and shoot in one motion with a quick release. Another objective is to develop your ability to start a jump shot in a balanced stance while facing the basket and to land in balance after the shot.

Start with the ball at the offensive left block outside the lane; your back is to the basket. Pass to yourself by tossing the ball high so it bounces high at the left elbow of the court. Run outside the lane to the left elbow and quickly jump behind the ball, turning to the middle to face the basket. Use a jump stop and land in balance. Have your hands and feet ready with your hands above your shoulders and your knees slightly flexed. Catch the ball with your shooting hand high, facing the front of the rim. Catch and shoot in one motion. Your knees should lower just before the catch and should extend upward on the catch in a quick, rhythmical down-and-up motion. Perform the same drill starting at the offensive right block and tossing the ball to the right elbow. Shoot 10 shots from the left elbow, then shoot 10 more from the right elbow.

To Increase Difficulty

Shoot from behind the three-point line.

Success Check

- Jump behind the ball with your hands high and in shooting position.
- Lower your knees just before the catch.
- Catch and shoot in one quick down-and-up motion.
- Use your key words, and use correct form.

Score Your Success

Record the number of shots you make from each elbow. Give yourself 1 point for each shot you make out of 10 attempts.

Made shots from left elbow ___;
points earned ___

Made shots from right elbow ___;
points earned ___

Your score ___ (20 points maximum)

Shooting off the Catch Drill. **FRONT-OF-BOARD SHOOTING**

This drill focuses on the fundamentals: shooting hand behind the ball, elbow-in alignment, release off the index finger, follow-through, and catching the ball in position to shoot.

Face the backboard. Pick a spot near the top corner of the front of the board to serve as your target. Using a spot on the front of the backboard is excellent for fostering a straight shot. Begin with the ball in shooting position above your shooting shoulder. Place your shooting hand behind the ball, with your hand facing the target and with your index finger at the ball's midpoint. Aim the ball at your target on the front of the board, and shoot a jump shot at that target with a full follow-through (full elbow extension); you want to make the ball return to your shooting position so you don't have to move your hands on the catch. Say your personalized key words in rhythm from the start of your shot to the release of the ball. If the ball does not return to your starting position, jump behind the ball and catch it in position to shoot. A shot that does not hit your target and does not come back directly to you is a missed shot. After a miss, visualize a successful shot with good form, again saying your key words. Use feedback from the feel and direction of the ball. For example, if the miss was caused by your arm going to the side, add the key word *straight*. Use *point* if the ball went off the wrong finger, creating sidespin. Use *hand* if you caught the ball with your hands on the sides.

Success Check

- Use proper technique for the jump shot.
- Catch the rebound in position to shoot.
- Your goal is to have 10 out of 10 shots hit the spot on the front of the board and return directly to you, allowing you to catch the ball in shooting position without having to move your hands.

Score Your Success

Record the number of shots that hit the target on the front of the board and then return directly to you, allowing you to make a good catch in shooting position. Give yourself 1 point for each successful shot with a good catch (out of 10 attempts).

Number of successful shots with good catches ___; points earned ___

Shooting off the Catch Drill. SIDE-OF-BOARD SHOOTING

This drill is the same as the front-of-board shooting drill except you use the side of the backboard. This drill puts more emphasis on a straight shot and good catch. On a shot that is slightly off, the rebound will go to the side. This enables you to practice jumping behind the ball to catch it in position to shoot.

Face the side of the backboard. Pick a spot near the top of the side of the board to serve as your target. Using a spot on the side of the backboard is excellent for fostering a straight shot. Aim the ball at your target on the side of the board, and shoot a jump shot at the target with a full follow-through (full elbow extension); you want to make the ball return to your shooting position so you don't have to move your hands on the catch. Catch the ball in position to shoot. Jump behind the ball on shots that rebound to your left or right side.

Success Check

- Use proper technique for the jump shot.
- Catch the rebound in position to shoot.
- Your goal is to have at least 8 out of 10 shots hit the spot on the side of the board and return directly to you, allowing you to catch the ball in shooting position without having to move your hands.

Score Your Success

Record the number of shots that hit the target on the side of the board and then return directly to you, allowing you to make a good catch in shooting position. Give yourself 1 point for each successful shot with a good catch (out of 10 attempts).

Number of successful shots with good catches ___; points earned ___

Shooting off the Catch Drill. POINT-OF-BOARD SHOOTING

This drill is the same as the front-of-board and side-of-board shooting drills except your target is the point of the backboard between the front and side of the board. This drill is obviously more difficult than the side-of-board shooting drill. It puts more emphasis on focusing and releasing the ball off your index finger. It also provides a greater challenge for jumping behind the ball in position to shoot. On shots that are off target, the rebound may go farther to the side than in the side-of-board shooting drill. This enables you to practice jumping behind the ball to catch it in position to shoot.

Face the point of the backboard. Pick a spot near the top of the point of the board to serve as your target. Focus on your target on the point of the board and shoot a jump shot to the target, emphasizing the release of the ball off your index finger. Catch the ball in position to shoot. Jump behind the ball on shots that rebound to your left or right side.

Success Check

- Use proper technique for the jump shot.
- Catch the rebound in position to shoot.
- Your goal is to have at least 6 out of 10 shots hit the spot on the point of the board and return directly to you, allowing you to catch the ball in shooting position without having to move your hands.

Score Your Success

Record the number of shots that hit the target on the point of the board and then return directly to you, allowing you to make a good catch in shooting position. Give yourself 1 point for each successful shot with a good catch (out of 10 attempts).

Number of successful shots with good catches ___; points earned ___

Shooting off the Catch Drill. PRESSURE THE SHOOTER

This drill requires two players: an offensive player and a defensive player. You start as the offensive player. Be in position to catch and shoot at the three-point line or within your shooting range. The defender starts under the basket and begins the drill by making a chest pass to your shooting hand. The defender then runs at you, attempting to pressure your shot without blocking it. You score a point each time you make a shot. After each attempt, switch roles with your partner. Each player takes 10 shots.

Success Check

- Catch and shoot in a smooth, fluid motion.
- Use proper shooting technique.

Score Your Success

This is a competitive drill in which you are trying to score more points than your partner. If you score more than your partner, give yourself 5 points.

Your score ___

Shooting off the Catch Drill. ONE-MINUTE SHOOT-OUT

This drill helps you to develop the ability to catch and shoot in one motion with a quick release. In addition, it helps you to develop the ability to shoot under pressure. The difference between good shooters and great shooters is the ability to shoot under pressure (in this drill, the pressure is the clock). Not only is this a good shooting drill, but it is also a good pass and catch drill (passing to the shooter's target) as well as a good rebounding drill (rebounding the ball with two hands without allowing the ball to hit the floor).

Select two players to work with you. One player keeps time. The timer blows a whistle to begin the drill, whistles again after 20 seconds at the first spot, whistles after 20 seconds at the second spot, and whistles at the 1-minute mark. The other player keeps score, rebounds the ball, and passes it back to you as you shoot.

You will shoot from three spots—9 feet (2.7 m) in front of the basket, with each made shot worth 1 point; 15 feet (4.6 m) in front of the basket (behind the free-throw line), with each made shot worth 2 points; and 21 feet (6.4 m) in front of the basket (or behind the three-point line), with each made shot worth 3 points.

Start in a balanced stance 9 feet in front of the basket with the ball in good shooting position in front of the shooting-side shoulder. On the first whistle, begin shooting and continue to shoot from the same spot until the second whistle. On the second whistle, move back until you are 15 feet in front of the basket, and continue to shoot from that spot until the third whistle. On the third whistle, move back until you are behind the three-point line in front of the basket. Continue to shoot from that spot until the final whistle. All shots count after the whistle except at the third spot, where the ball must be released before the final whistle.

After shooting for 1 minute, rotate positions with the other players. The shooter becomes the rebounder and passer, the rebounder and passer becomes the timer, and the timer becomes the shooter.

Success Check

- Catch and shoot with a quick release.
- Follow through until the ball reaches the net.
- A good rebounder and passer will help you achieve a good score.

Score Your Success

Record the number of shots made from each position on the court. Give yourself 1 point for each shot made from 9 feet, 2 points for each shot made from 15 feet (behind the free throw line), and 3 points for each shot made from 21 feet (or behind the three-point line).

Successful shots from 9 feet in 20 seconds (1 point for each made shot) ___; points earned ___

Successful shots from 15 feet in 20 seconds (2 points for each made shot) ___; points earned ___

Successful shots from 21 feet (or behind the three-point line) in 20 seconds (3 points for each made shot) ___; points earned ___

Total points earned in 1 minute ___; points earned ___ (40 points maximum)

Your score ___

RATE YOUR SUCCESS

Most of the shots in basketball are open shots. The ability to catch and shoot with a quick release is important for individual and team success. Remember that good passes and good catches make good shots. In the next step, we will look at creating your shot off the dribble, or what you should do if you are closely guarded. Before going to step 6, however, look back at how you performed the drills in this step. For each of the drills presented in this step, enter the points you earned, then add up your scores to rate your total success.

Shooting off the Catch Drills

	Drill	Score
1.	Catch and Shoot off Pass From in Front (Inside Out)	____ out of 25
2.	Catch and Shoot off Pass From Strong-Hand Side	____ out of 15
3.	Catch and Shoot off Pass From Weak-Hand Side	____ out of 15
4.	Catch and Shoot off Toss to Elbow	____ out of 20
5.	Front-of-Board Shooting	____ out of 10
6.	Side-of-Board Shooting	____ out of 10
7.	Point-of-Board Shooting	____ out of 10
8.	Pressure the Shooter	____ out of 5
9.	One-Minute Shoot-Out	____ out of 40
Total		____ **out of 150**

If you scored 80 or more points, congratulations! You have mastered the basics of this step and are ready to move on to step 6, creating your shot off the dribble. If you scored fewer than 80 points, you may want to spend more time on the fundamentals covered in this step. Practice the drills again to develop mastery of the techniques and increase your scores.

STEP

6

Creating Your Shot off the Dribble

Some players can score only when they get open shots. The best players are able to score when they are closely guarded. They develop offensive moves and become a triple threat to shoot, pass, or drive. To be a triple threat, you must be able to make the outside shot, pass to an open teammate in better scoring position, and drive to the basket to finish the play (either with a shot or a pass to an open teammate for the score). Every time you receive the ball, you have the opportunity to use offensive moves with the ball against your defender in a one-on-one confrontation. You can help or hurt your team, depending on what you do in this situation. A selfish one-on-one player guns the ball or drives into trouble. Team defense—in which defenders off the ball give help to the player defending the ball—prevents the selfish player from succeeding.

As an unselfish one-on-one player, you can gain an advantage over your defender by using a shot fake and a penetrating drive that forces defensive help from another defender and creates an opening that enables you to pass to your teammate for a score. This concept of one-on-one basketball, called *draw-and-kick,* is an integral part of team play. There is no greater offensive play than drawing another defensive player to help stop you and then passing to an open teammate who is spotting up for an easier shot. This method of creating openings for teammates is team basketball at its best. All-time greats Bob Cousy, Oscar Robertson, Jerry West, Elgin Baylor, Julius Erving, Magic Johnson, Larry Bird, and Michael Jordan were unselfish one-on-one players who used offensive moves to draw the defense and kick to open teammates.

CATCHING PASSES WHEN CLOSELY GUARDED IN THE SCORING AREA

You may be a fine shooter and may be able to execute good offensive moves, but if you cannot get open to receive the ball when you are being defended, all this ability with the ball is worthless. When you move to get open, you must see the ball, the basket, and your defender. If you don't see a ball being passed to you, the result will be a turnover and a missed scoring opportunity. Move to free yourself. You cannot stand still! Constantly change pace and direction. Creating space between players—an often neglected skill—is important. Work for 12 to 15 feet (3.7 to 4.6 m) of space, enough to keep one defender from guarding two offensive players. Try to move to an open area or create an angle for an open passing lane between you and the passer. When the defender is denying you a passing lane on the perimeter, overplaying the passing lane between you and the passer, you should make a *backdoor cut* to the basket. If you still do not receive a pass after the backdoor cut, change direction and cut back to the outside. This is called a *V-cut*. Get open to receive the ball within your shooting range. Your shooting range is the distance within which you can consistently make an outside shot. Have a trained observer such as a coach, a teacher, or a skilled player evaluate your ability to get open, your triple-threat stance, and your one-on-one moves. This observer can provide corrective feedback. Also, ask your coach to evaluate your decisions in reading your defender and reacting with the correct move.

Two methods are used for receiving the ball, depending on whether you are open or closely guarded. You read in step 5 about catching the ball when open in position to shoot. Catching the ball when you are closely guarded in the scoring area requires a different technique. When you are closely guarded, the passer will pass to your outside hand (the hand away from the defender). Go to the ball to meet the pass (figure 6.1, page 130). By meeting the pass, you can beat your defender to the ball. Give the passer a good target. Your hands should be above your waist for straight passes, above your head for lob passes, and below your waist and above your knees for bounce passes. Catch the ball with your hands in a relaxed position, giving with the ball as you catch it. Land with a one-two stop on your inside foot first (the foot closer to the basket), establishing it as the pivot foot. You can then protect the ball with your body while being in position to execute a reverse turn (drop step) with your opposite foot if your defender overcommits when going for the pass. After receiving the ball, use a front turn to the middle. Turning to the middle allows you to see more of the court. Face the basket and see the rim. Focusing on the rim allows you to see the total picture, including whether your defender is playing you for the shot, drive, or pass. Be a triple threat and a threat to shoot first.

Figure 6.1 **CATCHING A PASS WHEN CLOSELY GUARDED IN THE SCORING AREA**

Show hands

1. Eyes on ball
2. Balanced stance with feet shoulder-width apart
3. Knees flexed
4. Back straight
5. Hands up, ball-width apart, with fingers relaxed

Meet the ball

1. Come to meet ball
2. Make two-hand catch
3. Keep fingers relaxed
4. Give with ball on catch
5. Land with one-two stop on inside foot first, making it pivot foot

Follow through

1. Make front turn to middle, pivoting on inside foot
2. See rim
3. Be triple threat to shoot, pass, or drive
4. Be threat to shoot first
5. Feet shoulder-width apart
6. Knees flexed
7. Back straight

MISSTEP

You fumble the ball as you receive it.

CORRECTION

Keep your hands up. Watch the ball all the way into your hands. Keep your hands relaxed and give with the ball on the catch.

BEING A TRIPLE THREAT

When you receive the ball, you should face the basket and your defender (also called *squaring up*). Being square to the basket positions you well as a triple threat to shoot, pass, or drive (figure 6.2). Keep your eyes on the rim and your defender. By focusing on the rim, you can see more of the court and see whether a teammate is open in scoring position. You can also see your defender so that you can read whether the defender is playing you up close for a shot or playing you back for a pass or drive. Hold the ball high with your hands in shooting position. You must first be a threat to shoot before the options of passing or driving become viable. Make an aggressive *drive step* (also called a *jab step*). A drive step is a short, quick step with your nonpivot foot straight toward your defender. Your weight should be on your pivot foot, with your knees flexed and your upper body erect. A drive step is used to fake a drive and force your defender to react with a retreat step.

Figure 6.2 **BEING A TRIPLE THREAT**

Triple threat to shoot, pass, or drive

1. See rim and defender
2. Be threat to shoot first
3. Head over waist
4. Back straight
5. Knees flexed
6. Feet shoulder-width apart
7. Weight on pivot foot
8. Take short drive step with nonpivot foot

MISSTEP

You lower the ball, which takes away your option to shoot.

CORRECTION

Keep the ball high and be a threat to shoot first.

Reading the defense when you are being guarded on the perimeter entails first determining how your defender reacts to your aggressive drive step and then reacting with the correct offensive move. From your triple-threat stance, you can make one of four basic one-dribble moves, all starting with the drive step: the drive-step jump shot, the drive-step straight drive, the drive-step crossover drive, or the step-back jump shot. The move you choose depends on the defensive player's position in reaction to your drive step.

When your defender's hands are down, you should bring your drive-step foot back to shooting position and shoot a jump shot. When your defender has a hand up to play the shot, you should drive to the side of the raised hand. The weakness in a defender's stance is the lead foot (the foot that is forward or up). In a normal defensive stance, the defender's hand that is up will be on the same side as the lead foot. Rather than look down to check which foot is up, you can simply look at which hand is up and drive to that side. Stopping a drive toward the lead foot is more difficult for a defender because it requires the defender to make a long drop step with that foot while reverse pivoting on the back foot. On a drive toward the defender's back foot, the defender is only required to make a short retreat step. When the defender's hand is up on the side of your drive step, you should use a straight drive. When the defender's hand is up on the side away from your drive step, use a crossover drive.

Being a triple threat, making a drive step, and reading your defender's reaction and hand position are all extremely important. Do not rush. Keep your balance physically, mentally, and emotionally. Only by maintaining control and reading your defender can you successfully execute a one-on-one offensive move.

CREATING YOUR SHOT OFF ONE-DRIBBLE MOVES

A good shooter may be able to catch and shoot when open, but when closely guarded, this player may not be able to create space off the dribble to get a shot. The key to becoming a scorer and not just an open shooter is the ability to create space and to get your own shot off the dribble. The ability to create a shot off the dribble is particularly vital when the shot clock or game time is running down.

As mentioned, the four basic one-dribble moves are the drive-step jump shot, the drive-step straight drive, the drive-step crossover drive, and the step-back jump shot.

Drive-Step Jump Shot

If the defender's hands are down, you should quickly bring your drive-step foot back into a balanced shooting stance and shoot a jump shot (figure 6.3).

Figure 6.3 **DRIVE-STEP JUMP SHOT**

a

Read defender

1. Assume triple-threat stance
2. See rim and defender
3. Take short drive step
4. Read defender; hand is down

b

Shoot jump shot

1. Bring drive-step foot back
2. Shoot jump shot

c

Follow through

1. Land in balance
2. Follow through until ball reaches basket
3. Be ready to rebound or get back on defense

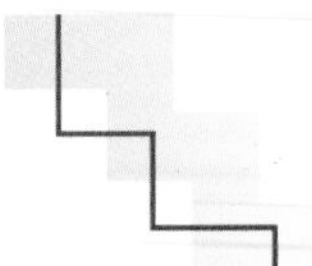

MISSTEP

You rush your move before reading your defender's position.

CORRECTION

After receiving a pass, take time to read the defender's position and then make your move.

Drive-Step Straight Drive

From a triple-threat stance, make an aggressive drive step (figure 6.4). Stop and read the defender's hand position. If the defender's hand is up on the *same side* as your drive step, you should take a longer step with your drive-step foot past your defender's lead foot. Take one long dribble with your outside hand (the hand away from the defender) and then push off your pivot foot. Dribble past your defender's body, keeping your eyes on the basket. Protect the ball with your inside hand and your body. Pick up the ball in front of your shooting-side knee with your shooting hand on top of the ball and with your balance hand under the ball. Protect the ball with your head and shoulders, and move the ball away from the defender's reach as you shoot a layup.

Figure 6.4 **DRIVE-STEP STRAIGHT DRIVE**

a

b

Read defender

1. Assume triple-threat stance
2. See rim and defender
3. Take short drive step
4. Read defender; hand is up on side of drive step

Straight drive

1. Take step past defender's lead foot
2. Keep weight on pivot foot and push off it before dribble
3. Dribble with outside hand
4. Protect ball with inside hand
5. When outside hand is right hand, prepare to shoot right-handed layup

c

d

Ball at shooting-side knee

1. Pick up ball at shooting-side knee
2. Shooting hand on top of ball; nonshooting hand under ball

Shoot layup

1. Protect ball
2. Move ball away from defender
3. Expect to be fouled
4. Shoot layup

MISSTEP

You commit a traveling violation because you drag your pivot foot or pick up your pivot foot before you release the ball on your dribble.

CORRECTION

Keep your weight on your pivot foot at the start of your drive in order to avoid dragging your pivot foot or picking it up before you release the ball on your dribble.

Drive-Step Crossover Drive

The crossover drive is similar to the straight drive and will also finish with a layup. If the defender's hand is up on the side *away* from your drive step, you should cross the ball over in front of your chest before the dribble (figure 6.5, page 136). Make a crossover step with your drive-step foot past your defender's lead foot.

Figure 6.5 **DRIVE-STEP CROSSOVER DRIVE**

a

Read defender

1. Assume triple-threat stance
2. See rim and defender
3. Take short drive step
4. Read defender; hand is up on side away from drive step

b

Crossover drive

1. Perform crossover step past defender's lead foot
2. Dribble past defender's body with outside hand
3. Push off pivot foot
4. Protect ball with inside hand and body
5. Drive to basket
6. When outside hand is left hand, prepare to shoot left-handed layup

c

Ball at shooting-side knee

1. Pick up ball at shooting-side knee
2. Shooting hand on top of ball; nonshooting hand under ball

d

Shoot layup

1. Protect ball
2. Move ball away from defender
3. Expect to be fouled
4. Shoot layup

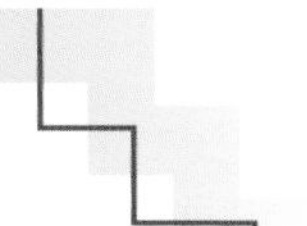

MISSTEP

You dribble too wide, giving the defender enough time and space to block the shot.

CORRECTION

Push the dribble straight out when creating space away from the defender. Protect the ball with your head and shoulders, and keep the ball away from the defender.

Step-Back Jump Shot

If the defender takes a retreat step, you should make a quick step back away from the defender on the same foot used for the drive step (figure 6.6). Dribble back with your strong hand, jump behind the ball, and pick up the ball in front of your shooting-side knee with your shooting hand on top of the ball. Shoot a jump shot. Maintain balance by picking up the ball at your knee and exaggerating the follow-through of your shoulders, head, and shooting hand toward the basket. This will counter any tendency to lean back or step back on your shot.

Figure 6.6 **STEP-BACK JUMP SHOT**

a

b

Read defender

1. Assume triple-threat stance
2. See rim and defender
3. Make short drive step
4. Read defender's retreat on drive step

Step-back dribble

1. Step back with drive-step foot
2. Dribble ball back with strong hand
3. Push off pivot foot
4. Protect ball with nondribbling hand

(continued)

(continued)

Ball at shooting-side knee

1. Pick up ball at shooting-side knee
2. Shooting hand on top of ball; nonshooting hand under ball

Shoot jump shot

1. Shoot jump shot
2. Exaggerate follow-through
3. Land in balance
4. Follow through until ball reaches basket

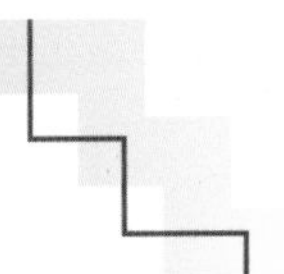

MISSTEP

When you jump behind the ball, you lean your head and shoulders back, causing you to fade back and miss short on your shot.

CORRECTION

When you jump behind the ball, keep your head and shoulders forward.

Creating Your Shot off the Dribble Drill. ONE-DRIBBLE MOVES OFF TOSS TO ELBOW

In this drill, you will practice four one-on-one moves off a drive step: drive-step jump shot, drive-step straight drive, drive-step crossover drive, and step-back jump shot. You will perform each move at the offensive left elbow and then perform each move at the offensive right elbow. Toss the ball so it bounces at the elbow. You are passing the ball to yourself. Use a toss back if one is available. Catch the ball while using a one-two stop. Your inside foot (the one closer to the basket) should land first, becoming your pivot foot. Make a front turn to the middle and see the rim. Be in a triple-threat stance and make a drive step.

Drive-step jump shot. After making a drive step, imagine that your defender's hands are down. Bring your drive-step foot back into a balanced shooting stance and shoot a jump shot.

Drive-step straight drive. After making a drive step, imagine that your defender's inside hand (the one closest to the middle) is up. Make an aggressive shot fake and then take a straight step past the imaginary defender with the same foot you used for the drive step. Keeping your weight on your pivot foot, push a long dribble past the imaginary defender using the hand away from the defender. Make sure your pivot foot doesn't leave the floor before you release the ball on the dribble. Keep your eyes on the basket. Protect the ball with your inside hand and your body. Pick up the ball in front of your shooting-side knee with your shooting hand on top of the ball and with your balance hand under the ball. Protect the ball with your head and shoulders, and move it away from the imaginary defender's reach as you shoot a layup. Land in balance.

Drive-step crossover drive. After executing a drive step, imagine that your defender's outside hand (the one away from the middle) is up. Make an aggressive shot fake and then make a crossover step past the imaginary defender with the same foot you used for the drive step. On the crossover step, aggressively move the ball across the front of your body. Dribble beyond the imaginary defender using the hand away from the defender. From this point, continue as when making a straight drive.

Step-back jump shot. After making a drive step, imagine that your defender takes a retreat step. Make a quick step back away from the imaginary defender on the same foot you used for the drive step. Dribble back with your strong hand, jump behind the ball, and pick up the ball in front of your shooting-side knee with your shooting hand on top of the ball. Shoot a jump shot. Maintain balance by picking up the ball at your knee and exaggerating the follow-through of your shoulders, head, and shooting hand toward the basket. This helps you counter any tendency to lean back or step back on your shot.

Success Check

- Be a triple threat to pass, shoot, or drive.
- Read the defender and react with the best move.
- Use correct shooting technique.

Score Your Success

Perform each move five times at each elbow. Record the number of shots you make off each move to each side. Give yourself 1 point for each shot made for each move.

Drive-step jump shot, left elbow ___ out of 5

Drive-step jump shot, right elbow ___ out of 5

Drive-step straight drive, left elbow ___ out of 5

Drive-step straight drive, right elbow ___ out of 5

Drive-step crossover drive, left elbow ___ out of 5

Drive-step crossover drive, right elbow ___ out of 5

Step-back jump shot, left elbow ___ out of 5

Step-back jump shot, right elbow ___ out of 5

Your score ___ (40 points maximum)

CREATING YOUR SHOT OFF DRIBBLE MOVES

The game of basketball has changed since the three-point shot was added. Many players have shown improvement in shooting the three-point shot and driving to the rim. However, fewer players have been able to master the in-between game—the ability to score by creating your own shot off the dribble using a variety of moves. Becoming a scorer and not just an open shooter requires creating space away from your defender by using two or more dribbles and finishing with a scoring move. The ability to score by creating your own shot is especially important when the shot clock is winding down or when under pressure near the end of the game.

Drive to Strong-Hand Side for Jump Shot

Creating a jump shot off the dribble is easier for most players when dribbling to the strong-hand side. Make an aggressive shot fake to get your defender to straighten up. Make your shot fake look like a shot. We like to say, "A shot fake is a shot not taken." From a triple-threat stance, make an aggressive drive step (figure 6.7). Keeping your weight on your pivot foot, create space away from your defender by pushing your dribble out to your strong-hand side using your outside hand (the hand away from the defender). Protect the ball with your inside hand and your body. When dribbling, always keep your eyes on your target, just over the front of the rim. Align your shooting-side knee with the ball as you jump behind the ball. Pick the ball up in front of your shooting-side knee with your shooting hand on top of the ball and with your nonshooting hand under the ball. When your shooting hand is on top of the ball, your shooting hand will face the rim when you raise the ball to shoot. By picking the ball up at your shooting-side knee, you are able to change sideward momentum to upward momentum and jump straight up on your shot, rather than float to the side. Shoot a jump shot and land in the same spot. Exaggerate your follow-through until the ball reaches the basket.

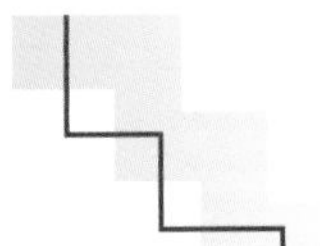

MISSTEP

You miss the shot because you float to the side.

CORRECTION

Pick the ball up at your shooting-side knee in order to change sideward momentum to upward momentum.

Figure 6.7 **DRIVE TO STRONG-HAND SIDE FOR JUMP SHOT**

Create space

1. Assume triple-threat stance
2. Take long step past defender's lead foot
3. Push dribble out with outside hand
4. Push off pivot foot
5. Protect ball with inside hand

Jump behind ball

1. Control second dribble
2. Jump-stop behind ball, aligning ball with shooting-side knee
3. Pick up ball at shooting-side knee
4. Shooting hand on top of ball; nonshooting hand under ball

Shoot jump shot

1. Raise ball up to shoot with shooting hand facing target
2. Shoot jump shot
3. Land in same spot
4. Follow through until ball reaches basket

Drive to Weak-Hand Side for Jump Shot

Creating a jump shot off the dribble is more difficult when driving to your weak-hand side, because you will have farther to go in order to pick up the ball in front of your shooting-side knee. Make an aggressive shot fake to get your defender to straighten up. Again, make your shot fake look like a shot. From a triple-threat stance, make an aggressive drive step (figure 6.8). Keeping your weight on your pivot foot, create space away from your defender by pushing your dribble out to your strong-hand side using your outside hand (the hand away from the defender). Protect the ball with your inside hand and your body. When dribbling, always keep your eyes on your target, just over the front of the rim. Align your shooting-side knee with the ball as you jump behind the ball. Because you have farther to go in order to pick up the ball in front of your shooting-side knee, you can make a crossover dribble to the front of your shooting-side knee on your last dribble. Pick the ball up in front of your shooting-side knee with your shooting hand on top of the ball and with your nonshooting hand under the ball. When your shooting hand is on top of the ball, your shooting hand will face the rim when you raise the ball to shoot. By picking the ball up at your shooting-side knee, you are able to change sideward momentum to upward momentum and jump straight up on your shot, rather than float to the side. Shoot a jump shot and land in the same spot. Exaggerate your follow-through until the ball reaches the basket.

Figure 6.8 **DRIVE TO WEAK-HAND SIDE FOR JUMP SHOT**

a

Create space

1. Assume triple-threat stance
2. Take long step past defender's lead foot
3. Push dribble out with outside hand
4. Push off pivot foot
5. Protect ball with inside hand

b

Jump behind ball

1. For second dribble, use crossover dribble to shooting-side knee
2. Jump-stop behind ball, aligning ball with shooting-side knee
3. Pick up ball at shooting-side knee
4. Shooting hand on top of ball; nonshooting hand under ball

Shoot jump shot

1. Raise ball up to shoot with shooting hand facing target
2. Shoot jump shot
3. Land in same spot
4. Follow through until ball reaches basket

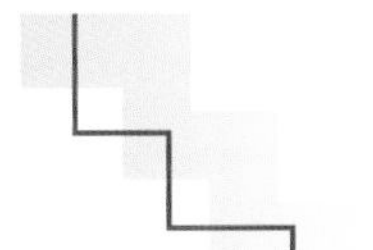

MISSTEP

The ball circles out of the basket because you picked the ball up with your hands on the sides of the ball, causing sidespin.

CORRECTION

Pick the ball up with your shooting hand on top of the ball so your shooting hand will face the rim when you raise the ball to shoot, leading to backspin.

Creating Your Shot off a Drive From the Top

To create your shot off a drive from the top, you can use two basic moves: (1) a drive off the pinch post for a jump shot and (2) a reverse dribble off the pinch post for a jump shot.

Drive Off Pinch Post for Jump Shot

When driving from the top off the pinch post to your strong-hand side, dribble with your strong (outside) hand. Use a change-of-pace dribble as you approach the pinch-post screen (figure 6.9, page 144). Create space away from your defender by using one or two dribbles to move away at a 45-degree angle with the basket, staying within your shooting range. Square up to the basket by jumping behind the ball or pivoting on your inside foot (the foot closest to the basket). Pick the ball up in front of your shooting-side knee with your shooting hand on top of the ball and with your nonshooting hand under the ball. When your shooting hand is on top of the ball, your shooting hand will face the target when you raise the ball to shoot. By picking the ball up at your shooting-side knee, you are able to change sideward momentum to upward momentum and jump straight up to shoot a jump shot, rather than float to the side. Shoot a bank jump shot, aiming for the top near corner of the box on the backboard. Jump and land in the same spot. Exaggerate your follow-through until the ball reaches the net.

When driving from the top off the pinch post to your weak-hand side, dribble with your weak (outside) hand. Shooting off the dribble is more difficult when you are going to your weak-hand side because you have farther to go to pick the ball up at your shooting-side knee. To help your pickup when going to your weak-hand side, you should make your last dribble a crossover dribble to the front of your shooting-side knee.

Figure 6.9 **DRIVE OFF PINCH POST FOR JUMP SHOT**

a

Create space

1. Assume triple-threat stance
2. Take long step past defender's lead foot
3. Push dribble out with outside hand
4. Push off pivot foot
5. Protect ball with inside hand

b

Jump behind ball

1. When driving to weak-hand side, make second dribble a crossover dribble to shooting-side knee
2. Jump-stop behind ball, aligning ball with shooting-side knee
3. Pick up ball at shooting-side knee
4. Shooting hand on top of ball; nonshooting hand under ball

Shoot jump shot

1. Raise ball up to shoot with shooting hand facing target
2. Shoot jump shot
3. Land in same spot
4. Follow through until ball reaches basket

MISSTEP

You miss the shot because you float to the side.

CORRECTION

Pick the ball up at your shooting-side knee in order to change sideward momentum to upward momentum.

Reverse Dribble off Pinch Post for Jump Shot

When driving from the top off the pinch post, use a change-of-pace dribble as you approach the pinch-post screen (figure 6.10, page 146). If your defender attempts to go over the top of the pinch-post screen, you should use a reverse dribble to the middle. Pivot on your inside foot (the foot closest to the basket), and square to the basket. Keep the ball in the same hand as you pull the ball close to your body on your reverse dribble. Pick the ball up between your knees with your shooting hand on top of the ball and with your nonshooting hand under the ball. If you lose balance on your reverse dribble, make a head and shoulder fake to regain balance before taking your shot. Shoot a jump shot. Jump and land in the same spot. Exaggerate your follow-through until the ball reaches the basket.

Figure 6.10 **REVERSE DRIBBLE OFF PINCH POST FOR JUMP SHOT**

a

Drive toward pinch post

1. Assume triple-threat stance
2. Drive with outside hand
3. Protect ball with inside hand

b

Read defender

1. Read defender; defender goes over top of pinch-post screen
2. Reverse dribble to middle
3. Stay outside foul lane

c

Pick ball up

1. Pick ball up between knees
2. Shooting hand on top of ball; nonshooting hand under ball

d

Shoot jump shot

1. Raise ball up to shoot with shooting hand facing target
2. Shoot jump shot
3. Land in same spot
4. Follow through until ball reaches basket

MISSTEP

You dribble too wide on the reverse and risk having the ball stolen.

CORRECTION

On the reverse dribble, keep the ball in the same hand and pull it close to your body.

Creating Your Shot off the Dribble Drill. MOVES OFF DRIVE FROM TOP OFF PINCH POST

In this drill, you will practice two moves off a drive from the top off the pinch post: (1) a drive off the pinch post for a jump shot and (2) a reverse dribble off the pinch post for a jump shot. You will practice each move on a drive off the offensive right pinch post and then on a drive off the offensive left pinch post. Toss the ball so it bounces above the top of the free-throw circle. You are passing the ball to yourself. Use a toss back if one is available.

Drive off pinch post for jump shot. When you practice driving off the pinch post, catch the ball with your back to the basket and land with a one-two stop on your inside foot (the one closer to the basket) first. Make a front turn to the middle, pivoting on your inside foot, and see the rim. Be in a triple-threat stance. Make an aggressive shot fake and then perform a crossover step to the outside. Use a change-of-pace dribble as you approach the pinch post. Create space away from your imaginary defender by using one or two dribbles to a 45-degree angle with the basket. When driving to your strong side, square up to the basket by jumping behind the ball or pivoting on your inside foot (the foot closest to the basket). Align your shooting-side knee with the ball as you jump behind the ball. When driving to your weak side, make your last dribble a crossover dribble to your shooting-side knee. Pick the ball up in front of your shooting-side knee with your shooting hand on top of the ball and with your nonshooting hand under the ball. If you are a left-handed shooter on the right side (or a right-handed shooter on the left side), you have farther to go in order to pick up the ball in front of your shooting-side knee, so make a crossover dribble to the front of your shooting-side knee on your last dribble. When your shooting hand is on top of the ball, your shooting hand will face the target when you raise the ball to shoot. By picking the ball up at your shooting-side knee, you are able to change sideward momentum to upward momentum and jump straight up on your shot, rather than float to the side. Shoot a bank jump shot, aiming for the top near corner of the box on the backboard. Jump and land in the same spot. Exaggerate your follow-through until the ball reaches the net. Perform five repetitions of this move driving right and five repetitions driving left.

Reverse dribble off pinch post for jump shot. When driving from the top off the pinch post, use a change-of-pace dribble as you approach the pinch-post screen. Imagine that your defender attempts to go over the top of the pinch-post screen. Use a reverse dribble to the middle. Pivot on your inside foot (the foot closest to the basket), and square up to the basket. Keep the ball in the same hand as you pull the ball close to your body on your reverse dribble. Stay outside the foul lane on your reverse dribble. Pick the ball up between your knees with your shooting hand on top of the ball and with your nonshooting hand under the ball. If you lose balance on your reverse dribble, make a head and shoulder fake to regain balance before taking your shot. Shoot a jump shot. Jump and land in the same spot. Exaggerate your follow-through until the ball reaches the net. Perform five repetitions of this move driving right and five repetitions driving left.

(continued)

Drive Baseline for Jump Shot

Creating a jump shot when driving from the wing to the baseline is the same as creating a jump shot off a drive to the middle except you will be driving to the baseline. Remember, making this move is more difficult when driving to your weak-hand side, because you will have farther to go in order to pick up the ball in front of your shooting-side knee. To help align your shooting-side knee with the ball and pick up the ball in front of your shooting-side knee, use a crossover dribble to your shooting-side knee on your last dribble.

Drive Middle for Step-Back Jump Shot

The step-back jump shot is used when you are closely guarded as you drive. From a triple-threat stance, make an aggressive drive step. Keeping your weight on your pivot foot, create space away from your defender by pushing your dribble out to the middle with your outside hand (the hand away from the defender). When your defender is able to stay with you, you should control your dribble. Lean your inside shoulder into your defender, then make an aggressive head and shoulder fake to straighten your defender's legs (figure 6.12). Create space away from your defender by dribbling back.

Jump behind the ball in balance by dipping your knees (to change backward momentum to upward momentum) while aligning your shooting-side knee with the ball. Keep your head and shoulders forward to counter the tendency to lean back. Pick up the ball in front of your shooting-side knee with your shooting hand on top of the ball and with your nonshooting hand under the ball for balance. Bring the ball straight up so your shooting hand faces the basket. Jump straight up and shoot a jump shot. Direct your head, shoulders, shooting hand, and fingers toward the basket to counter any tendency to lean your head and shoulders back on your shot. Hold your follow-through straight up until the ball goes through the net.

Figure 6.12 **DRIVE MIDDLE FOR STEP-BACK JUMP SHOT**

a

b

Read defender

1. Defender stays with you on drive to middle
2. Lean into defender
3. Make head and shoulder fake

Step-back dribble

1. Create space away from defender by dribbling back
2. Jump behind ball

Pick up ball

1. Align shooting-side knee with ball
2. Keep head and shoulders forward
3. Pick up ball in front of shooting-side knee
4. Shooting hand on top of ball; nonshooting hand under ball

Shoot jump shot

1. Raise ball up to shoot with shooting hand facing target
2. Direct head, shoulders, arm, and hand toward basket
3. Shoot jump shot
4. Land in same spot
5. Follow through until ball reaches basket

MISSTEP

Your shot is short because you float back.

CORRECTION

On the step-back dribble, jump behind the ball in balance by dipping your knees. Keep your head and shoulders forward to counter the tendency to lean back.

Drive Baseline for Step-Back Jump Shot

Creating a step-back jump shot when driving from the wing to the baseline is the same as creating a step-back jump shot off a drive to the middle except you will be driving to the baseline.

Drive Middle for Step-Back Drive

When you step back for a jump shot and your defender comes up on you, you should drive by your defender (figure 6.13). When your defender is able to stay with you as you dribble back, use a head and shoulder fake to straighten your defender's legs, then drive by your defender. Look for a help defender trying to block your shot. Continue your drive as close to the basket as possible to get the shot blocker's hand caught in the net (we call this "putting him in jail"). Shoot a hook shot over the reach of the shot blocker. Land in the same spot as your takeoff. Be ready to rebound a possible missed shot and score with a power move. You may also finish with a reverse layup, shoot a runner, or pass to the open teammate whom the shot blocker left.

Figure 6.13 **DRIVE MIDDLE FOR STEP-BACK DRIVE**

a

Read defender

1. Defender comes up on you as you dribble back
2. Make head and shoulder fake

b

Drive by defender

1. Drive by defender toward basket
2. Look for shot blocker

c

Shoot hook shot

1. Try to get shot blocker's hand caught in net
2. Shoot hook shot high over shot blocker
3. Land in same spot
4. Be ready to rebound

MISSTEP

Your shot is blocked as you drive.

CORRECTION

Continue your drive as close to the basket as possible to get the shot blocker's hand caught in the net. Shoot the hook shot over the reach of the shot blocker.

Drive Baseline for Step-Back Drive

Creating a step-back drive when driving from the wing to the baseline is the same as creating a step-back drive off a drive to the middle except you will be driving to the baseline. In addition, you will drive past the basket to get the shot blocker's hand caught in the net before shooting the hook shot over the reach of the shot blocker. You may also finish with a reverse layup.

Drive Middle for Runner

The runner, or extended layup shot, is used when you are farther from the basket and you need to take a quick shot off a cut or drive. It is often used when you have driven by your defender and you are being picked up by a taller opponent in the lane. The runner enables you to get the shot off quicker than a jump shot; therefore, the shot is less likely to be blocked by a shot blocker.

From a triple-threat stance, make an aggressive drive step (figure 6.14). Keeping your weight on your pivot foot, create space away from your defender by pushing your dribble out with your outside hand (the hand away from the defender) . Protect the ball with your inside hand and your body. When dribbling, always keep your eyes on your target just over the front of the rim. Use at least two dribbles. Control your speed on the approach and take a short step with your inside foot before you take your last dribble. Dip your inside (takeoff) knee in order to change forward momentum to upward momentum. Pick the ball up with your shooting (outside) hand on top and your nonshooting hand under the ball in front of your shooting-side knee. Lift your shooting-side knee and the ball straight up. Avoid swiveling the ball to the side, which can cause the ball to be stolen or can put sidespin on the shot. Shoot the ball with a soft touch over the reach of a shot blocker. Keep your balance hand on the ball until the release for protection. Follow through by keeping your arm up and fully extended at the elbow, with your index finger pointing straight over the front of the rim. Jump and land in the same spot as your takeoff; this will prevent you from charging into a help defender or floating into a shot blocker's reach. When you shoot the ball outside the lane, be ready to get back on defense. When you shoot the ball inside the lane, be ready to rebound the ball. When driving to the middle with your right hand, shoot a right-handed runner. When driving to the middle with your left hand, shoot a left-handed runner.

Figure 6.14 **DRIVE MIDDLE FOR RUNNER**

a

Create space

1. Assume triple-threat stance
2. Take long step past defender's lead foot
3. Push dribble out with outside hand
4. Push off pivot foot
5. Protect ball with inside hand

b

Pick up dribble

1. When outside hand is right hand, prepare to shoot right-handed runner
2. Take short step with inside foot before last dribble
3. Dip takeoff knee
4. Pick up ball at shooting-side knee
5. Shooting hand on top of ball; nonshooting hand under ball
6. Eyes on target

C

Shoot runner

1. Raise ball straight up to shoot with shooting hand facing target
2. Jump straight up, pushing off takeoff foot
3. Protect ball with nonshooting hand until release
4. Shoot runner high above shot blocker's reach
5. Land in balance at spot of takeoff
6. Be ready to rebound if shot is taken inside lane

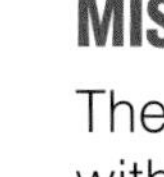

MISSTEP

The ball circles out of the basket because you picked the ball up with your hands on the sides of the ball, causing sidespin.

CORRECTION

Pick the ball up with your shooting hand on top of the ball so your shooting hand will face the rim when you raise the ball to shoot, leading to backspin.

Drive Baseline for Runner

Creating a runner when driving from the wing to the baseline is the same as creating a runner off a drive to the middle except you will be driving to the baseline. When driving to the baseline with your right hand, shoot a right-handed runner. When driving to the baseline with your left hand, shoot a left-handed runner.

Drive Middle and Reverse Dribble Down Lane for Hook

The reverse dribble down the lane for a hook is used when you are driving to the middle and your defender jumps in your path at the elbow. When driving to the middle with your right hand, reverse dribble down the lane and shoot a left-handed hook. When driving to the middle with your left hand, reverse dribble down the lane and shoot a right-handed hook.

From a triple-threat stance, make an aggressive drive step. Drive to the middle (figure 6.15, page 156). Keeping your weight on your pivot foot, create space away from your defender by pushing your dribble out with your outside hand (the hand away from the defender). Continue with a second dribble toward the elbow. When your defender jumps in your path at the elbow, use a reverse dribble. Pivot on your inside foot. Keep the ball in the same hand as you pull the ball close to your body on your reverse dribble. After the reverse dribble, switch hands and dribble with your outside hand. Use a control dribble down the lane with your outside hand. When you reach a spot above the block, shoot a hook shot.

As you start your hook shot, dip your takeoff knee in order to change forward momentum to upward momentum. Pick the ball up at your shooting-side knee with your shooting hand under the ball and with your nonshooting hand slightly behind and on top of the ball. Lift your shooting-side knee, pivot toward the basket, and lift the ball to the basket with an ear-to-ear motion of your arm. Aim for a spot on the top near corner of the box on the backboard. Keep your nonshooting hand on the ball until the release. Jump and land in the same spot. Be ready to rebound. On a missed shot, rebound the ball high with two hands, make a shot fake, and score with a power move. Do not fear missing a hook shot. Develop the attitude that "A hook is a pass to myself."

Figure 6.15 **DRIVE MIDDLE AND REVERSE DRIBBLE DOWN LANE FOR HOOK**

a

b

Drive to middle

1. Push dribble out with outside hand
2. Protect ball with inside hand
3. Continue dribble to elbow

Reverse dribble

1. See defender jump in your path at elbow
2. Reverse dribble down lane
3. Pivot on inside foot
4. Pull ball back with same hand
5. After reverse dribble, switch hands and dribble with outside hand

Pick up dribble

1. Use control dribble down lane
2. Continue dribble to spot above block
3. Dip takeoff knee
4. Pick up ball with shooting hand under ball; nonshooting hand slightly behind and on top of ball

Shoot hook shot

1. Lift shooting-side knee
2. Pivot toward basket
3. Aim for top near corner of box on backboard
4. Lift ball to basket
5. Use ear-to-ear motion of arm
6. Keep nonshooting hand on ball until release
7. Land in same spot as takeoff

MISSTEP

You miss the shot because you float to the side.

CORRECTION

Pick the ball up at your shooting-side knee in order to change sideward momentum to upward momentum.

Drive Baseline and Reverse Dribble to Middle for Bank Jump Shot

The reverse dribble to the middle for a bank jump shot is used when you are driving baseline and your defender gets in your path at the midpoint of the baseline.

Drive toward the baseline with your outside hand (the hand away from the defender) (figure 6.16). When your defender gets in your path at the midpoint of the baseline, pivot on your inside foot and make a reverse dribble to the middle, creating space away from your defender. The reverse dribble should take you to a 45-degree angle above the block. Keep the ball in the same hand as you pull the ball close to your body.

Pick the ball up between your knees with your shooting hand on top and your nonshooting hand under the ball. Aim for a spot above the top near corner of the box on the backboard. Shoot a bank jump shot. Jump and land in the same spot as your takeoff. Be ready to rebound. On a missed shot, catch the ball high with two hands, make a shot fake, and score with a power move.

Figure 6.16 **DRIVE BASELINE AND REVERSE DRIBBLE TO MIDDLE FOR BANK JUMP SHOT**

a

b

Drive baseline

1. Push dribble out with outside hand
2. Protect ball with inside hand
3. Continue drive to baseline

Reverse dribble

1. See defender cut off baseline
2. Pivot on inside foot
3. Reverse dribble to middle
4. Pull ball back with same hand
5. Create space, moving to bank shot angle

Pick up ball

1. Pick ball up between knees
2. Shooting hand on top of ball; nonshooting hand under ball

Shoot bank jump shot

1. Raise ball up to shoot with shooting hand facing target
2. Aim above top near corner of box on backboard
3. Shoot bank jump shot
4. Land in same spot
5. Follow through until ball reaches basket

MISSTEP

You dribble the ball too wide on your reverse dribble, and the ball is stolen by a help defender.

CORRECTION

Pick the ball up between your knees for protection.

Creating Your Shot off the Dribble Drill. MOVES OFF DRIVE FROM WING TO MIDDLE

In this drill, you will practice five moves: drive middle for jump shot, drive middle for step-back jump shot, drive middle for step-back drive, drive middle for runner, and drive middle and reverse dribble down lane for hook. You will perform each move at the offensive left wing and then perform each move at the offensive right wing. Toss the ball so it bounces at the wing. You are passing the ball to yourself. Use a toss back if one is available. Catch the ball while using a one-two stop. Your inside foot (the one closer to the middle) should land first, becoming your pivot foot. Make a front turn to the middle and see the rim. Be in a triple-threat stance, and make a drive step.

Drive middle for jump shot. After making a drive step, imagine that your defender's inside hand (the hand closest to the middle) is up. Make an aggressive shot fake. Make a straight drive to the middle, creating space with at least two dribbles using your outside hand. When driving to your strong-hand side, make a jump stop behind the ball, aligning your shooting-side knee with the ball. When driving to your weak-hand side, you have farther to jump in order to align your shooting-side knee with the ball; make an extra dribble (crossover dribble) to the front of your shooting-side knee. Pick up the ball in front of your shooting-side knee with your shooting hand on top of the ball and with your nonshooting hand under the ball. Shoot a jump shot. Perform five repetitions of this move from each wing.

Drive middle for step-back jump shot. After executing a drive step, imagine that your defender's inside hand (the hand closest to the middle) is up. Make an aggressive shot fake. Make a straight drive to the middle, creating space with at least two dribbles using your outside hand. Imagine that your defender stays with you. Create space away from the imaginary defender and shoot a step-back jump shot. Direct your head, shoulders, shooting hand, and fingers toward the basket to counter any tendency to lean your head and shoulders back on your shot. Land in balance at the spot of your takeoff. Perform five repetitions of this move from each wing.

Drive middle for step-back drive. After making a drive step, imagine that your defender's inside hand (the hand closest to the middle) is up. Make an aggressive shot fake. Make a straight drive to the middle, creating space with at least two dribbles using your outside hand. Imagine that your defender stays with you. Make a step-back dribble to try to create space for a jump shot. Imagine that your defender is able to stay with you as you dribble back. Use a head and shoulder fake to straighten your defender's legs, and then drive by your defender. Imagine that a help defender is trying to block your shot. Continue your drive as close to the basket as possible to get the shot blocker's hand caught in the net. Shoot a hook shot over the reach of the shot blocker. Land in the same spot as the takeoff. You may also finish with a reverse layup or shoot a runner. Perform five repetitions of this move from each wing.

Drive middle for runner. For this part of the drill, you will practice shooting a runner off a drive to the middle from the wing on each side. After making a drive step at the left wing, create space by pushing the first dribble out. Control the second dribble. Step into the lane at the left elbow and shoot a right-handed runner. When driving from the offensive right wing, step into the lane at the right elbow and shoot a left-handed runner. Perform five repetitions of this move from each wing.

Drive middle and reverse dribble down lane for hook. After making a drive step, imagine that your defender's inside hand (the hand closest to the middle) is up. Make an aggressive shot fake. Make a straight drive to the middle, creating space with at least two dribbles using your outside hand. At the elbow, imagine that your defender is playing you to the middle. Make a reverse dribble, keeping the ball in the same hand as you pull the ball close to your body. When driving from the offensive left wing and reversing down the lane, shoot a left-handed hook shot. When driving from the offensive right wing and reversing down the lane, shoot a right-handed hook shot. Perform five repetitions of this move from each wing.

Success Check

- When driving to your strong-hand side, jump behind the ball.
- When driving to your weak-hand side, use a crossover dribble to your shooting-side knee.
- Pick the ball up at your shooting-side knee.
- Place your shooting hand on top of the ball for a jump shot or runner.
- Place your shooting hand under the ball for a hook shot.

Score Your Success

Perform each move five times on each side. Record the number of shots you make off each move on each side. Give yourself 1 point for each shot made out of five attempts.

Drive from left wing to middle for jump shot ___ out of 5

Drive from right wing to middle for jump shot ___ out of 5

Drive from left wing to middle for step-back jump shot ___ out of 5

Drive from right wing to middle for step-back jump shot ___ out of 5

Drive from left wing to middle for step-back drive ___ out of 5

Drive from right wing to middle for step-back drive ___ out of 5

Drive from left wing to middle for runner ___ out of 5

Drive from right wing to middle for runner ___ out of 5

Drive from right wing to middle and reverse dribble down lane for hook ___ out of 5

Drive from left wing to middle and reverse dribble down lane for hook ___ out of 5

Your score ___ (50 points maximum)

Creating Your Shot off the Dribble Drill.
MOVES OFF DRIVE FROM WING TO BASELINE

In this drill, you will practice five moves: drive baseline for jump shot, drive baseline for step-back jump shot, drive baseline for step-back drive, drive baseline for runner, and drive baseline and reverse dribble to middle for bank jump shot. You will perform each move at the offensive left wing and then perform each move at the offensive right wing. Toss the ball so it bounces at the wing. You are passing the ball to yourself. Use a toss back if one is available. Catch the ball while making a one-two stop. Your inside foot (the one closer to the middle) should land first, becoming your pivot foot. Make a front turn to the middle and see the rim. Be in a triple-threat stance, and make a drive step.

Drive baseline for jump shot. After making a drive step, imagine that your defender's outside hand (the hand closest to the baseline) is up. Make an aggressive shot fake. Make a crossover drive to the baseline, creating space with at least two dribbles using your outside hand. When driving to your strong-hand side, make a jump stop behind the ball, aligning your shooting-side knee with the ball. When driving to your weak-hand side, you have farther to jump in order to align your shooting-side knee with the ball; make an extra dribble (crossover dribble) to the front of your shooting-side knee. Pick up the ball in front of your shooting-side knee with your shooting hand on top of the ball and with your nonshooting hand under the ball. Shoot a jump shot. Perform five repetitions of this move from each wing.

Drive baseline for step-back jump shot. This part of the drill is performed by shooting a step-back jump shot off a drive to the baseline from the wing on each side. After making a drive step, drive from the offensive left wing to the baseline and shoot a step-back jump shot, then drive from the offensive right wing and shoot a step-back jump shot. Perform five repetitions of this move from each wing.

Drive baseline for step-back drive. After making a drive step, imagine that your defender's outside hand (the hand closest to the baseline) is up. Make an aggressive shot fake. Make a crossover drive to the baseline, creating space with at least two dribbles using your outside hand. Imagine that your defender is able to stay with you as you dribble back for a step-back jump shot. Use a head and shoulder fake to straighten your defender's legs, then drive by your defender to the basket. Imagine that a help defender is trying to block your shot. Continue to drive past the basket to get the shot blocker's hand caught in the net. Shoot a hook shot over the reach of the shot blocker. Land in the same spot as the takeoff. You may also finish with a reverse layup or shoot a runner. Perform five repetitions of this move from each wing.

Drive baseline for runner. This part of the drill is performed by shooting a runner off a drive to the baseline from the wing on each side. After making a drive step at the left wing, create space by pushing the first dribble out. Control the second dribble. Step with your inside foot and shoot a left-handed runner. When driving from the offensive right wing, step with your inside foot and shoot a right-handed runner. Perform five repetitions of this move from each wing.

Drive baseline and reverse dribble to middle for bank jump shot. After making a drive step, imagine that your defender's outside hand (the hand closest to the baseline) is up. Make an aggressive shot fake. Make a crossover drive to the baseline, creating space with at least two dribbles using your outside hand. Imagine that your defender is cutting you off at the midpoint of the baseline, and reverse dribble toward the middle to a spot above the block. Shoot a bank jump shot. Perform five repetitions of this move from each wing.

Success Check

- When driving to your strong-hand side, jump behind the ball.
- When driving to your weak-hand side, use a crossover dribble to your shooting-side knee.
- Pick the ball up at your shooting-side knee.
- Place your shooting hand on top of the ball for a jump shot or runner.
- Place your shooting hand under the ball for a hook shot.

Score Your Success

Perform each move five times on each side. Record the number of shots you make off each move to each side. Give yourself 1 point for each shot made out of five attempts.

Drive from left wing to baseline for jump shot ___ out of 5

Drive from right wing to baseline for jump shot ___ out of 5

Drive from left wing to baseline for step-back jump shot ___ out of 5

Drive from right wing to baseline for step-back jump shot ___ out of 5

Drive from left wing to baseline for step-back drive ___ out of 5

Drive from right wing to baseline for step-back drive ___ out of 5

Drive from left wing to baseline for runner ___ out of 5

Drive from right wing to baseline for runner ___ out of 5

Drive from right wing to baseline and reverse dribble to middle for bank jump shot ___ out of 5

Drive from left wing to baseline and reverse dribble to middle for bank jump shot ___ out of 5

Your score ___ (50 points maximum)

Creating Your Shot off the Dribble Drill. VERSUS DEFENDER

This drill involves creating your shot off the dribble versus a defender.

Read the defense. This part of the drill gives you practice at reading how a defender is playing you and reacting with the correct move. Select a partner to be a defender. The defender defends you only until you read the defense and select the correct move, not while you make your move.

You start as an offensive player and take a position above the free-throw line. The defensive player takes a position below the free-throw line with a ball. The

(continued)

(continued)

defensive player tosses the ball to you. Catch the ball and take a triple-threat position, being a threat to shoot first. After you catch the ball, the defender varies the defensive position—hands down or one hand up—to give you practice at reading the defense and making the correct decision. If the defender's hands are down, you should shoot a jump shot. If one of the defender's hands is up, drive to the side of the raised hand with the appropriate straight drive or crossover drive. If the defender retreats on your drive step, use the step-back jump shot. Continue the drill until you have taken 10 shots. Then switch offensive and defensive roles. Keep track of the number of times you make a correct read of the defense and the number of shots you make. Each element is worth 1 point. Give yourself 1 point for each correct read and 1 point for each shot made out of 10 attempts (for a maximum of 20 points).

One-on-one in the free-throw circle (one dribble). This competitive game helps you develop the ability to read the defender and use fakes, pivots, and one-on-one moves to score or draw a foul. It also develops your defensive and rebounding skills. You will play offense against a defender. Your objective is to score with a one-on-one move. Use the top half of the free-throw circle as a boundary. The defender initiates play by getting in a defensive stance inside the free-throw line and handing you the ball at a position above the free-throw line. You may dribble once and may take one step outside the top half of the circle before releasing the shot. You get 2 points each time you score. If you get fouled on a successful shot, you get a free throw. If you get fouled but miss the shot, you get two free throws. If you miss the shot and get an offensive rebound, you can make a move and try to score from the spot where the ball was rebounded. Again, only one dribble is allowed. Continue play until you score or turn over the ball or until the defender gets the ball on a steal or rebound and dribbles back past the free-throw line. Then switch offensive and defensive roles. Play to 7 points. This is a competitive drill. The first player to score 7 points wins the game. Give yourself 5 points if you win the game.

Closeout one-on-one (three dribbles). This competitive game also helps you develop the ability to read a defender and create your shot off the dribble. Start on the perimeter within your shooting range. The defender starts under the basket and tosses a ball to you to begin the drill. The defender closes out on defense (runs at you and gets into a defensive stance within touching distance of you). You may use only three dribbles. You get 2 points each time you score. If you get fouled on a successful shot, you get a free throw. If you get fouled but the shot misses, you get two free throws. If you miss the shot and get the offensive rebound, you can make a move and try to score from the spot where the ball was rebounded. Again, only three dribbles are allowed. Continue play until you score or turn over the ball or until the defender gets the ball on a steal or rebound and dribbles back past the free-throw line. Then switch offensive and defensive roles.

For variety, the offensive player can start at a different position—such as the top, wing, or either corner—within the player's shooting range. This is a competitive drill. The first player to score 7 points wins the game. Give yourself 5 points if you win the game.

Block the shot. This part of the drill requires two players, one on offense and one on defense. Start as the offensive player. Be in position to catch and shoot at the three-point line or within your shooting range. The defender starts under the basket. The defender starts the drill by making a chest pass to your shooting hand. The defender attempts to block your shot and then runs past you. As the defender attempts to block your shot, you should make an aggressive shot fake, then take one dribble away from the shot blocker and shoot a jump shot. You score 1 point each time you make a shot. After each attempt, switch offensive and defensive roles. Each player makes 10 attempts. This is a competitive drill. Try to score more points than your partner, and give yourself 5 points if you succeed.

Dribble one-on-one. This part of the drill requires two players, one on offense and one on defense. Start as the offensive player. Be in position to catch the ball 10 feet (3 m) beyond the three-point line (outside your shooting range). The defender starts under the basket. The defender makes a chest pass to you before quickly moving to a defensive position at the three-point line. As the offensive player, you dribble at the defender and use a footfire dribble (page 59) as you meet. The footfire dribble normally causes a defender to freeze for a second, giving you time to gain balance, read the defender's position, and then make the appropriate decision to create your shot off the dribble. You get 2 points each time you score. If you get fouled on a successful shot, you get a free throw. If you get fouled but miss the shot, you get two free throws. If you miss the shot and get the offensive rebound, you can make a move and try to score from the spot where the ball was rebounded. Continue play until you score or make a turnover or until the defender gets the ball on a steal or rebound. Then switch offensive and defensive roles. This is a competitive drill. The first player to score 7 points wins the game. Give yourself 5 points if you win the game.

Success Check

- Read the defender and make the correct decision.
- Use proper technique for each one-on-one move and each shot.
- Be aggressive.

Score Your Success

Read the defender and make the correct move. Record the number of points you earned in each part of the drill.

Read the defense ___ out of 20

One-on-one in the free-throw circle (one dribble) ___ out of 5

Closeout one-on-one (three dribbles) ___ out of 5

Block the shot ___ out of 5

Dribble one-on-one ___ out of 5

Your score ___ (40 points maximum)

Creating Your Shot off the Dribble Drill. **BEAT THE PRO**

Beat the pro is a shooting game in which you practice under imaginary conditions and pressures similar to those that take place in a game. Use your imagination and pick your favorite pro to shoot against. For every shot that you make, you get 1 point. For every shot that you miss, the pro gets 2 points. Ten points wins.

(continued)

(continued)

Therefore, to win you must shoot at least 71 percent from the field. You must take game condition shots off individual offensive moves. Take jump shots and hook shots. Layups are not allowed. You are also not allowed to shoot from the same position twice in a row. You are allowed to take time between shots, but you must go hard when you make your move. Shoot from within your shooting range. Be confident. Work to develop shooting poise by controlling any thoughts that will upset your concentration. Learn not to worry about missed shots or the score. Think positive, and put your complete concentration into each shot. Use judgment in shot selection, and use your best move and shot when it is needed.

Success Check

- Take game-condition shots.
- Shoot from a different position on every shot.
- Use proper technique for each offensive move and each shot.
- Be confident.

Score Your Success

This is a competitive drill. Play five games. Give yourself 5 points for each game in which you beat the pro.

Your score ___ (25 points maximum)

RATE YOUR SUCCESS

Become a triple threat to score, pass, or drive. Learn to take on a defender one on one and win, opening up offensive opportunities for your team. In this step, we have covered various moves for creating your shot off the dribble. In the next step, we will look at scoring in the post. Before going to step 7, however, look back at how you performed the drills in this step. For each of the drills presented in this step, enter the points you earned, then add up your scores to rate your total success.

Creating Your Shot off the Dribble Drills

1. One-Dribble Moves off Toss to Elbow	____ out of 40
2. Moves off Drive From Top off Pinch Post	____ out of 20
3. Moves off Drive From Wing to Middle	____ out of 50
4. Moves off Drive From Wing to Baseline	____ out of 50
5. Versus Defender	____ out of 40
6. Beat the Pro	____ out of 25
Total	____ **out of 225**

If you scored 115 or more points, congratulations! You have mastered the basics of this step and are ready to move on to step 7, scoring in the post. If you scored fewer than 115 points, you may want to spend more time on the fundamentals covered in this step. Practice the drills again to develop mastery of the techniques and increase your scores.

STEP

7

Scoring in the Post

Players who can score in the post are very valuable to their team. You want to learn how to score on a post-up move or create an open shot for a teammate whose defender is drawn to you. When you are a threat to score in the post against your defender, a teammate's defender may be forced to leave an outside player to give defensive help on you. This creates an opening for you to pass to the open teammate on the outside. The strategy of getting the ball inside and then passing back to the outside is called *inside-out* basketball. An inside-out offense is considered by many teams to be the most consistent method for achieving scoring opportunities. When a team has the opposite approach—looking for an outside shot first—this makes it more difficult to get a high-percentage outside shot. Working the ball inside to a player who can score in the post will open up scoring opportunities both inside and out.

Post moves with the ball can be classified in three ways: (1) low-post moves made near the basket, (2) pinch-post moves made at the elbow area, and (3) midpoint moves made at the baseline midpoint.

LOW-POST MOVES

The basic low-post moves include the drop-step baseline power move, drop-step middle hook, front turn baseline for bank jump shot, and front turn baseline and crossover middle for hook. Countermoves include the spin-back power move, drive to opposite side for hook, drop-step to middle for one-dribble jump hook, and drop-step to middle for one-dribble shot fake and step-through.

Getting Open and Catching Passes in the Low Post

When you are in the low post, try to seal off your defender (keep the defender to one side) by using your back, shoulder, and upper arm on that side. Do not allow your defender to get a foot in front of your foot. Strategies will vary depending on whether you want to get open when denied or when fronted.

If your defender is in a denial position with a foot and hand in the passing lane between you and the ball, you should move a few steps away from the passer (figure 7.1). Quickly cut back on one side of your defender toward the ball. Work to get open using short, quick steps and get position in a strong, balanced stance, with your feet spread at least shoulder-width apart, your knees flexed, and your back straight. Your hands should be up and ball-width apart for a target.

On the pass, meet the ball, catching it with two hands. Use a jump stop, landing outside the lane and above the block. On the pro lane, land outside the lane and split the hash mark above the block. By catching the ball above the block, or splitting the hash mark above the pro lane, you will be able to shoot a bank shot after a front turn to the baseline. The feet land at the same time on a jump stop, enabling you to use either one as a pivot foot. To keep from stepping forward after the catch, land with your weight initially back on your heels. After landing, transfer your weight forward to the balls of your feet to get the balance you need to react and make an offensive move. Use a wide base and flex your knees. Protect the ball by keeping it in front of your forehead with your elbows out. Be strong both physically and mentally. We like to say, "When you have the ball, you have the power." Make sure that you read the position of your defender before making a move.

Figure 7.1 **GETTING OPEN FOR A PASS IN THE LOW POST WHEN DENIED**

Defender denies

1. Defender denies you the ball
2. See ball and defender
3. Offensive stance strong and balanced
4. Hands up

Move away, cut back

1. Take defender away
2. Cut back to ball
3. Keep hands up, ball-width apart

Catch ball

1. Catch ball with two hands
2. Protect ball in front of forehead
3. Keep elbows out
4. Jump-stop and land in balance outside lane above block

If a defender completely fronts you, take the defender high by moving up the lane with short, quick steps to a position above the middle hash mark (figure 7.2). Seal your defender by keeping your forearm on the defender's back. Signal for a lob pass with the hand closest to the basket. Cut to the basket and catch the lob pass that has been passed high toward the corner of the backboard. Jump-stop and land in balance, ready to score.

Figure 7.2 **GETTING OPEN FOR A PASS IN THE LOW POST WHEN FRONTED**

a

b

c

Defender fronts

1. Defender fronts you
2. See ball and defender
3. Offensive stance strong and balanced
4. Hand up

Take defender high

1. Take defender high (up lane)
2. Signal for lob pass with hand up
3. Cut to basket on pass

Catch lob

1. Catch ball with two hands
2. Protect ball in front of forehead
3. Jump-stop and land in balance, ready to score

Reading the defense means determining how your defender is playing you so you can react with the correct move. It involves seeing your opponent or feeling your defender's body against you. In the low post, you read the position by seeing or feeling whether your defender is on the *topside* (toward the foul line) or the *baseline side.* In both cases, you would drop-step with the foot opposite the side of your defender. If you cannot locate your defender or if you are in doubt, use a front turn toward the baseline to face the basket and see your defender's position.

Before receiving the ball, you can anticipate your defender's position by recognizing where the pass will be coming from (that is, the corner, wing, or high-post area) and by being aware of your defender's position in trying to prevent the pass.

Drop-Step Baseline Power Move

After catching the ball in the low post and reading your defender's position on the topside, make a ball fake to the middle by showing the ball above your shoulder (figure 7.3). After the fake, move the ball to a protected position in front of your forehead with your elbows out. Drop-step to the baseline with your inside foot (the one closer to the backboard). As you make the drop step, keep your weight on your pivot foot to avoid dragging it. Try to get your shoulders parallel to the backboard and get your defender on your back. Maintain a strong, balanced stance with your back straight and the ball protected in front of your forehead, away from your defender. Fake a shot, and then make a power move toward the basket, jumping off both feet. Shoot the ball with two hands, keeping your shoulders parallel to the board and without opening up on the shot. Aim the ball high above the box. Land in balance and be ready to rebound the ball with two hands after a possible missed shot. Go up again with as many power moves as it takes to score.

Figure 7.3 **DROP-STEP BASELINE POWER MOVE**

a

Defender topside

1. Jump-stop as you catch ball, landing in balanced stance
2. Protect ball in front of forehead
3. Keep elbows out
4. Read defender topside
5. Make ball fake to middle

b

Drop-step baseline

1. Drop-step to baseline and maintain balanced stance
2. Protect ball in front of forehead
3. Keep elbows out
4. Fake shot

c

Power move

1. Make power move
2. Jump off both feet
3. Shoot with two hands
4. Follow through by landing in balance with hands up, ball-width apart, ready to rebound

MISSTEP

You land with a one-two stop on the catch and can only pivot on the foot that landed first.

CORRECTION

Land with a jump stop so you have the option to choose which foot you will use as a pivot foot.

Drop-Step Middle Hook

After catching the ball in the low post and reading your defender's position on the baseline side, make a ball fake to the baseline by showing the ball above your shoulder (figure 7.4). After the fake, drop-step to the middle with your outside foot (the one away from the backboard). As you make the drop step, move the ball to hook shot position, with your shooting hand under the ball and your balance hand behind and slightly on top of the ball. Hold the ball back, protecting it with your head and shoulders rather than leading with it. Pivot in toward the basket. Shoot a hook shot. Keep your nonshooting hand on the ball until release for protection. Land in balance, ready to rebound a possible miss with two hands. If you rebound a missed shot, use a power move to score.

Figure 7.4 **DROP-STEP MIDDLE HOOK**

a

Defender baseline

1. Jump-stop as you catch ball, landing in balance
2. Protect ball in front of forehead
3. Keep elbows out
4. Read defender baseline side
5. Ball fake to baseline

b

Drop-step middle

1. Drop-step to middle and maintain balanced stance
2. Get hands in hook shot position
3. Hold ball back and protect it with head and shoulders

c

Hook shot

1. Shoot hook shot
2. Keep nonshooting hand on ball until release for protection
3. Land in balance with hands up, ball-width apart, ready to rebound

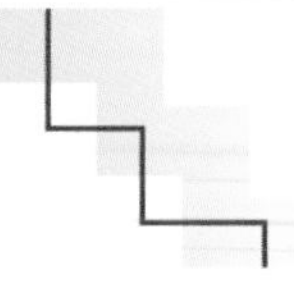

MISSTEP

You rush into the move before reading the defender's position.

CORRECTION

After receiving the pass in the low post, stop for at least one count to take time to read your defender's position. Then make your move.

Front Turn Baseline for Bank Jump Shot

If you cannot see or feel your defender after catching the ball in the low post, your defender is behind you (figure 7.5). Make a front turn to the baseline to see your defender. On the front turn, make an aggressive drive step. A drive step is a short (8- to 10-inch [20 to 25 cm]) jab step with one foot straight at the basket. The drive step should make your defender react with a retreat step.

Keep your eyes on the rim and your defender. Be a triple threat to shoot, pass, or drive. Hold the ball high with your hands in shooting position. Be sure to maintain your balance, and don't rush. Depending on your defender's reaction, you can then shoot a bank jump shot or make a crossover step to the middle for a hook.

If the defender's hands are down or the defender retreats on your drive step, shoot a bank jump shot. Aim for the top near corner of the box on the backboard. Land in balance, ready to rebound a possible miss with two hands. When you rebound a missed shot, use a power move to score.

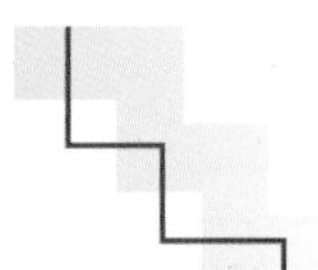

MISSTEP

Still in doubt about the defender's position, you make a front turn to the middle, which limits your moves to a jump shot in the middle or a crossover and hook from the baseline, both of which are difficult.

CORRECTION

When in doubt, always make a front turn to the baseline so you can use the bank jump shot or use the crossover step to the middle for a hook.

Figure 7.5 **FRONT TURN BASELINE FOR BANK JUMP SHOT**

Defender behind

1. Jump-stop as you catch ball, landing in balanced stance
2. Protect ball in front of forehead
3. Keep elbows out
4. Read defender behind you

Front turn baseline

1. Make front turn to baseline
2. Hold ball high with hands in shooting position
3. Make drive step
4. See rim and defender
5. Read that defender's hands are down or defender retreats on drive step

Bank jump shot

1. Shoot bank jump shot
2. Aim for top near corner of box on backboard
3. Follow through by landing in balance with hands up, ball-width apart, ready to rebound

Front Turn Baseline and Crossover Middle for Hook

If you cannot see or feel your defender after catching the ball in the low post, your defender is behind you (figure 7.6, page 174). Make a front turn to the baseline to see the rim and your defender. On the front turn, make an aggressive drive step and show the ball high. Be a triple threat to shoot, pass, or drive. Hold the ball with your hands in shooting position. Be sure to maintain your balance, and don't rush. If your defender extends on your shot fake with hands up, hold for a count of one before making your next move. Take a crossover step to the middle with the same foot you used for the drive step. As you cross over to the middle, aggressively move the ball across the front of your body to hook shot position with your shooting hand under the ball. Hold the ball back, protecting it with your head and shoulders. Pivot in toward the basket and shoot a hook shot. Land in balance, ready to rebound a possible miss with two hands. When you rebound a missed shot, use a power move to score.

Figure 7.6 **FRONT TURN BASELINE AND CROSSOVER MIDDLE FOR HOOK**

Defender behind

1. Jump-stop as you catch ball, landing in balanced stance
2. Protect ball in front of forehead
3. Keep elbows out
4. Read defender behind you

Front turn baseline and fake shot

1. Make front turn to baseline
2. Perform drive step
3. See rim and defender's hands up
4. Fake shot

Crossover middle

1. Perform crossover step to middle
2. Get hands in hook shot position
3. Hold ball back and protect it with head and shoulders

Shoot hook shot

1. Pivot in toward basket
2. Shoot hook shot
3. Keep both hands on ball until release
4. Be ready to rebound

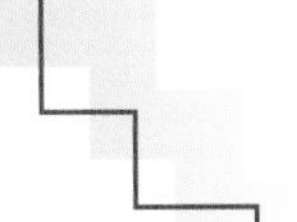

MISSTEP

You dribble the ball before making your move.

CORRECTION

Make your move without dribbling. Learn to save the dribble until after your crossover step. This gives you the option of faking a hook and then either making a spin-back (reverse) dribble for a power move or making a one-dribble drive across the lane to the opposite side for a baby hook.

Spin-Back Power Move

After you make a front turn and crossover step, your defender may anticipate your move to shoot a hook shot and jump in your path. If this occurs, you can fake a hook shot and counter with a spin-back power move (figure 7.7, page 176). Dribble the ball between your knees as you reverse pivot (spin back) on the same foot that you used for your crossover step. Dribbling the ball between your knees protects the ball from a help defender trying to flick it away. Pick up the ball with two hands. Keep your weight on your pivot foot to avoid dragging it. Try to get your shoulders parallel to the backboard and get your defender on your back. Maintain a strong, balanced stance with your back straight and the ball protected in front of your forehead, away from your defender. Make a power move toward the basket, jumping off both feet. Aim the ball high above the box on the backboard. Shoot the ball with two hands, keeping your shoulders parallel to the board and without opening up on the shot. Land in balance, ready to rebound a possible miss with two hands. When you rebound a missed shot, use a power move to score.

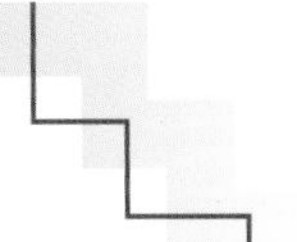

MISSTEP

You dribble the ball too wide, allowing a help defender to flick the ball away.

CORRECTION

Dribble the ball between your knees to protect the ball from a help defender.

Figure 7.7 **SPIN-BACK POWER MOVE**

Defender anticipates hook

1. Defender anticipates hook and jumps in your path
2. Fake hook shot

Spin back

1. Reverse pivot (spin back)
2. Dribble ball between knees
3. Pick up ball with two hands
4. Protect ball from help defenders

Power move

1. Back parallel to backboard
2. Protect ball in front of forehead with elbows out
3. Make power move to basket, jumping off both feet
4. Aim ball high above box on backboard
5. Shoot ball with two hands
6. Be ready to rebound

Drive to Opposite Side for Hook

This is another counter you can use when your defender anticipates your move to shoot a hook shot and jumps in your path. In this case, you fake a hook and then counter with a one-dribble drive across the lane to the opposite side for a hook (figure 7.8). Look for an opening to the opposite side of the basket. Be alert for help-side defenders. If you see an opening, fake a hook shot and then create space away from your defender by using a one-dribble drive to the opposite side of the basket. Keep your weight on your pivot foot to avoid dragging it. Make sure you push the dribble out away from your defender. Use the basket for protection against a possible blocked shot—this is called "putting the defender in jail." Pick the ball up off the dribble with your shooting hand under the ball and with your nonshooting hand slightly above and behind the ball for protection. Aim for a spot high above the top near corner of the box on the backboard, and shoot a baby hook. Land in balance, ready to rebound a possible miss with two hands. When you rebound a missed shot, use a power move to score.

Figure 7.8 **DRIVE TO OPPOSITE SIDE FOR HOOK**

a

Defender anticipates hook

1. Defender anticipates hook and jumps in path
2. Look for opening to opposite side of basket

b

Drive to opposite side

1. Be alert for help-side defenders
2. Fake hook shot
3. Create space away from defender by pushing ball out with one dribble
4. Use basket for protection against possible blocked shot

c

Shoot hook shot

1. Pick ball up off dribble
2. Shooting hand under ball; nonshooting hand slightly above and behind ball for protection
3. Aim for spot high above top near corner of box on backboard
4. Shoot hook shot
5. Keep both hands on ball until release

MISSTEP

Defender stays with you as you dribble.

CORRECTION

Push dribble out to create space away from the defender.

Drop-Step to Middle for One-Dribble Jump Hook

When you are being guarded by a physical defender who wants to knock you off balance, the one-dribble jump hook can be more effective than the one-foot hook. After catching the ball in the low post and reading your defender's position on the baseline side, make a ball fake to the baseline by showing the ball above your shoulder (figure 7.9). After the fake, make a drop step to the middle with your outside foot. Create space with one dribble and then jump-stop. The dribble should be between your knees for protection against a help defender. Pick the ball up with your hands in hook shot position; your shooting hand is under the ball, and your nonshooting hand is behind and slightly on top of the ball. Protect the ball with your head and shoulders. Jump off both feet and shoot a hook shot. Be strong, expect to be fouled, and complete the shot for a possible three-point play. Land in balance, ready to rebound a possible miss with two hands. When you rebound a missed shot, use a power move to score.

Figure 7.9 **DROP-STEP TO MIDDLE FOR ONE-DRIBBLE JUMP HOOK**

a

Defender baseline

1. Jump-stop as you catch ball, landing in balance
2. Protect ball in front of forehead
3. Keep elbows out
4. Read defender baseline side
5. Make ball fake to baseline

b

Drop-step middle

1. Drop-step to middle
2. Make one dribble, with ball between knees
3. Make jump stop

Pick ball up in hook shot position

1. Pick ball up in hook shot position
2. Protect ball with head and shoulders

Jump hook

1. Jump off both feet
2. Shoot jump hook
3. Keep two hands on ball until release
4. Be strong; expect to be fouled
5. Land in balance with hands up, ready to rebound

MISSTEP

As you dribble, the ball is deflected by a help defender.

CORRECTION

Make sure the dribble is close to your body.

Drop-Step to Middle for One-Dribble Shot Fake and Step-Through

This move is another low-post option. Make a drop step to the middle, make one dribble, and jump-stop (figure 7.10, page 180). When your defender is overly aggressive and plays you for a jump hook with both hands up, you should make a shot fake and then step through with your outside foot past the defender's foot. Move your head and shoulders under the defender's arm. Protect the ball with your head and shoulders, moving the ball away from your defender's reach, and score with a power move. Be strong. Expect to be fouled and complete the shot for a possible three-point play. This move is also called the up-and-under move. Land in balance, ready to rebound a possible miss with two hands. When you rebound a missed shot, use a power move to score.

Figure 7.10 **DROP-STEP TO MIDDLE FOR ONE-DRIBBLE SHOT FAKE AND STEP-THROUGH**

a

b

c

Read defender

1. Defender's hands up
2. Read defender aggressively over-playing jump hook
3. Make shot fake

Step through

1. Step through past defender's lead foot
2. Move head and shoulders under defender's arm
3. Move ball away from defender's reach

Power move

1. Lean in toward basket
2. Jump off both feet
3. Score with power move
4. Be strong; expect to be fouled
5. Land in balance, ready to rebound

MISSTEP

Your shot is blocked.

CORRECTION

When making the step-through, move your head and shoulders under your defender's arm and move the ball away from your defender's reach. Lean in toward the basket as you shoot.

Low-Post Drill. **Low-Post Moves**

In this drill, you will practice eight low-post moves: drop-step baseline power move, drop-step middle hook, front turn baseline for bank jump shot, front turn baseline and crossover middle for hook, spin-back power move, drive to opposite side for hook, drop-step to middle for one-dribble jump hook, and drop-step to middle for one-dribble shot fake and step-through. You will perform each move at the offensive left low post and then perform each move at the offensive right low post. Start under the basket. Toss the ball to the offensive left side so it will bounce outside the lane and above the block on the lane line. On the pro lane, the ball should be tossed so it splits the hash mark above the block on the lane line. Catch the ball with two hands as you jump-stop, landing outside the lane with your back to the basket.

Drop-step baseline power move. After catching the ball in the low post, imagine that you feel or see your defender on your middle side. Make a shot fake to the middle and then protect the ball at your forehead. Make a drop step toward the baseline with your inside foot (the one closest to the basket), followed by another shot fake. Make a strong power move, jumping off both feet and keeping your shoulders parallel to the backboard as you shoot the ball with two hands. Aim the ball high above the box on the backboard. Land in balance. Perform five repetitions of this low-post move from each side.

Drop-step middle hook. After catching the ball in the low post, imagine that you feel or see your defender on your baseline side. Make a shot fake to the baseline, and then drop-step to the middle with your outside foot (the one away from the baseline). As you make the drop step, move the ball to hook shot position, with your shooting hand under the ball and your balance hand behind and slightly on top of the ball. Hold the ball back, protecting it with your head and shoulders rather than leading with it. Pivot in toward the basket. Shoot a hook shot. Land in balance. Perform five repetitions of this low-post move from each side.

Front turn baseline for bank jump shot. After catching the ball in the low post, imagine that you cannot see or feel your defender. Make a front turn to the baseline to see the rim and your imaginary defender. On the front turn, make an aggressive drive step and shot fake. Hold the ball with your hands in shooting position. Be sure to maintain your balance, and don't rush.

Imagine that your defender's hands are down. Shoot a bank jump shot. Aim for the top near corner of the box on the backboard. Land in balance. Perform five repetitions of this low-post move from each side.

Front turn baseline and crossover middle for hook. After catching the ball in the low post, imagine that you cannot see or feel your defender. Make a front turn to the baseline to see your imaginary defender. On the front turn, make an aggressive drive step and shot fake. Hold the ball with your hands in shooting position. Be sure to maintain your balance, and don't rush. Hold for a count of one before making your next move.

Imagine that in reaction to your shot fake, your defender puts a hand up on the side of your drive step. Take a crossover step to the middle with the same foot you used for the drive step. As you cross over to the middle, aggressively move the ball across the front of your body to hook shot position with your shooting hand under the ball. Hold the ball back, protecting

(continued)

(continued)

it with your head and shoulders. Pivot in toward the basket and shoot a hook shot. Keep your nonshooting hand on the ball until the release for protection. Land in balance. Perform five repetitions of this low-post move from each side. From the left low post, shoot a right-handed hook. From the right low post, shoot a left-handed hook.

Spin-back power move. After you make a front turn to the baseline and a crossover step to the middle, imagine that your defender anticipates your move to shoot a hook shot and jumps in your path. Fake a hook shot and counter with a spin-back power move. Dribble the ball between your knees as you reverse pivot (spin back) on the same foot you used for your crossover step. Dribbling the ball between your knees protects the ball from an imaginary help defender trying to flick it away. Keep your weight on your pivot foot to avoid dragging it. Try to get your shoulders parallel to the backboard and get your imaginary defender on your back. Maintain a strong, balanced stance with your back straight and the ball protected in front of your forehead, away from your imaginary defender. Make a power move toward the basket, jumping off both feet. Aim the ball high above the box on the backboard. Shoot the ball with two hands, keeping your shoulders parallel to the board and without opening up on the shot. Land in balance. Perform five repetitions of the spin-back power move from each side.

Drive to opposite side for hook. After you make a front turn to the baseline and a crossover step to the middle, imagine that your defender anticipates your move to shoot a hook shot and jumps in your path. Imagine that you see an opening to drive to the opposite side of the basket. Fake a hook shot and counter with a one-dribble drive to the opposite side. Then shoot a hook shot. Keep your nonshooting hand on the ball until the release for protection. Land in balance. Perform five repetitions of this low-post move from each side. When driving from the offensive left side, shoot a right-handed hook. When driving from the offensive right side, shoot a left-handed hook.

Drop-step to middle for one-dribble jump hook. After making a drop step to the middle, imagine that you are guarded by a physical defender who wants to knock you off balance. Make one dribble and jump-stop. The dribble should be between your knees for protection against an imaginary help defender. Pick the ball up with your hands in hook shot position; your shooting hand is under the ball, and your nonshooting hand is behind and slightly on top of the ball. Protect the ball with your head and shoulders. Jump off both feet and shoot a hook shot. Be strong. Land in balance. Perform five repetitions of this low-post move from each side. From the left low post, shoot a right-handed jump hook. From the right low post, shoot a left-handed jump hook.

Drop-step to middle for one-dribble shot fake and step-through. After making a drop step to the middle, imagine that you are guarded by an overly aggressive defender who plays you for a jump hook with both hands up. Make a shot fake and then step through with your outside foot past the imaginary defender's foot. Move your head and shoulders under the defender's arm. Protect the ball with your head and shoulders, moving the ball away from your imaginary defender's reach, and score with a power move. Be strong. Land in balance. Perform five repetitions of this low-post move from each side.

Success Check

- Be a triple threat to pass, shoot, or drive.
- Use correct shooting technique.

Score Your Success

Perform each low-post move five times on each side. Record the number of shots you make off each move to each side. Give yourself 1 point for each shot made for each move.

Drop-step baseline power move, left low post ___ out of 5

Drop-step baseline power move, right low post ___ out of 5

Drop-step middle hook, left low post ___ out of 5

Drop-step middle hook, right low post ___ out of 5

Front turn baseline for bank jump shot, left low post ___ out of 5

Front turn baseline for bank jump shot, right low post ___ out of 5

Front turn baseline and crossover middle for hook, left low post ___ out of 5

Front turn baseline and crossover middle for hook, right low post ___ out of 5

Spin-back power move, left low post ___ out of 5

Spin-back power move, right low post ___ out of 5

Drive to opposite side for hook, left low post ___ out of 5

Drive to opposite side for hook, right low post ___ out of 5

Drop-step to middle for one-dribble jump hook, left low post ___ out of 5

Drop-step to middle for one-dribble jump hook, right low post ___ out of 5

Drop-step to middle for one-dribble shot fake and step-through, left low post ___ out of 5

Drop-step to middle for one-dribble shot fake and step-through, right low post ___ out of 5

Your score ___ (80 points maximum)

Low-Post Drill. **Read the Defense**

This drill gives you practice reading defenders in the low post and reacting with the correct move. Select a partner to be a defensive player. The defensive player defends you only until you read the defense and select the correct move, not while you make your move. After you catch the ball in the low post, the defender will vary the defensive position—baseline side, topside, or off you—to give you practice making the correct decision.

When you see or sense that your defender is on the topside (toward the foul line) or on the baseline side, make a drop step with the foot opposite the side of the defender and make the appropriate move. If you cannot locate the defender or if you are in doubt, use a front turn toward the baseline to face the basket and see the defender's position. After the front turn, the defender will play you with hands up or hands down. If the defender's hands are down, shoot a bank jump shot. If the defender's hands are up, use a crossover step to the middle and shoot a hook shot. Continue the drill for 10 shots, 5 from each side.

Success Check

- Read the defender and make the appropriate move.
- Use correct technique for each low-post move.

Score Your Success

Make five reads resulting in five shots from each side. Give yourself 1 point for each correct read of your defender and 1 point for each shot you make.

Number of correct reads and made shots from offensive left side ___; points earned ___

Number of correct reads and made shots from offensive right side ___; points earned ___

Your score ___ (20 points maximum)

Low-Post Drill. **One-on-One in Half Circle**

This competitive game helps you develop the ability to read the defender and use fakes, pivots, and various low-post moves to score or draw a foul. It also develops your defensive and rebounding skills. You will play offense against a defender. On a pro court, use the lower half of the free-throw circle as a boundary. On a college or high school court, use the imaginary lower half of the free-throw circle as a boundary. Your objective is to score with a low-post move. You may not dribble the ball, but you may take one step outside the lower half of the circle before shooting the ball.

The defender initiates play by getting in a defensive stance and then handing you the ball. You get 2 points each time you score. If you get fouled while making the shot, you get a free throw. If you get fouled but miss the shot, you get two free throws. If you miss the shot but get an offensive rebound, you may make a move and score from the spot where the ball was rebounded. Again, dribbling is not allowed. Continue play until you score or turn the ball over or until the defender gets the ball on a steal or rebound and dribbles back past the free-throw line. Then switch offensive and defensive roles. Play to 7 points.

Use a variation by having the offensive player start with a ball. The offensive player's back is to the basket in the low-post area in the middle of the lane. The defender initiates play by touching the offensive player. In this variation, the offensive player could also start with a ball in the low post on either side of the lane.

Success Check

- Read the defender and use the best low-post move.
- Do not dribble the ball.
- Be aggressive.

Score Your Success

This is a competitive drill. The first player to score 7 points wins the game. Play three games. Give yourself 5 points each time you win a game.

Your score ___ (15 points maximum)

PINCH-POST MOVES

The pinch post is the area just above the elbow on either side. Basic pinch-post moves include the shot fake jump shot, step-back jump shot, step-through leaner, drive across lane for hook, crossover drive layup, crossover drive bank jump shot, crossover drive step-back jump shot, and crossover drive step-through leaner.

Getting Open and Catching Passes at the Pinch Post

If your defender is in a denial position with a foot and hand in the passing lane between you and the ball, you should use your outside hand (the hand away from the defender) for a target (figure 7.11, page 186). Take your defender away, then cut to the elbow. Show the passer a target with your outside hand. On the pass, meet the ball, catching it with two hands. Use a one-two stop, landing at the elbow with your inside foot (the foot closest to the middle) first. Make a front turn to the middle to see the rim and your defender. Make an aggressive drive step and show the ball high. Be a triple threat to shoot, pass, or drive. Be a threat to shoot first. Make sure you read the position of your defender before making a move.

Figure 7.11 **GETTING OPEN FOR A PASS AT THE PINCH POST WHEN DENIED**

a

Defender denies

1. Defender denies you the ball
2. Eyes on ball and opponent
3. Offensive stance strong and balanced

b

Cut to elbow

1. Take defender away
2. Cut to elbow
3. Show passer target with outside hand

c

Catch ball

1. Catch ball with two hands
2. Land with one-two stop, inside foot landing first

d

Front turn to middle and read defender

1. Make front turn to middle to see rim and defender
2. Make aggressive drive step
3. Be triple threat to shoot, pass, or drive; be threat to shoot first
4. Read position of defender before making move

Shot Fake Jump Shot

After catching the ball at the pinch post, you want to be a triple threat and a threat to shoot first. See the rim and your defender. If you are closely guarded and your defender's hand is up, you should make a drive step, keeping your weight on your pivot foot (figure 7.12). Make an aggressive shot fake to make your defender react by straightening his legs. This will enable you to jump higher than your defender and get your shot off over your defender's reach. After the fake, move the ball to shooting position with your shooting hand behind the ball and facing the front of the rim. Shoot a jump shot. Follow through until the ball reaches the net. Land in balance and be ready to rebound the ball if the shot is missed.

Figure 7.12 **SHOT FAKE JUMP SHOT**

a

b

c

Defender's hand up

1. Assume triple-threat position; be threat to shoot first
2. Perform drive step
3. Weight on pivot foot
4. Read defender before making move

Shot fake

1. Execute aggressive shot fake, making it look like shot
2. Read defender's legs straighten

Jump shot

1. Shoot jump shot
2. Follow through until ball reaches net
3. Land in balance, ready to rebound

MISSTEP

Your defender does not react to your fake.

CORRECTION

Make an aggressive shot fake, making it look like a shot. Remember, a shot fake is a shot not taken.

Step-Back Jump Shot

After you make a drive step, the defender may take a retreat step. If this occurs, make a quick step back away from the defender on the same foot used for the drive step, and at the same time dribble back (figure 7.13). Jump behind the ball in balance by dipping your knees (to change backward momentum to upward momentum) while aligning your shooting-side knee with the ball. Keep your head and shoulders forward to counter the tendency to lean back. Pick the ball up in front of your shooting-side knee with your shooting hand on top of the ball; your nonshooting hand should be under the ball for balance. Bring the ball straight up so your shooting hand faces the basket. Jump straight up and shoot a jump shot. Direct your head, shoulders, shooting hand, and fingers toward the basket to counter any tendency to lean your head and shoulders back on your shot. Hold your follow-through straight up until the ball goes through the net. Land in balance at the spot of your takeoff, and be ready to get back on defense if the shot is missed.

Figure 7.13 **STEP-BACK JUMP SHOT**

a

Defender's hand up

1. Assume triple-threat position; be threat to shoot first
2. Make drive step
3. Weight on pivot foot
4. Read defender before making move

b

Dribble back

1. Read defender's retreat step
2. Dribble back with strong hand

Pick up dribble

1. Jump behind ball
2. Align shooting-side knee with ball
3. Keep head and shoulders forward
4. Pick ball up in front of shooting-side knee
5. Shooting hand on top of ball; nonshooting hand under ball

Jump shot

1. Raise ball up to shoot with shooting hand facing target
2. Shoot jump shot
3. Follow-through with shoulders, head, shooting hand, and fingers until ball reaches net
4. Land in balance at spot of take-off and be ready to get back on defense

---

MISSTEP

Your shot misses short because you lean your shoulders back on the backward dribble or you step back on the shot.

CORRECTION

Maintain balance by picking up the ball at your knee and exaggerating the follow-through of your shoulders, head, and shooting hand toward the basket.

Step-Through Leaner

After catching the ball at the pinch post, make a front turn to the middle, pivoting on your inside foot. See the rim and your defender. Be a triple threat and a threat to shoot first. Make a drive step, keeping your weight on your pivot foot. When your defender is overly aggressive, read the defender's hand position. If the defender's hand is up (most often on the same side as the defender's lead foot), step through with your inside foot past the defender's lead foot (figure 7.14). Move your head and shoulders under the defender's arm, and move the ball away from the defender's reach. Lean in toward the basket, jump off both feet, and shoot. This is called a leaner. Be strong. Expect to be fouled and complete the shot for a possible three-point play. Land in balance, ready to rebound a possible miss with two hands. When you rebound a missed shot, use a power move to score.

Figure 7.14 **STEP-THROUGH LEANER**

a

Read defender

1. Assume triple-threat position; be threat to shoot first
2. Make drive step
3. Read defender aggressively over-playing jump shot
4. Read defender's hand up

b

Step through

1. Step through with inside foot past defender's lead foot
2. Move head and shoulders under defender's arm
3. Move ball away from defender's reach

c

Shoot leaner

1. Lean in toward basket
2. Jump off both feet
3. Shoot leaner
4. Be strong; expect to be fouled
5. Land in balance, ready to rebound

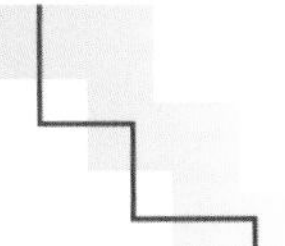

MISSTEP

Your shot is blocked.

CORRECTION

When making the step-through, move your head and shoulders under your defender's arm, and move the ball away from your defender's reach. Lean in toward the basket as you shoot.

Drive Across Lane for Hook

After catching the ball at the pinch post, make a front turn to the middle, pivoting on your inside foot. See the rim and your defender. Be a triple threat and a threat to shoot first. Make a drive step, keeping your weight on your pivot foot. After the drive step, you may read your defender's position as having the lead foot forward and hand up on the side of your drive step (figure 7.15, page 192). If this occurs, take a long step with your drive-step foot past your defender's lead foot while keeping your weight on your pivot foot. Push a dribble out with your outside hand (the hand away from the defender) to create space past your defender, keeping your eyes on the basket and looking for defensive help. Protect the ball with your inside hand and your body. Drive across the lane, past your defender's retreat step. Dip your takeoff knee. Pick the ball up at your shooting-side knee with your shooting hand under the ball and with your nonshooting hand slightly behind and on top of the ball. Explode off your takeoff foot to elevate. Bring the ball straight up. Avoid swiveling the ball into your defender. Shoot a hook shot over the reach of your defender. Be strong as you shoot the hook, protecting the ball with your nonshooting hand until the release. Land in balance and be ready to rebound the ball on a possible missed shot. Go up again with as many power moves as it takes to score.

MISSTEP

Your hook shot is blocked.

CORRECTION

Lift the ball high over the reach of the shot blocker.

Figure 7.15 **DRIVE ACROSS LANE FOR HOOK**

a

Defender's hand up and foot forward on side of drive step

1. Assume triple-threat position; be threat to shoot first
2. Make drive step
3. Weight on pivot foot
4. Read defender's hand up and foot forward on side of drive step

b

Drive across lane to basket

1. Take long step past defender's lead foot
2. Create space
3. Protect ball with inside hand
4. Drive across lane to basket

c

Pick up dribble

1. Dip takeoff knee
2. Pick ball up at shooting-side knee
3. Shooting hand under ball; nonshooting hand slightly behind and on top of ball

d

Shoot hook shot

1. Bring ball straight up; avoid swiveling
2. Protect ball with nonshooting hand
3. Shoot hook shot over defender
4. Be ready to rebound

Crossover Drive Layup

After catching the ball at the pinch post, make a front turn to the middle, pivoting on your inside foot. See the rim and your defender. Be a triple threat and a threat to shoot first. Make a drive step, keeping your weight on your pivot foot. After the drive step, you may read your defender's position as having the lead foot forward and hand up on the side away from your drive step (figure 7.16, page 194). If this occurs, make a crossover step past your defender's lead foot while keeping your weight on your pivot foot. Push a dribble out with your outside hand (the hand away from the defender) to create space past your defender. Keep your head up and eyes on the basket. Protect the ball with your inside hand and your body. Drive in a straight line, closing the gap between your body and the defender's retreat step. Be aware that a help defender may leave a teammate to defend your layup. In this case, pass off to your open teammate. When going for the layup, pick the ball up in front of your shooting-side knee with your shooting hand on top of the ball and with your nonshooting hand under the ball. Explode off your takeoff foot to elevate on your layup. Bring the ball straight up. Avoid swiveling the ball into your defender. Be strong as you shoot the layup, protecting the ball with two hands until the release. Land in balance at the spot of your takeoff, and be ready to rebound the ball on a possible missed shot.

MISSTEP

Your defender steals the ball because you swivel it in when shooting the layup.

CORRECTION

When shooting the layup, raise the ball straight up while protecting it with two hands.

Figure 7.16 **CROSSOVER DRIVE LAYUP**

a

Defender's hand up on side away from drive step

1. Assume triple-threat position; be threat to shoot first
2. Drive-step; weight on pivot foot
3. Read defender's hand up on side away from drive step

b

Crossover drive

1. Make crossover step past defender's lead foot
2. Create space
3. Protect ball with inside hand
4. Drive in straight line to basket

c

Close gap

1. Close gap between your body and defender's retreat step
2. Pick ball up at shooting-side knee
3. Shooting hand on top of ball; nonshooting hand under ball

d

Shoot layup

1. Go strong to the basket for layup
2. Bring ball straight up; avoid swiveling
3. Protect ball with two hands
4. Be ready to rebound

Crossover Drive Bank Jump Shot

After catching the ball at the pinch post, make a front turn to the middle, pivoting on your inside foot. See the rim and your defender. Be a triple threat and a threat to shoot first. Make a drive step, keeping your weight on your pivot foot. After the drive step, you may read your defender's position as having the lead foot forward and hand up on the side away from your drive step (figure 7.17, page 196). If this occurs, make a crossover step and push a long dribble out with your outside hand (the one away from the defender), and then push off your pivot foot. Aim the dribble for a spot at a 45-degree angle with the backboard. Keep your eyes on the target. Protect the ball with your inside hand and your body. When driving to your strong-hand side, make a jump stop behind the ball, aligning your shooting-side knee with the ball. When driving to your weak-hand side, you have farther to jump in order to align your shooting-side knee with the ball; make a second dribble (crossover dribble) to the front of your shooting-side knee. Pick up the ball in front of your shooting-side knee with your shooting hand on top of the ball and with your nonshooting hand under the ball. Avoid reaching for the ball and picking it up with your hands on the sides of the ball, which leads to sidespin. Aim for the top near corner of the box on the backboard, and shoot a jump shot. Land in balance at the spot of your takeoff, and be ready to get back on defense if the shot is missed.

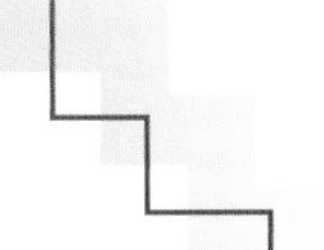

MISSTEP

You miss the shot because you float to the side.

CORRECTION

Pick the ball up at your shooting-side knee in order to change sideward momentum to upward momentum.

MISSTEP

The ball circles out of the basket because you picked the ball up with your hands on the sides of the ball, causing sidespin.

CORRECTION

Pick the ball up with your shooting hand on top of the ball so your shooting hand will face the rim, leading to backspin on the shot.

Figure 7.17 **CROSSOVER DRIVE BANK JUMP SHOT**

a

Defender's hand up on side away from drive step

1. Assume triple-threat position; be threat to shoot first
2. Drive-step; weight on pivot foot
3. Read defender's hand up on side away from drive step

b

Crossover step and drive

1. Make crossover step past defender's lead foot
2. Create space
3. Protect ball with inside hand
4. Drive to spot at 45-degree angle with backboard

c

Pick up dribble

1. Jump behind ball
2. On drive to weak-hand side, make crossover dribble to shooting-side knee
3. Pick ball up at shooting-side knee
4. Shooting hand on top of ball; nonshooting hand under ball

d

Shoot bank jump shot

1. Bring ball straight up; avoid swiveling
2. Aim for top near corner of box on backboard
3. Shoot bank jump shot

Crossover Drive Step-Back Jump Shot

After catching the ball at the pinch post, make a front turn to the middle, pivoting on your inside foot. See the rim and your defender. Be a triple threat and a threat to shoot first. Perform a drive step, keeping your weight on your pivot foot. After the drive step, you may read your defender's position as having the lead foot forward and hand up on the side away from your drive step. Make a crossover step past the defender's lead foot. Keeping your weight on your pivot foot, create space away from your defender by pushing your dribble out with your outside hand (the hand away from the defender).

The step-back jump shot is used when you are closely guarded as you drive. When your defender is able to stay with you, use a control dribble (figure 7.18, page 198). Lean your inside shoulder into the defender and then make an aggressive head and shoulder fake to straighten your defender's legs. Create space by taking a quick step back away from your defender, and at the same time, dribble back with your outside hand.

Jump behind the ball in balance by dipping your knees (to change backward momentum to upward momentum), while aligning your shooting-side knee with the ball. Keep your head and shoulders forward to counter the tendency to lean back. Pick up the ball in front of your shooting-side knee with your shooting hand on top of the ball; your nonshooting hand should be under the ball for balance. Bring the ball straight up so your shooting hand faces the basket. Jump straight up and shoot a jump shot. Direct your head, shoulders, shooting hand, and fingers toward the basket to counter any tendency to lean your head and shoulders back on your shot. Hold your follow-through straight up until the ball goes through the net. Land in balance at the spot of your takeoff, and be ready to get back on defense if the shot is missed.

MISSTEP

You miss the shot because you float back.

CORRECTION

When making the step-back dribble, jump behind the ball in balance by dipping your knees, and keep your head and shoulders forward to counter the tendency to lean back.

Figure 7.18 **CROSSOVER DRIVE STEP-BACK JUMP SHOT**

Read defender

1. Assume triple-threat position; be threat to shoot first
2. Defender stays with you on drive toward basket
3. Lean inside shoulder into defender
4. Make head and shoulder fake to straighten defender's legs

Make step-back dribble

1. Create space with step back and dribble back
2. Jump behind ball, aligning shooting-side knee with ball
3. Keep head and shoulders forward
4. Pick up ball in front of shooting-side knee
5. Shooting hand on top of ball; nonshooting hand under ball

Shoot jump shot

1. Raise ball up to shoot with shooting hand facing target
2. Direct head, shoulders, and hand toward basket
3. Follow through until ball reaches basket
4. Land in same spot

Crossover Drive Step-Through Leaner

After catching the ball at the pinch post, make a front turn to the middle, pivoting on your inside foot. See the rim and your defender. Be a triple threat and a threat to shoot first. Make a drive step, keeping your weight on your pivot foot. After the drive step, you may read your defender's position as having the lead foot forward and hand up on the side away from your drive step. Make a crossover step past the defender's lead foot. Keeping your weight on your pivot foot, create space away from your defender by pushing your dribble out with your outside hand (the hand away from the defender). The step-through leaner is used when your defender stays with you as you drive and is overly aggressive. Use a control dribble (figure 7.19, page 200). When your defender is overly aggressive, read the defender's hand position. When the defender's hand is up, step through with your inside foot past the defender's lead foot. Move your head and shoulders under your defender's arm, and move the ball away from your defender's reach. Lean in toward the basket, jump off both feet, and shoot. This is called a leaner. Be strong. Expect to be fouled and complete the shot for a possible three-point play. Land in balance, ready to rebound a possible miss with two hands. When you rebound a missed shot, use a power move to score.

MISSTEP

Your shot is blocked.

CORRECTION

When making the step-through, move your head and shoulders under your defender's arm, and move the ball away from your defender's reach. Lean in toward the basket as you shoot.

Figure 7.19 **CROSSOVER DRIVE STEP-THROUGH LEANER**

a

b

c

Read defender

1. Assume triple-threat position; be threat to shoot first
2. Drive toward basket
3. Read defender being overly aggressive with hand up

Step through

1. Step through with inside foot past defender's lead foot
2. Move head and shoulders under defender's arm
3. Move ball away from defender

Shoot leaner

1. Lean in toward basket
2. Jump off both feet
3. Shoot leaner
4. Be strong; expect to be fouled
5. Be ready to rebound

Pinch-Post Drill. Pinch-Post Moves

In this drill, you will practice eight pinch-post moves: shot fake jump shot, step-back jump shot, step-through leaner, drive across lane for hook, crossover drive layup, crossover drive bank jump shot, crossover drive step-back jump shot, and crossover drive step-through leaner. You will perform each move at the offensive left elbow and then perform each move at the offensive right elbow. Toss the ball so it bounces at the elbow. You are passing the ball to yourself. Use a toss back if one is available. Catch the ball while using a one-two stop. Your inside foot (the one closer to the basket) should land first, becoming your pivot foot. Make a front turn to the middle and see the rim. Be in a triple-threat stance, and execute a drive step.

Shot fake jump shot. After you make a drive step and shot fake, imagine that your defender's hands are down. Bring your drive-step foot back into a balanced shooting stance and shoot a jump shot. Perform five repetitions of this move from each pinch post.

Step-back jump shot. After you make a drive step, imagine that your defender takes a retreat step. Step back and dribble back at the same time, and shoot a jump shot. Maintain balance by picking up the ball at your knee and exaggerating the follow-through of your shoulders, head, and shooting hand toward the basket. This will counter any tendency to lean back or step back on your shot. Perform five repetitions of this move from each pinch post.

Step-through leaner. After you make a drive step, imagine that your defender aggressively overplays you for a jump shot with either or both hands up. Step through with your drive-step foot past the imaginary defender's lead foot, and move your head and shoulders under the defender's arm. Protect the ball with your head and shoulders, moving the ball away from your imaginary defender's reach. Lean in toward the basket, jump off both feet, and shoot a leaner. Be strong and land in balance. Perform five repetitions of the step-through leaner from each pinch post.

Drive across lane for hook. After you make a drive step, imagine that your defender's inside hand (the hand closest to the middle) is up. Make an aggressive shot fake. Then make a one-dribble drive across the lane with your outside hand and shoot a hook shot. On the hook, lift the ball high over the reach of an imaginary shot blocker. Land in balance. Perform five repetitions of this move from each side. When driving from the offensive left pinch post, shoot a right-handed hook shot. When driving from the offensive right pinch post, shoot a left-handed hook shot.

Crossover drive layup. After you make a drive step, imagine that your defender's lead foot and hand are up on the side away from your drive step. Make a crossover step past your imaginary defender's lead foot. Make a one-dribble drive to the basket and shoot a layup. Be strong as you shoot the layup, protecting the ball with two hands until the release. Land in balance at the spot of your takeoff. Perform five repetitions of the crossover drive layup from each pinch post. When driving from the offensive left pinch post, shoot a left-handed layup. When driving from the offensive right pinch post, shoot a right-handed layup.

Crossover drive bank jump shot. After you make a drive step, imagine that your defender's lead foot and hand are up on the side away from your drive step. Make a crossover step past your

(continued)

(continued)

imaginary defender's lead foot, and dribble with your outside hand to a spot at a 45-degree angle with the backboard. When driving to your strong-hand side, make a jump stop behind the ball, aligning your shooting-side knee with the ball. When driving to your weak-hand side, you have farther to jump in order to align your shooting-side knee with the ball; take a second dribble (crossover dribble) to the front of your shooting-side knee. Pick up the ball in front of your shooting-side knee with your shooting hand on top of the ball and with your nonshooting hand under the ball. Aim for the top near corner of the box on the backboard, and shoot a bank jump shot. Land in balance at the spot of your takeoff. Perform five repetitions of this move from each pinch post.

Crossover drive step-back jump shot. After you make a drive step, imagine that your defender's lead foot and hand are up on the side away from your drive step. Make a crossover step past your imaginary defender's lead foot, and use a control dribble with your outside hand down the outside of the lane. Lean your inside shoulder into your imaginary defender, and make an aggressive head and shoulder fake. Create space away from the defender, and shoot a step-back jump shot.

Direct your head, shoulders, shooting hand, and fingers toward the basket to counter any tendency to lean your head and shoulders back on your shot. Land in balance at the spot of your takeoff. Perform five repetitions of this move from each pinch post.

Crossover drive step-through leaner. After you make a drive step, imagine that your defender's lead foot and hand are up on the side away from your drive step. Make a crossover step past your imaginary defender's lead foot, and dribble with your outside hand down the outside of the lane. Imagine that your defender is overly aggressive with either or both hands up. Step through with your inside foot past the imaginary defender's lead foot. Move your head and shoulders under your defender's arm, and move the ball away from your defender's reach. Lean in toward the basket, jump off both feet, and shoot a leaner. Be strong and land in balance. Perform five repetitions of this move from each pinch post.

Success Check

- Be a triple threat to pass, shoot, or drive.
- Use correct technique on each pinch-post move.
- Use correct shooting technique.

Score Your Success

Perform each move five times at each elbow. Record the number of shots you make off each move to each side. Give yourself 1 point for each shot made for each move.

Shot fake jump shot, left pinch post ___ out of 5

Shot fake jump shot, right pinch post ___ out of 5

Step-back jump shot, left pinch post ___ out of 5

Step-back jump shot, right pinch post ___ out of 5

Step-through leaner, left pinch post ___ out of 5

Step-through leaner, right pinch post ___ out of 5

Drive across lane for hook, left pinch post ___ out of 5

Drive across lane for hook, right pinch post ___ out of 5

Crossover drive layup, left pinch post ___ out of 5

Crossover drive layup, right pinch post ___ out of 5

Crossover drive bank jump shot, left pinch post ___ out of 5

Crossover drive bank jump shot, right pinch post ___ out of 5

Crossover drive step-back jump shot, left pinch post ___ out of 5

Crossover drive step-back jump shot, right pinch post ___ out of 5

Crossover drive step-through leaner, left pinch post ___ out of 5

Crossover drive step-through leaner, right pinch post ___ out of 5

Your score ___ (80 points maximum)

Pinch-Post Drill. **One-on-One at Pinch Post**

This competitive game helps you develop the ability to read the defender and use fakes, pivots, and various pinch-post moves to score or draw a foul. It also develops your defensive and rebounding skills. The drill starts at either pinch post. You will play offense against a defender. Your objective is to score with a pinch-post move. You may use no more than two dribbles before shooting the ball. The defender initiates play by getting in a defensive stance and then handing you the ball. You get 2 points each time you score. If you get fouled while making the shot, you get a free throw. If you get fouled but miss the shot, you get two free throws. If you miss the shot but get an offensive rebound, you may make a move and score from the spot where the ball was rebounded. Again, no more than two dribbles are allowed. Continue play until you score or turn the ball over or until the defender gets the ball on a steal or rebound and dribbles back past the free-throw line. Then switch offensive and defensive roles. Play to 7 points.

Success Check

- Read the defender and use the best pinch-post move.
- Use only two dribbles.
- Be aggressive.

Score Your Success

This is a competitive drill. The first player to score 7 points wins the game. Play four games, two games at the offensive left pinch post and two games at the offensive right pinch post. Give yourself 5 points each time you win a game.

Your score ___ (20 points maximum)

MIDPOINT MOVES

The midpoint is a spot 5 feet (1.5 m) from the baseline and halfway between the basket and the sideline on either side. The midpoint is also called the short corner. Basic midpoint moves include the shot fake jump shot, straight one-dribble drive middle for hook, and crossover one-dribble drive for reverse layup.

Getting Open and Catching Passes at the Midpoint

The best way to get open at the midpoint is to set a screen outside the lane and above the block for a teammate (figure 7.20). The teammate curls around the screen to the basket. Your defender will usually give defensive help on the player making the curl, and that will enable you to quickly pop out and be open at the midpoint. As you pop out, get open using short, quick steps. Use the far hand as a target for the passer.

Face the basket. On the pass, let the ball come to you; avoid reaching for the ball. Jump behind the ball and catch it in position to shoot. The feet land at the same time on a jump stop, enabling you to use either one as a pivot foot. After catching the ball, make sure you read the position of your defender before making a move.

Figure 7.20 **GETTING OPEN FOR A PASS AT THE MIDPOINT AFTER SETTING A SCREEN**

a

Set screen

1. Set screen outside lane above block
2. Teammate curls around screen to elbow

b

Defender gives defensive help

1. Teammate's defender trails your body around screen on curl
2. Your defender gives defensive help on curl

Pop to midpoint

1. Pop out to midpoint
2. Get open using short, quick steps.
3. Use far hand as target for passer

Catch ball at midpoint

1. Face basket
2. Let ball come to you; avoid reaching for ball
3. Jump behind ball
4. Catch ball in position to shoot
5. Read position of defender before making move

Shot Fake Jump Shot

This is the same technique as described under pinch-post moves earlier (figure 7.12, page 187), but it takes place at the midpoint. After catching the ball at the midpoint, assume a triple-threat position. Be a threat to shoot first. See the rim and your defender. If you are closely guarded and your defender's hand is up, make a drive step, keeping your weight on your pivot foot. Use an aggressive shot fake to make your defender react by straightening the legs. This will enable you to jump higher than your defender and get your shot off over your defender's reach. After the fake, move the ball to shooting position with your shooting hand behind the ball and facing the front of the rim. Shoot a jump shot. Follow through until the ball reaches the net. Land in balance and be ready to rebound the ball if the shot is missed.

MISSTEP

Your defender does not react to your fake.

CORRECTION

Make an aggressive shot fake, making it look like a shot.

Straight One-Dribble Drive Middle for Hook

Catch the ball at the midpoint while using a jump stop. Pivot on your inside foot (the foot closest to the baseline) to face the basket. See the rim and your defender. Be a triple threat and a threat to shoot first. Make a drive step, keeping your weight on your pivot foot. After the drive step, you may read your defender's position as having the lead foot forward and hand up on the side of your drive step (figure 7.21). If this occurs, make a straight step with your drive-step foot past your defender's lead foot while keeping your weight on your pivot foot. Push a dribble out with your outside hand (the hand away from the defender) to create space past your defender, keeping your eyes on the basket and looking for defensive help. Protect the ball with your inside hand and your body. Dip your takeoff knee. Pick the ball up at your shooting-side knee with your shooting hand under the ball; your nonshooting hand should be slightly behind and on top of the ball. Explode off your takeoff foot to elevate. Bring the ball straight up. Avoid swiveling the ball into your defender. Shoot a hook shot over the reach of your defender. Be strong as you shoot the hook, protecting the ball with your nonshooting hand until release. Land in balance and be ready to rebound the ball on a possible missed shot. Go up again with as many power moves as it takes to score.

Figure 7.21 **STRAIGHT ONE-DRIBBLE DRIVE MIDDLE FOR HOOK**

a

b

Defender's hand up on side of drive step

1. Assume triple-threat position; be threat to shoot first
2. Make drive step with weight on pivot foot
3. Read defender's hand up on side of drive step

One-dribble drive middle to basket

1. Make straight step past defender's lead foot
2. Create space
3. Protect ball with inside hand
4. Drive middle to basket

c

d

Pick up dribble

1. Dip takeoff knee
2. Pick ball up at shooting-side knee
3. Shooting hand under ball; nonshooting hand slightly behind and on top of ball

Shoot hook shot

1. Bring ball straight up; avoid swiveling
2. Protect ball with nonshooting hand
3. Shoot hook shot over defender
4. Be ready to rebound

MISSTEP

Your hook shot is blocked.

CORRECTION

Lift the ball high over the reach of the shot blocker.

Crossover One-Dribble Drive for Reverse Layup

Catch the ball at the midpoint while using a jump stop. Pivot on your inside foot (the foot closest to the baseline) to face the basket. See the rim and your defender. Be a triple threat and a threat to shoot first. Make a drive step, keeping your weight on your pivot foot. After the drive step, you may read your defender's position as having the lead foot forward and hand up on the side away from your drive step (figure 7.22, page 208). If this occurs, make a crossover step past your defender's lead foot while keeping your weight on your pivot foot. Push one dribble out with your outside hand (the hand away from the defender) to create space past your defender. Keep your head up and eyes on the basket. Protect the ball with your inside hand and your body. Drive in a straight line, closing the gap between your body and the defender's retreat step.

RATE YOUR SUCCESS

If you are able to score in the post against your defender, this can force a teammate's defender to leave an outside player in order to give defensive help on you, opening up a pass to that outside teammate. In this step, we have covered various post moves with the ball that will turn you into a post-up threat. In the next step, we will look at rebounding. Before going to step 8, however, look back at how you performed the drills in this step. For each of the drills presented in this step, enter the points you earned, then add up your scores to rate your total success.

Low-Post Drills	
1. Low-Post Moves	___ out of 80
2. Read the Defense	___ out of 20
3. One-on-One in Half Circle	___ out of 15
Pinch-Post Drills	
1. Pinch-Post Moves	___ out of 80
2. One-on-One at Pinch Post	___ out of 20
Midpoint Drills	
1. Midpoint Moves	___ out of 30
2. One-on-One at Midpoint	___ out of 20
Total	___ **out of 265**

If you scored 135 or more points, congratulations! You have mastered the basics of this step and are ready to move on to step 8, rebounding. If you scored fewer than 135 points, you may want to spend more time on the fundamentals covered in this step. Practice the drills again to develop mastery of the techniques and increase your scores.

STEP

8

Rebounding

Rebounding is the one fundamental that you cannot overdo. You can shoot too often, dribble too much, pass too much, and try to steal the ball or block shots too much, but you can never rebound too much. The team that controls the backboards usually controls the game.

Possession of the ball comes from missed shots more often than any other way. Offensive rebounding adds to your team's scoring opportunities, and defensive rebounding limits your opponent's scoring opportunities.

Offensive rebounding takes desire, effort, and anticipation. Attacking the offensive glass for rebounds enables your team to create second-chance scoring opportunities. More often than not, these second shots are high-percentage inside shots, and many result in three-point plays. Also, getting an offensive rebound gives a team a "bonus" possession, which can inspire an offense and, conversely, demoralize a defense that has just fought hard to prevent a score and failed to gain possession.

That is why coaches and players believe that defensive rebounds are so essential to success. If you control the defensive backboard, your opponent will have fewer opportunities to gain second shots, which often result in easy scores and three-point plays. Defensive rebounding not only limits your opponent's second-chance scoring opportunities, but it also creates more opportunities for your team to initiate a fast break.

REBOUNDING ESSENTIALS

Unlike most fundamentals that contribute to basketball success, effective rebounding requires at least as much toughness as it does technique. Being a good rebounder involves emotional and mental factors in addition to skill and physicality.

Emotional

Desire. Wanting the ball is the most important factor in rebounding. Assume that every shot will be missed, and develop the attitude that you will go after every rebound. Because many rebounds are not obtained by the first player to touch the ball, second effort is truly needed. The difference between good and great rebounders is that the great ones go after more rebounds.

Jerry Wachter/Getty Images

Wes Unseld averaged 18.2 rebounds a game and was the NBA's Most Valuable Player in his rookie season.

David Sherman/NBAE via Getty Images

A self-educated sense of where opponents' and teammates' shots are likely to rebound off the rim has served Kevin Love well in becoming a top rebounder.

Courage. The physical contact of rebounding demands courage. Your greatness as a rebounder can be measured by the amount of physical contact you can take. To be a great rebounder, you must be eager to get into the battle of the boards. There is often no glory in rebounding, just victory. Wes Unseld was a player whom few opponents challenged, not only because of his tree-trunk torso, but also because of his determination and will to dominate the boards. Unseld is still widely regarded as one of the best outlet passers ever to play the game.

Mental

Anticipation. Check the rims, backboards, and bracing to determine how hard or soft the ball will rebound. Know your teammates' shooting techniques and study your opponents' shooting to anticipate where shots will rebound. Observe the angle and distance of shots: Most shots rebound to the opposite side, and three-point shot attempts tend to rebound longer. Kevin Love demonstrates a keen understanding of where a player's shot is most likely to carom off the rim—and how to get to that spot before anyone else. In a December 20, 2010 *Sports Illustrated* article by Lee Jenkins, Love said, "A different sense knocks into me when the ball is in the air. I know where it will hit and where it will land. I'm playing percentages, but it's not a guessing game. Most of the time I'm right" (p. 63).

Knowledge. Use your experience of playing and practicing with teammates to your advantage. Pay attention to scouting reports and examine the players you are likely to match up against. Assess their height, strength, jumping ability, quickness, aggressiveness, blockout technique, and second-effort tendencies. Also, study other great rebounders. You'll be amazed at how much you'll learn.

Physical

Quickness. Move! On offense, move quickly around your opponent and go for the ball. On defense, move quickly to block out your opponent and then go for the ball. Watch videos of yourself to identify any wasted movements and practice maneuvers that will allow you to get to the ball more effectively.

Jumping ability. Work continually to improve your jumping height and the quickness and explosiveness of your jump. A quick second jump is a great asset for rebounding. Off-season plyometric training is a great way to develop the powerful, repetitive jumping ability needed to be a real force on the boards.

Strength. A well-conceived conditioning program will improve your total body strength so you can withstand the body contact under the boards. Legs and hips must provide a solid base, and wrists and hands should be like a vise gripping the ball.

Fernando Medina/NBAE via Getty Images

Despite being more than a little unorthodox on and off the court, Dennis Rodman was a relentless rebounder.

Muscular endurance. Improve muscular endurance in your legs: You want to improve not just how high you jump but also how often you jump. Dennis Rodman had an all-time high 23.4 percent rebounding rate for his career—meaning he claimed more than one of every four missed shots while on the court. Rodman was like a pogo stick, seemingly indefatigable as he bounded repeatedly until gaining possession of the ball.

Height. You cannot change how tall you are or how long your arms are, but you can control all the other qualities that determine your success as a rebounder.

Photo by Dick Raphael/NBAE via Getty Images

Paul Silas mastered all rebounding fundamentals. Here he establishes proper position, boxing out his former Boston Celtics teammates for a rebound.

Skill

Vision. Use peripheral vision to see the total picture, including the ball and your opponent. When you play defense, after the shot, you should watch your opponent, block out, and go for the ball. When you play offense, after the shot, you should determine how your opponent blocks out, use the correct method to get by the blockout, and go for the ball. Paul Silas, one of the greatest rebounders of all time, *averaged* 21.6 rebounds a game during his 3-year career at Creighton University. He was both an artist and a technician on the boards. Although barely 6-foot-7 and a mediocre leaper, Silas's well-crafted skills and dedication to his role allowed him to capture more than a rebound every three minutes throughout his 16-year NBA career.

Position. Anticipate your opponent's move and work to establish inside position.

Balance. Maintain a balanced stance to counter any physical play such as bumping, shoving, and pushing. Be on the balls of your feet, with your feet shoulder-width apart, your knees flexed, your back straight, your head up, and your hands above your shoulders. Also, after claiming the ball, land in a balanced stance. On offense, be ready to score with a power move or to pass out to a teammate. On defense, be ready to pivot and use a quick outlet pass to start a fast break.

Hands up. Move both hands to a position above your forehead, placing your hands ball-width apart. When gaining possession of the rebound, catch the ball with two hands and aggressively protect it in front of your forehead and away from your opponent.

Timing. Time your jump to reach the ball at the maximum height of your jump.

Jumping often. In rebounding, it is not how high but how often you jump that is crucial for success.

Rebounding Drill. **Backboard Rebounding**

Start in a balanced stance 8 feet (2.4 m) in front of the backboard and to the side of the rim. Make a two-hand chest pass, aiming high on the backboard. Rebound the ball with two hands and land in balance. Protect the ball above your forehead with elbows out, and do not lower the ball. Repeat 10 times.

Success Check

- Use two hands to rebound the ball.
- Protect the ball on the rebound.
- Land in balance.

Score Your Success

8 to 10 successful rebounds = 5 points

6 or 7 successful rebounds = 3 points

4 or 5 successful rebounds = 1 point

3 or fewer successful rebounds = 0 points

Your score ___

Rebounding Drill. **Superman or Wonder Woman Rebounding**

Start in a balanced stance with one foot outside the lane line and above the block. Make a strong two-hand chest pass, aiming high on the opposite corner of the backboard. Pass the ball so that it rebounds above the box to the opposite side of the lane. Rebound the ball with two hands and land in balance on two feet with at least one foot landing outside the lane and above the block. Protect the ball above your forehead with your elbows out. Repeat to the opposite side. Perform the drill for 30 seconds.

Success Check

- Use two hands to rebound the ball.
- Protect the ball on the rebound.
- Land in balance.

Score Your Success

10 or more successful rebounds in 30 seconds = 5 points

8 or 9 successful rebounds in 30 seconds = 3 points

6 or 7 successful rebounds in 30 seconds = 1 point

5 or fewer successful rebounds in 30 seconds = 0 points

Your score ___

DEFENSIVE REBOUNDING

The key to defensive rebounding is getting inside position on your opponent and going for the ball. When playing defense, you usually have the inside position between your opponent and the basket, giving you the early advantage in the ensuing battle for the rebound.

Coaches teach two strategies for defensive rebounding. The most commonly used philosophy is to *block out* (often called *box out*) the opponent. Blocking out involves first blocking your opponent's path to the ball by putting your back to your opponent's chest and then going for the ball. The other philosophy, espoused by John Wooden (the great UCLA coach of 10 NCAA championship teams), is simply to step in your opponent's path and go for the ball. Wooden's method, called the *check-and-go,* might be best when your quickness and leaping ability are far superior to your opponent's. Blocking out is recommended for most players.

Players use two methods for blocking out: the front turn and the reverse turn. Putting your back on your opponent's chest and going for the ball are more important than which blockout method you use.

The front turn method (figure 8.1) is best for blocking out the shooter. Be in a defensive stance with your hand up. Once the shot is taken, front pivot on your back foot, aggressively step forward toward the shooter, and block out. Use a wide base for balance. Keep your back on your opponent's chest and keep your hands up. Be physically and mentally strong to resist the force of your opponent trying to go by you. Go for the ball and catch it with two hands. Land in balance. Protect the ball in front of your forehead.

The reverse turn (figure 8.2, page 220) is best when you are defending a player without the ball. When guarding a player without the ball, take a defensive stance that allows you to see the ball and your opponent. To guard a player on the ball side of the basket (also called the strong side), take a denial stance with one hand up and one foot in the passing lane. To guard a player on the opposite side of the basket (called the help side or weak side), take a defensive stance several steps away that allows you to see the ball and the player you are guarding. When you defend a player off the ball and a shot is taken, first observe your opponent's cut and then make a reverse turn, dropping your foot back away from your opponent's cut. Block out and get the rebound.

Develop the attitude that you are going to go after every ball. Always try to catch the ball with two hands, but if you cannot make a two-hand catch, use one hand to try to keep it alive until you or a teammate can grab it.

Figure 8.1 **FRONT TURN**

a

b

c

Front turn

1. Defensive stance with hand up in passing lane
2. Front pivot on back foot
3. Aggressively step forward toward opponent

Block out

1. Wide base
2. Back on opponent's chest
3. Hands up
4. Be physically and mentally strong
5. Resist force of opponent trying to go by you

Go for ball

1. Go for ball and catch it with two hands
2. Protect ball in front of forehead
3. Land in balance

MISSTEP

You watch the ball, and your opponent cuts by you.

CORRECTION

Locate your opponent first, get inside position, block out or check, and then go for the ball.

Figure 8.2 **REVERSE TURN**

Reverse pivot

1. Defensive stance with hand up in passing lane
2. Reverse pivot on foot closest to opponent's cut
3. Drop other foot back

Block out

1. Hands up
2. Wide base
3. Back on opponent's chest

Go for ball

1. Go for ball and catch it with two hands
2. Protect ball in front of forehead
3. Land in balance

MISSTEP

You lose balance when your opponent fakes.

CORRECTION

Use a wide base and keep moving on the balls of your feet.

Defensive Rebounding Drill. Block Out the Shooter

This drill requires two players. Begin as the defensive player and have your partner start as the shooter. The shooter starts outside the free-throw line with the ball, and you take a defensive stance facing your partner. Allow the shot and then use a front turn to block out the shooter and get the rebound if the shot misses. Meanwhile, the shooter tries to get an offensive rebound. If the offensive player secures the rebound, he can shoot again from the spot of the rebound. Continue until you get the rebound. Once you get the rebound, take a 10-second rest interval. After the rest interval, the offensive player starts outside the free-throw line again, and the drill is repeated four more times. Rotate from defense to offense.

Success Check

- On defense, block out the shooter using good technique.
- On offense, try to get past the defender's blockout using good offensive rebounding technique.

Score Your Success

Record the number of defensive rebounds you get. Give yourself 5 points if you get five defensive rebounds, 1 point if you get three or four defensive rebounds, and 0 points if you get fewer than three defensive rebounds. On offense, record the number of offensive rebounds you get. Give yourself 5 points if you get at least two offensive rebounds.

Your score for defensive rebounds

___

Your score for offensive rebounds

___

Defensive Rebounding Drill. Block Out the Player Without the Ball

This drill requires three players: a defensive player, an offensive player, and a shooter. Assume the role of the defensive player first; you will be rebounding against the offensive player without the ball. The third player acts as the shooter only. Shooting on one side of the floor from at least 15 feet (4.6 m), the shooter intentionally tries to miss. On the opposite side of the basket, you should take a defensive stance that allows you to see the ball and the player without the ball, whom you are guarding.

On the shot, first observe your opponent's cut and then perform a reverse turn, dropping your foot away from your opponent's cut in a backward direction. Block out and get the rebound. The offensive player will try to get an offensive rebound. If successful, the offensive player can shoot again from the spot of the rebound. Continue until you get the rebound. Once you get the rebound, take a 10-second rest interval. After the rest interval, the ball is returned to the shooter, and the drill is repeated four more times. After five total repetitions, players rotate: The defender becomes the offensive player without the ball, the offensive player without the ball becomes the shooter, and the shooter becomes the defender.

Success Check

- On defense, watch the player you are defending and the ball.
- Block out the offensive player using good technique.

Score Your Success

Record the number of defensive rebounds you get. Give yourself 5 points if you get five defensive rebounds, 1 point if you get three or four defensive rebounds, and 0 points if you get fewer than three defensive rebounds. On offense, record the number of offensive rebounds you get. Give yourself 5 points if you get at least two offensive rebounds.

Your score for defensive rebounds ___

Your score for offensive rebounds ___

OFFENSIVE REBOUNDING

The key to offensive rebounding is to move. Develop the attitude and will to move and go after every ball. Move to outmaneuver the defender, who is usually between you and the basket. Make a quick, aggressive move to get past the defender and jump to get the ball, always trying to catch it with two hands. If you cannot catch the ball with two hands, use one hand to try to tip the ball into the basket or keep it alive until you or a teammate can grab it. To avoid being blocked out, keep moving.

If you are blocked out, use every effort to get around the blockout. Even great rebounders get blocked out, but they keep moving to outmaneuver the opponent. It is not a mistake to be blocked out, but it is a mistake to stay blocked out.

Four methods of moving past the blockout are the straight cut, the fake-and-go, the spin, and the step back.

Straight Cut

Use the straight cut (figure 8.3) when your opponent blocks you out with a front turn. Quickly cut by before the blockout can be set. Keep your hands up, ball-width apart. Go for the ball and catch it with two hands. Land in balance and protect the ball in front of your forehead.

Figure 8.3 **STRAIGHT CUT**

a

Hands up

1. View of ball and opponent
2. Offensive stance
3. Hands up

b

Straight cut

1. Opponent uses front turn
2. Cut straight by opponent
3. Keep hands up, ball-width apart
4. Go for ball

c

Rebound

1. Catch ball with two hands
2. Protect ball in front of forehead
3. Land in balance

MISSTEP

You have trouble holding on to rebounds.

CORRECTION

Catch the ball with two hands.

Fake-and-Go

Use the fake-and-go (figure 8.4) when your opponent blocks you out with a reverse turn. Fake in the direction of your opponent's reverse step and then cut by the opposite side. Keep your hands up, ball-width apart. Go for the ball and catch it with two hands. Land in balance and protect the ball in front of your forehead.

Figure 8.4 **FAKE-AND-GO**

a

b

c

Fake

1. Offensive stance with hands up
2. Opponent uses reverse turn
3. Fake in direction of opponent's reverse step

Cut opposite

1. Cut to opposite side
2. Keep hands up, ball-width apart
3. Go for ball

Rebound

1. Catch ball with two hands
2. Protect ball in front of forehead
3. Land in balance

MISSTEP

Your opponent uses a reverse step and blocks you out.

CORRECTION

Fake in the direction of your opponent's reverse step, and cut to the opposite side.

Spin

Use the spin (figure 8.5) when your opponent blocks you out and holds your body or arm. Place your forearm on your opponent's back, reverse pivot on your lead foot, hook your arm over your opponent's arm for leverage, and cut by. Keep your hands up, ball-width apart. Go for the ball and catch it with two hands. Land in balance and protect the ball in front of your forehead.

Figure 8.5 **SPIN**

Forearm on back

1. Offensive stance with hands up
2. Opponent holds your body or arm
3. Place forearm on opponent's back

Reverse pivot

1. Reverse pivot
2. Hook arm over opponent's arm
3. Go for ball

Rebound

1. Catch ball with two hands
2. Protect ball in front of forehead
3. Land in balance

MISSTEP

You hold your opponent, and your opponent hooks an arm over yours for leverage.

CORRECTION

Keep your hands up.

Step Back

Use the step back (figure 8.6) when your opponent leans back on you while blocking out. Simply step back so your opponent loses balance and falls back, then cut by. Keep your hands up, ball-width apart. Go for the ball and catch it with two hands. Land in balance and protect the ball in front of your forehead.

Figure 8.6 **STEP BACK**

a

Opponent leans on you

1. View of ball and opponent
2. Offensive stance
3. Hands up
4. Opponent leans on you

b

Step back

1. Step back
2. Opponent falls back
3. Go for ball

c

Rebound

1. Catch ball with two hands
2. Protect ball in front of forehead
3. Land in balance

MISSTEP

After gaining the rebound, you have it stripped by an opponent.

CORRECTION

Keep the ball protected above your forehead and away from your opponent. Keep your elbows out.

Offensive Rebounding Drill. One-Versus-Two Offensive Rebound and Score

Start in a balanced stance 8 feet (2.4 m) in front of the backboard and to the side of the rim. Two players take positions on either side of you. Make a two-hand chest pass, aiming high on the backboard. Rebound the ball with two hands and land in balance. Instead of lowering the ball below your forehead and keeping your elbows out, try to score with a power move such as a strong two-hand shot. The other players will give you some resistance by slightly bumping your arms, trying to knock the ball out of your hands after your rebound and during your scoring attempt. Perform 10 repetitions.

Success Check

- Focus on getting the rebound and making the shot.
- Use both hands to rebound the ball.

Score Your Success

6 to 10 successful rebounds and scores = 5 points

4 or 5 successful rebounds and scores = 3 points

2 or 3 successful rebounds and scores = 1 point

0 or 1 successful rebound and score = 0 points

Your score ___

Offensive Rebounding Drill. Tipping

Stand in a balanced stance in front of the backboard and to the side of the rim. Using only one hand, shoot the ball high and softly on the backboard. Time the shot so that you can tip the ball with one hand at the top of your jump. Using your strong hand, tip the ball high on the board five times in succession and then tip it into the basket to score. Use your weak hand next, tipping the ball five times in succession and then into the basket.

For variety and to add difficulty to the drill, try alternating hands on each tip. Stand in a balanced stance in front of the backboard and to the side of the rim. Use your weak hand to shoot the ball high and softly on the backboard so it rebounds to the opposite side. Move quickly to the other side of the basket, jump, and tip the ball using your strong hand so it rebounds to the opposite side. Move quickly back to the first side of the basket, jump, and tip the ball using your weak hand. Continue tipping the ball high across the board, alternating hands as you tip. After three successive alternate-hand tips, score on your last tip.

(continued)

(continued)

Success Check

- Perform the drill with both your strong hand and your weak hand.
- Tip the ball at the top of your jump.

Score Your Success

For the tipping drill, attempt five sets (a set is five consecutive tips, then a score) with each hand. Give yourself 1 point each time you successfully complete five consecutive tips and put the ball in the basket.

Your score ___

For the alternate-hand tipping drill, attempt five sets (a set is three consecutive alternate-hand tips, then a score). Give yourself 1 point each time you successfully complete three consecutive tips and put the ball in the basket.

Your score ___

Offensive and Defensive Rebounding Drill. Circle Rebounding

Three players are needed for this drill. Begin with a ball placed inside the free-throw or center circle. Start as a defensive player. Assume a rebounding stance outside the circle, facing the ball. An offensive player gets in a balanced stance behind you. The third player gives commands. On the "Go!" command, the offensive player will use offensive rebounding methods to try to get to the ball while you block out. Try to keep the offensive player from getting the ball for 3 seconds. The "Stop!" command stops the drill after 3 seconds. Take a 10-second rest interval and then perform the drill for another 3 seconds. Complete five repetitions of 3 seconds each with 10-second rest intervals in between. Players then rotate: The defensive player becomes the offensive player, the offensive player moves into position to give commands, and the player who gave commands becomes the defender.

To add variety to the drill, add a front turn to the block out. Begin as the defender in a defensive stance facing the offensive player, who is assumed to be the shooter. On the "Go!" command, block out the offensive player using a front turn. The offensive player uses an offensive rebounding method to try to get the ball while you block out. Try to keep the offensive player from getting the ball for 3 seconds. The "Stop!" command stops the drill after 3 seconds. After a 10-second rest interval, perform the drill for another 3 seconds. Complete five repetitions of 3 seconds each with 10-second rest intervals in between. Players then rotate: The defensive player becomes the offensive player, the offensive player moves into position to give commands, and the player who gave commands becomes the defender.

Success Check

- On defense, use good technique for blocking out.
- On offense, use good offensive rebounding strategies to get past the blockout.
- Go for the ball.

Score Your Success

On defense, keep track of the number of times you are able to block out the offensive player. Give yourself 5 points if you complete at least three blockouts in five attempts. On offense, keep track of the number of times you are able to get past the blockout set by the defensive player. Give yourself 5 points if you are able to get past at least three times in five attempts.

Your score on defense ___

Your score on offense ___

RATE YOUR SUCCESS

No matter how good the shooters are, not every shot is going to go in the basket. Strong rebounding skills are essential to maintaining possession of the ball (offensive rebounds) or taking possession of the ball (defensive rebounds).

In the next step, we will look at the fast break. Before going to step 9, however, look back at how you performed the drills in this step. For each of the drills presented in this step, enter the points you earned, then add up your scores to rate your total success.

Rebounding Drills

1. Backboard Rebounding	___ out of 5
2. Superman or Wonder Woman Rebounding	___ out of 5

Defensive Rebounding Drills

1. Block Out the Shooter	___ out of 10
2. Block Out the Player Without the Ball	___ out of 10

Offensive Rebounding Drills

1. One-Versus-Two Offensive Rebound and Score	___ out of 5
2. Tipping	___ out of 10

Offensive and Defensive Rebounding Drill

1. Circle Rebounding	___ out of 10
Total	___ **out of 55**

If you scored 40 or more points, congratulations! You have mastered the basics of this step and are ready to move on to step 9, fast break. If you scored fewer than 40 points, you may want to spend more time on the fundamentals covered in this step. Practice the drills again to develop mastery of the techniques and increase your scores.

STEP

9

Fast Break

The fast break is exciting for both players and fans. The objective of the fast break is to advance the ball up the court for a high-percentage shot, either by outnumbering the defense or by denying the defense an opportunity to get set.

The fast break is important for several strategic reasons. It creates the easiest way to score. A team that has to work hard for every shot against a set five-on-five half-court defense will have trouble beating a team that consistently gets fast-break baskets. Creating an easy scoring opportunity by numerical advantage is the first objective of the fast break. The two-on-one and three-on-two, which are the most common numerical advantages, often result in a layup. The four-on-three usually leads to an inside post-up shot. The five-on-four often allows for an easy swing of the ball away from the side of defensive pressure for a possible open shot on the weak side.

A second objective is to attack before the opponents are set to play team defense or rebound. The fast break works well against zone defenses because the defenders do not have time to get set in their positions. A fast-breaking team is also more effective than a half-court team in combating pressing defenses. A fast-breaking team is better prepared to inbound the ball quickly before the press is set. A fast-breaking team is more experienced in passing on the move and generally looks to score against the press rather than just get the ball past half-court, posing a greater threat to the pressing team. A fast-break attack can also create mismatches against man-to-man defenses.

Another important objective of playing fast-break basketball is motivating the fast-breaking team to play tough defense and to rebound. Good defense and rebounding are the best ways to start the fast break. A fast-breaking team also discourages its opponents from sending too many players to rebound an offensive board for fear of not having players back to defend against the break. A fast-break style is very demanding and encourages a team to be in top physical condition.

The fast break places a premium on physical conditioning, fundamentals, teamwork, and intelligent decisions. Have a trained observer such as a coach, a teacher, or a skilled player subjectively evaluate your skills and decision making at different fast-break positions.

THREE-LANE FAST BREAK

The most common fast-break attack is the controlled three-lane fast break. In the controlled fast break, fundamental execution and good decision making matter more than speed. The controlled fast break has three phases: starting the fast break, getting into position, and finishing the break with the correct scoring option.

To start the fast break, you must first gain possession of the ball, which requires good defense and rebounding. Aggressive defense creates opportunities to get the ball after missed shots, blocked shots, steals, interceptions, or violations by an opponent. Inbounding the ball quickly after an opponent scores from the field or on a free throw also provides an opportunity to start the fast break.

After gaining possession, yell a key word such as *ball!* Immediately look upcourt for the possibility of passing ahead to an open teammate for an uncontested breakaway layup. When the opportunity for a quick pass ahead is not there, a quick outlet pass to the point guard (the best ball handler and playmaker) is needed. As shown in figure 9.1, the rebounder (5) uses the outlet pass to get the ball to the point guard (1). Players 2 and 3 sprint ahead and fill the outside lanes. The quicker you outlet the ball, the better, provided the pass can be completed. If there is too much congestion or you are trapped under your opponent's basket after a rebound, use one or two strong power dribbles up the middle and then look to complete an outlet pass to the point guard. If the point guard is not open, pass to another teammate on the weak side of the court.

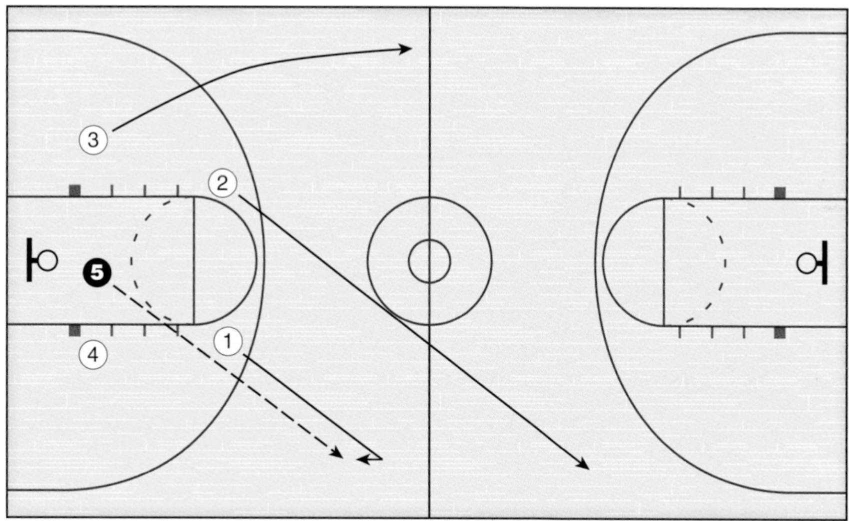

Figure 9.1 Fast break: The rebounder outlets to the point guard.

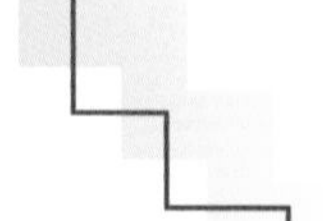

MISSTEP

As the point guard receiving an outlet pass, you dribble before looking upcourt.

CORRECTION

Catch the ball while using a one-two stop, pivot to the middle, see the rim, and then look to advance the ball up the court quickly with a pass or dribble.

The point guard will handle the ball in the middle of the fast break. The point guard should get open to receive an outlet pass in the area between the top of the circle and half-court on the side the ball was rebounded, calling for the ball by using a key word such as *outlet*. If denied a pass in this area, the point guard should look to make a backdoor cut toward the basket. As shown in figure 9.2, the point guard (1) makes a backdoor cut when denied the pass. When the rebounder is in a congested area or trapped, the rebounder (5) power dribbles up the middle and makes an outlet pass to player 1 or 3. When the point guard is denied, a teammate, particularly a player on the weak-side wing, should flash back to the ball; this player should receive the ball and then pass to the point guard on a backdoor cut toward the basket or on a front cut toward the ball. If the rebounder is in trouble and cannot make an outlet pass, the point guard should come back to that player to receive a short pass or handoff. The point guard should demand the ball and come to meet the pass, catching the ball while using a one-two stop. The point guard should pivot to the middle, locate the rim, and then look to advance the ball quickly up the court with either a pass or a dribble.

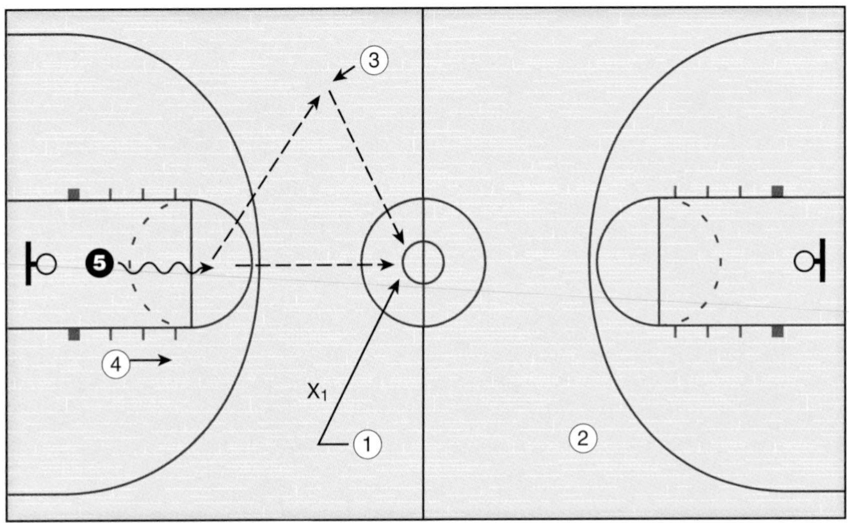

Figure 9.2 Fast break: The point guard cuts backdoor when denied the pass.

MISSTEP

As the point guard, you are denied from receiving the outlet pass.

CORRECTION

When you are denied from receiving a pass, make a backdoor cut toward your basket. Signal your backdoor cut with a key word—for example, call out "Eyeball!" If the rebounder is in trouble, come back to the ball for a short pass or handoff, calling out "Ball!" to demand the ball.

After receiving the outlet pass, immediately look upcourt for the possibility of passing ahead to an open teammate for an uncontested breakaway layup or a two-on-one scoring opportunity. If you are the point guard and a quick pass ahead is not there, push the dribble upcourt into the middle of the floor. Signal your move by yelling "Middle!" If you are not the point guard and a quick pass ahead is not there, look to pass the ball to the point guard in the middle of the floor.

To execute the controlled three-lane fast break (figure 9.3), think of the court as being divided by imaginary lines into three lanes. During the fast break, the point guard (1) will handle the ball in the middle lane, signaling this with the key word *middle.* The shooting guard (2) will be a wing and will fill one of the outside lanes. The small forward (3) will also be a wing, filling the other outside lane.

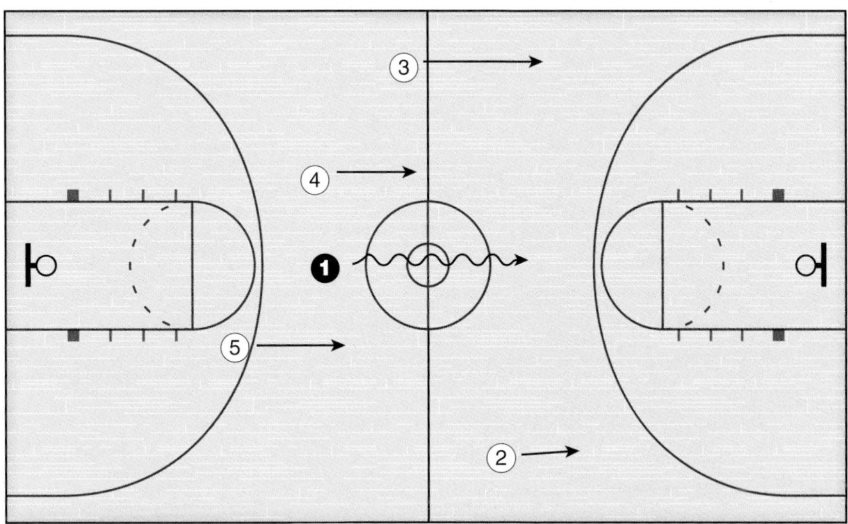

Figure 9.3 Fast break: filling lanes.

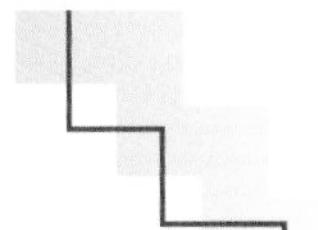

MISSTEP

A player other than the best ball handler dribbles in the middle lane, resulting in a possible turnover and missed scoring opportunity.

CORRECTION

The point guard should demand the ball, and if necessary, take the ball out of a teammate's hands.

If two players find themselves in the same lane, whoever gets there second must cut across to the lane on the other side of the court. Players should call out their lanes. The player filling the right lane yells "Right!" and the player filling the left lane yells "Left!" The wings should stay wide, about 5 feet (1.5 m) from the sideline, and should run ahead of the ball. The remaining players, usually the power forward (4) and center (5), will be trailers. The first trailer (usually your best post-up player) takes a position several feet to the rear and left side of the middle player and yells "Trailer left!" The second trailer (usually the best passer and outside shooter among your big players) follows the play upcourt, serving as a defensive safety.

Three-Lane Fast-Break Drill. Parallel Lane Passing

This drill requires three players. The players get in three lanes evenly spaced along the baseline. The player in the middle lane starts with the ball. The middle player tosses the ball high on the backboard and rebounds with two hands while yelling "Ball!" On the rebound, the wing on the right runs to an outlet position past the foul line extended while yelling "Outlet!" The rebounder makes a two-hand overhead outlet pass to the right wing beyond the foul line extended. The rebounder sprints up the middle while yelling "Middle!" and receives a return chest pass. The left wing sprints up the court while yelling "Left!" The player in the middle makes a chest pass to the left wing, who has sprinted ahead. Continue the drill up the court with the players passing and sprinting in parallel lanes while calling out lanes. At the foul line extended, each wing should cut at a sharp 45-degree angle to the basket. When the ball is received above the free-throw line in the scoring area, the middle player makes a bounce pass to one of the wings for a bank jump shot. The wing who receives the pass shoots a bank jump shot from 15 to 18 feet (4.6 to 5.5 m). The other wing should follow in, prepared to rebound a possible miss and score with a power move. After a score, switch lanes: The middle player moves to the right, the right player moves to the left, and the left player moves to the middle. Continue the drill back down the court. Each player should attempt three bank jump shots from each side of the basket (a total of six bank jump shots for each player).

Success Check

- Verbally communicate lanes with your teammates.
- Maintain proper spacing in the lanes.
- Make accurate passes.

Score Your Success

Give yourself 1 point for each bank jump shot you make from each side, for a maximum of 6 points. A score of 5 or 6 points is excellent.

Your score ___

Three-Lane Fast-Break Drill. Pass and Go Behind

This drill requires three players; the players set up as in the previous drill (the parallel lane passing drill). After making a two-hand overhead outlet pass to the player in the right lane, the rebounder follows the pass by sprinting behind the player passed to, filling the right lane and yelling "Right!" The player in the left lane then sprints to the middle lane and yells "Middle!" The player in the right lane makes a chest pass to the player now in the middle, then follows the pass by sprinting behind the player passed to, filling the left lane and yelling "Left!" Continue the drill up the court with each player passing and going behind the player who receives the pass, making a weave pattern and filling and calling out a lane. At the foul line extended, each wing should cut at a sharp 45-degree angle to the basket. When the ball is received above the free-throw line in the scoring area, the middle player makes a bounce pass to one of the wings for a bank jump shot. The wing who receives the pass shoots a bank jump shot from 15 to 18 feet (4.6 to 5.5 m). The other wing should follow in, prepared to rebound a possible miss and score with a power move. After a score, switch lanes: The middle player moves to the right, the right player moves to the left, and the left player moves to the middle. Continue the drill back down the court. Each player should attempt three bank jump shots from each side (a total of six bank jump shots for each player).

Success Check

- Verbally communicate lanes with your teammates.
- Maintain proper spacing in the lanes.
- Make accurate passes.

Score Your Success

Give yourself 1 point for each bank jump shot you make from each side, for a maximum of 6 points. A score of 5 or 6 points is excellent.

Your score ___

TWO-ON-ONE FAST BREAK

The two-on-one fast break is a quick way to move the ball upcourt and should result in a layup. When executed properly, the two-on-one is a fine example of teamwork and one of the most exciting plays in basketball. When you gain possession of the ball, you should immediately look upcourt, read the offensive situation, and react to it. See whether the two-on-one fast break—a quick scoring option—is available.

When you and a teammate recognize a two-on-one fast-break situation, you should immediately alert each other by yelling "Two-on-one!"

Move the ball upcourt, quickly passing back and forth to each other while maintaining lane-wide position (about 12 feet [3.7 m] apart, or the width of the free-throw lane). Being wider than that results in longer passes that are easily intercepted and creates a slower break. Being any narrower than that, however, allows the defender to guard both offensive players more easily.

When you have the ball as you reach the scoring area just above the top of the circle, you must decide whether to pass or drive. Good decisions come from reading the defense. When the defender attacks you and is in your driving line, pass to an open teammate cutting to the basket (figure 9.4). If you are passing to a smaller teammate, use a quick inside-hand bounce pass. If you are passing to a taller teammate or one with great leaping ability, use a two-hand lob pass. Both the bounce and lob passes have less chance of being intercepted than a chest pass.

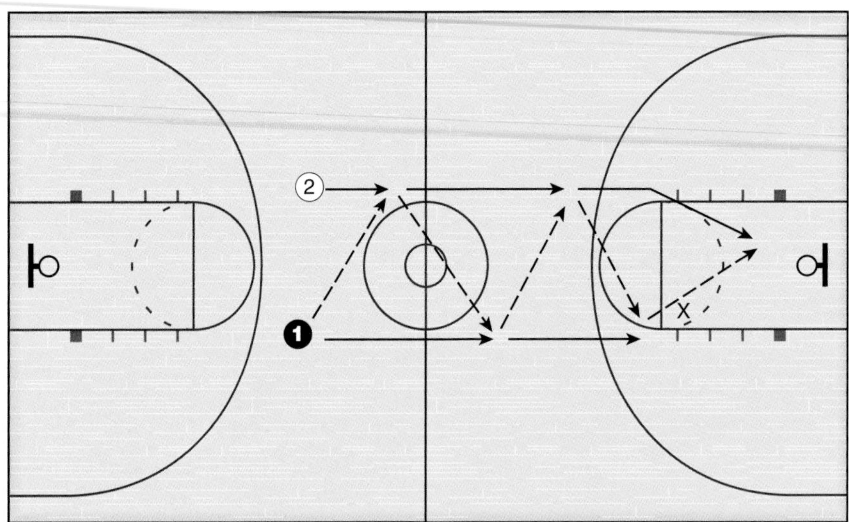

Figure 9.4 Two-on-one fast break: Player 1 sees the defender in the driving line and passes to the cutting teammate.

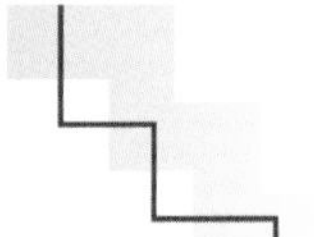

MISSTEP

In the scoring area, you penetrate past the foul line before passing, which creates congestion and allows one defender to guard two players or results in an interception or a charging foul.

CORRECTION

Only penetrate past the foul line to score if the defense gives you an open driving line to the basket.

When the defender is off the driving line, you should drive to the basket (figure 9.5). The usual defensive adjustment is to stop the ball high, a step above the foul line. On a pass to the cutter, a shot blocker will react by trying to block the shot from behind the shooter's head. A smaller player will attempt to draw a charge or steal the ball. As you drive to the basket, you should react to the defense and take the ball to the basket with a strong two-hand layup. Your teammate should follow, prepared to rebound a possible miss and score with a power move.

Within the scoring area, penetrate past the foul line to score only if the defense gives you an open driving line to the basket. Penetrating past the foul line and then attempting to pass creates congestion and allows one defender to guard two players. This can result in an interception or a charging foul.

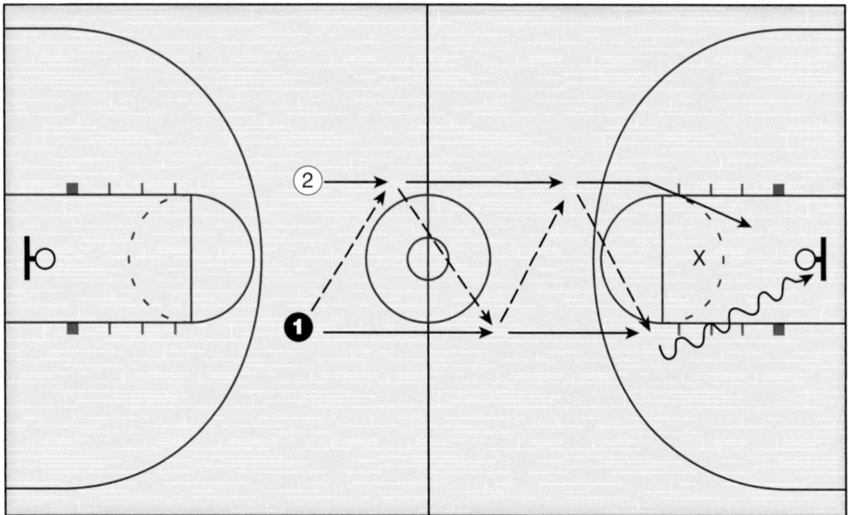

Figure 9.5 Two-on-one fast break: Player 1 sees the defender off the driving line and drives to the basket.

MISSTEP

When you reach the scoring area just above the top of the circle, you fail to read the defense and make a poor decision on whether to pass or drive.

CORRECTION

Read the defense when you reach the scoring area. If your defender is on your driving line, pass to the cutter. If your defender is off your driving line, drive to the basket.

Two-on-One Fast-Break Drill. **Two-on-One**

This drill requires three players, two on offense and one on defense. The two offensive players start at the blocks outside the lane on their defensive end, and the defensive player starts with the ball just inside the foul line. The defender starts the drill by passing to one of the offensive players and then sprinting back to the free-throw line in the offense's scoring area.

Both offensive players yell "Two-on-one!" and move the ball upcourt, quickly passing back and forth while maintaining positions 12 feet (3.7 m) apart (the width of the free-throw lane). If you have the ball as you reach the scoring area just above the top of the circle, read the defense and decide whether to pass or drive. If the defender attacks you in your driving line, you should pass to the teammate who is cutting to the basket. Use a quick, inside-hand bounce pass if the teammate is a smaller player. Use a two-hand lob if the teammate is a taller player or one with great leaping ability.

When the defender is off the driving line, you should drive to the basket, scoring with a strong two-hand layup. The offense scores 1 point when either offensive player makes a basket.

When you play on defense, stop the ball high, a step above the foul line. React on a pass to the cutter by trying to block the shot (from behind the shooter's head), draw a charge, or steal the ball. The defensive player scores 1 point each time she stops the offense from scoring. Play to 5 points.

(continued)

(continued)

Success Check

- Offensive players should communicate with each other as they move upcourt.
- The defender should try to stop the ball high.
- Offensive players should react to the defender's actions and make the correct decision on whether to pass or drive to the basket.

Score Your Success

The offense scores 1 point when either offensive player makes a basket. The defensive player scores 1 point each time she stops the two offensive players from scoring. This is a competitive drill. The first team to score 5 points wins the game. Give yourself 5 points if your team wins the game.

Your score ___

THREE-ON-TWO FAST BREAK

The three-on-two is a classic fast-break situation. The point guard should have the ball and should read the situation when the fast-breaking team enters the scoring area (normally a step outside the three-point line). The point guard with the ball must make good decisions on whether to penetrate to the basket or pass to the wing. The point guard should penetrate past the foul line and drive for a score only if the defense gives an open driving line to the basket. Otherwise, it is always better to stop above the foul line. Too much penetration causes congestion and may result in a charging foul.

The two defenders will normally be in tandem, with the top defender meeting the player with the ball slightly ahead of the foul line. When the wings reach the foul line extended, they should cut toward the basket at a 45-degree angle. When attacked by the top defender, the point guard should pass to the open wing player and cut to the ball-side elbow. In turn, the wing player should catch the pass in position to shoot and react to the defense. If the back defender does not come out, the wing should be in position for a catch-and-shoot bank jump shot, a short drive for a pull-up bank jump shot in rhythm and range, or a drive to the basket.

As shown in figure 9.6, the wings (2 and 3) make sharp 45-degree cuts to the basket at the foul line extended. The point guard (1) makes a bounce pass to the open wing (2) and then cuts to the ball-side elbow. Player 4 trails the play and then spots up at the weak-side elbow. Player 5 trails and acts as the defensive safety.

The normal defensive adjustment is for the back player to yell "Ball!" and cover the pass to the wing while the top player yells "You have help!" and drops back to give help on a drive or to block out on a shot. When this occurs, the wing should reverse the ball to the point guard, who may shoot or pass to the weak-side wing for a jump shot. The offense should not only get an open shot, but should also establish offensive rebounding position.

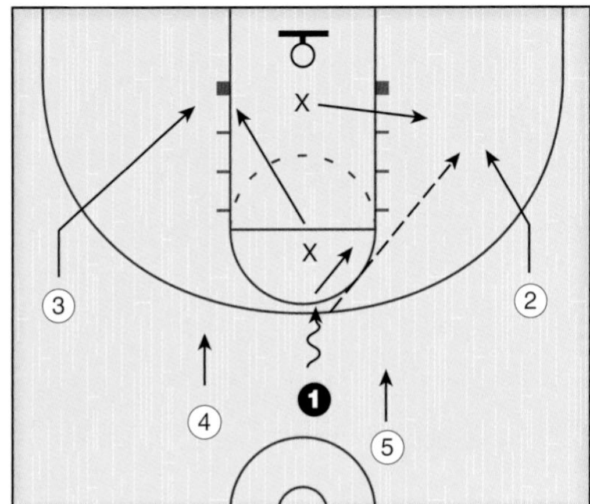

Figure 9.6 Three-on-two fast break.

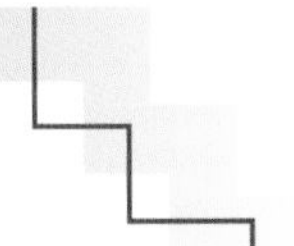

MISSTEP

The wings cut to the corners, making for a difficult corner jump shot rather than an easier bank jump shot.

CORRECTION

The wings should cut at a 45-degree angle so they are in position for a catch-and-shoot bank jump shot, a short drive for a pull-up bank shot in rhythm and range, or a drive to the basket.

Three-on-Two Fast-Break Drill. **Three-on-Two**

This drill requires five players, three on offense and two on defense. The defensive players start at half-court and sprint in tandem to the defensive positions just inside the free-throw line in the scoring area. The offensive players are evenly spaced along the baseline in three lanes. The offensive player in the middle lane has the ball. The middle player starts the drill by tossing the ball high on the backboard and then rebounding it with two hands while yelling "Ball!" On the rebound, the right wing runs to an outlet position past the foul line extended and yells "Outlet!" The rebounder makes a two-hand overhead outlet pass to the right wing beyond the foul line extended. The rebounder then sprints up the middle while yelling "Middle!" and receives a return chest pass. The left wing sprints up the court while yelling "Left!" The middle player makes a chest pass to the left wing, who has sprinted ahead. Continue the drill up the court, with the players passing and sprinting in parallel positions while calling out their lanes.

The defensive players should be in tandem in the scoring area, one on top and one behind. The defensive player on top defends the player with the ball, yelling "I've got the ball!" The bottom defender near the basket yells, "I've got the hole!" On a pass to the wing, the bottom defender takes the ball, and the top defender retreats to defend the basket or block out the weak-side wing and rebound a possible missed shot.

At the foul line extended, each wing should cut at a sharp 45-degree angle to the basket. The offensive player in the middle makes a bounce pass to one of the wings for a bank jump shot from 15 to 18 feet (4.6 to 5.5 m) or for a driving layup. The other wing follows in, prepared to rebound a miss and score with a power move. The middle player stays back for a swing of the ball (in case the wing decides not to shoot) or for defensive balance on a shot.

The offense earns 1 point for every basket; the defense earns 1 point for every stop. After a score, switch lanes: The middle player moves to the right, the right player moves to the left, and the left player moves to the middle. Continue the drill back down the court. Play to 5 points.

(continued)

(continued)

Success Check

- Offensive players should communicate with each other as they move upcourt.
- Wings should cut at a 45-degree angle to the basket at the foul line extended.
- Offensive players, especially the middle player, should read the defenders' actions.

Score Your Success

The offense earns 1 point each time they make a basket. The defense earns 1 point each time they stop the three offensive players from scoring. This is a competitive drill. The first team to score 5 points wins the game. Give yourself 5 points if your team wins the game.

Your score ___

Three-on-Two Fast-Break Drill.
Continuous Three-on-Two, Two-on-One

This drill requires at least 5 and no more than 15 players. Two defensive players start in tandem just inside the free-throw line in the scoring area (figure 9.7). Three offensive players are evenly spaced along the opposite baseline in three lanes. The offensive player in the middle lane has the ball. The middle player starts the drill by tossing the ball high on the backboard and rebounding it with two hands while yelling "Ball!" On the rebound, the right wing runs to an outlet position past the foul line extended and yells "Outlet!" The rebounder makes a two-hand overhead outlet pass to the right wing beyond the foul line extended. After the rebound and outlet pass, the three offensive players move up the court to the scoring area, where they attempt to score against the two defenders.

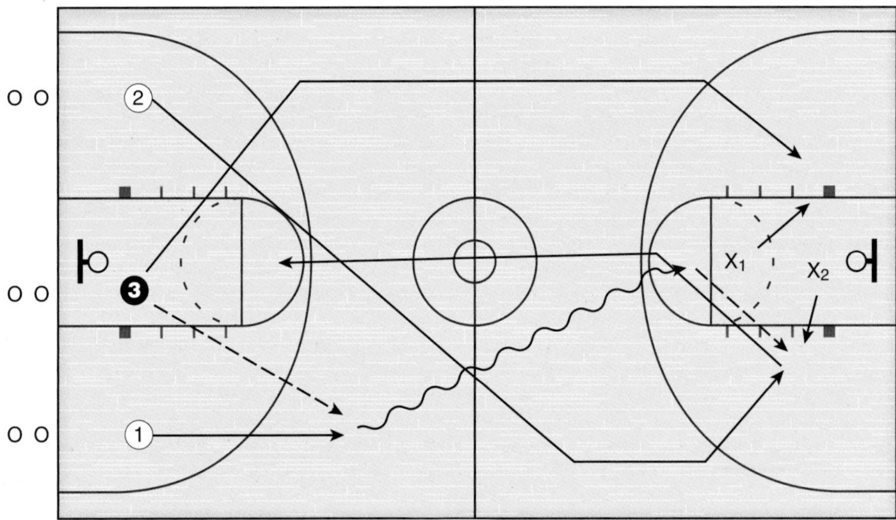

Figure 9.7 Continuous three-on-two, two-on-one fast-break drill.

When the offense scores (for 1 point) or the defense gains possession via an interception or rebound (for 1 point), the original two defenders start a two-on-one fast break against one of the original offensive players. The other two original offensive players stay back as the defense for the next three-on-two fast break. When the offense scores (for 1 point) or the defense gains possession via an interception or rebound (for 1 point), a three-lane fast break begins in the other direction with the two offensive players and the defender or with three new players. The drill becomes a three-on-two and two-on-one continuous fast-break. Play to 5 points.

Success Check

- Offensive players should communicate with each other as they move upcourt.
- Offensive players should read the defenders' actions and make the right decisions.
- Players should aggressively go for the rebounds.

Score Your Success

Each time you are on offense and your group scores, you and each member of your group earn 1 point. Each time you are on defense and your group stops the offensive players from scoring, you and each member of your group earn 1 point. This is a competitive drill. The first player to score 5 points wins the game. Give yourself 5 points if you win the game, 3 points if you are second in scoring, and 1 point if you are third in scoring.

Your score ___

Three-on-Two Fast-Break Drill. Three-on-Two With Defensive Trailer

This drill requires at least 9 but no more than 15 players. Group players into three or more teams. Put three players on each team. Team 1 starts on offense; the three players on this team are evenly spaced along the baseline in three lanes (figure 9.8, page 242). The middle player has the ball. Team 2 starts out of bounds at half-court, ready to jump in on defense. The remaining teams wait their turn.

The middle player on team 1 starts the drill by tossing the ball high on the backboard and then rebounding it with two hands. As the ball is rebounded, two defensive players from team 2 run and touch a foot in the center circle before sprinting back to tandem defensive positions just inside the free-throw line in the scoring area. The three offensive players move up the court to the scoring area and attempt to score. After one of the offensive players crosses half-court, the remaining defensive player from team 2 runs and touches the center circle and then sprints back as a defensive trailer. After team 1 scores (for 1 point) or team 2 obtains possession via an interception or a rebound, team 1 gets off the court and becomes the last team waiting out of bounds at half-court.

Team 2, the original defensive team, now starts a three-lane fast break in the other direction. Two players from team 3 run and touch a foot in the center circle and sprint back on defense. The third player from team 3 runs and touches a foot in the center circle after a player from the offensive team crosses half-court. The drill becomes a continuous three-on-two fast break with a defensive trailer. The first team to score 7 points wins the game.

(continued)

(continued)

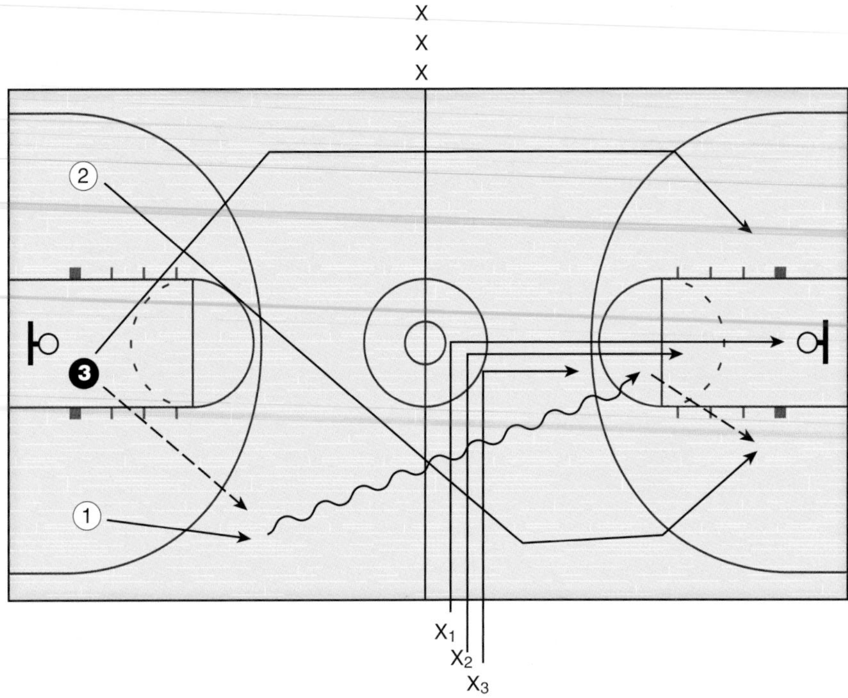

Figure 9.8 Three-on-two with defensive trailer drill.

To Increase Difficulty

After a team scores, that team can press up to half-court, and if they gain possession by a steal, interception, or turnover, they can attempt to score again.

Success Check

- Communicate with the players on your team.
- On offense, read and react to the defenders' actions.
- On defense, work hard to deny the pass and deny the drive.

Score Your Success

Each made basket is worth 1 point. This is a competitive drill. The first team to score 7 points wins the game. Give yourself 5 points if your team wins the game.

Your score ___

FOUR-ON-THREE FAST BREAK

The four-on-three fast break uses the first trailer. When the defense gets three players back, the wing player should dribble to the corner and look to pass to the first trailer, cutting to the ball-side block. The wing player should keep the dribble alive until he is able to pass to the trailer or reverse the ball to the middle. The first trailer should cut to the weak-side elbow and then make a diagonal cut to a post-up position above the ball-side block, looking to receive a pass from the wing. After beating the defense to the block, the trailer should seal a retreating defender on the topside and look for a pass from the baseline side. The wing should then pass to the trailer using a sidearm bounce pass from the baseline side.

As shown in figure 9.9, the point guard (1) makes a bounce pass to the open wing (2) and then cuts to the ball-side elbow. The first trailer (4) makes a diagonal cut to the low post at the ball-side block. The second trailer (5) follows as a defensive safety. Wing 2 dribbles to the corner, then makes a sidearm bounce pass to the first trailer (4). Wing 3 prepares to rebound the ball.

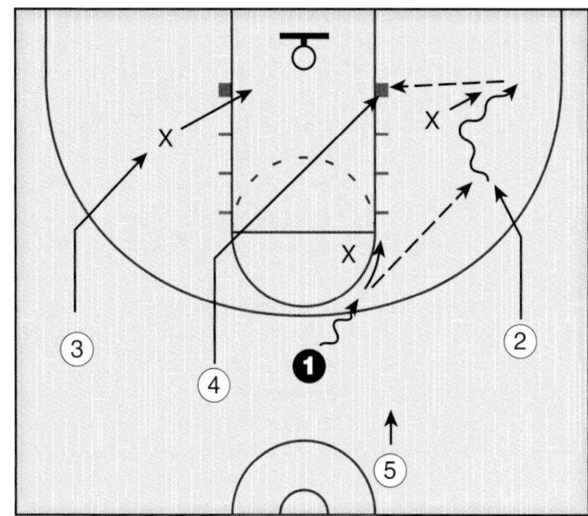

Figure 9.9 Four-on-three fast break.

MISSTEP

The wing stops dribbling and is unable to pass to the trailer or pass back to the point guard.

CORRECTION

The wing player should keep the dribble alive until he is able to pass to the trailer or reverse the ball back to the point guard.

Four-on-Three Fast-Break Drill. **Four-on-Three With Defensive Trailer**

This drill requires 12 to 16 players grouped into three or four teams, with 4 players on each team. Team 1 starts on offense (figure 9.10, page 244). Team 2 starts on defense. The action is similar to the three-on-two with defensive trailer drill. Three players from team 2 run and touch a foot in the center circle before sprinting back to defensive position as the offensive players of team 1 move up the court. Again, as one of the offensive players crosses half-court, the remaining defensive player runs and touches a foot in the center circle and sprints back as a defensive trailer. After team 1 scores (for 1 point) or team 2 obtains possession via an interception or a rebound, team 1 gets off the court and becomes the last team waiting out of bounds at half-court. The drill becomes a continuous four-on-three fast break with defensive trailer. The first team to score 7 points wins the game.

(continued)

(continued)

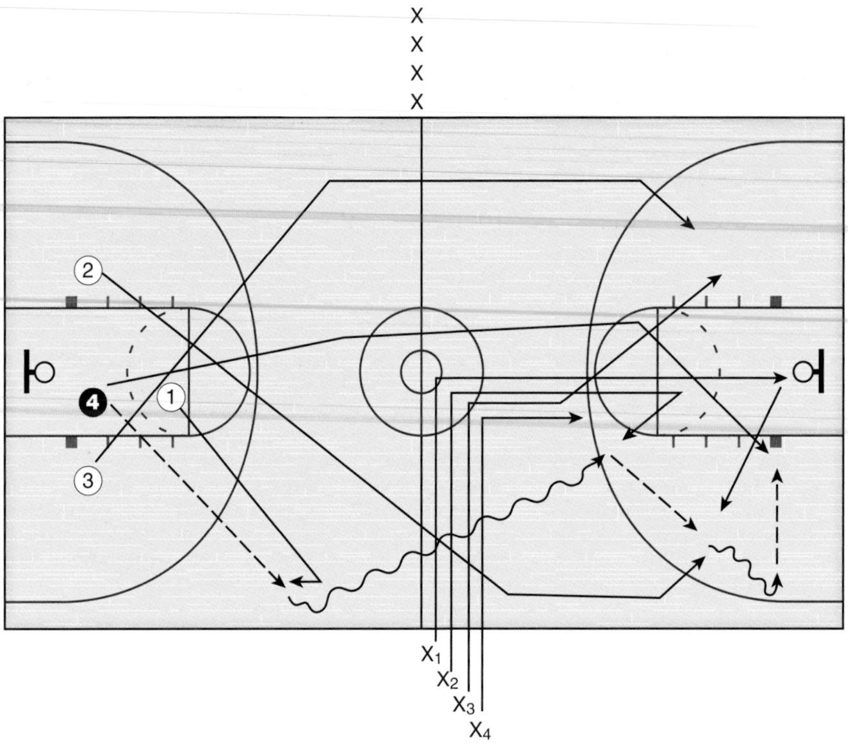

Figure 9.10 Four-on-three with defensive trailer drill.

Success Check

- Communicate with the players on your team.
- On offense, read and react to the defenders' actions.
- On defense, work hard to deny the pass and deny the drive.

Score Your Success

Each made basket is worth 1 point. This is a competitive drill. The first team to score 7 points wins the game. Give yourself 5 points if your team wins the game.

Your score ___

FAST-BREAK SWING

In the fast-break swing, the second trailer receives a pass and swings the ball from the ball side to the weak side. When the defense gets four or five players back and the wing player cannot pass to the first trailer in the post, each of the other players should spot up within shooting range in order to swing (reverse) the ball to the weak side (figure 9.11). The point guard should spot up above the ball-side elbow while the second trailer spots up above the weak-side elbow. Meanwhile, the weak-side wing should maintain spacing at the imaginary foul line extended. After receiving a swing pass, each perimeter player's options, in order, are as follows: to pass inside to the post-up player moving across the lane, to swing the ball to the weak side, and to shoot the outside shot. During the swing of the ball, the post-up player should move on each pass across the lane to the weak-side box.

The second trailer has an important role during the swing. If the defense denies the first swing pass to the point guard (figure 9.12), the point guard should either cut through to the weak-side corner or pull out to the ball-side sideline. As this happens, the second trailer must immediately flash to the ball-side elbow to receive a pass from the wing. After receiving the pass, the second trailer's options, in order, are as follows: to pass inside, to pass to the weak-side wing, and to shoot.

When a swing of the ball to the weak side does not produce an open inside or outside shot, the team can get into a passing game offense, or the point guard can demand the ball and run a set play.

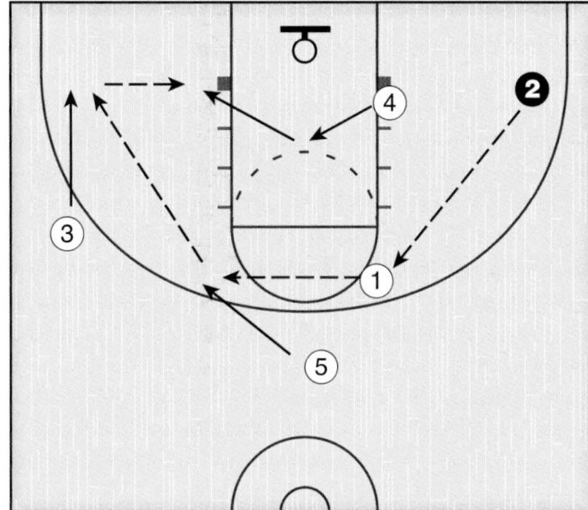

Figure 9.11 Fast-break swing: The post-up player (4) moves from block to block as the ball is passed (swings) to players spotting up on the perimeter.

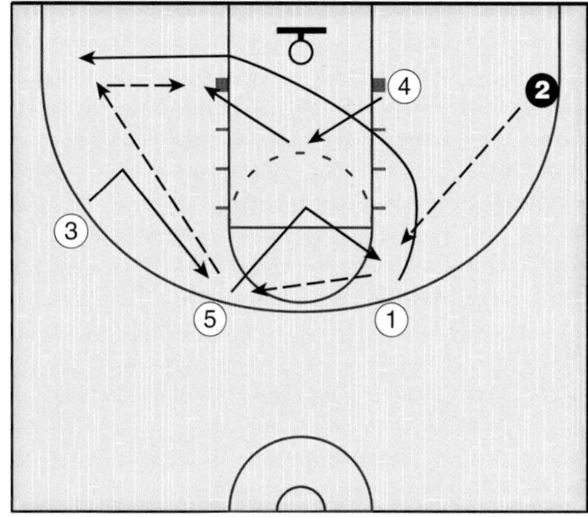

Figure 9.12 Fast-break swing: The defense denies the first swing pass, so the point guard (1) cuts through or pulls out, and the second trailer (5) flashes to the ball side.

MISSTEP

On a swing of the ball, the perimeter players first look to shoot, rather than looking inside first and weak side second.

CORRECTION

The swing players' options, in order, are as follows: to look to pass inside, to look weak side to continue the swing of the ball, and finally, to look to shoot.

Complete Fast-Break Drill. Five-on-Zero Fast-Break Options

This drill requires 5 to 15 players grouped into one or more teams of 5 players each. Each team will run the fast break using a different scoring option down the court each time. The scoring options include the following:

- Pass to the strong-side wing for a bank jump shot.
- Pass to the weak-side wing for a bank jump shot.
- Pass to the strong-side wing, who then passes to the first trailer at the strong-side block for a low-post move.
- Pass to the strong-side wing, who then passes back to the point guard at the strong-side elbow for a jump shot.
- Pass to the strong-side wing. The point guard cuts through to the weak-side corner or pulls out to the ball-side sideline. The strong-side wing then passes to the second trailer, who is flashing to the ball-side elbow for a jump shot.
- Pass to the strong-side wing. The point guard cuts through to the weak-side corner or pulls out to the ball-side sideline. The strong-side wing then passes to the second trailer flashing to the ball-side elbow, who then passes inside to the first trailer for a low-post move.
- Pass to the strong-side wing. The point guard cuts through to the weak-side corner or pulls out to the ball-side sideline. The strong-side wing then passes to the second trailer flashing to the ball-side elbow, who then passes to the weak-side wing. The weak-side wing takes a jump shot or passes inside to the first trailer, who moves high across the lane on each pass from the strong-side block to the weak-side block.

The drill starts with the fast-breaking team in defensive position at the defensive end. Either the center or power forward tosses the ball to the backboard, rebounds it, and makes an outlet pass to the point guard. The selected scoring option is then executed. Repeat each scoring option twice.

Success Check

- Use the correct technique for each scoring option.
- Communicate with your teammates during the fast break.

Score Your Success

Each trip down the court can result in 2 points, 1 point for correctly executing the fast-break scoring option and 1 point for making the shot at the end of the scoring option. If more than one team is playing, make it a competitive game. The first team to score 14 points wins. If only one team is playing, try to make 12 out of 14 points. If you are playing a competitive game against another team, give yourself 5 points if your team wins. If you are playing with only one team, give yourself 5 points if you make 12 to 14 points, 3 points if you make 10 or 11 points, and 0 points if you make fewer than 10 points.

Your score ___

Complete Fast-Break Drill. Five-on-One Deny the Point Guard

This drill requires 10 players grouped into two teams of 5 players each. Select a player from the off-court team to play defense on the middle player (point guard). Only the point guard is allowed to score. The point guard can practice moving without the ball (cutting through to the weak-side corner or pulling out to the ball-side sideline) while being denied from receiving a return pass at the ball-side elbow. The other offensive players practice options such as flashing to the ball when the point guard is denied from receiving the ball.

Each offensive team will run a fast-break swing option, looking to get the ball inside to the first trailer, who attempts to get open by moving high across the lane on each pass from the strong-side block to the weak-side block. After receiving a pass, the first trailer will make a front turn to the baseline and then attempt to pass the ball out to the point guard, who is working to get open on the perimeter or with a backdoor cut or front cut to the basket. If the point guard cannot get open, the first trailer passes to another perimeter player, and the drill continues. Once open, the point guard attempts to score. The offensive team earns 1 point for each shot made by the point guard. Switch out teams after each shot attempt. Play to 5 points.

To Increase Difficulty

Make the drill a five-on-two fast-break drill by using two defenders. The two defenders can be assigned to defend the point guard and the first trailer, the two wings, or any other two offensive players. Only the defended players may score.

Success Check

- Each perimeter player looks first to pass inside to the first trailer, who then attempts to pass to the point guard on a backdoor cut or front cut. If the point guard is not open, the first trailer passes out to another perimeter player, and the drill continues.
- The offensive team swings the ball around the perimeter until the point guard gets open.

Score Your Success

The fast-breaking team earns 1 point for each shot made by the point guard. This is a competitive drill. The first team to score 5 points wins the game. Give yourself 5 points if your team wins the game.

Your score ___

Complete Fast-Break Drill.

Five-on-Two Plus One Plus Two Fast Break

This drill gives a fast-breaking team practice at reading and reacting to various defensive options. The drill requires 10 players, 5 on offense and 5 on defense. As the offensive team runs a fast break, the defensive team will choose defensive options to defend it.

Divide the full court into three equal areas: area I (initial area), area II (secondary area), and area III (scoring area) (figure 9.13). The defense spreads into a two-one-two alignment with two defenders in area I, one defender in area II, and two defenders in area III. The drill starts with a coach, teacher, or extra player intentionally missing a shot. The players on the fast-breaking team start in defensive positions, block out their two opponents, and rebound the ball. The defenders in area I can go for the rebound, trap the rebounder, steal the ball from the rebounder, drop back to deny a passing lane to the favorite or other potential outlet receiver, or intercept the outlet pass.

Once the fast-breaking team advances the ball into area II, the secondary area, the single defender in area II can overplay the outlet receiver and deny the outlet pass. The single defender can also allow the outlet pass and pop up on the offensive player who receives the ball with the intent to draw a charge, pressure the dribbler to delay the fast break, or allow the dribbler to go by and try to steal the ball by flicking it from behind.

Once the fast-breaking team advances the ball into area III, the scoring area, the two defenders in area III can trap the player with the ball, play a tandem defense inside the free-throw lane, pressure the shooter, or rebound a possible missed shot.

The offensive team gets 1 point each time it scores. If the defense commits a foul, the offense gets the ball and starts again. If an offensive player misses a shot and a teammate gets an offensive rebound, play continues. The defense gets 1 point if it steals the ball, rebounds the ball, or forces the offense into a violation. Play to 5 points, and then switch roles.

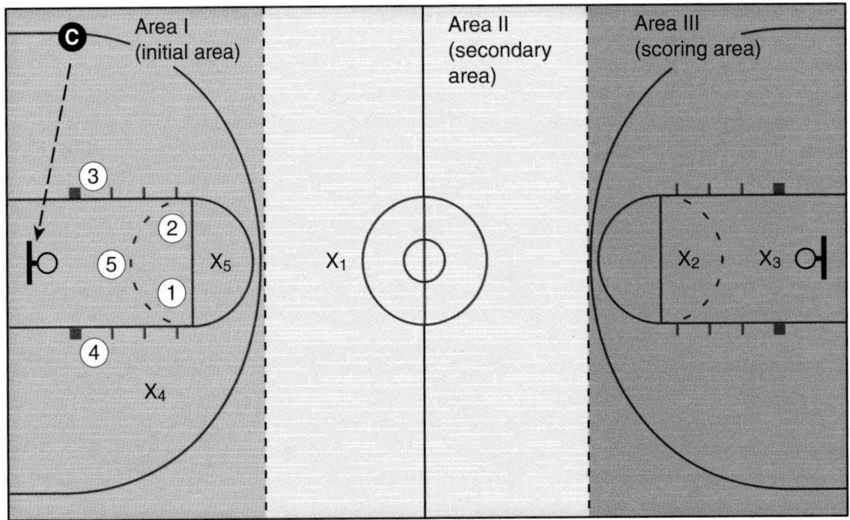

Figure 9.13 Five-on-two plus one plus two fast-break drill.

Success Check

- On offense, read the defense's actions and react accordingly.
- On defense, choose the best option and communicate with teammates.

Score Your Success

This is a competitive drill. Try to win more games than your opponent, playing each game to 5 points. Give yourself 5 points if your team wins the most games.

Your score ___

Complete Fast-Break Drill. Five-on-Five Fast Break

In this drill, the offensive team practices running a fast break, and the defensive team practices defending against the fast break. This drill requires 10 players grouped into two teams of 5 players each. One team plays offense, and the other team plays defense.

To defend against the fast break, the defensive team should have the player nearest the rebounder pressure the outlet pass. They should also have a defender deny a passing lane to the favorite or other potential outlet receiver. The other defenders should quickly retreat to the scoring area by sprinting back on the ball side of the floor while calling out their individual assignments in order. The first player back takes the most dangerous offensive player, usually the one near the basket. The second player back takes the second most dangerous player, usually the player with the ball. The third player back takes the third most dangerous player, the other team's best shooter. (Instead, you can choose to have your defensive center always take the offensive center.) Once two defensive players are back, a defensive guard can attack the offensive player who receives the ball; this defender pressures the dribbler in order to delay the fast break.

The offensive team gets 1 point each time it scores. If the defense commits a foul, the offense gets the ball and starts again. If an offensive player misses a shot and a teammate gets an offensive rebound, play continues. The defense gets 1 point if it steals the ball, rebounds the ball, or forces the offense into a violation. Play to 5 points, and then switch roles.

Success Check

- On defense, pressure the rebounder and the outlet pass.
- Communicate your defensive assignment.
- On offense, read the defense and react with the best option.

Score Your Success

This is a competitive drill. Try to win more games than your opponent, playing each game to 5 points. Give yourself 5 points if your team wins the most games.

Your score ___

RATE YOUR SUCCESS

A well-executed fast break is an exciting play to watch and participate in. You can swing the momentum of a game in your favor if you and your teammates can run the fast break effectively.

In the next step, we will look in more detail at two- and three-man plays. Before going to step 10, however, look back at how you performed the drills in this step. For each of the drills presented in this step, enter the points you earned, then add up your scores to rate your total success.

Three-Lane Fast-Break Drills	
1. Parallel Lane Passing	____ out of 6
2. Pass and Go Behind	____ out of 6
Two-on-One Fast-Break Drill	
1. Two-on-One	____ out of 5
Three-on-Two Fast-Break Drills	
1. Three-on-Two	____ out of 5
2. Continuous Three-on-Two, Two-on-One	____ out of 5
3. Three-on-Two With Defensive Trailer	____ out of 5
Four-on-Three Fast-Break Drill	
1. Four-on-Three With Defensive Trailer	____ out of 5
Complete Fast-Break Drills	
1. Five-on-Zero Fast-Break Options	____ out of 5
2. Five-on-One Deny the Point Guard	____ out of 5
3. Five-on-Two Plus One Plus Two Fast Break	____ out of 5
4. Five-on-Five Fast Break	____ out of 5
Total	____ **out of 57**

If you scored 45 or more points, congratulations! You have mastered the basics of this step and are ready to move on to step 10, two- and three-man plays. If you scored fewer than 45 points, you may want to spend more time on the fundamentals covered in this step. Practice the drills again to develop mastery of the techniques and increase your scores.

STEP

10

Two- and Three-Man Plays

Basketball is a team game. Having the most talented players does not guarantee that your team will win. To win, you must play as a team. A team's success depends on all players working together so all team members fully utilize their offensive talents. On offense, the goal is to score. This means helping each other create opportunities to get the best shot possible each time your team has possession of the ball.

Success on offense depends mainly on sound offensive fundamentals—footwork, passing, dribbling, shooting, and offensive moves with the ball. You have worked to improve these fundamentals in the previous steps. In this step, we will progress to moving without the ball and executing two- and three-man plays, which are the foundation of team offense.

To help your team create scoring opportunities, you must be able to move without the ball. Only one of the team's five players can have the ball at a time, so about 80 percent of the time you will be playing without the ball. Moving without the ball includes helping yourself or a teammate get open by setting or cutting off a screen and keeping your defender focused on your movements away from the ball, thus limiting defensive help on the ball.

When you learn to move without the ball, you will not only make yourself a better player, but will also have more fun. The knowledge that you are helping your teammates brings its own satisfaction in addition to the acknowledgment you receive from an appreciative coach, teammates, and fans.

No matter how good your offensive skills with the ball are, they will not help if you cannot get open to use them. First, you must move to get open to receive the ball where you can be in position as a triple threat to shoot, drive, or pass. You must also move without the ball to provide opportunities for the shots you and your teammates want, such as an inside post-up, a one-on-one drive, or a jump shot that you can shoot in rhythm and range.

Moving without the ball is also important when you are away from the ball. When your defender is uncertain of your position, the defender will not be as alert to giving defensive help to a teammate guarding the player with the ball.

Here are some specific opportunities for moving without the ball:

- To use various maneuvers to get open to receive the ball in position to be a triple threat to shoot, pass, or drive
- To set a screen on or off the ball, enabling a teammate to get open or forcing a switch that will get you open
- To cut off a screen to get yourself open or to force a switch that will get the screener open
- To keep moving away from the ball to make it difficult for your defender to see both you and the ball or to make it difficult for the defender to be in position to give defensive help to a teammate guarding the ball
- To be alert to go after loose balls or to change from offense to defense when your team loses possession
- To move on a shot to get into offensive rebounding position or to get back on defense

Have a trained observer such as a coach, a teacher, or a skilled player evaluate and provide corrective feedback on your ability to move without the ball and to execute two- and three-man plays.

V-CUT

When your defender has a foot and hand in the passing lane to deny you the pass, you should take your opponent toward the basket and then sharply change direction, cutting back to the outside. This is called a V-cut (figure 10.1) and is the most commonly used way to get open. You can use a V-cut from any position on the floor if an opponent is overplaying the passing lane between you and the passer.

The effectiveness of a V-cut depends on deception, timing, and changing direction sharply from cutting toward the basket to cutting back out. When you take a defender toward the basket, be deceptive before changing direction to cut back to the outside. Time your cut back out so that it coincides with the delivery of the pass.

As you change direction, use a two-count move. Step first with your inside foot (the foot closer to the basket) and then with your outside foot, without crossing your feet. On your first step, use a three-quarter step rather than a full step, and flex your inside knee as you plant your foot firmly to stop your momentum.

Turn on the ball of your inside foot and push off toward the outside. Shift your weight and take a long step with your outside foot, toes pointing to the outside. Continue to move out, going to meet the ball as it is passed.

When you move to get open, keep the ball, the basket, and the defender in view. When you fail to see the ball being passed to you, this usually results in a turnover and a missed scoring opportunity. After making the V-cut, get your lead hand up as a target for the pass. Beat your defender to the ball by going to meet the pass, and catch it with two hands.

Make a one-two stop, landing first on your inside foot (the one closer to the basket) and establishing it as your pivot foot. You can then protect the ball with your body and still be in position to execute a reverse turn (drop step) with your opposite foot if your defender overcommits when going for the pass. After receiving the pass, use a front turn to the middle, face the basket, look for the rim, and be a triple threat to shoot, drive, or pass.

Figure 10.1 **V-CUT**

Cut to basket

1. Cut to basket, using three-quarter step with inside foot
2. Use deception and timing, and use two-count move
3. Flex inside knee

V-cut out

1. Turn on ball of inside foot and push off to outside
2. Shift weight and take long step with outside foot
3. Have outside hand up as target
4. Continue to cut to outside

Catch and front turn

1. Meet pass and catch it with both hands
2. Use one-two stop, landing on inside foot first
3. Make front turn to middle
4. Keep rim and defender in view
5. Get in triple-threat stance

MISSTEP

You circle your change of direction rather than make a sharp cut.

CORRECTION

Use a two-count move, first taking a three-quarter step and flexing your inside knee to pivot sharply and push off in the direction you want to go. Shift your weight and take a long second step.

BACKDOOR CUT

When your defender has a foot and hand in the passing lane to deny you the pass to the outside, you should change direction and cut behind the defender toward the basket. This is called a backdoor cut (figure 10.2). You can use the backdoor cut from any position on the floor if an opponent is overplaying the passing lane between you and the passer.

With experience, you will be able to use a backdoor cut automatically any time you are denied a pass on the outside. Also use this move when you see your defender's head turned away from you and toward the ball. That momentary loss of vision can cause your defender to miss seeing you cut backdoor to the basket for a pass and possible layup.

The success of a backdoor cut comes from communicating with the passer and sharply changing direction to the basket. The passer may throw the ball away when a backdoor cut is not made. Eliminate guesswork by using a designated key word to indicate to the passer that you are going backdoor. This key word signals that, once you start, you will continue your backdoor cut to the basket. A sharp, two-syllable word (for example, *New York, LA,* or *ice cream*) works well because it coincides with your two-count footwork. Set up the backdoor cut by taking your defender high. On the wing, take the defender at least a step above the foul line extended; at the point, take the defender a step above the free-throw circle. Shout the key word to indicate your backdoor cut just before changing direction and cutting to the basket. Use a two-count move to change direction, stepping first with your outside foot and then with your inside foot (see the V-cut to review how to do this).

The backdoor cut appears to be a relatively simple move but requires concentrated practice to execute sharply and effectively. Concentrate on the two-count move. When changing direction from right to left, you would concentrate on a two-count *right-left;* when going from left to right, you would concentrate on a two-count *left-right.*

As with the V-cut, when you cut backdoor, you should keep the ball, the basket, and other defenders in view. You must also be alert for help-side defenders rotating to you and possibly trying to draw a charge after your cut. After making your backdoor cut, get your lead hand up as a target. After receiving the pass, look to shoot, drive to the basket for a layup, or, if picked up by another defender, pass to the teammate who has been left open.

Figure 10.2 **BACKDOOR CUT**

Take defender high

1. Take defender high
2. Concentrate on two-count move
3. Shout key word for backdoor cut
4. Take three-quarter step with outside foot
5. Flex outside knee

Cut to basket

1. Turn on ball of foot and push off to inside
2. Shift weight and take long step with inside foot
3. Have inside hand up as target
4. Continue cut to basket

Catch the pass

1. Catch ball with two hands
2. Shoot layup
3. Protect ball with two hands until release
4. Follow through by landing in balance, ready to rebound

MISSTEP

You do not have enough space on your backdoor cut to get open.

CORRECTION

Take the defender high. On the wing, take the defender at least a step above the foul line extended; at the point, take the defender a step above the free-throw circle.

Backdoor Cut Drill. Two-on-Zero

This drill requires two players. Start with the ball at a block outside the lane and with your back to the basket. Pass to yourself by tossing the ball diagonally across the lane to the opposite elbow. Catch the ball while using a one-two stop with your inside foot landing first. Pivot to the middle, find the rim, and take a drive step. Be a triple threat to shoot, pass, or drive.

On your toss of the ball, your teammate runs to the opposite block, makes a sharp change of direction, and runs up the lane line to the elbow on the side opposite you. On reaching the elbow, your teammate assumes that a defender is denying a pass at the elbow (a chair can represent a defender) and makes a backdoor cut to the basket, giving a verbal signal just before the backdoor cut. A two-syllable word such as *eyeball* or *onion* is recommended to coincide with the sharp two-step change of direction needed to make a successful backdoor cut. Make a bounce pass to your teammate, who will receive the pass and shoot a layup.

Follow the shot to rebound a possible miss and make a power move to score. Change positions and continue the drill; each player should make five backdoor cuts and five layups on each side.

Success Check

- Use a one-two stop when you catch the ball, landing on your inside foot first.
- Verbally signal the backdoor cut to your teammate.
- Get in triple-threat position when you have the ball.

Score Your Success

Perform five backdoor cuts on each side.

8 to 10 successful backdoor cuts and layups = 5 points

6 or 7 successful backdoor cuts and layups = 3 points

3 to 5 successful backdoor cuts and layups = 1 point

2 or fewer successful backdoor cuts and layups = 0 points

Your score ___

FLASH AND BACKDOOR CUT

A flash is a quick cut toward the ball. The flash and backdoor cut (figure 10.3, page 258) involves three players: a passer, an overplayed receiver who is being denied the ball, and a player who will flash. When a defender is denying a teammate from catching the ball and you are the next closest player to the denied receiver, you should automatically flash to an open area between the passer and your overplayed teammate. Flashing to the ball relieves defensive pressure on your two teammates by giving the passer another outlet. A flash can help prevent a possible turnover, and it can also create a scoring opportunity when you combine it with the overplayed receiver's well-timed backdoor cut.

As you flash, signal the cut with the key word *flash*. On the flash, go hard with two hands up to receive the pass. When you receive the ball, use a one-two stop with your inside foot (the one closer to the basket) landing first. Catch the ball and look for your overplayed teammate, who should be setting up to make a backdoor cut toward the basket. Your overplayed teammate should set up the defense by taking a step away from the basket before the backdoor cut. Use a reverse pivot and make a bounce pass to your teammate cutting backdoor for a layup. If your teammate is covered on the backdoor cut, use a front turn and get into a triple-threat position for a possible shot, drive, or pass.

You should automatically flash whenever you see a teammate being overplayed. Usually, you will flash high when your teammate is prevented from receiving a pass on the perimeter. You can also flash to the high post when a teammate is being fronted in the low post, or you can flash to the low post when a teammate is being denied at the high post.

The success of the flash and backdoor cut is based on communication between teammates and the timing of the overplayed receiver's backdoor cut. Using the key word signals to the passer that you are flashing and alerts your overplayed teammate to cut backdoor after you receive the pass. Alertness and timing are required in order to execute this play sharply and effectively.

MISSTEP

The backdoor cut is made too soon.

CORRECTION

Your teammate can time the backdoor cut correctly by stepping away from the basket just as the ball is caught by the flash cutter and then cutting backdoor.

Figure 10.3 **FLASH AND BACKDOOR CUT**

a

See teammate denied

1. See overplayed teammate
2. Fake away

b

Flash

1. Shout "Flash!" and flash to ball
2. Catch pass
3. Make one-two stop, landing on inside foot first
4. Overplayed teammate steps high

c

Cut backdoor

1. Overplayed teammate executes backdoor cut
2. Reverse pivot
3. Bounce pass to backdoor cutter

Flash and Backdoor Cut Drill. Flash Backdoor (Three-on-Zero)

Start with the ball at the point position at the top of the free-throw circle. The other two players start at the right and left wing positions (foul line extended), respectively. After passing to either the right or left wing, fake a screen away before cutting to the basket. The weak-side wing moves out to replace you at the point. Assume that an imaginary defender is denying a swing pass back toward the weak-side point, and flash to the ball-side elbow to receive a pass, shouting the *flash* signal. When you receive the pass at the elbow after you flash, the player at the point should make a backdoor cut to the basket. Reverse pivot on your inside foot and make a bounce pass to your teammate, who is cutting backdoor to the basket. On receiving the pass, the cutter shoots a layup. If the shot is missed, the cutter rebounds the ball and scores with a power move.

Change positions and continue the drill. Each player completes three repetitions at each position on each side.

Success Check

- Verbally signal your teammates when you flash to the ball-side elbow.
- Make the right decision in reaction to what your teammates are doing and what the imaginary defense is doing.

Score Your Success

Each player plays each position on each side. When a correct flash, correct reverse pivot and bounce pass to the backdoor cutter, and a made layup are completed, 1 point is earned.

16 to 18 points = 5 points

14 or 15 points = 3 points

12 or 13 points = 1 point

11 or fewer points = 0 points

Your score ___

GIVE-AND-GO

The give-and-go, the most basic play in basketball, has been part of the game since it was first played. The name comes from the action: You give (pass) the ball to your teammate and then go (cut) to the basket, looking to receive a return pass for a layup. The give-and-go exemplifies team play. By passing the ball and then moving without it, you create an opportunity to score on a return pass. Even if you do not get open on the cut, you at least give your teammate a better opportunity to initiate a one-on-one move because your defender will be in a less advantageous position to give defensive help.

After initiating the give-and-go with a pass, be sure to read the defender's position before cutting to the basket. If the defender moves with you, continuing to guard you closely, you should simply make a hard cut to the basket. But if your opponent drops off you, you should move toward the ball after your pass (as most players learn to do), setting up your defender with a fake before you cut. Take a step or two away from the ball, as though you are not involved in the play. As the defender moves with you, make a sharp change of direction and front cut to the basket (figure 10.4). You can also fake by taking a step or two toward the ball, as though you are going to set a screen for or take a handoff from the player with the ball. Then, as the defender moves with you, you make a sharp change of direction and backdoor cut all the way to the basket (figure 10.5, page 262). As you gain experience in executing the give-and-go, you will learn to read your defender, use deception, and time your cut.

Figure 10.4 **STEP AWAY AND FRONT CUT**

a

Pass

1. See rim and teammate
2. Pass to teammate

b

Fake away

1. Read defender
2. Fake with step away from ball

c

Front cut

1. Change direction and make front cut to basket
2. Have lead hand up
3. Catch ball with two hands
4. Shoot layup

MISSTEP

You do not have enough space to get open.

CORRECTION

When you are at the point, start the give-and-go at least a step above the free-throw circle. When you are on the wing, start the give-and-go at least a step above the foul line extended.

Figure 10.5 **STEP TO BALL AND BACKDOOR CUT**

a

Pass

1. See rim and teammate
2. Pass to teammate

b

Fake toward ball

1. Read defender
2. Fake with step toward ball

c

Backdoor cut

1. Change direction and make backdoor cut all the way to basket
2. Have lead hand up
3. Catch ball with two hands
4. Shoot layup

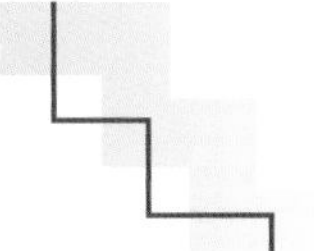

MISSTEP

After starting your backdoor cut, you stop cutting, causing the pass to be thrown away.

CORRECTION

On a backdoor cut, you must cut all the way to the basket. The passer should only pass if you are open. This will eliminate a turnover on the pass.

Give-and-Go Drill. **Two-on-Zero**

Select a teammate to be your partner. Start with the ball at a block outside the lane and with your back to the basket. Your partner starts at the opposite block across the lane. Pass to yourself by tossing the ball diagonally across the lane to the opposite elbow. Catch the ball while using a one-two stop with your inside foot landing first. Pivot to the middle, find the rim, and make a drive step. Be a triple threat to shoot, pass, or drive.

On your toss of the ball, your teammate runs to the other block, makes a sharp change of direction, and runs up the lane line to the elbow on the side opposite you. You make a chest pass to your teammate and cut to the basket (give-and-go). Your teammate makes a return bounce pass to you as you cut. Receive the pass and shoot a layup. Your teammate follows to rebound a possible miss and to make as many power moves as necessary to score.

Change positions and continue the drill; each player should cut and shoot five layups on each side (for a total of 10 layups for each player).

Success Check

- Use a one-two stop, landing on your inside foot first.
- Get in triple-threat position when you have the ball.

Score Your Success

9 or 10 made layups = 5 points

7 or 8 made layups = 3 points

5 or 6 made layups = 1 point

Fewer than 5 made layups = 0 points

Your score ___

Give-and-Go Drill.
Pass and Cut (Three-on-Zero)

This drill requires three players. Start with the ball at the point position at the top of the free-throw circle. The other two players start at the right and left wing positions (foul line extended). Pass to the player at either wing, then take one or two steps away from the ball toward the weak-side wing. Execute a sharp change of direction and cut toward the basket. As you cut to the basket, the weak-side wing replaces you at the point. The wing who received the pass should fake a bounce pass to you as you cut to the basket, and then pass to the player now occupying the point. When the ball is passed to the point, move to the open wing position that was vacated when the player moved to the point. Continue the drill: The player at the point passes to either wing and cuts to the basket, and the wing fakes a pass to the cutter before passing back to the player who replaces the cutter at the point. The group should make at least 5 passes before passing the ball to a player cutting from the point to the basket for a layup. Continue the drill for a total of 30 passes and 6 layups.

Success Check

- Pass and cut with precision.
- Run the drill smoothly and continuously.
- Try to complete 30 consecutive passes and 6 layups without error.

Score Your Success

30 passes and 6 made layups without error = 5 points

25 to 29 passes and 5 made layups without error = 3 points

20 to 24 passes and 4 made layups without error = 1 point

Fewer than 20 passes and 4 made layups without error = 0 points

Your score ___

SETTING A SCREEN AWAY FROM THE BALL

Setting a screen (also called a *pick*) is a maneuver to position your body to block the path of a teammate's defender. Screens may be set for a player with or without the ball.

The pass and screen away is basic to team play in basketball. It involves at least three players: screener, cutter, and passer. You set a screen for a teammate, who cuts off the screen to get open to receive a pass for a shot or drive. If your defender switches to your cutting teammate, you will be momentarily open on the ball side of the defender whom you screened.

Screening involves four steps: setting the screen, seeing the screen, using the screen, and freeing the screen.

Setting the screen. When setting a screen, align the center of your body on your teammate's defender at an angle that can prevent the defender from going through it. Taking a few steps toward the basket before setting the screen enables you to get a better angle on your teammate's defender. To avoid an illegal moving block, use a wide two-foot jump stop to establish a stationary position. You will be taking the blow of your teammate's defender moving into you, so you need good balance, with your feet more than shoulder-width apart and your knees flexed. While your teammate uses the screen, you are not allowed to move any body part into the defender. Keep one arm in front of your crotch and the other in front of your chest for protection.

Seeing the screen. When you are using the screen, you must be sure to wait until the screen is set. This will prevent an illegal moving block. Be patient. Read how the defense is playing the screen. Most mistakes in using screens occur either because you do not read the defense or because you move too fast without setting up the defense.

Using the screen. Approach the screen under control before you use it. You can never be late, but you can be too early when you cut off a screen. You can actually walk your defender into the screen while gaining a good angle for cutting off the screen. First, move slowly in the direction your defender plays you before cutting hard off the screen in the opposite direction. As you cut off the screen, go shoulder to shoulder with the screener so your defender cannot get between you and the screen. Be sure to cut far enough away from the screen so that one defender cannot guard both you and the screener and so you create space for a pass to the screener when there is a defensive switch.

Freeing the screen. When you set a good screen, this will have one of two outcomes: Either you or your teammate using the screen will be open. If your teammate cuts off your screen correctly, your defender's usual reaction is to give defensive help or switch. This momentarily gives you inside position on the defender who has given defensive help or, after a switch, on your new defender.

You can keep your open position by using a roll. A roll is executed by pivoting on your inside foot (the foot closest to the basket) and opening your body in the direction of the ball, putting your defender on your back. If your teammate cuts to the outside, you will be free to roll in toward the basket and receive a pass for an inside shot. If your teammate cuts to the basket, you will be free to step back and receive a pass for an outside shot.

You can also fake a screen and make a cut (called slipping the pick or early release). This maneuver is effective if your defender decides to give help by stepping out hard to slow your teammate's cut off your screen. If your defender leaves you to step out toward the cutter as you go to set the screen, you can make a quick cut to the basket to receive a pass for an inside shot.

If both defenders are trying to take the cutter, you should move to an open area. After receiving the pass, you will have the defense outnumbered and will be in position to drive or pass to a teammate for an open shot.

You have four basic options for cutting off a screen, depending on how it is defended: pop-out, curl, backdoor cut, and fade.

Pop-Out

When the screener's defender drops back to allow your defender to slide behind the screen, you should pop out to receive a chest or overhead pass for a catch-and-shoot jump shot in your rhythm and range (figure 10.6).

Figure 10.6 **POP-OUT**

a

Defender goes under screen

1. Screener sets screen
2. Cutter fakes in
3. Cutter's defender slides under screen

b

Cutter pops out

1. Read defense
2. Cutter pops out
3. Screener rolls in toward basket

c

Cutter catches and shoots

1. Ball is passed to cutter
2. Cutter shoots jump shot

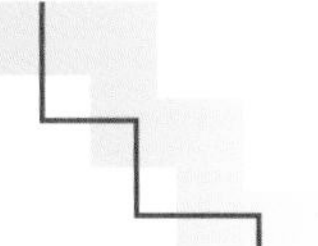

MISSTEP

As you cut off the screen, you do not create enough space to get open, and you allow the screener's defender to guard you and the screener.

CORRECTION

Cut far enough past the screen to create operating space for you or the screener to get open.

Curl

If your defender trails your body over the top of the screen, you should curl (cut in front and completely around the screen) toward the basket to receive an overhead or bounce pass for an inside baby hook shot. Signal this move by putting your arm around your screener's body as you curl. If the screener's defender helps slow your cut, the screener will then pop out for an open catch-and-shoot jump shot (figure 10.7).

Figure 10.7 **CURL**

a

Defender trails cutter's body

1. Screener sets screen
2. Cutter fakes in
3. Defender trails cutter's body

b

Cutter curls

1. Read defense
2. Cutter signals curl with arm around screener
3. Cutter curls in toward basket

(continued)

(continued)

Cutter catches and shoots

1. Screener pops out
2. Ball is passed to cutter on curl
3. Cutter shoots baby hook shot

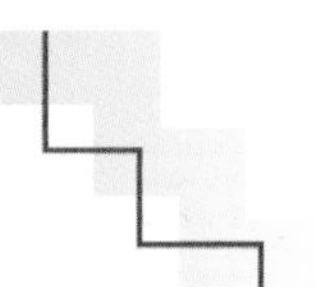

MISSTEP

You predetermine the cut when a screen is set for you and do not read your defender's position. For example, you pop out when you should curl.

CORRECTION

For your cut to be successful, you must read the defense and react to how your defender plays the screen. Do not predetermine or rush your cut. If your defender drops back, you should pop out. If your defender trails you, you should curl to the basket. If your defender steps out, anticipating your cut, you should use a backdoor cut. If your defender takes a shortcut behind the screener and the screener's defender, you should fade.

Backdoor Cut

If your defender tries to anticipate your move over the top of the screen before you make your cut, you should step out above the screen with your outside foot and then sharply change direction for a backdoor cut (behind the screen and toward the basket) to receive a lob or bounce pass for a layup. Signal the backdoor cut before your jab step by using a two-syllable key word such as *eyeball*. At the same time, provide a target for the passer with your inside hand; this hand should be pointing toward the basket for a bounce pass or pointing up in the air for a lob pass. If the screener's defender helps on the backdoor cut, the screener will then pop out and be open for a catch-and-shoot jump shot in rhythm and range (see figure 10.8).

Figure 10.8 **BACKDOOR CUT**

a

Defender steps out

1. Screener sets screen
2. Defender steps out to deny pass

b

Cutter cuts backdoor

1. Read defense
2. Cutter shouts key word for backdoor cut
3. Cutter steps out before backdoor cut to basket
4. Screener pops out

c

Cutter catches and shoots

1. Cutter receives bounce pass or lob pass
2. Cutter shoots layup

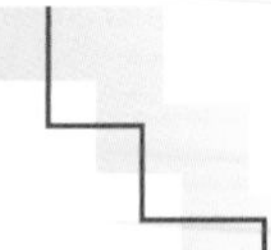

MISSTEP

The screener does not set a strong pick, and the defender is able to stay with you.

CORRECTION

The screener must set the screen at an angle that makes the defender go under the screen. The screener should use a wide base with the knees flexed to maintain balance. In addition, the screener should keep one arm in front of the crotch and keep the other arm in front of the chest for protection as the defender fights to get through the pick.

Fade (Bump)

If your defender takes a shortcut to your anticipated cut by moving behind the screener's defender on the basket side of the screen, you should fade away from the screen. Signal this move by putting your hands on your screener's hip before you fade (also called *bump*). You can also signal the fade with the key word *bump*. Prepare to receive an overhead skip pass to the far side of the screen for a catch-and-shoot jump shot in your rhythm and range. If the screener's defender switches out to pressure your shot, the screener pops out (figure 10.9).

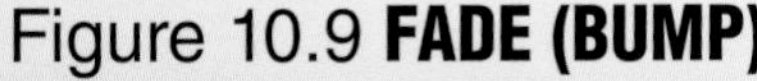

Figure 10.9 **FADE (BUMP)**

a

Defender takes shortcut under both screener and screener's defender

1. Screener sets screen
2. Defender takes shortcut under both screener and screener's defender
3. Read defense
4. Cutter signals fade with hands on screener's hip and calls out "Bump!"

b

Cutter fades

1. Cutter fades away from ball
2. Screener pops out

c

Cutter catches and shoots

1. Ball is passed to cutter on fade
2. Cutter shoots jump shot

MISSTEP

When you are the cutter, you fail to read your defender's shortcut and do not get open.

CORRECTION

Be sure to read your defender. When you see your defender take a shortcut underneath, fade away from the screen. Signal by putting your hands on the screener's hip and calling "Bump!"

As you and your teammates practice the screen away from the ball, you will learn to read the defense and react with the best option to create an opening for a shot. Properly executed, the screen away from the ball is a beautiful example of teamwork. By setting a screen for your teammate away from the ball, you create an opportunity for your teammate or you to score.

Screening Drill.
Pass and Screen Away (Three-on-Zero)

This drill requires three players. Start with the ball at the point position at the top of the free-throw circle. The other two players start at the right and left wing positions (foul line extended), respectively. Pass to the player at either wing, then fake a cut to the basket before setting a screen away from the ball on the inside of an imaginary defender on the weak-side wing (a chair can represent the defender). The weak-side wing has four options when using the screen: curl, backdoor cut, pop-out, or fade. If the weak-side wing uses your screen by cutting to the basket with a curl or backdoor cut, you should pop back out to the ball. If the weak-side wing pops out toward the ball to receive a possible pass for an outside jump shot, you should roll to the basket by opening to the ball with a reverse pivot on your inside foot (the one closer to the basket) and sealing out an imaginary defender. If the weak-side wing fades away from the ball, you can pop out or roll to the basket, depending on how you imagine the defense is being played.

The wing who receives the pass can make a bounce pass to a player cutting to the basket, pass to a player popping out, throw a skip pass (a pass that bypasses the next closest receiver) to a player fading, or pass or dribble the ball out to the point. A player receiving the pass on a cut to the basket should shoot a layup; if the shot is missed, the player should rebound and score with a power move. After a pop-out or fade, a receiver may take the outside shot or pass back to the point to restart the pass and screen play.

Change positions and continue the drill. Each player should execute five screens and reactions to how the screens are used.

Success Check

- Communicate with teammates.
- Use proper screening technique.
- Make the right decision in reaction to what your teammates are doing and what the imaginary defense is doing.

Score Your Success

Give yourself 1 point for each correct screen and for each correct reaction to the use of the screen.

12 to 15 correct screens and reactions = 5 points

9 to 11 correct screens and reactions = 3 points

6 to 9 correct screens and reactions = 1 point

Fewer than 6 correct screens and reactions = 0 points

Your score ___

SETTING A SCREEN ON THE BALL

The pick-and-roll is another basic play that has been part of basketball since the game was first played. Its name comes from the action of the play. You set a pick (also called a *screen*) for a teammate with the ball who dribbles by it for an outside shot, drive, or pass back to you or another teammate. Screening on the ball, as in screening away from the ball, involves four steps: setting the screen, seeing the screen, using the screen, and freeing the screen.

When a pick is set, the player with the ball should use at least two dribbles going by the pick to create space for a pass to the picker, who rolls to the basket. As you and your teammates become experienced in executing the pick-and-roll, you will learn to read how the pick is being defended and react with a roll, pop-out, slip, or stretch dribble to create an opening for a shot. This play is another example of good teamwork.

Pick-and-Roll

On the basic pick-and-roll play, a pick is set for the player with the ball. The pick should be set on the inside (lane side) of the defender guarding the ball handler. The player with the ball should wait until the pick is set and read how it is being defended. When dribbling off the pick, the dribbler should brush the outside shoulder of the picker to prevent the defender from getting over the screen and staying with the dribbler. When the pick is defended by a switch, the player with the ball should take at least two dribbles by the pick to create space for a pass to the picker, who rolls to the basket. The picker executes the roll by opening to the ball with a reverse pivot on the inside foot (the one closer to the basket) and sealing out the defender. The dribbler then makes a bounce or lob pass to the picker rolling to the basket to receive a pass and score (figure 10.10).

Figure 10.10 **PICK-AND-ROLL**

a

Defenders switch

1. Dribbler waits for pick to be set
2. Defenders switch
3. Read defense

(continued)

(continued)

b

Dribbler drives off pick

1. Dribbler drives off pick shoulder to shoulder
2. Dribbler takes two dribbles past pick

c

Picker rolls to basket

1. Picker rolls to basket
2. Dribbler makes bounce or lob pass to picker for layup

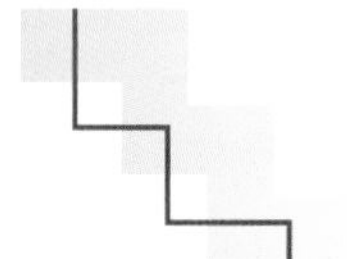

MISSTEP

You are called for a foul because you move your body or a body part into the path of the defender as your teammate dribbles off your pick.

CORRECTION

Before your teammate dribbles, you should use a wide, two-foot jump stop in order to avoid an illegal moving block. Keep your arms and knees in as the defender fights to get through your pick.

Pick-and-Roll Drill. **Two-on-Zero**

This drill requires two players. Start with the ball at a block outside the lane and with your back to the basket. Pass to yourself by tossing the ball diagonally across the lane to the opposite elbow. Catch the ball while using a one-two stop with your inside foot landing first. Pivot to the middle, find the rim, and make a drive step. Be a triple threat to shoot, pass, or drive.

Your teammate starts at the opposite block. On your toss of the ball, your teammate runs to the other block, makes a sharp change of direction, and runs up the lane line to the elbow on the side opposite you. Make a chest pass to your teammate and then set a screen on the inside (lane side) of your teammate's imaginary defender. Your teammate uses the screen, brushing your outside shoulder to prevent an imaginary defender from getting over the screen and staying with the dribbler.

Your teammate dribbles at least twice in moving past your screen in order to create space for a pass as you roll to the basket. Execute the roll by opening to the ball with a reverse pivot on your inside foot (the one closer to the basket) and sealing out an imaginary defender. Your teammate makes a bounce or lob pass to you as you cut to the basket. Shoot a layup. Your teammate follows to rebound a possible miss and make a power move to score. Change positions and continue the drill. Each player should execute five pick-and-rolls and five layups on each side.

To Increase Difficulty

Add a third player, a defender, to the drill. After executing the chest pass, set a screen on the inside of the receiver's defender.

Success Check

- Use a one-two stop when you catch the ball, landing on your inside foot first.
- Get in triple-threat position when you have the ball.
- When using the screen, brush the screener's outside shoulder to keep an imaginary defender from getting over the screen.

Score Your Success

Each player plays each position on each side. Give yourself 1 point for each successful pick-and-roll and for each made layup.

9 or 10 successful pick-and-rolls and made layups = 5 points

7 or 8 successful pick-and-rolls and made layups = 3 points

5 or 6 successful pick-and-rolls and made layups = 1 point

Fewer than 5 successful pick-and-rolls and made layups = 0 points

Your score ___

Pick-and-Roll Drill. Switching Defense (Two-on-Two)

This drill provides practice in executing the pick-and-roll against a switching defense. The drill requires four players, two on offense and two on defense. Start with the ball at a block outside the lane and with your back to the basket. Pass to yourself by tossing the ball diagonally across the lane to the opposite elbow. Catch the ball while using a one-two stop with your inside foot landing first. Pivot to the middle, find the rim, and perform a drive step. Be a triple threat to shoot, pass, or drive.

Your teammate starts at the opposite block. On your toss of the ball, your teammate runs to the other block, makes a sharp change of direction, and runs up the lane line to the elbow on the side opposite you. Make a chest pass to your teammate and then set a screen on the inside (lane side) of your teammate's defender. The defenders should switch as your partner dribbles past your screen. Roll to the basket. If the defender you screen defends your roll by quickly spinning around the pick toward the basket, rather than rolling in, you may pop out to receive a pass for a jump shot.

Each basket is worth 2 points. If an offensive player is fouled and the shot goes in, a free throw is awarded. An offensive player who is fouled on a missed shot gets two free throws. If the offense gets the rebound on a missed shot, they may continue playing offense until they score or until the defense gets the ball on a steal or rebound and dribbles back past the free-throw line. Switch sides. Play until one team scores 7 points.

Success Check

- Use a one-two stop when you catch the ball, landing on your inside foot first.
- Go after the rebound and keep playing until the defense gets the ball or you make the shot.
- Communicate with your partner.

Score Your Success

This is a competitive drill. The first team to score 7 points wins the game. Give yourself 5 points if your team wins the game.

Your score ___

Pick-and-Pop

The pick-and-pop (figure 10.11) is used when your defender opens (drops back) to allow the defender you screened to slide under your pick. Rather than roll in, you can pop out to receive a pass for a jump shot. You can also do this when the defense switches and the defender you screen quickly spins around your pick toward the basket.

Figure 10.11 PICK-AND-POP

a

Defenders open and go under

1. Dribbler waits for pick to be set
2. Picker's defender opens (drops back), and dribbler's defender slides under pick
3. Read defense

b

Dribbler drives off pick

1. Dribbler drives off pick, shoulder to shoulder
2. Dribbler takes at least two dribbles past pick

c

Picker pops out for jump shot

1. Picker pops out
2. Dribbler passes to picker for open jump shot

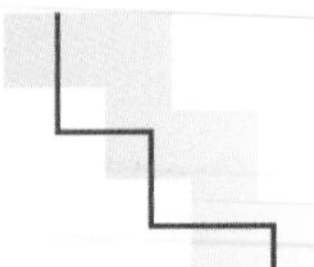

MISSTEP

As the dribbler drives off your pick, not enough space is created, allowing one defender to guard both the dribbler and you.

CORRECTION

The dribbler should take at least two dribbles past the pick in order to create space to shoot or pass back to you for an open shot.

Pick-and-Pop Drill. Open and Slide Under Defense (Two-on-Two)

In this drill, you will practice executing the pick-and-pop against a sliding defense. The drill requires four players, two on offense and two on defense. Start with the ball at a block outside the lane and with your back to the basket. Pass to yourself by tossing the ball diagonally across the lane to the opposite elbow. Catch the ball while using a one-two stop with your inside foot landing first. Pivot to the middle, find the rim, and make a drive step. Be a triple threat to shoot, pass, or drive.

Your teammate starts at the opposite block. On your toss of the ball, your teammate runs to the other block, makes a sharp change of direction, and runs up the lane line to the elbow on the side opposite you. Make a chest pass to your teammate and then set a screen on the inside (lane side) of your teammate's defender. Your defender opens (drops back) to allow the defender being screened to slide under the screen and stay with the dribbler. After dropping back, the first defender recovers to a defensive position on the screener.

When you set a pick and your defender opens (drops back), allowing the screened defender to slide under your pick, you should pop out to receive a pass for a jump shot (rather than roll in). Your partner can either take a jump shot or pass to you for a jump shot if your defender fails to recover after dropping back.

Each basket is worth 2 points. If an offensive player is fouled and the shot goes in, a free throw is awarded. An offensive player who is fouled on a missed shot gets two free throws. If the offense gets the rebound on a missed shot, they may continue playing offense until they score or until the defense gets the ball on a steal or rebound and dribbles back past the free-throw line. Switch sides. Play until one team scores 7 points.

Success Check

- After setting the pick, pop out for the return pass.
- Communicate with your partner.

Score Your Success

This is a competitive drill. The first team to score 7 points wins the game. Give yourself 5 points if your team wins the game.

Your score ___

Slip the Pick

Slipping the pick (also called early release) is a move you can use when your defender reacts to the pick-and-roll by stepping out hard to make your teammate using your screen veer out (figure 10.12). If your defender leaves you to step out toward the dribbler as you go to set the pick, you should slip (release early) and make a basket cut for a pass from your teammate.

Figure 10.12 **SLIP THE PICK**

a

Picker's defender steps out

1. Dribbler waits for pick to be set
2. Picker's defender steps out
3. Read defense

b

Picker slips the pick

1. Picker slips the pick and cuts to basket
2. Dribbler makes overhead lob pass to picker

MISSTEP

You do not read your defender, and you slip the pick before your defender steps out, enabling your defender to stay with you.

CORRECTION

Read your defender. Wait for your defender to step out before you slip the pick and cut to the basket.

Slip the Pick Drill. Help-and-Recover Defense (Two-on-Two)

This drill requires four players, two on offense and two on defense. The two defenders use a help-and-recover defense as an offensive player dribbles past the screen set by the other offensive player. Start with the ball at a block outside the lane and with your back to the basket. Pass to yourself by tossing the ball diagonally across the lane to the opposite elbow. Catch the ball while using a one-two stop with your inside foot landing first. Pivot to the middle, find the rim, and make a drive step. Be a triple threat to shoot, pass, or drive.

Your teammate starts at the opposite block. On your toss of the ball, your teammate runs to the other block, makes a sharp change of direction, and runs up the lane line to the elbow on the side opposite you. Make a chest pass to your partner and then set a screen on the inside (lane side) of your teammate's defender. If your defender decides to defend the pick-and-roll by stepping out early to slow down your teammate before the dribble, you should slip the pick and make a basket cut for a pass from your teammate. If after stepping out, the first defender recovers to a defensive position on you, your teammate can then drive to the basket for a layup or shoot a jump shot.

Each basket is worth 2 points. If an offensive player is fouled and the shot goes in, a free throw is awarded. An offensive player who is fouled on a missed shot gets two free throws. If the offense gets the rebound on a missed shot, they may continue playing offense until they score or until the defense gets the ball on a steal or rebound and dribbles back past the free-throw line. Switch sides. Play until one team scores 7 points.

Success Check

- Use a one-two stop when you catch the ball, landing on your inside foot first.
- Communicate with your partner.
- Read the defense and react to what the defenders are doing.

Score Your Success

This is a competitive drill. The first team to score 7 points wins the game. Give yourself 5 points if your team wins the game.

Your score ___

Stretch the Trap

When both defenders react to the pick-and-roll by trapping the player with the ball as you set the pick, a different adjustment, called *stretch the trap* (figure 10.13), is advantageous. When the trap occurs, the player with the ball should use at least two retreat dribbles to stretch the defense and create space. The dribbler can then split the trap or pass to you as you move to an open area. You will have the defense outnumbered and will be in position to drive or pass to a teammate for an open shot.

Figure 10.13 **STRETCH THE TRAP**

a

Defenders trap ball

1. Dribbler waits for pick to be set
2. Defenders trap ball
3. Read defense

b

Dribbler stretches trap

1. Dribbler uses at least two retreat dribbles to stretch trap
2. Picker cuts to open area and calls for ball

c

Dribbler passes to picker

1. Dribbler makes overhead pass to picker or splits trap with dribble to basket
2. Picker receives ball and drives to basket or passes to open teammate

---

MISSTEP

The dribbler stops dribbling and is trapped.

CORRECTION

The dribbler should keep the dribble alive by making at least two retreat dribbles to stretch the trap and create space to pass to the picker or split the trap with a dribble drive.

Stretch the Trap Drill. Two-on-Two

This drill requires four players, two on offense and two on defense. The two defenders use a trap against your pick. Start with the ball at a block outside the lane and with your back to the basket. Pass to yourself by tossing the ball diagonally across the lane to the opposite elbow. Catch the ball while using a one-two stop with your inside foot landing first. Pivot to the middle, find the rim, and make a drive step. Be a triple threat to shoot, pass, or drive.

Your teammate starts at the opposite block. On your toss of the ball, your teammate runs to the other block, makes a sharp change of direction, and runs up the lane line to the elbow on the side opposite you. Make a chest pass to your partner and then set a screen on the inside (lane side) of your teammate's defender. If both defenders trap the dribbler during the screen, you should adjust by stretching the trap. Your teammate should use at least two retreat dribbles to stretch the defense. The dribbler can split the trap with a dribble drive or pass to you as you move to an open area. After receiving the pass, you will have the defense outnumbered and will be in position to drive to the basket.

Each basket is worth 2 points. If an offensive player is fouled and the shot goes in, a free throw is awarded. An offensive player who is fouled on a missed shot gets two free throws. If the offense gets the rebound on a missed shot, they may continue playing offense until they score or until the defense gets the ball on a steal or rebound and dribbles back past the free-throw line. Switch sides. Play until one team scores 7 points.

Success Check

- Use a one-two stop when you catch the ball, landing on your inside foot first.
- Communicate with your partner.
- Stretch the defense.

Score Your Success

This is a competitive drill. The first team to score 7 points wins the game. Give yourself 5 points if your team wins the game.

Your score ___

DRIBBLE SCREEN AND WEAVE

A dribble screen occurs when you dribble toward your teammate to hand the ball off while you screen your teammate's defender. To execute the play, dribble to the inside of your teammate. Your teammate fakes in and then cuts to the outside and behind you to receive the handoff. To hand off the ball, pivot on your inside foot (the one closer to the basket), placing your body in the path of your teammate's defender. Be prepared for contact during the handoff. Maintain a strong, balanced stance and use your body and two hands to protect the ball. After receiving the handoff, your teammate should be a triple threat to shoot, drive, or pass. After you make the handoff, you should read the defense and roll to the basket, pop out, or move away from the ball to an open area.

The dribble screen is used to execute a *weave,* which is another basic basketball play. In a weave, at least three players set dribble screens for each other. For example, you start the weave with a dribble screen and hand off to your teammate. The recipient of the handoff has several options: shoot from behind the screen, drive to the basket, or continue for a dribble screen and handoff (figure 10.14). The weave continues until someone takes advantage of an opening for a shot or drive to the basket.

With experience, you and your teammates will learn to read how the weave is being defended so you can choose whether to react with a handoff, fake handoff, or backdoor cut to create an opening for a shot. The weave creates a variety of scoring opportunities and is yet another beautiful example of teamwork.

Figure 10.14 **SHOOT, DRIVE, OR CONTINUE WEAVE**

a

Defenders open and go under

1. Dribbler starts weave by dribbling inside teammate, setting dribble screen
2. Receiver steps away before cutting outside dribbler for handoff
3. Dribbler's defender opens (drops back), and receiver's defender slides under screen
4. Read defense
5. Dribbler hands off ball to receiver

b

Receiver shoots, drives, or continues weave

1. Dribbler cuts away from ball
2. Receiver shoots jump shot, drives to basket, or continues weave

---

MISSTEP

As you dribble toward your teammate to set the dribble screen, you bump into each other.

CORRECTION

To avoid bumping into each other, remember that the dribbler goes to the inside and the receiver cuts behind the dribbler and to the outside.

One way to defend either the dribble screen or the weave is for the defender to get in the path of the receiver in order to prevent the handoff (figure 10.15). When you are the potential receiver and a defender gets in your path, you should take a step to the outside and make a backdoor cut to the basket for a possible pass and layup.

Figure 10.15 **CUT BACKDOOR**

Defender denies handoff

1. Dribbler starts weave by dribbling inside teammate, setting dribble screen
2. Receiver steps away before cutting to dribbler's outside for handoff
3. Receiver's defender denies handoff
4. Read defense
5. Receiver shouts key word for backdoor cut

Receiver cuts backdoor

1. Receiver cuts backdoor
2. Dribbler makes overhead pass to receiver for layup

MISSTEP

When a dribble screen is set for you, you do not read the defense. For example, your defender steps in the path of the handoff, and you fail to make a backdoor cut.

CORRECTION

For the weave to be successful, you must read and react to how the defense plays it. Learn to read how the dribble screen is being defended and when to react with a handoff, a fake handoff, a backdoor cut, or a retreat dribble to create an opening for a shot.

A second defense is to jump switch into the path of the receiver (figure 10.16). A jump switch is an aggressive early switch made to draw a charge or to change the direction of the player receiving the ball. To combat a jump switch, make a short 5- to 10-foot (1.5 to 3 m) cut to an open area after you hand off. Then look for a quick return pass. When you anticipate a jump switch, you can also fake the handoff and drive to the basket.

Figure 10.16 **FAKE HANDOFF AND DRIVE**

Defenders jump switch

1. Dribbler starts weave by dribbling inside teammate to set dribble screen
2. Receiver steps away before cutting outside dribbler for handoff
3. Defenders jump switch
4. Read defense

Dribbler fakes handoff and drives

1. Dribbler fakes handoff while continuing to dribble
2. Dribbler drives between defenders to basket

MISSTEP

When you set the dribble screen, you get knocked off balance.

CORRECTION

Expect to be bumped. Maintain your balance by widening your base and flexing your knees as you fake the handoff.

Another way to defend the weave is to have both defenders trap the player receiving the handoff (figure 10.17). When the opponents trap, your teammate should use a retreat dribble to stretch the defense and then pass to you while you make a short 5- to 10-foot (1.5 to 3 m) cut to an open area. After receiving the pass, you will outnumber the defense and will be in position to drive or pass to a teammate for an open shot.

Figure 10.17 **STRETCH TRAP**

Defenders trap

1. Dribbler starts weave by dribbling inside teammate, setting dribble screen
2. Receiver steps away before cutting outside dribbler for handoff
3. Defenders trap receiver
4. Read defense

Receiver stretches trap

1. Receiver uses retreat dribble to stretch trap
2. Screener makes short cut to open area
3. Screener calls for ball
4. Receiver makes overhead lob pass to screener or splits trap with dribble drive

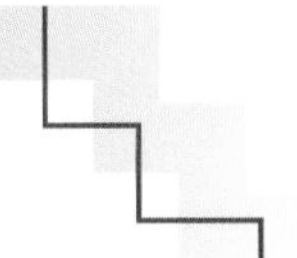

MISSTEP

The receiver stops his dribble and allows himself to be trapped.

CORRECTION

The receiver should keep his dribble alive and use a retreat dribble to stretch the trap, creating space to pass to the screener or split the trap with a dribble drive.

Dribble Screen and Weave Drill. **Three-on-Zero**

This drill requires three players. Start with the ball at the point position at the top of the free-throw circle. The other two players start at the right and left wing positions (foul line extended).

Begin the weave by dribbling toward one of the wings. Screen the wing's imaginary defender and dribble to the inside. The wing cuts to the outside and behind you to receive the handoff. The wing should then be a triple threat to shoot, drive, or pass.

After the handoff, imagine how the defense is playing the move, and then roll to the basket, pop out, or move away from the ball to an open area. The recipient of the handoff has the option of shooting from behind the screen, driving to the basket, or continuing the weave by dribbling toward the other teammate for a dribble screen and handoff.

The weave continues until a member of your team takes advantage of an opening for a shot or a drive to the basket. The group should make at least 5 handoffs before passing to a player cutting to the basket for a layup. Continue the drill for a total of 30 correct handoffs and layups.

Success Check

- Read the defense.
- Communicate with your teammates.
- Use the correct technique when doing the weave.

Score Your Success

25 to 30 correct consecutive handoffs and layups = 5 points

20 to 24 correct consecutive handoffs and layups = 3 points

15 to 19 correct consecutive handoffs and layups = 1 point

Fewer than 15 correct consecutive handoffs and layups = 0 points

Your score ___

Three-Player Drill. **Half-Court Offense Versus Passive Defense (Three-on-Three)**

This drill requires six players, three on offense and three on defense. The players will play a half-court three-on-three game. The three defenders will play passive (half-speed) defense to allow the offense to practice executing offensive options in three-on-three situations. Having the defense play at half speed helps the offensive players recognize which defense is being played, react with the correct offensive option, and develop confidence. The offensive options are to pass and cut (the give-and-go), pass and screen away, pass and go to the ball for a pick-and-roll, flash backdoor, or weave. The defensive options are to switch, slide, help and recover, or trap.

The drill starts when the defensive team gives the offensive team the ball at half-court. The offensive team gets 1 point each time it scores. If the defense commits a foul, the offense gets the ball and starts again. If an offensive player misses a shot and a teammate gets an offensive rebound, play continues. The defense gets 1 point if it gets the ball on a steal or rebound and makes an outlet pass past the free-throw line or if it forces the offense into a violation. The first team to score 5 points wins the game. The defense then goes to offense, and the offense goes on defense.

To Increase Difficulty

- Practice against an active (full-speed) defense.
- Practice the drill without dribbling. This creates more opportunities to practice passing and cutting, especially using the backdoor cut and flash backdoor.

Success Check

- Read and react to the defense.
- Communicate with teammates.
- Go after rebounds to keep the ball alive.

Score Your Success

This is a competitive drill. The first team to score 5 points wins the game. Give yourself 5 points if your team wins the game.

Your score ___

RATE YOUR SUCCESS

Moving effectively without the ball and executing two- and three-man plays will make you a better player and improve your team. In the next step, we will look at team offense. Before going to step 11, however, look back at how you performed the drills in this step. For each of the drills presented in this step, enter the points you earned, then add up your scores to rate your total success.

Backdoor Cut Drill

1. Two-on-Zero ____ out of 5

Flash and Backdoor Cut Drill

1. Flash Backdoor (Three-on-Zero) ____ out of 5

Give-and-Go Drills

1. Two-on-Zero ____ out of 5
2. Pass and Cut (Three-on-Zero) ____ out of 5

Screening Drill

1. Pass and Screen Away (Three-on-Zero) ____ out of 5

Pick-and-Roll Drills

1. Two-on-Zero ____ out of 5
2. Switching Defense (Two-on-Two) ____ out of 5

Pick-and-Pop Drill

1. Open and Slide Under Defense (Two-on-Two) ____ out of 5

Slip the Pick Drill

1. Help-and-Recover Defense (Two-on-Two) ____ out of 5

Stretch the Trap Drill

1. Two-on-Two ____ out of 5

Dribble Screen and Weave Drill

1. Three-on-Zero ____ out of 5

Three-Player Drill

1. Half-Court Offense Versus Passive Defense (Three-on-Three) ____ out of 5

Total ____ **out of 60**

If you scored 30 or more points, congratulations! You have mastered the basics of this step and are ready to move on to step 11, team offense. If you scored fewer than 30 points, you may want to spend more time on the fundamentals covered in this step. Practice the drills again to develop mastery of the techniques and increase your scores.

STEP

11

Team Offense

At its best, basketball is a team game played unselfishly by five players moving the ball, moving without the ball, and making quick, intelligent decisions, especially with regard to shot selection. Team offense depends on the sound execution of offensive fundamentals, including shooting, passing, dribbling, making moves with the ball, and moving without the ball. Basketball includes several positions, each with different responsibilities; the level to which each fundamental skill must be mastered varies with each position. The positions are often defined as point guard (playmaker), two guard (shooting guard), small forward (best shooter and ball handler of the two forwards), power forward (best inside scorer and rebounder of the two forwards), and center (best inside scorer and rebounder on the team). Obviously, you should be better skilled in the fundamentals that are needed for your position.

In today's game, more emphasis is placed on the spread offense. The international emphasis on using dribble penetration to draw defenders and then passing the ball out to players for open three-point shots has become a trend. The NBA rule changes that do not allow hand-checking have also contributed to this trend. The pick-and-roll and the pick-and-pop have become popular methods for gaining dribble penetration and then drawing and kicking to open shooters.

Versatility has also become more important. Taller players are not simply playing inside but are also being asked to perform farther out while facing the basket. Perimeter players must now be able to score and pass from the inside. As you mature as a player, you should attempt to become a more complete player. Once you have mastered the fundamental skills for your position, work to improve in other fundamental skills so that you are prepared to play any position. This will enable you to alternate positions on the court. The mark of a complete player is versatility.

MOTION OFFENSE

The motion offense (or passing game) is one of the most popular man-to-man offenses in basketball. In the motion offense, players are guided more by principles than by a strict set of specific assigned responsibilities. Every player should learn to execute the motion offense because it teaches team play and is an offense used by many teams.

The motion offense can be started from a variety of offensive formations, or sets, including the 3-2, 2-3, 1-3-1, 2-1-2, and 1-4. The 3-2 open set (figure 11.1), also called the spread formation, is the most basic formation for learning to play team offense. It involves three perimeter players and two baseline players. The point position (player 1 in figure 11.1) is above the top of the circle. The wing positions (players 2 and 3) are at the imaginary foul line extended on each side. The baseline positions (players 4 and 5) are at the midpoint between the corner and the basket on each side.

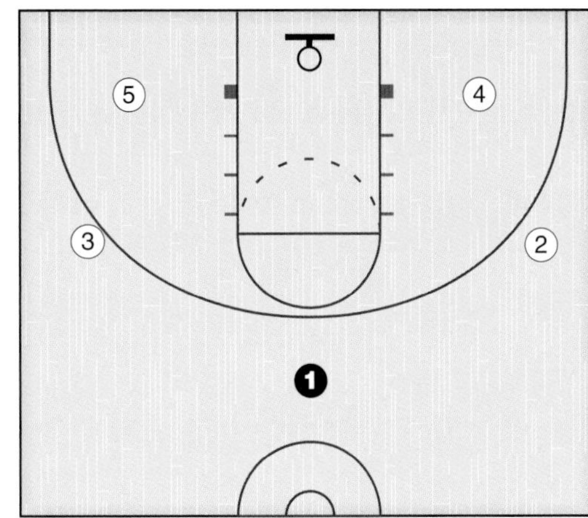

Figure 11.1 The 3-2 open set or spread formation.

MISSTEP

Players on your team tend to crowd together near the ball or too close to the basket.

CORRECTION

Maintain spacing and balance in an open formation, with players spread 15 to 20 feet (4.6 to 6.1 m) apart. Keep the middle open. When you cut to the basket and do not receive a pass, continue through and fill a spot on the side with fewer players.

The 3-2 open set encourages versatility rather than forcing players into restricted roles as center, power forward, small forward, shooting guard, or point guard. It gives each player the opportunity to handle the ball, cut, screen, and move outside and inside. The 3-2 set provides initial structure and spacing that allow players to execute basic two- and three-man plays and plays that involve all five players, such as a five-player weave or five-player give-and-go offense.

When executing the motion offense, keep in mind these basic principles of good teamwork:

- **Talk.** Communication is important to all aspects of team offense. The motion offense is not a set-play offense, and players are not assigned a specific set of responsibilities. Therefore, continual communication between players becomes especially important when executing the motion offense.

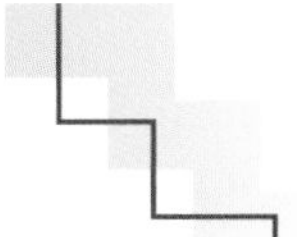

MISSTEP

You and your teammates get confused about what one another is doing.

CORRECTION

Talk! The motion offense is not a set-play offense in which each player has a specific assignment or set of responsibilities. Communication is especially important in a motion offense, so use designated key words for basic actions within the motion offense.

- **See the rim.** By having the rim in view, you see the entire court. When you have the ball, keep the rim in view and look for teammates cutting to the basket, posting up, and cutting off screens. When you do *not* have the ball, you should keep the rim and the player with the ball in view.
- **Maintain spacing and court balance.** Start in an open formation with players spread 15 to 20 feet (4.6 to 6.1 m) apart. Players should be spaced high at the top, wide on the wing, and at the baseline midpoint (halfway between the basket and corner).
- **Cut backdoor when overplayed.** When overplayed by a defender who denies you the pass, you should make a backdoor cut all the way to the basket. When backdoor cuts are used frequently, the motion offense becomes a great offense for beating pressure defenses.
- **Flash between the passer and the overplayed receiver.** When a defender denies your teammate the pass and you are the next player away from the receiver, you should automatically flash to an open area between the passer and the overplayed receiver. Flashing to the ball helps relieve defensive pressure on your teammates by giving the passer another outlet. A flash can prevent a possible turnover, and it may also create a scoring opportunity if the overplayed receiver makes a well-timed backdoor cut.
- **Keep the middle open.** When you cut to the basket and do not receive a pass, you should continue on through and fill an open spot on the side of the court with fewer players. This will keep the middle open and the floor balanced. Do not stay in the post area for more than one count.
- **Move to a vacated spot quickly.** When you are the next player away from a cutting player, you should quickly move to the vacated spot. This is especially important when the player is cutting from the point or top position. To replace the player at the point, cut high above the three-point line, creating a better passing angle to receive a swing pass from a wing and a better angle to reverse the ball to the weak side. This will also force the defense to cover more of the court, thus providing more space for cutting, driving, and posting up.
- **Know your options at the wing position.** When you are on the wing or cutting to the wing, your options are to catch and shoot within your rhythm and range or to continue your cut out wide. When you catch the ball outside of your range, look to pass inside to a cutter or a player posting up. On the wing, hold the ball for a count or two to give cutters and post players time to get open. If you are unable to pass to an open teammate cutting or posting up, look to penetrate and pass (draw and kick) or try to balance the court by quickly dribbling to the point. Look to pass to a baseline player only if that teammate is open for a catch-and-shoot jump shot within rhythm and range or can make an easy pass to a player cutting inside or posting up. You can move the ball more quickly if you swing it from wing to point to wing and keep it off the baseline.
- **Know your options at the point position.** When you are at the point position, your options, in order, are as follows: to reverse the ball quickly to the weak side, to look inside for a pass to a post-up player, to penetrate and pass (draw and kick), or to fake a pass to the weak side and make a quick snapback pass to the wing on the side from which you received the pass.

- **Know your options at the baseline position.** When you are at a baseline position, look to set up your defender for a cut off a down screen, or look to set a back pick for a wing player. On the baseline, you should be especially alert to flash to the ball when a wing is denied the pass. Look to receive a pass on the baseline only when you are in an open catch-and-shoot position within your rhythm and range or when you can make an easy pass to a player cutting inside or posting up. The ball can be moved more quickly if it is kept off the baseline.
- **Know your options as a post-up player.** When you receive the ball in the low post, you should read the defense and look to score before passing out to a perimeter player. When you do not receive a pass in the low post, look to set a back pick for a perimeter player. After setting the back pick, pop out to receive a pass on the perimeter for a possible jump shot within your rhythm and range.
- **Maintain rebounding and defensive balance.** On a shot inside, three players should rebound, and the point guard and another outside player should get back for defensive balance. When you take a shot outside of the lane area, you should get back for defensive balance. Any time the player at the point drives to the basket, players at the wings should get back for defensive balance.

A member of your team, usually the point guard, signals the start of the motion offense with a simple verbal call such as "Motion" or with a hand signal such as circling one finger upward. The best way to start is to pass the ball to the wing and then work together using basic actions of the motion offense. After receiving a pass on the wing, you should be a triple threat to pass, shoot, or drive to the basket. On a drive, look to score or draw and kick in or out to an open teammate.

When the ball is at the point, the closest wing player should initiate movement by cutting through to create an open area for a baseline player, who will cut to the wing for a pass from the point (figure 11.2). When you are at the point and cannot pass to the wing, initiate movement by dribbling at the wing and using a dribble screen or weave action (figure 11.3).

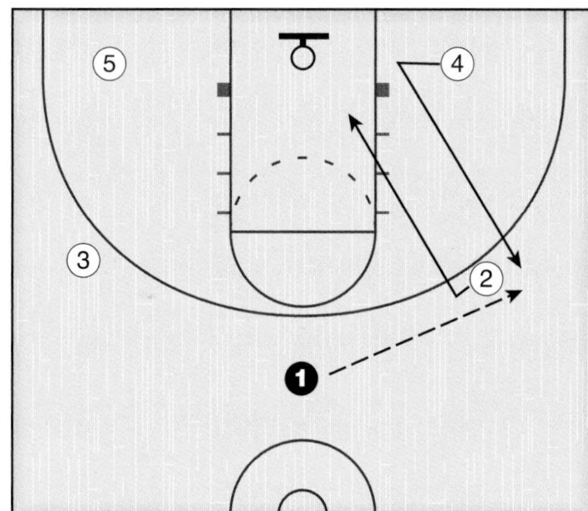

Figure 11.2 Start of motion offense: Wing player 2 cuts through to create an opening for player 4.

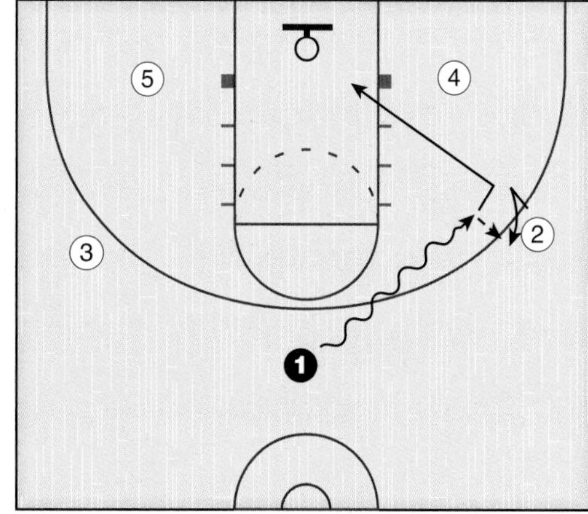

Figure 11.3 Start of motion offense: The player at the point (1) sets a dribble screen for wing 2 and then cuts to the basket.

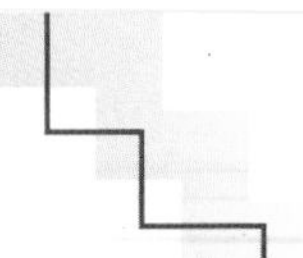

MISSTEP

You and your teammates have difficulty seeing each other when you get open on a cut, off a screen, or when posting up.

CORRECTION

Players with the ball should see the rim and the entire court. When you see the rim, you can see when your teammates are open.

Some of the basic actions used in the motion offense are the backdoor cut, the flash, the give-and-go, the dribble screen or weave, the down screen, the elbow curl, the back pick, the cross screen, the pick-and-roll, and the draw-and-kick.

Backdoor Cut

You should automatically use a backdoor cut any time you are overplayed by a defender and prevented from receiving a pass. You should also use a backdoor cut when your defender's head is turned away from you, causing a momentary loss of visual contact. Use a designated key word such as *eyeball* to signal the passer that you are going backdoor. The designated word indicates that you will continue your backdoor cut to the basket once you start it. When you are on the wing, set up your defender by taking a step above the foul line extended (figure 11.4). When you are at the point, set up the defender by taking a step above the free-throw circle (figure 11.5). After receiving the pass, look to shoot, drive to the basket for a layup, or penetrate and pass (draw and kick).

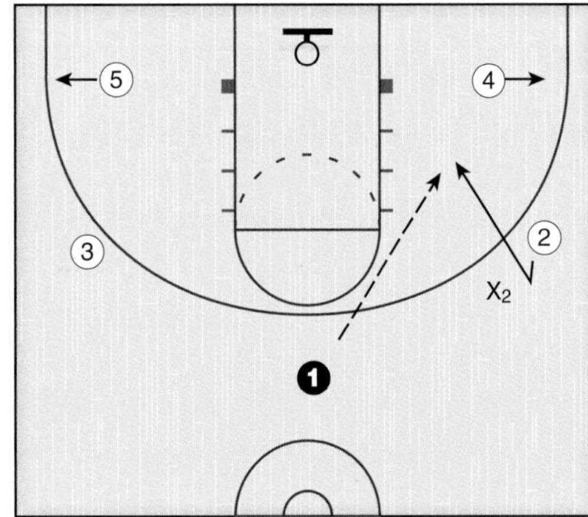

Figure 11.4 Backdoor cut: Player 2, denied a pass at the wing, cuts backdoor.

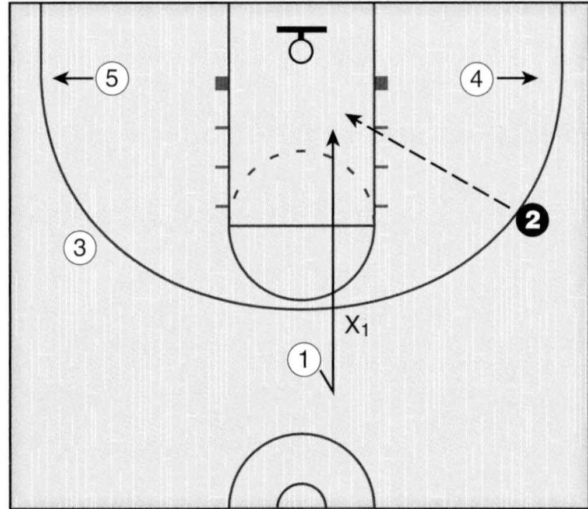

Figure 11.5 Backdoor cut: Player 1, denied a pass at the top, cuts backdoor.

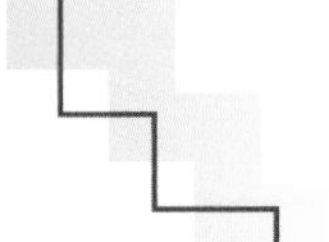

MISSTEP

Your team has difficulty moving the ball from the ball side to the weak side, resulting in your swing passes being intercepted easily.

CORRECTION

When replacing the point from the weak side, cut high above the circle to receive a pass. If you use a shallow cut, this gives your defender a good angle to deny and intercept a pass. If you cut high and your defender continues to go with you, you should cut backdoor.

Flash

Any time you see a teammate being denied the pass and you are the next player away, you should automatically flash to an open area between the passer and the overplayed teammate. Flashing to the ball relieves defensive pressure on your teammates by giving the passer another outlet. A flash can prevent a possible turnover, and when combined with a well-timed backdoor cut by the overplayed teammate, the flash can also create a scoring opportunity. Signal your flash cut with the key word *flash!* As you receive the pass, look to pass to your overplayed teammate cutting backdoor to the basket. If your teammate is covered on the backdoor cut, you should front turn into a triple-threat position for a possible shot, drive to the basket, or pass.

Flash high when your teammate is prevented from receiving a pass on the perimeter (figure 11.6). You can also flash to the high post when your teammate is being fronted in the low post (figure 11.7), and you can flash to the low post if your teammate is being denied at the high post (figure 11.8).

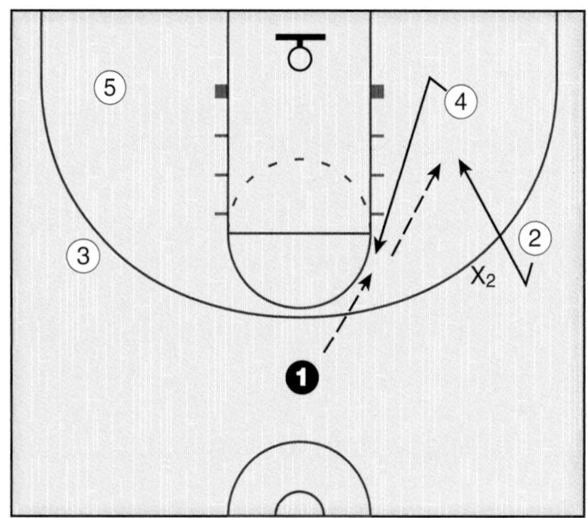

Figure 11.6 Flash: Player 4 sees wing 2 being denied, flashes high, receives a pass from player 1, and passes to 2, who is cutting backdoor.

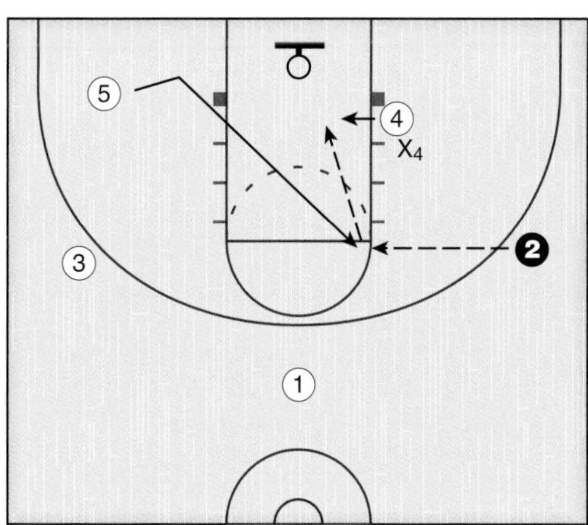

Figure 11.7 Flash: Player 5 sees low post 4 being denied, flashes high, receives a pass from player 2, and passes to 4, who is cutting to the basket.

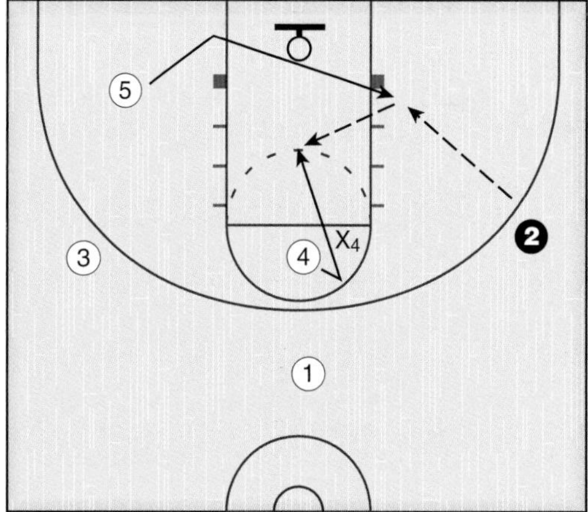

Figure 11.8 Flash: Player 5 sees high post 4 being denied, flashes to the low post, receives a pass from player 2, and passes to 4, who is cutting backdoor.

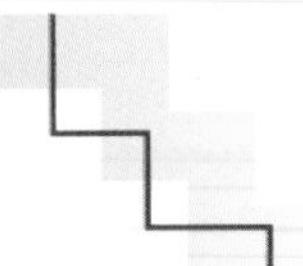

MISSTEP

Pressure defense prevents you and your teammates from getting open to receive a pass.

CORRECTION

When your defender overplays you and denies you from receiving a pass, you should make a backdoor cut to the basket. When you see a defender denying your teammate from receiving a pass, you should automatically flash.

Give-and-Go

The give-and-go is the most basic play in basketball. Give (pass) the ball to your teammate and then go (cut) to the basket, looking to receive a return pass for a layup. Read and set up your defender with a well-timed fake before the cut. Fake as if you are not involved in the play by taking a step or two away from the ball. Then, as your defender moves with you, change direction sharply and use a front cut to the basket. Another way to fake is by taking a step or two toward the ball as if you are going to set a screen for or take a handoff from the player with the ball. As your defender moves with you, you should change direction sharply and make a backdoor cut behind (refer to figures 10.4 and 10.5, beginning on page 260). Figure 11.9 shows a five-player give-and-go offensive pattern.

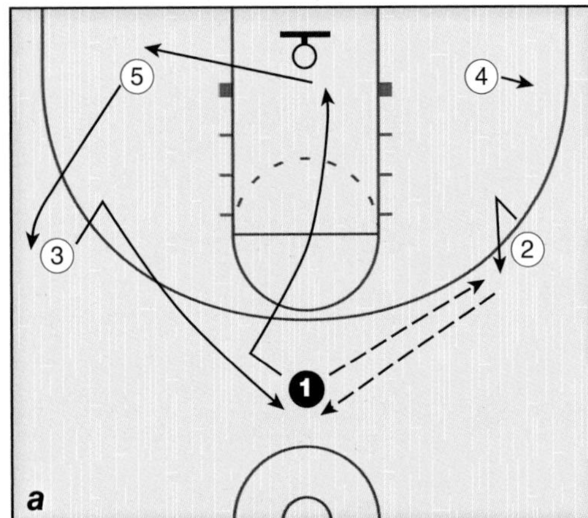

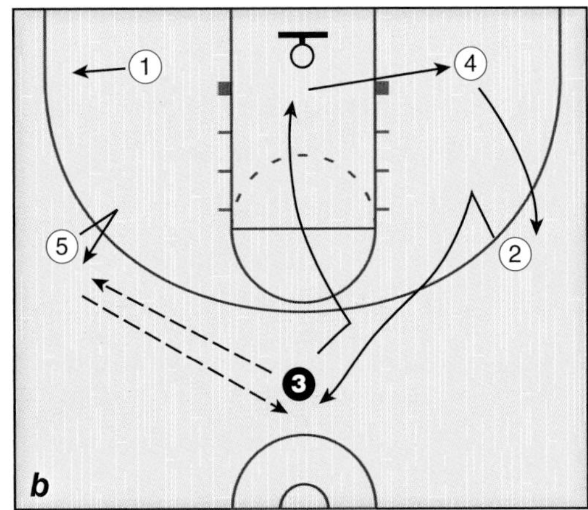

Figure 11.9 Five-player give-and-go: *(a)* To start the give-and-go, the point player (1) passes to wing 2 and cuts to the basket. The weak-side wing (3) quickly replaces the point and receives the pass from 2. *(b)* Player 3 passes to opposite wing 5 (who has replaced 3) and cuts to the basket. The weak-side wing (2) quickly replaces the point and receives the pass from 5. Player 4 replaces player 2 at the wing, and cutter 3 replaces 4.

Give-and-Go Drill. **Five-on-Zero, No Dribble**

This drill requires five players. Set up in a 3-2 open set with three perimeter players and two baseline players. This is the most basic formation and is good for learning to play team offense. Run the give-and-go (pass-and-cut) offense against an imaginary defense. The offense may not dribble the ball except on a drive to the basket.

A team member, usually the point guard, signals the start of the offense with a simple verbal call, such as "Pass and cut!" or "Give and go!" When the ball is at the point, the closest wing player should initiate movement by cutting through to the basket. This creates an open area at the wing for the baseline player to cut to for a pass from the point. When the baseline player cuts to the wing, the wing player who had cut to the basket moves to the open area at the baseline. After passing the ball to the wing, the point cuts to the basket, looking to receive a return pass for a layup.

Use your imagination, deception, and timing before cutting. Set up a fake either by taking a step or two away from the ball or by taking a step or two toward the ball before sharply changing direction and cutting to the basket. As you cut to the basket, the weak-side wing replaces you at the point, and the weak-side corner replaces the weak-side wing.

After receiving a pass on the wing, be a triple threat. The wing may make a bounce pass to a player cutting to the basket, pass to the player now occupying the point, or drive to the basket. If the ball is passed to the point, the cutter moves to the corner position that has been vacated.

Continue the drill with the player at the point passing to either wing, cutting to the basket, and having the wing fake a pass to the cutter before passing back to the point. Make at least five passes before passing to the cutter or driving to the basket. On a drive from the wing, you can look to score, or you can draw and kick to a teammate. Again, use your imagination! At times, assume defensive pressure and use the backdoor cut and flash backdoor options. Continue the drill for a total of 30 passes and 6 layups without error.

Success Check

- Communicate verbally with teammates by using key words.
- When in possession of the ball, be a triple threat to pass, drive, or shoot.
- Imagine the presence of the defense, and use fakes to get open or help a teammate get open.
- Pass at least five times before driving to the basket.

Score Your Success

25 to 30 consecutive passes and 6 layups without error = 5 points

20 to 24 consecutive passes and 5 layups without error = 3 points

15 to 19 consecutive passes and 3 layups without error = 1 point

Fewer than 15 consecutive passes and 3 layups without error = 0 points

Your score ___

Give-and-Go Drill. **Five-on-Two, No Dribble**

This drill requires 10 players divided into two teams of 5 players each. One team is on offense, and the other is on defense. Select two players from the defensive team to play defense on two selected players from the offensive team. The other three defenders are not on the court at this time. Only the defended players are allowed to score. This drill gives the two defended offensive players practice in moving without the ball (e.g., cutting backdoor), and all players practice in flashing backdoor.

Use a backdoor cut automatically any time a defender overplays and prevents you from receiving a pass. Use a designated key word such as *eyeball!* to indicate to the passer that you are going backdoor. A flash and backdoor cut is also effective against a defender denying a teammate from catching the ball when you are the next closest player. Flash to an open area between the passer and the overplayed receiver. As you flash, signal your cut with the key word *flash!* Catch the ball and look for your overplayed teammate, who should make a backdoor cut toward the basket.

The offensive team may not dribble the ball. If the ball touches the floor on a missed or deflected pass, this is not counted as a dribble. The offensive team is awarded 1 point for a made basket. The defensive team is awarded 1 point for each steal, turnover, or defensive rebound. Change from offense to defense after a made basket or after the defense obtains possession. Rotate in new defensive players after each made basket or after the defense obtains possession. Play to 3 points.

Success Check

- Communicate verbally with teammates by using key words.
- Read the defenders and use fakes to get open or help a teammate get open.
- Only the players who are defended can score.

Score Your Success

This is a competitive drill. The first team to score 3 points wins the game. Give yourself 5 points if your team wins the game.

Your score ___

Give-and-Go Drill. **Five-on-Five, No Dribble**

This drill requires 10 players divided into two teams of 5 players each. One team will play offense, and the other will play defense.

The offense may not dribble the ball. If the ball touches the floor on a missed or deflected pass, this is not counted as a dribble. This drill gives the offense practice at moving without the ball and using the give-and-go, backdoor cut, and flash backdoor. When the defensive team is instructed to pressure the ball and deny all passes, the drill also becomes an extremely challenging team defensive drill.

The offensive team gets 1 point each time it scores. If the defense commits a foul, the offense gets the ball and starts again. If an offensive player misses a shot and a teammate gets an offensive rebound, play continues. The defense gets 1 point if it gets the ball on a steal or rebound or if it forces a violation. Play to 5 points. Teams then switch roles.

Success Check

- The offense may not dribble the ball.
- Communicate verbally with teammates.
- Read the defenders and use the right move to get open.

Score Your Success

This is a competitive drill. The first team to score 5 points wins the game. Give yourself 5 points if your team wins the game.

Your score ___

Dribble Screen or Weave

A dribble screen is set by dribbling toward a teammate and screening the defender while handing off the ball to the teammate (refer to figures 10.14 through 10.17, beginning on page 283). On a dribble screen, the defensive reaction will usually be for the screener's defender to give defensive help or switch.

Before receiving the handoff, you must read the defensive positioning. If your defender attempts to prevent the handoff by getting in your path, you should make a backdoor cut to the basket. After you receive a handoff on a dribble screen, you must again read the defense. If the defenders do not switch and your defender is slow getting over the screen, you should turn the corner and drive to the basket. If your defender slides behind the screen, you should look to take the outside shot. If your teammate's defender switches to you as you receive the handoff for an outside shot, you should go at least two dribbles past the screen and pass back to the screener, who is either rolling to the basket or popping out.

One way to defend the dribble screen is for the dribble screener's defender to use a jump switch. The jump switch is an aggressive early switch before the receiver gets to the screen. The defender jumps into the path of the receiver with the intent of drawing a charge or changing the direction of the player receiving the ball. To combat the jump switch after the handoff, make a short 5- to 10-foot (1.5 to 3 m) cut to an open area and look for a quick return pass. If you anticipate a jump switch, fake the handoff and drive to the basket.

Another way the defense may try to overcome the dribble screen is for both defenders to trap the player receiving the ball on the handoff. If the defenders trap you, you should use at least two retreat dribbles to stretch the defense. You can then pass to your teammate, who is making a short 5- to 10-foot (1.5 to 3 m) cut to an open area. The defense will then be outnumbered, and the player with the ball will be able to drive or pass to an open teammate for a shot.

The dribble screen is used to execute a weave, which is a basic play in basketball. A weave (figure 11.10) involves at least three players who set dribble screens for each other. It starts with your teammate setting a dribble screen and handing off to you. After receiving the handoff, you can shoot from behind the screen, drive to the basket, or continue the weave by dribbling toward another teammate for another dribble screen and handoff. The weave continues until you or a teammate can take advantage of an opening for a shot or drive to the basket.

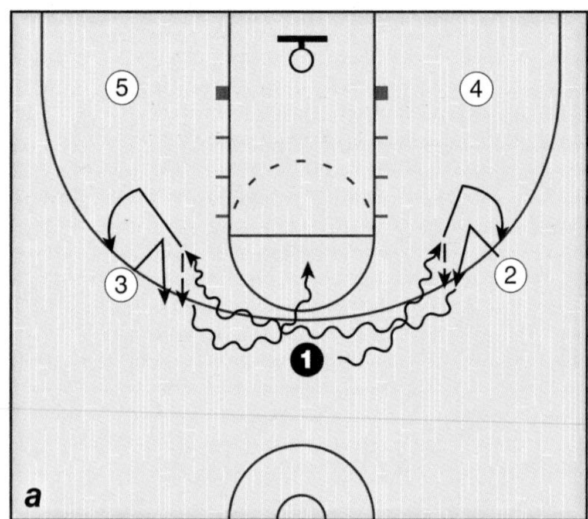

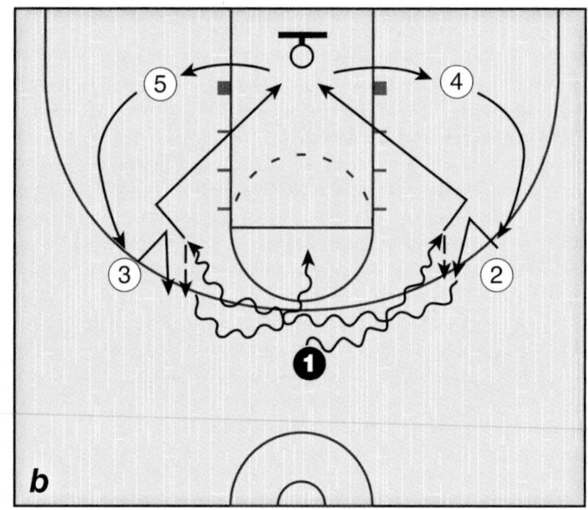

Figure 11.10 Dribble screen: *(a)* three-player weave; *(b)* five-player weave.

Weave Drill. **Five-on-Zero Weave**

This drill requires five players. Set up in a 3-2 open set, or spread formation, with three perimeter players and two baseline players. Run a weave offense against an imaginary defense.

A member of the team, usually the point guard, signals the start of the weave with a simple verbal call such as "Weave!" or "Figure!" The point guard initiates the weave by dribbling to the inside of one of the wings. The wing should create an opening by faking away and then cutting to the outside of the dribbler for a handoff. The point guard hands off and cuts to the basket, looking to receive a return pass for a layup.

Use imagination, deception, and timing before cutting. As the point player cuts to the basket, the weak-side wing replaces the point, and the weak-side corner replaces the weak-side wing. After receiving the handoff, the wing should be a triple threat. The wing can either bounce pass to the cutter, shoot, drive, or continue the weave by dribbling to the inside of the player now occupying the point. If the weave is continued, the cutter moves to the vacated corner position.

Continue the weave, making at least five handoffs before passing to a player cutting or driving to the basket. When you drive or receive a pass on a cut, you can look to score, or you can draw and kick to a teammate. Use your imagination to mix in various offensive options off the weave. You might assume that your defender is attempting to get in your path to prevent the handoff. In that case, you should make a backdoor cut before the handoff. After the handoff, you might assume that the defense is jump switching or trapping. You can then make a short 5- to 10-foot (1.5 to 3 m) cut to an open area, look for a quick return pass, and drive to the basket. Continue the drill for a total of 30 handoffs and 6 layups without error.

Success Check

- Make at least five handoffs before driving to the basket.
- Communicate verbally with teammates.
- Imagine various defensive tactics and use fakes and moves to overcome them.

Score Your Success

25 to 30 consecutive handoffs and 6 layups without error = 5 points

20 to 24 consecutive handoffs and 5 layups without error = 3 points

15 to 19 consecutive handoffs and 3 layups without error = 1 point

Fewer than 15 consecutive handoffs and 3 layups without error = 0 points

Your score ___

Weave Drill. **Five-on-Five Weave**

This drill requires 10 players divided into two teams of 5 players each. One team plays offense, and the other plays defense.

This drill gives the offense practice in executing the weave against various defensive strategies. Practice different defensive options against the weave, such as opening up and sliding, pressuring the ball and denying all passes, jump switching, and trapping. The offensive team gets 1 point each time it scores. If the defense commits a foul, the offense gets the ball and starts again. If an offensive player misses a shot and a teammate gets an offensive rebound, play continues. The defense gets 1 point if it gets the ball on a steal or rebound or if it forces the offense into a violation. Play to 5 points. Teams then switch roles.

Success Check

- Communicate verbally with teammates during the weave.
- Read the defenders and react to how they are playing the weave.
- Have the rim and the players on the court in view.

Score Your Success

This is a competitive drill. The first team to score 5 points wins the game. Give yourself 5 points if your team wins the game.

Your score ___

Down Screen

A screen set by a player toward the baseline for a teammate is called a down screen. By setting a down screen for a teammate, you create a scoring opportunity. Your teammate can cut off your down screen to get open to receive a pass for a shot or drive. If your defender switches to your cutting teammate, you will be on the ball side of the defender you screened, and you will be open momentarily. Taking a few steps toward the basket before setting the screen enables you to get a better angle on the defender. You want the defender to go under the pick. As you set the down screen, communicate with your teammate by using a designated key word such as *down!*

Use one of the four basic options for cutting off a screen, depending on how it is defended: pop-out, curl, backdoor cut, or fade (see figures 10.6 through 10.9, beginning on page 266). Be patient. Wait until the screen is set. This will prevent an illegal moving block and will enable you to read how the defense is playing the screen. Before using the screen, slowly set up your move off it. Set a good angle for cutting off the screen by first moving slowly in the direction your defender plays you and then cutting hard off the screen in the opposite direction. Cut far enough away from the screen so that one defender cannot guard both you and the screener. This creates space for a pass to the screener if there is a defensive switch.

When you cut off a screen correctly, the screener's defender will usually give defensive help or switch. If you cut to the outside, the screener will be free to roll in toward the basket and receive a pass for an inside shot (figure 11.11). If you curl to the basket, the screener becomes free to pop to the midpoint and receive a pass for an outside shot.

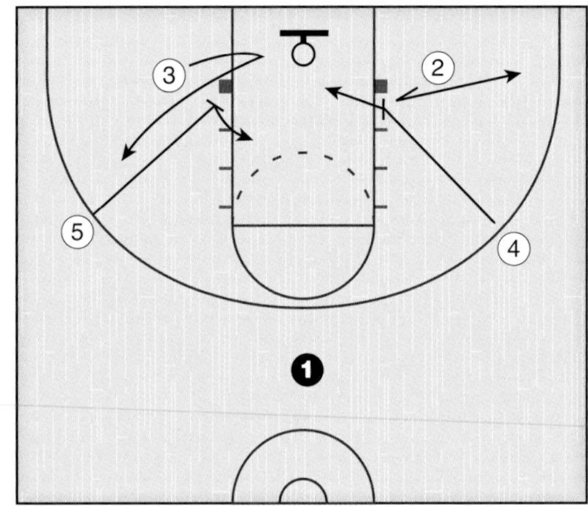

Figure 11.11 Down screen, pop and fade options: Players 5 and 4 set down screens for players 3 and 2. Cutter 3 pops out, and screener 5 rolls. Cutter 2 fades, and screener 4 cuts to the basket.

MISSTEP

Fouls are called on you and your teammates for setting illegal screens.

CORRECTION

Be patient. When setting a screen, use a jump stop to avoid moving when your teammate uses your screen. When a screen is being set for you, wait until it is set before using it. You can be late to cut or dribble off a screen, but you should never be early. Waiting for the screen to be set prevents an illegal moving screen and gives you time to read the defense.

Elbow Curl

When you pass and then screen away for a teammate positioned at the elbow, your teammate should look to curl off your screen. As your teammate curls off your screen at the elbow (figure 11.12), your defender will usually give defensive help or switch. This momentarily frees you to pop out and receive a pass for a jump shot. The screen away at the elbow is often used when a smaller player sets the screen for a bigger player. The bigger player can curl to the basket, and the smaller player can pop out for a catch-and-shoot jump shot. To set the screen at the elbow, again take a few steps toward the basket to get a better angle on the defender. Signal to your teammate to curl off your screen by shouting the key word *curl!*

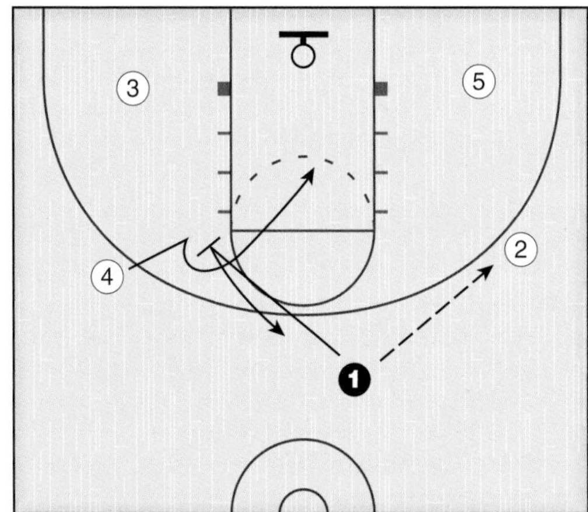

Figure 11.12 Elbow curl: Player 1 passes to player 2 and sets a screen at the weak-side elbow for player 4. Player 4 curls to the basket, and screener 1 pops out to receive a pass for a jump shot.

Back Pick

When you screen for a teammate by setting a pick behind the teammate's defender, this is called a *back pick* or *up screen* (figure 11.13). By setting a back pick for a teammate, you create the opportunity for either the teammate or you to score. Your teammate can cut off your back pick to get open to receive a pass for a layup or drive. If your defender switches to the cutter, you will be on the ball side of your teammate's defender, free to pop out to the ball to receive a pass for a jump shot. Before setting the screen, take a few steps toward the basket to get a better angle on the defender you will back pick, communicating to your teammate by shouting a designated key word such as *up!*

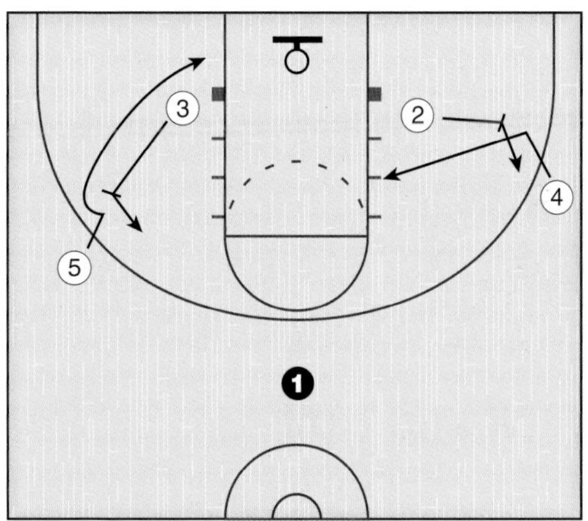

Figure 11.13 Back pick: Players 2 and 3 set back picks for players 4 and 5. Cutter 5 goes backdoor, and screener 3 pops out. Cutter 4 makes a front cut, and screener 2 pops out.

Make sure you set a legal screen. With a back pick, you are not allowed to be closer than a normal step from a stationary opponent if that opponent is unaware of your screen. In addition, you may not be so close that a moving opponent cannot avoid contact without changing direction or stopping. Your opponent's speed determines what your screening position should be. This position will vary and might be one or two normal steps away.

As with the down screen, you should wait until the back pick is set before cutting off it. This prevents an illegal screen and enables you to read the defense. Slowly set up a good angle for your move off the screen before you cut hard off it in the opposite direction. If you cut to the basket with a front cut or backdoor cut, the screener will be free to pop out and receive a pass for an outside shot. If you fake a cut to the basket and pop out, or if you fake to receive a pass for an outside shot, the screener should cut to the basket. The four basic options for cutting off a back pick (depending on how it is defended) are the front cut, backdoor cut, pop-out, and fade.

Cross Screen

A cross screen (figure 11.14) is set by starting on one block and screening across the lane for a teammate at the opposite block. On a cross screen, the screener's defender usually reacts by giving defensive help or switching. When you cut off a cross screen, you should read the defensive positioning and cut either over or under the screen. When you set a cross screen and your teammate cuts low to the block by cutting over or under the cross screen, you should pop out high to the elbow area and receive a pass for an outside shot. If your teammate flashes high to the elbow to receive a pass for an outside shot, you should roll back to the ball-side block.

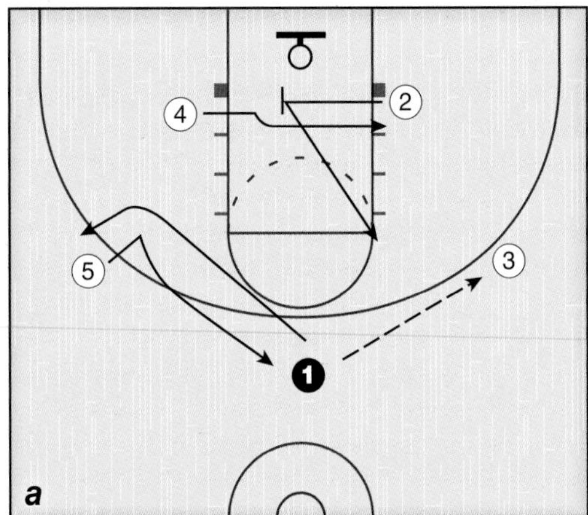

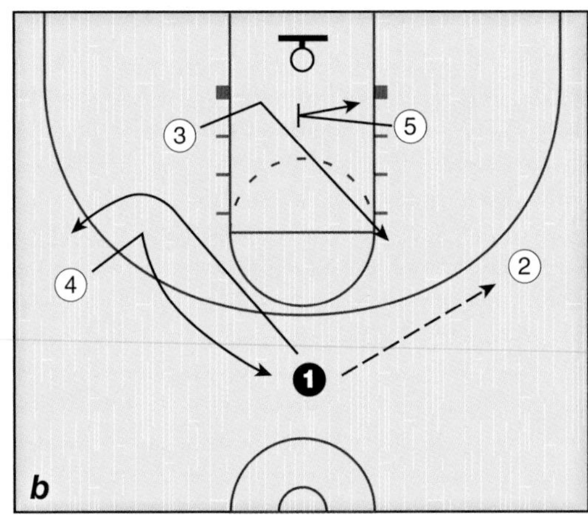

Figure 11.14 Cross screen: *(a)* Player 2 sets a cross screen for player 4. Cutter 4 cuts low to the block, and screener 2 rolls high. *(b)* Player 5 sets a cross screen for player 3. Cutter 3 cuts high, and screener 5 rolls low to the block.

Pick-and-Roll

The pick-and-roll (figure 11.15), which is another basic basketball play, gets its name from the action. You set a pick (screen) for your teammate, who dribbles past it for an outside shot or drive. If your defender switches to your teammate, you will momentarily be inside the defender you screened and will be free to roll toward the basket, looking to receive a return pass from the dribbler for a layup. Four options with the pick-and-roll, depending on how it is defended, are pick-and-roll, pick-and-pop, slip the pick (early release), and stretch the trap (see figures 10.10 through 10.13, beginning on page 273). Figure 11.15 shows the basic option when defenders switch.

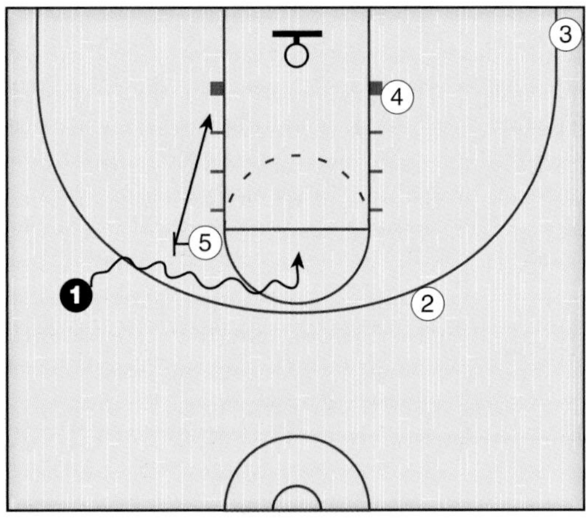

Figure 11.15 Pick-and-roll: Player 5 sets a pick for player 1 and rolls to the basket.

Draw-and-Kick

In today's game, a great emphasis is placed on players driving to the basket to score inside or pass back out to a teammate for a three-point shot. When you penetrate past a defender and a teammate's defender leaves to give defensive help on you, an open passing lane to your teammate is created. This action of penetrating and passing is called the draw-and-kick. Always be alert for an opportunity to drive past a defender to score or create an open shot for a teammate whose defender is drawn to you. Also look for an opening or gap between two defenders that will enable you to penetrate the gap with one or two dribbles and draw the defenders to you.

Effective use of the draw-and-kick depends on correctly judging when and where to penetrate. But it also depends on players without the ball moving to open spots. Because the motion offense depends primarily on moving the ball, overdribbling becomes counterproductive. The draw-and-kick is best used from the wing after a swing of the ball from ball side to weak side. Options for a penetrating player include driving to the basket, shooting an in-between runner or pull-up jump shot, penetrating and passing inside (draw and kick in; figure 11.16), and penetrating and passing outside (draw and kick out; figure 11.17).

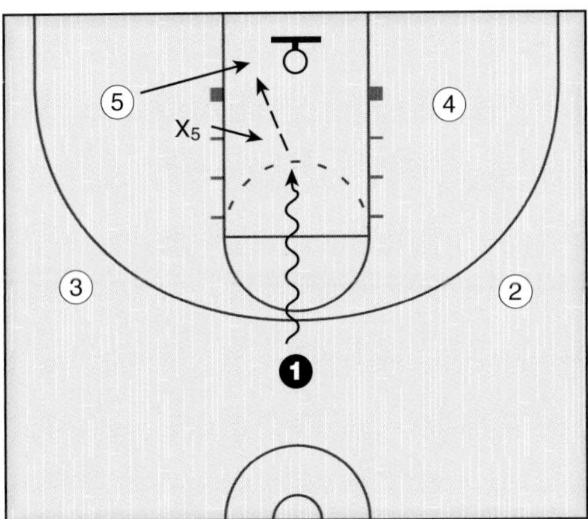

Figure 11.16 Draw and kick in: Player 1 penetrates, drawing the defender off player 5, and then passes (kicks in) to player 5, who is cutting to the basket.

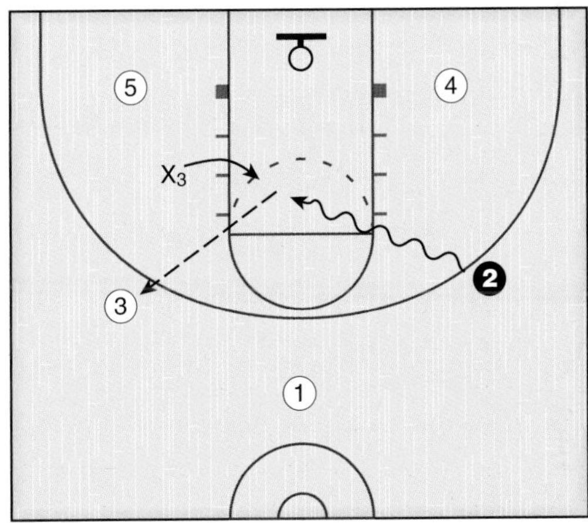

Figure 11.17 Draw and kick out: Player 2 penetrates, drawing the defender off player 3, and then passes (kicks out) to player 3, who is spotting up outside.

MISSTEP

You and your teammates overuse the dribble without a plan. You do not move the ball enough—and players do not move enough—to break down the defense.

CORRECTION

The motion offense is most effective when there is both ball and player movement. Too much dribbling is counterproductive. Reverse the ball to the weak-side wing before using the draw-and-kick.

Motion Drill. **Five-on-Zero**

This drill requires five players. Set up in a 3-2 open set, or spread formation, with three perimeter players and two baseline players. Run a motion offense against an imaginary defense.

One player, usually the point guard, signals the start of the drill with a simple verbal call such as "Motion!" or a hand signal such as circling one finger upward. The point passes the ball to the wing, and the players work together using basic actions of the motion offense. After receiving a pass on the wing, the wing should be a triple threat.

Continue the offense, making at least five passes before taking a shot. Use your imagination to mix in various offensive options, such as the backdoor cut, flash, give-and-go, weave, down screen, back pick, cross screen, screen away, pick-and-roll, and draw-and-kick. Work on the basic options for cutting off a screen: pop-out, curl, backdoor cut, and fake. Practice communicating by using designated key words such as *flash!, down!, cut!, up!, cross!, pick!,* and *weave!* Continue for a total of 30 passes and 6 made shots without error.

Success Check

- Communicate with teammates by using key words.
- Use various offensive options, including the backdoor cut, flash, give-and-go, weave, down screen, screen away, back pick, and cross screen.

Score Your Success

25 to 30 consecutive passes and 6 made shots without error = 5 points

20 to 24 consecutive passes and 4 made shots without error = 3 points

15 to 19 consecutive passes and 3 made shots without error = 1 point

Fewer than 15 consecutive passes and 3 made shots without error = 0 points

Your score ___

Motion Drill. **Five-on-Two**

This drill requires 10 players divided into two teams of 5 players each. One team plays offense, and the other plays defense. Select two players from the defensive team to play defense on two selected offensive players. The other three defenders are off the court. Only the defended players may score.

This drill focuses on the two defended offensive players as they practice executing various motion options and the basic options for cutting off a screen. Again, practice communicating to teammates with designated key words. The two defenders can practice pressuring the ball, strong-side denial, weak-side help, and combating screens with a slide, jump switch, or trap. Change from offense to defense after a made basket or after the defense obtains possession. Rotate in new defensive players after each made basket or after the defense obtains possession. The offense is awarded 1 point for each basket made by a defended player. The defense is awarded 1 point for each steal, turnover, or defensive rebound. Play to 5 points.

Success Check

- Communicate with teammates by using designated key words.
- On offense, use various options in the motion offense, and use various methods for cutting off a screen.
- On defense, work on pressuring the ball, strong-side denial, weak-side help, and beating screens.

Score Your Success

This is a competitive drill. The first team to score 5 points wins the game. Give yourself 5 points if your team wins the game.

Your score ___

Motion Drill. **Five-on-Five**

This drill requires two teams of five players each. One team plays offense, and the other plays defense.

The offensive team practices using various options within the motion offense and communicating with designated key words. The defense practices pressuring the ball, strong-side denial, weak-side help, and combating screens with help-and-recover, switch, or trap options.

The offensive team gets 1 point each time it scores. If the defense commits a foul, the offense gets the ball and starts again. If an offensive player misses a shot and a teammate gets an offensive rebound, play continues. The defense gets 1 point if it gets the ball on a steal or rebound or if it forces the offense into a violation. Play to 5 points. Teams then switch roles.

Success Check

- On offense, read the defense and use the correct option to create a good scoring opportunity.
- On defense, use various options to combat the screen and pressure the ball.
- Communicate with teammates by using key words.

Score Your Success

This is a competitive drill. The first team to score 5 points wins the game. Give yourself 5 points if your team wins the game.

Your score ___

PICK-AND-ROLL OFFENSE

As mentioned at the beginning of this step, greater emphasis is being placed on the open or spread offense, dribble penetration, and the ability to draw and kick to three-point shooters. The pick-and-roll (also called the ball screen) is one of the oldest plays in basketball, but it is now being used more than ever. The pick-and-roll has become popular as a method for gaining dribble penetration and then drawing and kicking—either kicking in to a player near the basket or kicking out to a three-point shooter.

At the professional level, the pick-and-roll has become a primary part of the offense for most teams. It has also become a part of college and high school play. *Pick-and-roll* is a broad term for many actions. In the pick-and-roll, the picker sets the pick and then rolls (cuts to the basket) for a possible inside shot off a pass from the ball handler. If the picker is a good shooter, a pick-and-pop may be used; this play has the picker popping out for an outside shot rather than rolling to the basket.

Pick-and-roll plays may be a part of a set offensive attack or a part of an early offense at the end of a fast break. Several types of pick-and-roll plays may be used, and they can take place in various spots on the court, including the top, side, elbow, and corner. The following are some common pick-and-roll plays.

High pick-and-roll. Refer to figure 11.18. Player 5 sets a pick at the top for player 1. Player 1 dribbles off the pick, forcing player 5's defender to give help. Player 1 takes at least two dribbles past the pick to create space. Player 1 can then shoot a jump shot, pass to player 5 rolling to the basket, pass to player 4 cutting up to the weak-side elbow, pass to player 2 in the strong-side corner, or pass to player 3 in the weak-side corner.

High pick-and-pop. See figure 11.19. Player 4 sets a pick at the top for player 1. Player 1 dribbles off the pick, forcing player 4's defender to give help. Player 1 takes at least two dribbles past the pick to create space. Player 1 can then shoot a jump shot, pass to player 4 popping to the weak-side elbow area, pass to player 5 cutting to the strong-side low post, pass to player 2 in the strong-side corner, or pass to player 3 in the weak-side corner.

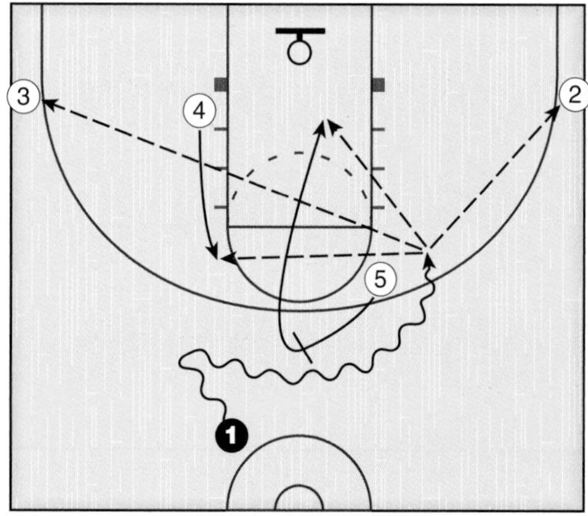

Figure 11.18 High pick-and-roll.

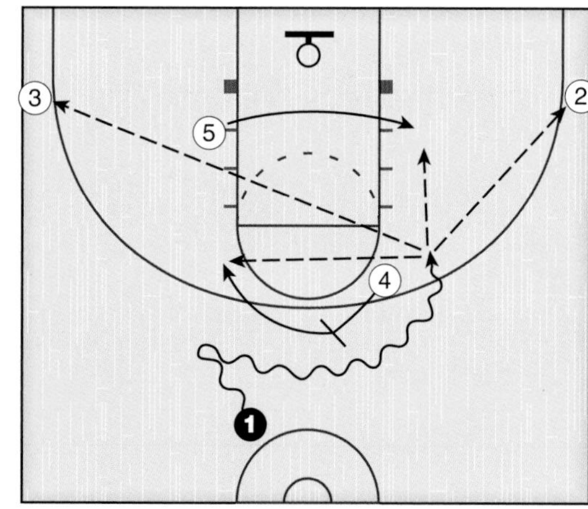

Figure 11.19 High pick-and-pop.

Side pick-and-roll. In figure 11.20, player 4 sets a pick at the wing for player 1. Player 1 dribbles off the pick, forcing player 4's defender to give help. Player 1 takes at least two dribbles past the pick to create space. Player 1 can then shoot a jump shot, pass to player 4 rolling to the basket, or pass to one of the other players (2, 3, or 5) set up in a triangle formation on the weak side.

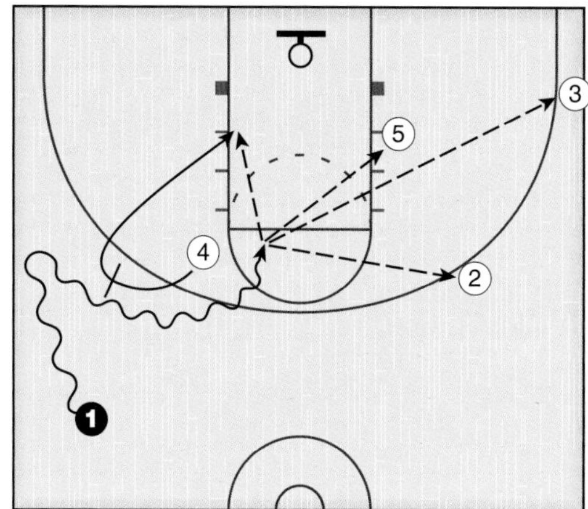

Figure 11.20 Side pick-and-roll.

Side pick-and-pop. See figure 11.21. Player 4 sets a pick at the wing for player 1. Player 1 dribbles off the pick, forcing player 4's defender to give help. Player 1 takes at least two dribbles past the pick to create space. Player 1 can then shoot a jump shot, pass to player 4 popping to the corner, pass to player 5 ducking into the lane, or pass to player 2 or 3 spaced out on the weak-side perimeter.

Elbow pick-and-roll. In figure 11.22, player 4 sets a pick at the elbow for player 1. Player 1 dribbles off the pick, forcing player 4's defender to give help. Player 1 takes at least two dribbles past the pick to create space. Player 1 can then shoot a jump shot, pass to player 4 rolling to the basket, pass to player 5 ducking into the lane, or pass to player 2 or 3 spaced out on the weak-side perimeter.

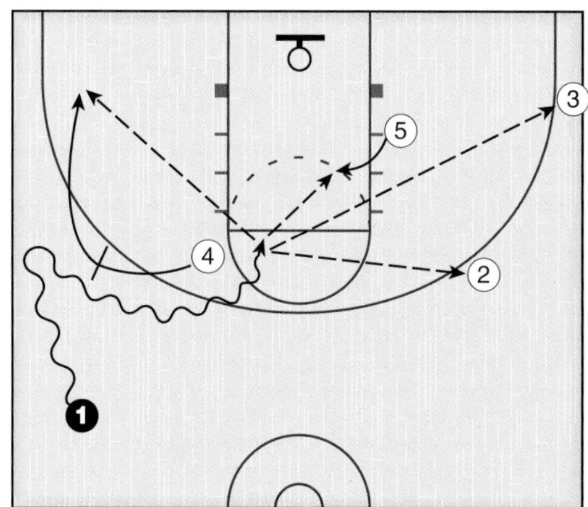

Figure 11.21 Side pick-and-pop.

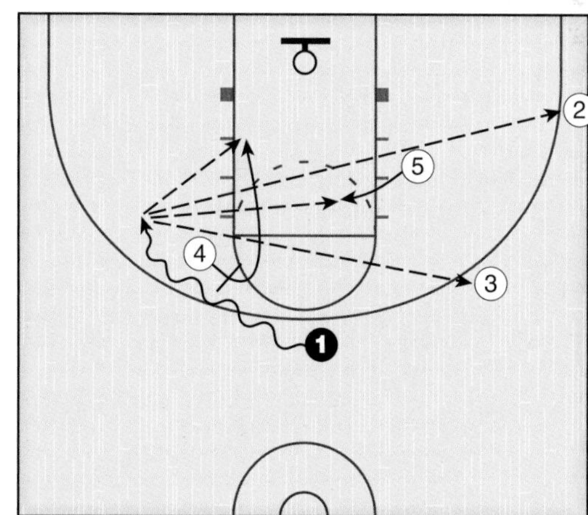

Figure 11.22 Elbow pick-and-roll.

Elbow pick-and-roll to high-low. Refer to figure 11.23. Players 4 and 5 set picks at each elbow. Player 1 dribbles off player 4's pick, forcing player 4's defender to give help. Player 1 takes at least two dribbles past the pick to create space for a pass to player 4 rolling to the basket or to player 5 popping high to the top. When the pass is made to player 5 at the top, player 5 looks first to pass to player 4 posting low in front of the basket; player 5 may also shoot a jump shot. Players 2 and 3 position themselves in each corner to spread the floor.

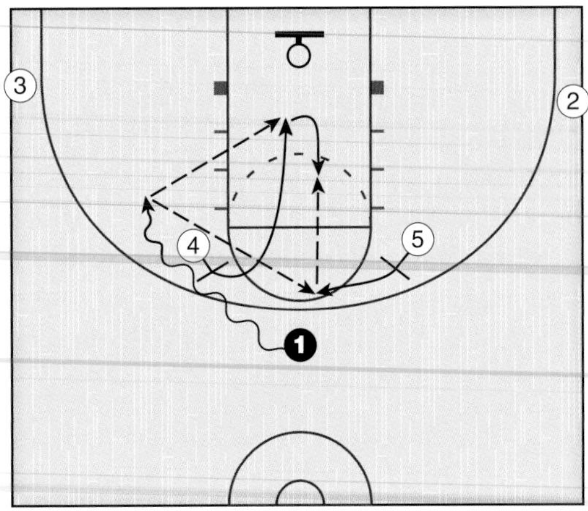

Figure 11.23 Elbow pick-and-roll to high-low.

MISSTEP

You fail to create space when dribbling by the pick, thus allowing the help defender to defend you and the pass back to the picker.

CORRECTION

You must take at least two dribbles past the pick to create space for a pass back to the picker.

Pick-and-roll plays may also be a part of an early offense at the end of a fast break. Various early-offense plays use the pick-and-roll in different spots on the court, including the top, side, corner, and elbow. The following are some common early-offense pick-and-roll plays:

Early drag (pick-and-roll). Refer to figure 11.24. Player 5 sets a pick at the top or side for player 1. Player 1 dribbles off the pick, forcing player 5's defender to give help. Player 1 takes at least two dribbles past the pick to create space. Player 1 can then shoot a jump shot, pass to player 5 rolling to the basket, or pass to player 2, 3, or 4 spaced out on the perimeter.

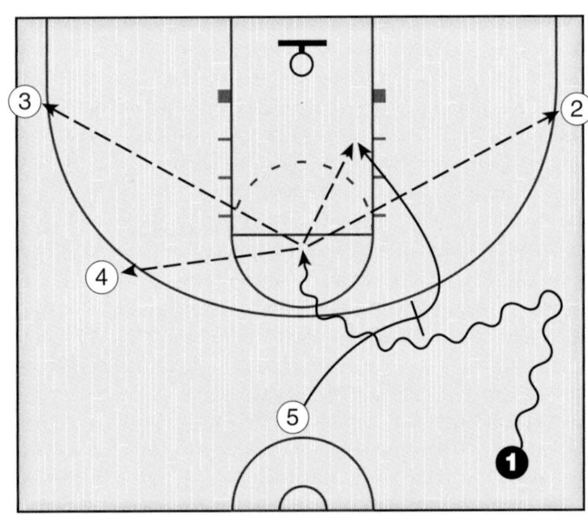

Figure 11.24 Early drag (pick-and-roll).

Early dribble drag (pick-and-roll). In figure 11.25, player 1 makes a dribble handoff to player 2. Player 5 sets a pick at the top or side for player 2. Player 2 dribbles off the pick, forcing player 5's defender to give help. Player 2 takes at least two dribbles past the pick to create space. Player 2 can then shoot a jump shot, pass to player 5 rolling to the basket, or pass to player 3 or 4 spaced out on the perimeter.

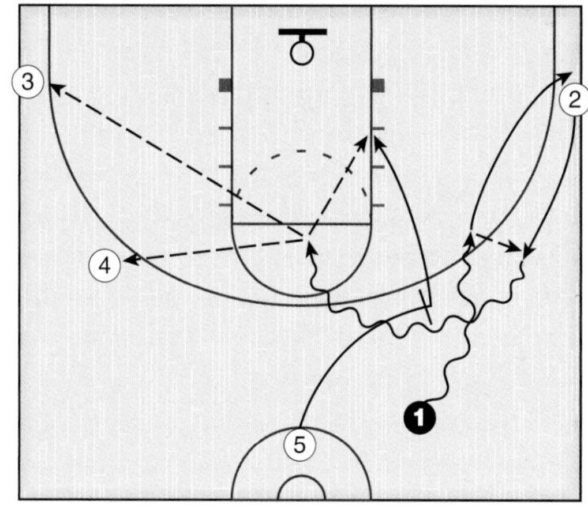

Figure 11.25 Early dribble drag (pick-and-roll).

Early double drag (pick-and-roll and pick-and-pop). See figure 11.26. Players 5 and 4 set picks at the top or side for player 1. Player 1 dribbles off the picks, forcing player 5's and player 4's defenders to give help. Player 1 takes at least two dribbles past player 4's pick to create space. Player 1 can then shoot a jump shot, pass to player 5 rolling to the basket, pass to player 4 popping to the elbow, or pass to player 2 in the corner.

Early wing pick-and-roll. Refer to figure 11.27. Player 1 passes to player 2 and cuts outside player 2 to the corner. Player 5 sets a pick at the wing for player 2. Player 2 dribbles off player 5's pick, forcing player 5's defender to give help. Player 2 takes at least two dribbles past the pick to create space. Player 2 can then shoot a jump shot, pass to player 5 rolling to the basket, or pass to player 1, 3, or 4 spaced out on the perimeter.

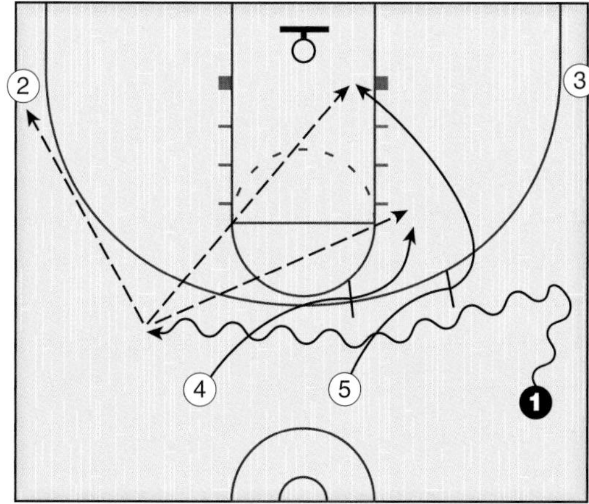

Figure 11.26 Early double drag (pick-and-roll and pick-and-pop).

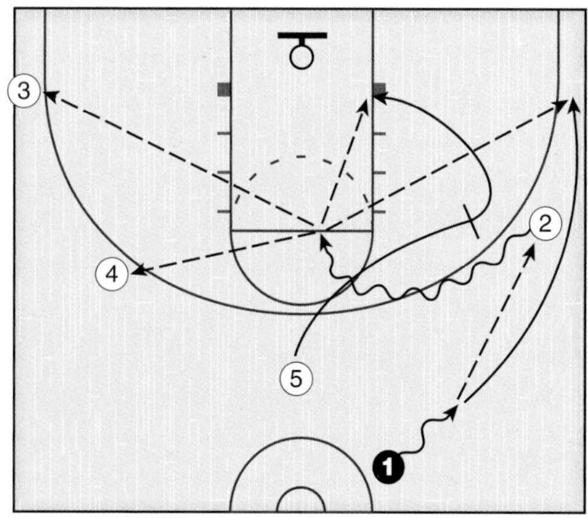

Figure 11.27 Early wing pick-and-roll.

Early step-up to pick-picker pick flare. See figure 11.28. Player 2 sets a step-up pick above the wing for player 1. Player 1 dribbles off player 2's pick, forcing player 2's defender to give help. Player 5 sets a pick at the wing for player 2 (called *pick the picker*). Player 2 flares off player 5's pick, forcing player 5's defender to give help. Player 1 passes to player 2. Player 2 looks to shoot a jump shot, pass to player 5 rolling to the basket, or pass to player 1, 3, or 4 spaced out on the perimeter.

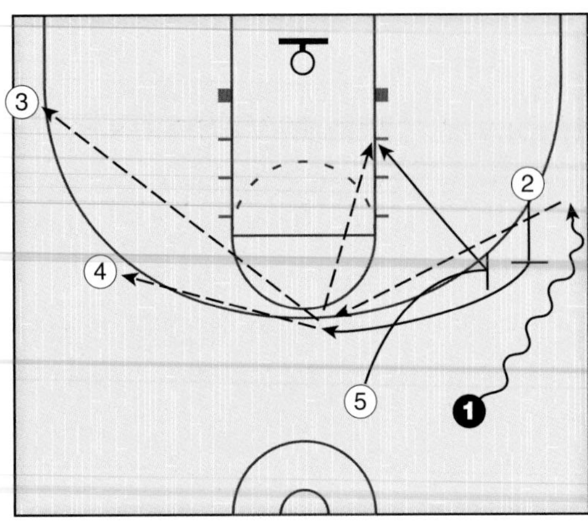

Figure 11.28 Early step-up to pick-picker pick flare.

Early step-up pick to corner pick-and-roll. In figure 11.29, player 2 sets a step-up pick above the wing for player 1. Player 1 dribbles off player 2's pick, forcing player 2's defender to give help. Player 1 continues to dribble to the corner. Player 5 sets a pick at the corner for player 1. Player 1 dribbles off player 5's pick, forcing player 5's defender to give help. Player 1 looks to shoot a jump shot, pass to player 5 rolling to the basket, pass to player 4 cutting to the weak-side post area, or pass to player 2 or 3 spaced out on the perimeter.

Early backdoor to corner pick-and-roll. Refer to figure 11.30. Player 2 cuts backdoor. If player 2 gets open on the backdoor cut, player 1 will pass to player 2. If player 2 is not open, player 2 continues to cut to the weak-side corner, and player 1 continues to dribble toward the strong-side corner. Player 5 sets a pick near the corner for player 1. Player 1 dribbles off player 5's pick, forcing player 5's defender to give help. Player 1 looks to shoot a jump shot, pass to player 5 rolling to the basket, or pass to player 2, 3, or 4 spaced out on the perimeter.

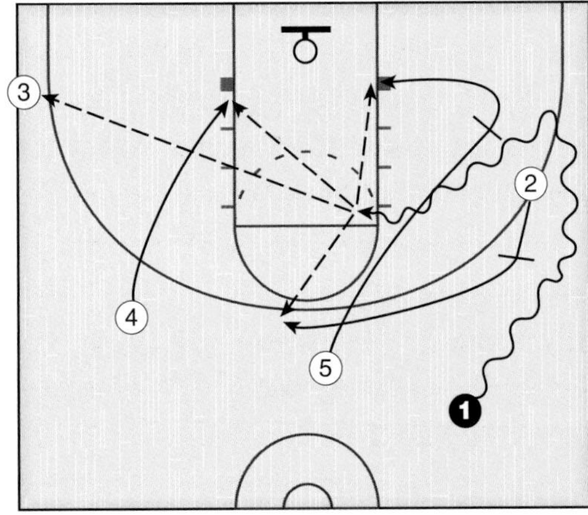

Figure 11.29 Early step-up pick to corner pick-and-roll.

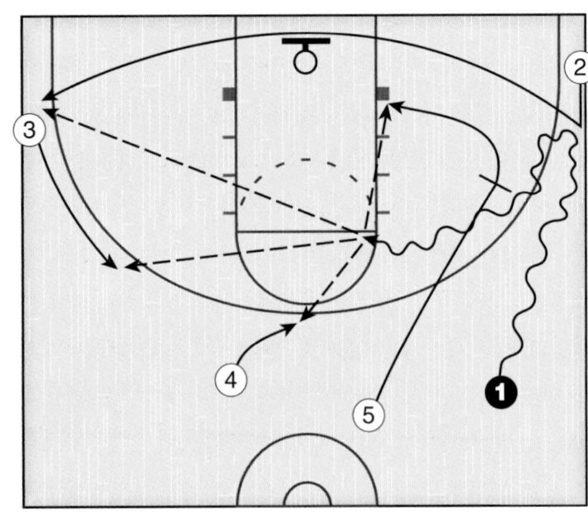

Figure 11.30 Early backdoor to corner pick-and-roll.

ZONE OFFENSE

In zone defenses, defenders are assigned to a designated area of the court rather than an individual offensive opponent. When you attack zone defenses, you should understand the type of zone you are playing against. Different zones employ different strategies, from sagging inside to pressuring outside shots, overplaying passing lanes, or trapping the ball. Zone defenses are named according to the alignment of players from the top toward the basket; these alignments include the 2-1-2, 2-3, 1-2-2, 3-2, and 1-3-1 zones.

Several common set offenses are used against zones. One method of attacking a zone is to use an offset alignment. Attack a zone that has an even front (two players) with an odd front (one player), and vice versa. This allows you to get into the gaps or seams of the zone—the areas between defensive players—where the defenders may be indecisive or late in covering. Other set attacks against the zone include sending a cutter or cutters through to open areas on the weak side and inside and overloading a zone area.

The basic principles for attacking zones are more important than those for a set zone offense that includes plays and options that can be diagrammed because knowing the basic principles will help in any set zone offense.

- **Fast break.** Beat the zone upcourt and attack it before the defenders get to their zone positions.
- **Use good spacing.** Spread the zone. Three-point shooters should spot up behind the three-point line.
- **Move the ball.** The ball can move faster than the zone can shift. Pass the ball from the ball side to the weak side. Move the ball inside, then out.
- **Reverse the ball.** Pass the ball to make the defense move in one direction, then quickly reverse the ball back (snap-back pass) to the opposite side.
- **Be a triple threat.** Square up to the basket and be a threat to score. Make use of shot fakes and pass fakes.
- **Split the zone.** Outside players should move into the gaps or seams of the zone (between defenders) and within shooting range.
- **Draw and kick.** Penetrate between defenders to draw your teammate's defender to you and create an open passing lane to your teammate.
- **Use cuts.** Send a cutter or cutters through to the weak side or to the inside behind the defense. It is very difficult for the defense to have visual contact with both the ball and an offensive player cutting through and from behind.
- **Show patience, poise, and good shot selection.** When you are patient, the defense can become fatigued and make mistakes.
- **Attack the offensive boards.** Although the opponent's better rebounders can be positioned in the inside zone areas, they have a more difficult time matching up to block out aggressive offensive rebounders.

Zone Offense Shell Drill. **Draw and Kick**

This is a good offensive drill for working on establishing a triple-threat position and being able to draw and kick (penetrate and pass). Divide eight players into two teams of four players each, one offensive team and one defensive team. The defense sets up with two players on the elbows and two on the blocks. The offensive team starts with two guards at the top of the circle and two forwards at the wing positions. Any offensive player with the ball is allowed one penetrating dribble. When the defender nearest the ball moves to help stop penetration, the offensive player with the ball passes out to whichever player the help defender left. The offensive player receiving the pass should be a triple threat to shoot, pass, or drive.

The offensive team gets 1 point for each basket made. If the defense commits a foul, the offense gets the ball and starts again. If an offensive player misses a shot and a teammate gets an offensive rebound, play continues. The defense gets 1 point when it gets the ball on a steal or rebound or when it forces the offense into a violation. Play to 5 points. Teams then switch roles.

Success Check

- The offensive player who receives the pass must be a triple threat.
- The offensive player with the ball must be aware of which teammate is open when the defensive player moves to help stop the penetration.

Score Your Success

This is a competitive drill. The first team to score 5 points wins the game. Give yourself 5 points if your team wins the game.

Your score ___

RATE YOUR SUCCESS

After you master individual skills, you are ready to apply them in a team environment. Basketball is the ultimate team game, and a well-executed team offense will lead to more point production and better teamwork. In the next step, we will look in more detail at team defense. Before going to step 12, however, look back at how you performed the drills in this step. For each of the drills presented in this step, enter the points you earned, then add up your scores to rate your total success.

Give-and-Go Drills

1. Five-on-Zero, No Dribble ____ out of 5
2. Five-on-Two, No Dribble ____ out of 5
3. Five-on-Five, No Dribble ____ out of 5

Weave Drills

1. Five-on-Zero Weave ____ out of 5
2. Five-on-Five Weave ____ out of 5

Motion Drills

1. Five-on-Zero ____ out of 5
2. Five-on-Two ____ out of 5
3. Five-on-Five ____ out of 5

Zone Offense Shell Drill

1. Draw and Kick ____ out of 5

Total ____ **out of 45**

If you scored 25 or more points, congratulations! You have mastered the basics of this step and are ready to move on to the final step, team defense. If you scored fewer than 25 points, you may want to spend more time on the fundamentals covered in this step. Practice the drills again to develop mastery of the techniques and increase your scores.

STEP

12

Team Defense

You win with defense. Even more than skill, defense requires desire and intelligence. The best defensive players play with heart, giving maximum effort every second on the court. Defense is mostly desire, but the desire to play defense is limited by physical conditioning. As fatigue sets in, you lose your ability to execute skills, which leads to a more harmful loss in the desire to compete. You also have to be smart to play winning defense. Coaches look for good decision makers who will stay in position, avoid fouling, help teammates, and wisely choose their opportunities for charges, steals, and shot blocks.

Good defense inhibits an opponent by limiting uncontested open shots. Good team defense not only reduces scoring opportunities for an opponent, but also creates them for your team. An aggressive pressure defense leads to steals, interceptions, and missed shots that enable your team to create scoring opportunities. More often than not, steals and interceptions lead to high-percentage shots at the end of fast breaks.

Playing tough defense seldom brings the public acclaim afforded to successful offense, but most coaches recognize the value of defensive stoppers and tough team defense. You can make your team better by being a great defender, even if your offensive skills haven't developed. Defensive skills take less time to develop, but they require hard work.

Teams with less than average offensive talent can be successful by playing hard, intelligent team defense. Defense is more consistent than offense because it is based mostly on desire and effort, whereas offense is based on a high degree of skill. The ball might not be dropping for you in a given game, but with sufficient effort, you'll never have an off game defensively.

Striving on defense not only helps you become a better player, but also helps you contribute to your team's success. Enthusiasm, intelligence, and maximum effort on defense can be contagious. These characteristics can foster a greater team defensive effort and team spirit. The old saying is true: Defense wins championships.

FACTORS OF CHAMPIONSHIP DEFENSE

Great defense involves much more than skill. The factors that determine defensive success may be classified as emotional, mental, and physical.

Emotional

Desire. Wanting to play great defense is most important. Offense is mostly fun. Defense, while hard work, can also be fun as you stop what your opponent wants to do. Desire on defense is giving maximum effort and concentration on each play. Playing defense with intensity involves giving great effort in many areas—running full speed in transition from offense to defense, maintaining a defensive stance with your hands up at all times, drawing the charge, diving for loose balls, blocking out for defensive rebounds, and communicating with your teammates by using key words.

Discipline. Desire is a start, but you must discipline yourself to stick with your goal of becoming a great defensive player. The hard work of developing superior physical condition, practicing defensive skills, and playing tough defense in games requires continuous self-discipline. Defense cannot be part-time. Defense must be played hard all of the time. This takes discipline, and tough defenders have learned to appreciate and gain satisfaction from discipline.

Aggressiveness. Defense is a battle. In playing offense, you have the advantage of knowing what your next move will be. In playing defense, the tendency is to react to the offensive player's moves. This is a negative approach. Take the positive approach of being aggressive on defense, thereby forcing the offensive player to react to you. Being an aggressive defender means that you have the attitude to dominate your opponent in all ways. You do not allow the moves your opponent wants to make. You take the initiative. Aggressive defense forces your opponent to react to what you do. Examples of aggressive defense include pressuring the dribbler, fighting over the top of screens, pressuring the shooter, denying passes and going for interceptions, taking the charge, diving for loose balls, and rebounding missed shots.

Mental toughness. The physical demands of aggressive defense can exhaust even the most highly conditioned athlete. The progressive discomfort of defensive movements—plus the physical pain of fighting over screens, drawing the charge, diving for loose balls, and battling for rebounds—can take a toll. Being a mentally tough defender means overcoming this physical discomfort and pain. You bounce up from the floor each time you are knocked down. You do not need excessive encouragement from your coach. On the contrary, your mental toughness inspires others, including coaches, teammates, and fans.

Joe Murphy/NBAE/Getty Images

Shane Battier has become one of the best defenders in the NBA by being in great physical condition, playing with heart, and giving maximum effort on every defensive play. Here he stops Tracy McGrady of the Orlando Magic with a quick vertical jump and clean block.

Mental

Knowledge of your opponent. Successful defense requires analyzing your opponent and your opponent's team offense. Prepare by studying scouting reports, watching videos, and observing your opponent during the game's early stages. Judge your opponent's quickness and strength. Ask yourself questions. What are your opponent's offensive tendencies? Does your opponent want to shoot or drive? What are your opponent's offensive moves and which direction is favored on each? If your opponent is great with the ball, should you overplay, or does your opponent also move well without the ball? Maybe the place to be alert is in preventing your opponent from scoring on rebounds and loose balls near the basket.

From a team standpoint, would your opposition rather beat you on fast breaks or with a set offense? Which plays will the opposing team run against your team, and which plays will they run when they need a key basket? Who are their outside shooters, drivers, and post-up players?

Study both your individual opponent and the team. Know what your opponent does best—and work to take it away.

Anticipation. Anticipation is knowing tendencies and adjusting to each situation to gain an advantage. Playing offense gives you the advantage of knowing your next move, but in playing defense you must react to the offensive player's move—that is, you react unless you use anticipation. By knowing your opponent's tendencies, you can adjust accordingly and anticipate the next move. You should not guess on defense, but you should make a calculated move based on intelligent study of your individual opponent and the opponent's team.

Concentration. To concentrate is to focus completely on the assignment and not be distracted. Potential distractions include the opponent's trash talk, the actions of fans, an official's call, and your own negative thoughts. When you recognize that you are being distracted or are thinking negatively, interrupt the distraction by saying a key word to yourself, such as *stop!* Then replace the distraction with a positive statement to yourself. Concentrate on your defensive assignment, rather than allowing yourself to be distracted.

Alertness. Alertness involves being in a state of readiness at all times, able to react instantly. On the ball, you must be ready to defend your opponent's shot, drive, or pass. You must also remain alert to being screened. Off the ball, you should see the ball and your opponent. Be ready to stop a cut, defend a screen, go for an interception, dive for a loose ball, or rebound a missed shot.

Judgment. Judgment is the ability to size up the game situation and decide on the appropriate action. Numerous situations on defense call for good judgment. One example is deciding whether to pressure the ball on the perimeter or to drop back to prevent a pass inside. Another example is deciding whether to go for an interception or to play it safe. The decision will involve comparing your ability with your opponent's. You will also need to consider the tempo of the game, the score, and the time remaining. Using good defensive judgment is particularly important near the end of close games.

Physical

Physical condition. Physical condition is a prerequisite to good defense. Over the course of a game, your desire to compete will be proportional to your level of physical condition. The physical condition needed to play defense develops through specific physical conditioning programs and, even more, through expending great effort both in practice and games. Dominating an opponent requires strength, muscular endurance, and circulatory–respiratory endurance. Work to improve your total body strength so you can particularly withstand the body contact in defending a low-post player. You must also improve the muscular endurance of your legs. Being a good defensive player is not just about how quickly you can move but also whether you can move quickly throughout the game.

Quickness and balance. Quickness refers to speed of movement in performing a skill, not simply running speed. Moving your feet quickly is the most important physical skill for a defensive player, and you must develop this ability. Being able to change direction laterally is very important. Although many people consider it difficult to make great improvements in quickness, three factors can help. First, you can improve speed through hard work on defensive footwork drills and by jumping rope. Second, you can be mentally quick, using intelligence to anticipate your opponent's offensive moves, and thus get more quickly to the right place at the right time. Knowing and anticipating your opponent's moves can compensate for less physical quickness. Third, being balanced and under control is critical: Quickness without balance can be useless. Because defensive quickness involves the ability to start, stop, and change direction, you must also have control. Quickness under control, or quickness with balance, is essential to good defense.

PLAYING DEFENSE ON THE BALL

The most vital aspect of playing great defense is pressuring the dribbler. Pressuring the offensive point guard (and best ball handler) throughout the game prevents your opponent from focusing on running an offense.

Where on the court you will pick up the dribbler (e.g., full court, half-court, top of the circle) will be determined by team strategy. When you are guarding an opponent with the ball, you should maintain a position between your opponent and the basket. Strive to give ground grudgingly. Whenever possible, you should force your opponent to pick up (stop) the dribble. Then you can apply more pressure against a shot or a pass—with both your hands up.

Four basic positions can be used against the dribbler depending on your team's defensive strategy. These positions include turning the dribbler, forcing the dribbler to the sideline, funneling the dribbler to the middle, and forcing the dribbler to use the weak hand.

Turning the Dribbler (Forcing the Reverse Dribble)

The basic idea in turning the dribbler is to dominate your opponent by applying maximum pressure on the ball. Work to establish defensive position a half body ahead in the direction the dribbler wants to go. This position is called *chest on the ball.* The objective is preventing another dribble in the same direction and forcing the dribbler into a reverse dribble. With good anticipation, you may even draw a charge.

If the dribbler tries a front crossover dribble, you should be able to steal the ball with a quick flick upward of your near hand. On the dribbler's reverse dribble, quickly change direction and again move into chest-on-the-ball position, at least a half body ahead of the direction the dribbler wants to go. Continue forcing the dribbler to reverse dribble.

Forcing the Dribbler to the Sideline

When forced to the sideline, the dribbler can pass in only one direction, and the sideline can serve as a defensive aid. Work for position a half body to the inside of the court, with your inside foot (the one closer to the middle) forward and your outside foot back. Force the dribbler to the sideline. Then maintain your defensive position, keeping your feet moving close to the floor and not allowing a reverse dribble back to the middle of the court. By dribbling to the middle, the dribbler has more options for passing to either side or attempting a high-percentage shot.

Funneling the Dribbler to the Middle

By taking a defensive position a half body to the outside of the court, you can funnel the dribbler to the middle. This strategy will move the dribbler toward your defensive teammate off the ball. In turn, your teammate may use one of several teaming tactics, including a switch, fake switch (hedge), trap, or steal.

If your team has a shot blocker, you may benefit by funneling the dribbler in the direction of the shot blocker. The danger in funneling the dribbler to the middle is allowing that player to penetrate by you into the lane for a high-percentage shot or a pass to either side.

Forcing the Dribbler to Use the Weak Hand

Few dribblers can drive with their weak hand as effectively as with their strong hand. By overplaying the dribbler's strong hand, you force the opponent to dribble with the weak hand. Overplay the dribbler by taking a position a half body to the dribbler's strong-hand side, with your forward foot outside and your back foot aligned with the middle of the dribbler's body.

PLAYING DEFENSE OFF THE BALL

Positioning off the ball is an important part of team defense. To better understand team defensive positioning, think of how the court is divided from basket to basket into a strong side (also called ball side) and weak side (also called help side). The strong side refers to the ball side of the court, and the weak side refers to the side of the court away from the ball.

Playing good defense involves defending your opponent, the ball, and the basket. To accomplish this, you will move continually from one defensive responsibility to another. The phrase *help and recover* refers to being in good defensive position off the ball to help stop a penetrating pass or dribble by the player with the ball and then recovering to your own opponent.

When you are off the ball, you should take a position off your opponent and toward the ball so that you are able to see both the ball and your opponent. This is called the *ball–you–man principle.* You want to form an imaginary triangle between you, the ball, and your opponent. The closer your opponent is to the ball, the closer you should be to your opponent. The farther the ball is from your opponent, the farther away you can play from your opponent and still give help to your teammate guarding the ball.

Strong-Side Wing Denial Defensive Positioning

When you are off the ball on the strong side, you should work to deny a penetrating pass to a receiver on the wing inside the foul line extended (figure 12.1, page 322). To deny a pass to the ball-side wing, first take a ball–you–player position within touching distance from your opponent. Overplay your opponent by using a closed stance, with your lead foot and hand up in the passing lane. See the ball and your opponent by keeping your head up and looking over the shoulder of your lead arm. Be ready to knock away a pass by having the palm of your lead hand facing out with your thumb down. Your back arm should be flexed and close to your body. Having your back hand touching your opponent can help you monitor movement. Be ready to move, keeping a wide base and flexed knees. React to your opponent's movements by using short, quick steps. As you move, keep your feet close to the floor and at least shoulder-width apart. Do not cross your feet or hop. Keep your head steady and over your waist, with your back straight, to keep from leaning off balance. Be alert and ready to knock away an outside pass to your opponent.

On a backdoor pass, open to the ball on the pass and knock the pass away. Open to the ball by pivoting on your inside foot while dropping your lead foot back and toward the ball.

Weak-Side Help Defensive Positioning

When you are on the weak side, sag off your opponent and form an imaginary flat triangle between you, your opponent, and the ball (figure 12.1, page 322). Be in an open stance to see both the ball and your opponent without turning your head. The farther the ball is from your opponent, the farther away you can play from your opponent, but still be in position to give help to your teammate guarding the ball. Point your inside hand (the one closest to your opponent) at your opponent and your outside hand at the ball. Be ready to move, keeping a wide base and flexed knees. React to your opponent's movements by using short, quick steps. As you move, keep your feet close to the floor and at least shoulder-width apart. Do not cross your feet or hop. Keep your head steady and over your waist, with your back straight, to keep from leaning off balance. Be able to help on a drive or pass inside by the player with the ball. Communicate that you are in position to help, yelling to your teammate on the ball, "You've got help!"

Figure 12.1 **DEFENSIVE POSITIONING**

Strong-side denial

1. Touching distance from opponent
2. Ball–you–player position
3. Closed stance
4. Lead hand and foot up in passing lane; lead hand knocks ball away
5. Wide base with knees flexed
6. Short, quick steps as feet move shoulder-width apart (do not cross feet)
7. Prepared to open to ball and knock it away on backdoor pass

Weak-side help

1. Sagging off opponent
2. Ball–you–player position
3. Open stance
4. Inside hand pointed at opponent; outside hand pointed at ball
5. Wide base with knees flexed
6. Short, quick steps as feet move shoulder-width apart (do not cross feet)
7. Ready to help teammate on drive or backdoor pass; yell to teammate, "You've got help!"

MISSTEP

Defending on the strong side, you are unable to deny the pass after the wing fakes a step to the basket and cuts back for the ball.

CORRECTION

Learn to ignore the wing's first step to the basket and understand that you will have defensive help from weak-side defenders on a backdoor pass.

MISSTEP

When defending on the weak side, you are too close to your opponent and not in position to give help on a drive or pass inside.

CORRECTION

When defending on the weak side, sag off your opponent and form an imaginary flat triangle between you, your opponent, and the ball. Be in an open stance to see both the ball and your opponent. Communicate to your teammate on the ball that you are in position to help by yelling "You've got help!"

Defending Ball-Side Guard With Ball at Wing

When you are defending the ball-side guard while the wing has the ball, you can choose from two options, depending on your team's defensive strategy. One option is to prevent ball reversal to the ball-side guard by overplaying the guard with a closed stance, lead foot and hand up in the passing lane. As shown in figure 12.2*a*, defensive player X1 takes a closed-stance position to prevent the ball reversal from the wing (3) to the ball-side guard (1).

The other option is getting into a help-and-recover position to help on a drive to the middle by the wing and to discourage a pass to the high post. As shown in figure 12.2*b*, defensive player X1 takes an open stance, sagging off the ball-side guard (1) to help teammate X3 on the drive to the middle by the wing (3). X1 then recovers on the pass to the ball-side guard. Be alert and ready to prevent the ball-side guard from receiving a pass on a possible front or backdoor cut to the basket.

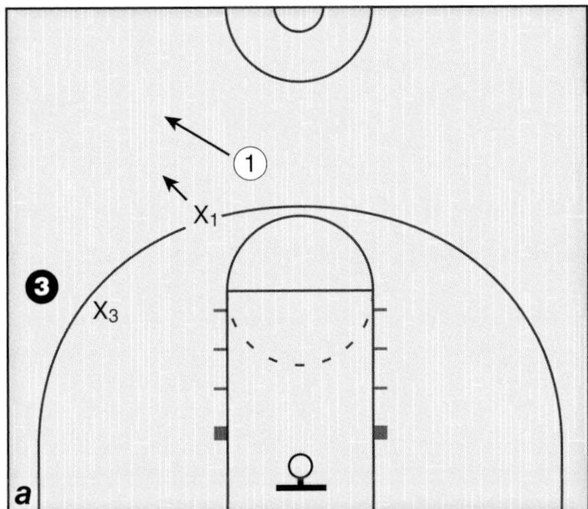

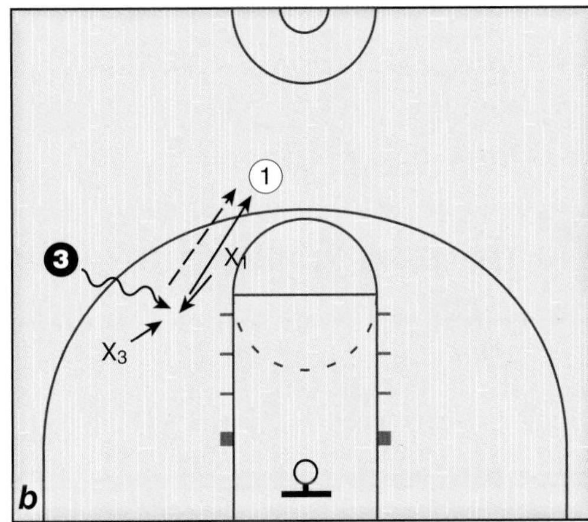

Figure 12.2 Defending the ball-side guard when the wing has the ball: *(a)* denial defensive position; *(b)* help-and-recover defensive position.

Defending Weak-Side Guard When Other Guard Has Ball

Be in an open stance at least one step off an imaginary line between your opponent and the basket. You should be in a ball–you–player position and in position to see both the ball and your opponent without turning your head. Point one hand at the ball, and point the other hand at your opponent. Get in a help-and-recover position, and communicate to your teammate on the ball that you are in position to help by yelling "You've got help!"

In figure 12.3, defensive player X2 takes an open stance, sagging off the weak-side guard (2) to prevent the front cut by 2, give help on a drive to the middle by 1, and recover on a pass to 2.

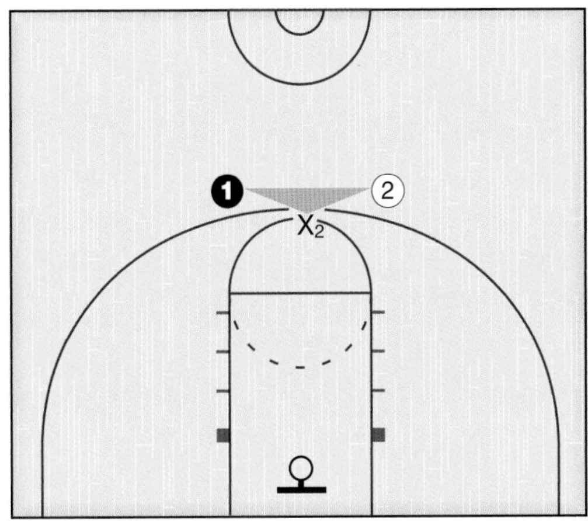

Figure 12.3 Defending the weak-side guard when the other guard has the ball.

Defending Weak-Side Wing When Guard Has Ball

Sag off your opponent in a ball–you–player position. Be in an open stance with at least one foot in the lane. You should be able to see both the ball and your opponent without turning your head. Point one hand at the ball, and point the other hand at your opponent. Communicate to your teammate on the ball that you are in position to help by yelling "You've got help!"

As shown in figure 12.4, defensive player X4 takes an open stance, sagging off the weak-side wing (4) to prevent 4's flash cut, give help on a drive to the middle or a pass inside by player 1, and recover on a pass to 4.

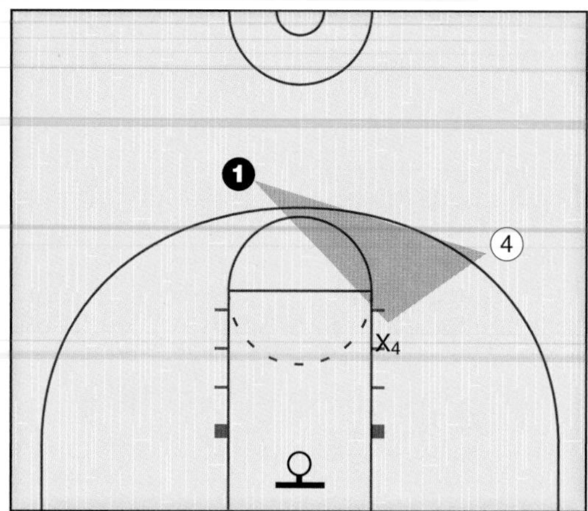

Figure 12.4 Defending the weak-side wing when the guard has the ball.

Defending Weak-Side Guard With Ball at Wing

Sag off your opponent in a ball–you–player position. Be in an open stance, one step to the weak side of the basket. You should be able to see both the ball and your opponent without turning your head. Point one hand at the ball, and point the other hand at your opponent. Communicate to your teammate on the ball that you are in position to help by yelling "You've got help!" Be alert and ready to prevent the weak-side guard from receiving a pass on a possible cut to the basket.

As shown in figure 12.5, defensive player X2 takes an open stance, sagging farther off the weak-side guard (2) to prevent 2's cut to the basket, give help on a drive to the middle by player 3, and recover on a pass to 2.

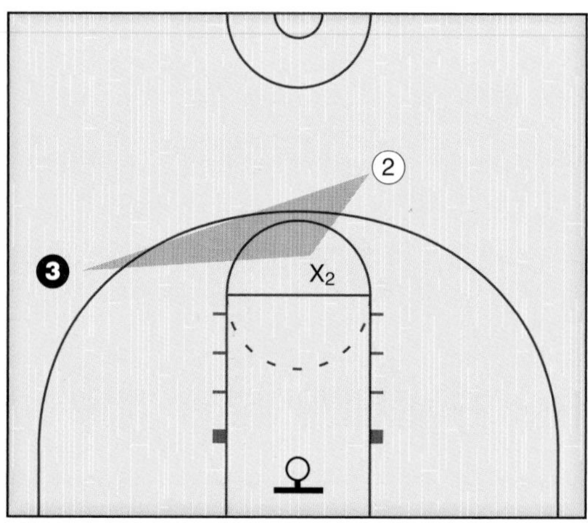

Figure 12.5 Defending the weak-side guard with the ball at the wing.

Defending Weak-Side Wing With Ball at Wing

Sag off your opponent in a ball–you–player position. Be in an open stance, one step to the weak side of the basket. You should be able to see both the ball and your opponent without turning your head. Point one hand at the ball, and point the other hand at your opponent. Communicate to your teammate on the ball that you are in position to help by yelling "You've got help!" Be alert and ready to prevent the weak-side wing from receiving a pass on a possible flash cut to the ball-side elbow or a cut to the low post.

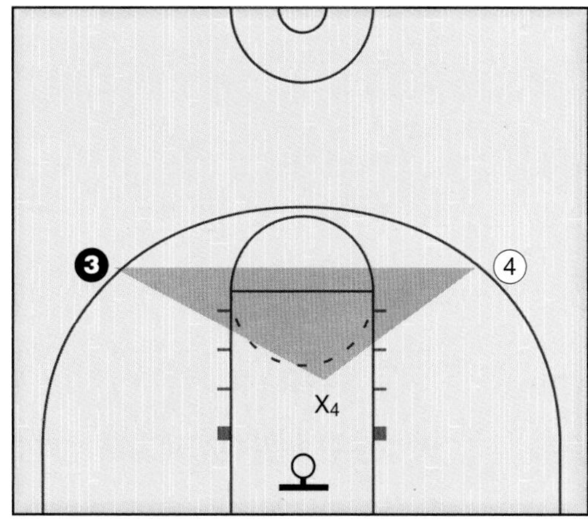

Figure 12.6 Defending the weak-side wing with the ball at the wing.

As shown in figure 12.6, defensive player X4 takes an open stance, sagging farther off the weak-side wing (4) to prevent 4 from flashing to the ball-side elbow or cutting to the low post, give help on a drive to the baseline or backdoor cut by player 3, and recover on a pass to 4.

Defense off the Ball Drill. **Wing Denial**

A good defender is able to pressure and deny a penetrating pass to the ball-side wing. The wing denial drill provides practice at denying a pass inside the foul line extended. The drill requires three players, two on offense and one on defense. Offensive player 1 starts with the ball at the point position at the top of the circle. Offensive player 2 plays at the ball-side wing, starting at the foul line extended. You begin as the defensive player and take a denial defensive position on player 2.

To deny a pass to the ball-side wing, first take a ball–you–player position. Overplay your opponent by using a closed stance, with your lead foot and hand up in the passing lane. Keep the ball and your opponent in sight by keeping your head up and looking over the shoulder of your lead arm. Be ready to knock away a pass by having the palm of your lead hand out with your thumb down. Player 2, the ball-side wing, attempts to get open, moving in the area within the following boundaries: one step above the foul line extended, the lane line, the baseline, and the sideline. React to player 2's movements using short, quick steps, with your feet at least shoulder-width apart. Stay alert and be ready to knock away an outside pass to your opponent. On a backdoor pass, open to the ball and knock the pass away by pivoting on your inside foot while dropping your lead foot back and toward the ball.

When the offensive wing receives the ball, the drill becomes a one-on-one drill. Continue the drill until the wing scores or you obtain possession via a rebound, steal, or interception. Go for 30 seconds before changing positions. You and your partners should play wing denial defense three times each.

(continued)

(continued)

Success Check

- Keep your head up to see the ball and your opponent.
- Read and react to the offensive players.
- Use short, quick steps.

Score Your Success

Give yourself 1 point each time you stop the wing from scoring. This is a competitive drill, so try to score more points than your opponents. Give yourself 5 points if you score more than your opponents.

Your score ___

Defense off the Ball Drill. **Weak-Side Help and Recover**

In this drill, you will practice opening up on the weak side, helping on a penetrating drive by the ball-side wing, and then, when the ball is passed out, recovering to the player you are guarding. The drill requires three players, two offensive players and one defender. Offensive player 1 starts with the ball at the foul line extended. Offensive player 2 starts as a weak-side wing at the opposite foul line extended. You take a weak-side defensive position on player 2, the weak-side wing.

From the weak side, sag off your opponent in a ball–you–player position, forming an imaginary flat triangle between you, your opponent, and the ball. Be in an open stance, one step to the weak side of the basket. Position yourself to see both the ball and your opponent without turning your head. Point one hand at the ball, and point the other hand at your opponent. Communicate to your imaginary teammate on the ball that you are in position to help by yelling "You've got help!"

Player 1 drives past an imaginary ball-side defensive wing on the baseline side toward the basket. Give help to this imaginary ball-side defensive wing by moving to the ball side of the basket to stop the drive or draw a charge. As you move, player 1 passes to player 2, the weak-side wing, who is flashing to the weak-side elbow. On the pass, recover quickly but under control to player 2. When player 2 receives the ball at the weak-side elbow, player 1 steps off the court, and the drill becomes a one-on-one contest between you and player 2.

Continue until the wing scores or you obtain possession of the ball via a rebound, steal, or interception. Change positions and continue the drill. Allow each player to play weak-side help-and-recover defense three times.

Success Check

- Use a ball–you–player position.
- Use verbal signals to let your imaginary teammate know that you are available to help.
- Try to draw a charge when the offensive player with the ball drives to the basket.

Score Your Success

Give yourself 1 point each time you stop the weak-side wing from scoring. This is a competitive drill, so try to score more points than your opponents. Give yourself 5 points if you score more than your opponents.

Your score ___

DEFENDING THE LOW POST

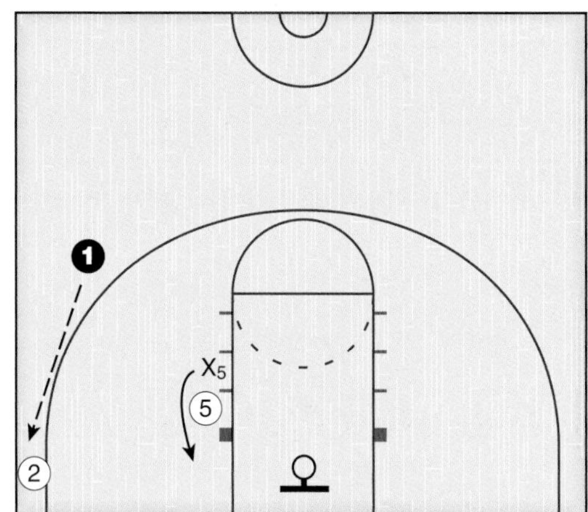

Figure 12.7 Low-post defensive positioning: changing sides.

Always attempt to keep your opponent from receiving a pass in good low-post position. Use a closed stance with your body in three-quarter defensive position between the ball and your opponent. When the ball is above the imaginary foul line extended, deny your low-post opponent from the topside. When the ball is below the imaginary foul line extended, deny your low-post opponent from the baseline side.

When a wing above the foul line extended passes the ball to a player in the corner below the foul line extended or in the reverse direction, from the corner to the wing, you should move quickly from one side of the low post to the other. A denial defensive position can be maintained by stepping in front of the low-post player as you change sides. Use quick footwork. Step through first with your inside foot (the one closer to the opponent) and then with your outside foot.

As shown in figure 12.7, as the ball is passed from player 1 to corner player 2, X5 quickly changes from topside to baseline side, stepping in front of low-post player 5.

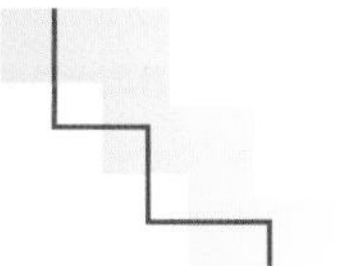

MISSTEP

When the ball is passed from wing to corner, or vice versa, you are unable to deny a pass to the low post.

CORRECTION

As the ball is passed, change sides but maintain denial position by stepping in front of the low-post player with a quick two-step move.

Defending the Low Post Drill. Low-Post Denial

You should always attempt to deny your opponent from receiving a pass in good low-post position, and this drill gives you practice. The drill requires four players. You will start on defense, and the other three players will be on offense.

Offensive player 1 starts with the ball above the foul line extended on the ball side. Offensive player 2 takes a position below the foul line extended in the corner. Offensive player 3 takes a position in the low post above the block outside the lane. As the defensive player, you take a position denying a pass to player 3 in the low post. Use a closed stance with your body in three-quarter defensive position between the ball and your opponent. Players 1 and 2 attempt to pass the ball inside to the low post, and you attempt to deny each pass to the low post. Players 1 and 2 should pass the ball to each other, and player 3 should get good low-post position by sealing you off.

(continued)

(continued)

When the ball is above the imaginary foul line extended, you should deny the low post from the topside. When the ball is below the imaginary foul line extended, you should deny the low post from the baseline side. As player 1 (above the foul line extended) passes the ball to player 2 in the corner below the foul line extended, or as player 2 passes to player 1, you should move quickly from one side of the low post to the other. Maintain your denial defensive position by stepping in front of the low-post player as you change sides.

Quick footwork is needed. Step through first with your inside foot and then with your outside foot. When player 3 receives the ball in the low post, the drill becomes a one-on-one drill until either the low post scores or you obtain possession via a rebound, steal, or interception. Allow each player to play low-post denial defense three times, then change sides.

Success Check

- Use a closed stance with your body in three-quarter defensive position between the ball and your opponent.
- Maintain correct denial defensive positioning.
- Use quick footwork.

Score Your Success

Give yourself 1 point each time you stop the low post from scoring. This is a competitive drill, so try to score more points than your opponents. Give yourself 5 points if you score more than your opponents.

Your score ___

DEFENDING THE CUTTER

When the opponent you are closely guarding on the perimeter passes the ball, you must move off your opponent in the direction of the pass. This is called *jumping to the ball.* Jumping to the ball positions you to defend a give-and-go cut by your opponent and allows you to give help on the ball.

You must move on the pass to establish ball–you–player position. If you wait for your opponent to cut before you move, you will get beat. The pass-and-cut is the most basic offensive play in basketball: It is as old as the game itself.

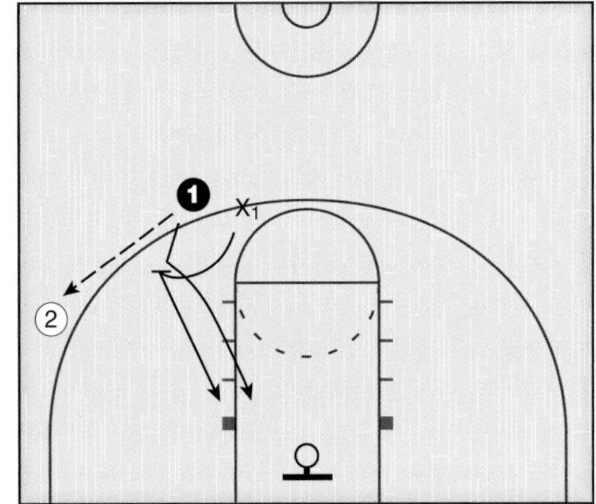

Figure 12.8 Defending the cutter.

For playing defense off the ball, you should be in position to see both the ball and your opponent. To defend a cutter, position yourself off the cutter and toward the ball. Do not allow the cutter to move between you and the ball. Be in a strong, balanced stance, ready to withstand any contact that may occur as you prevent the cutter from going between you and the ball.

When the cutter approaches the lane area, you should be in position to bump the cutter. Use a bump-and-release technique. Bump the cutter with the inside part of your body, and release to a position between the cutter and the ball. If your opponent makes a backdoor cut to the basket, you should maintain a closed stance as you move with your opponent on the cut and then open to the ball as the pass is thrown. Use your lead hand to knock away a pass.

As shown in figure 12.8, as offensive player 1 passes to player 2, X1 quickly jumps to the ball and uses the bump-and-release technique, staying between the ball and player 1 on that player's cut.

MISSTEP

On a cut, you allow the cutter to get between you and the ball.

CORRECTION

Change to a closed stance and get your lead foot and hand into the passing lane. Force the cutter to go behind you.

DEFENDING THE FLASH CUT

A flash cut is a quick move by an opponent from the weak side toward the ball. Most offenses use a flash cut from the weak side into the high-post area. As a defender on the weak side, you should be in an open stance and in position to see both the ball and the opponent. As shown in figure 12.9, if player 1 has the ball on the opposite-side wing, when your opponent flashes to the high-post area, you must be alert to move and stop the flash. Change to a closed stance with your lead foot and hand in the passing lane. Be in a strong, balanced stance, ready to withstand any contact that may take place as you stop the flash cut. Use your lead hand to knock away a pass.

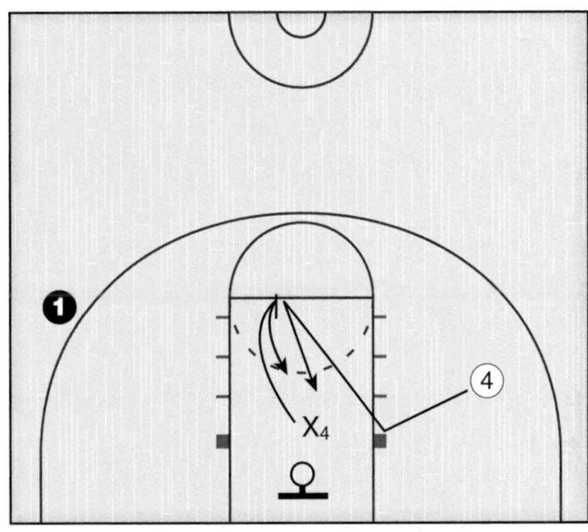

Figure 12.9 Defending the flash cut.

If your opponent flashes high and then makes a backdoor cut to the basket, you must first get in a closed stance to deny the flash high. On the backdoor cut to the basket, you should maintain a closed stance as you move with your opponent on the cut. Be alert and ready to intercept or deflect the ball when the pass is thrown.

MISSTEP

Your opponent flashes high and then beats you on a backdoor cut to the basket.

CORRECTION

First, you need to get in a closed stance to deny the flash high. Maintain a closed stance as you move with your opponent on a backdoor cut, then open to the ball as the pass is thrown.

Defending the Flash Drill. Deny the Flash and Deny the Backdoor Cut

This drill gives you practice denying both a flash cut and a backdoor cut. The drill requires three players, two on offense and one on defense. Offensive player 1 starts with two balls at the foul line extended. Offensive player 2 is a weak-side wing, starting at the weak-side foul line extended. As the defensive player, you take a weak-side defensive position on player 2. Use an open stance and point one hand at the ball and the other hand at your opponent. Communicate to your imaginary teammate on the ball that you are in position to help by yelling "You've got help!"

Player 2 starts the drill by cutting toward the basket for a few steps and then flashing to the ball-side elbow. React to stop the flash by changing to a closed stance and beating the weak-side wing to the ball-side elbow; your lead foot and hand should be up in the passing lane to deny a pass. Be strong and ready to withstand any contact that may take place as you stop player 2's flash. Use your lead hand to knock away a pass.

Player 1 attempts to pass the first ball to player 2 at the ball-side elbow. React to a pass on the flash cut by deflecting the ball. Once you deny the flash, player 2 cuts backdoor to the basket. Player 1 then attempts to pass the second ball to player 2 cutting backdoor. React to a pass on the backdoor cut by opening up as the pass is thrown and then deflecting the ball. Change positions and continue the drill until each player has had three turns denying the flash cut and the backdoor cut.

Success Check

- Begin in an open stance, and then react to the flash with a closed stance.
- Communicate verbally with your imaginary teammate on the ball.
- Be ready for contact as you stop the flash.

Score Your Success

Five or six denials = 5 points

Three or four denials = 1 point

Fewer than three denials = 0 points

Your score ___

Defending the Flash Drill. **Six Points**

This drill adds practice at stopping the drive, blocking out, rebounding, making an outlet pass, and converting from defense to offense. You will practice six points of defense: deny the wing; deny the low post; assume weak-side help position; deny the flash; stop the drive; and block out, rebound, outlet, and convert to offense.

The drill requires three players, one on defense and two on offense. Start by playing defense on player 2, who is the ball-side wing and starts at the foul line extended. Offensive player 1 starts with the ball at the point position at the top of the circle and gives commands. The drill begins when player 1 calls out "Deny!" On this command, player 2 works to get open on the wing, and you work to deny the pass.

Player 1 then yells "Low post!" and dribbles from above the foul line extended to below it while player 2 moves to get open in the low post on the ball side. You should deny a pass to the low post by moving from the topside to the baseline side of the low post as the ball is dribbled from above the foul line extended to below it.

Player 1 then yells "Away!" On this command, player 2 moves away from the ball to the weak side. You should now move to a weak-side help-and-recover position only one step to the weak side of the basket. Be in an open stance, pointing one hand at the ball and one hand at your opponent. Say your key phrase to communicate to the imaginary teammate on the ball that you are in position to help.

Player 1 then calls out "Flash!" and player 2 cuts a few steps toward the basket before flashing to the ball-side elbow. You should react to stop the flash by closing your stance and beating player 2 to the ball-side elbow; your lead foot and hand should be up in the passing lane to deny a pass.

Player 1 next yells "Out!" and player 2 moves out to the top of the circle. You should allow the pass to player 2 but then stop the one-on-one drive to the basket. On a shot, block out and go for the rebound. On a missed shot, rebound and make an outlet pass to player 1 on the wing. On a made shot, take the ball out of the net, run out of bounds, and make the outlet pass to player 1. Then run to the foul line for a return pass. Change positions and continue the drill, allowing each player to play defense.

Success Check

- Execute the correct defensive reaction to each of the offensive moves.
- On a shot, block out and be aggressive when going for the rebound.

Score Your Success

Give yourself 1 point for each correct defensive reaction to each of the six offensive moves.

6 correct reactions = 6 points

5 correct reactions = 3 points

4 correct reactions = 1 point

Fewer than 4 correct reactions = 0 points

Your score ___

DEFENDING THE PICK-AND-ROLL

As mentioned earlier, the pick-and-roll (also called a ball screen) is one of the oldest plays in basketball and is currently being used more than ever. At the professional level, the pick-and-roll has become a primary part of the offense for most teams. It has also become a part of college and high school play. In the pick-and-roll, the picker sets the pick and then rolls (cuts to the basket) for a possible inside shot off a pass from the ball handler. If the picker is a good shooter, a pick-and-pop may be used; in this option, the picker pops out for an outside shot rather than rolling to the basket. The pick-and-roll—whether the offense uses the pick to penetrate and pass inside to a post player or to pass outside to an open three-point shooter—has become arguably the most difficult play to defend in today's game.

Various methods are used for defending the pick-and-roll. Regardless of the method of defense being used, it takes all five defenders to defend a well-executed pick-and-roll. Two primary defensive players defend the pick-and-roll: (1) the player guarding the player with the ball and (2) the player guarding the player setting the pick. The other defensive players, most often positioned on the weak side, must move into help positions and be able to give help as needed. However, a weak-side help defender cannot move too far away from a hot shooter positioned behind the three-point line and give that shooter an open three-point shot. How you defend the pick-and-roll action is determined by the abilities of your opponents and how they want to use the pick-and-roll to score.

To defend the pick-and-roll, you and your teammates must be able to communicate and help each other. The defender on the opponent who is setting the screen must alert the defender being screened by calling out the direction of the screen. The defender should call out "Screen right!" or "Screen left!" The defender on the screener should also communicate how the screen will be defended by calling out the defensive coverage that will be used. For example, if your teammate is defending a good shooter and you want this teammate to fight over the top of the screen, you would call out "Get over!" If your teammate is defending a good driver, you would call out "Go under!"

Four players are directly involved in the pick-and-roll, two offensive players (the screener and the player with the ball, who will use the screen) and their two defenders. To make it easier to understand the methods for defending a pick-and-roll, we always refer to the player with the ball (the player who will use the screen) as the first player. If the defender on the ball goes over the screen, this is called fighting over the top or simply going second. If the defender on the ball goes under the screen, this is called going under or third. If the defender on the ball goes under both the screener and the screener's defender, this is called going fourth.

You have numerous ways to defend the pick-and-roll, but you should master one standard tactic first before learning other methods. Most coaches want defensive players to master the hard help-and-recover method before making an adjustment in pick-and-roll coverage by using another method. Six basic methods for defending the pick-and-roll are covered in this section: hard help and recover, soft help and recover, trap, squeeze, force down sideline or baseline, and switch.

Hard Help and Recover

When your opponent sets a screen on a teammate who is guarding a good shooter within shooting range, you should use a defensive tactic called *hard help and recover* to help your teammate stay with the shooter. Call out the screen and get right up on

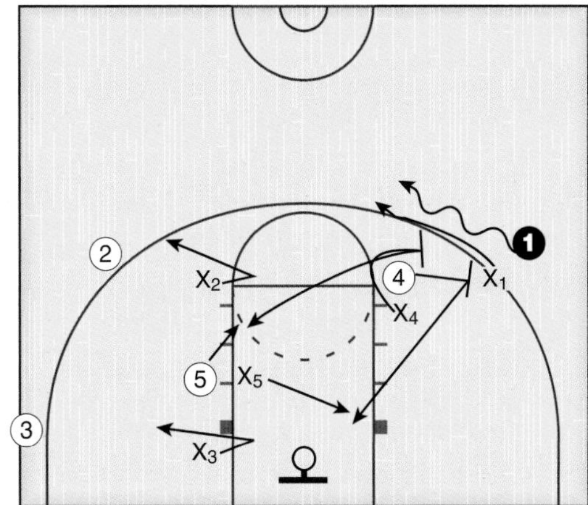

Figure 12.10 Hard help and recover.

the screener in order to jump out into the ball handler's path. This "showing hard" action will prevent the ball handler from getting into the middle, called *turning the corner.* By showing hard, you will delay the ball handler or force her to veer wide when dribbling. This will give your teammate time to stay with the dribbler (go second). When you show hard, you should keep a hand on the screener so you can stay with the screener if the screener releases early or slips to the basket. After giving hard help, recover back to the screener, unless you get too extended and another teammate rotates up to pick up the screener. In this case, you should rotate back toward the basket and look for an open offensive player.

When you are the defensive player being screened, you should work hard to stay with the dribbler by fighting over the top of the screen. Work to get over the screen by first getting a foot over the screen and then the remainder of your body. You will be more difficult to screen when you are fighting hard to stay with the dribbler rather than being soft when screened.

As shown in figure 12.10, offensive player 4 sets a screen for offensive player 1. Defender X4 shows hard by stepping into offensive player 1's path, giving teammate X1 time to fight over the top of the screen (go second) and stay with the dribbler. Defender X5 rotates to screener 4 rolling to the basket, and defender X4 rotates back to offensive player 5. Weak-side defenders X2 and X3 give help and then recover to the players they were originally guarding.

MISSTEP

When you give hard help to your teammate who is attempting to fight over the top of the screen, you get beat by the screener releasing early on a slip to the basket.

CORRECTION

When you show hard, keep a hand on the screener so you can stay with the screener if the screener releases early or slips to the basket.

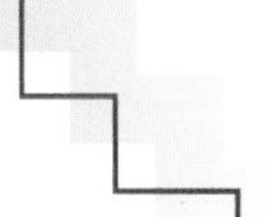

MISSTEP

Your teammate attempts to fight over the top of the screen but gets beat by the ball handler driving off the screen.

CORRECTION

Show hard by stepping out into the path of the dribbler to delay the dribbler or force her to veer wide. This will give your teammate time to stay with the dribbler. When you are the defensive player being screened, work hard to stay with the dribbler by fighting over the top of the screen.

Soft Help and Recover

When your opponent sets a screen on a teammate who is guarding a good penetrator within shooting range, you should use a defensive tactic called *soft help and recover* to help your teammate stay with the penetrator. Call out the screen and drop back off the screener in order to cover the turn of the ball handler's path. This soft help action will allow you to be in better position to defend the roll of the picker and also help your teammate when the dribbler attempts to penetrate with a drive. However, this tactic provides less help against the ball handler, who can create a jump shot off the dribble. After giving soft help, you should recover back to the screener, unless another teammate rotates to pick up the screener. In this case, you should rotate back toward the basket and look for an open offensive player.

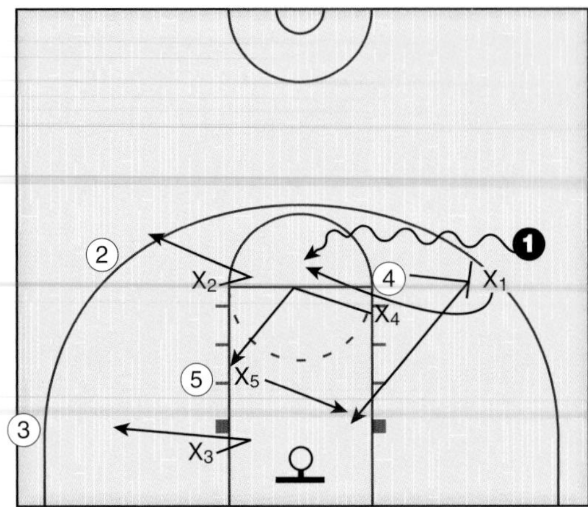

Figure 12.11 Soft help and recover.

When you are the defensive player being screened while guarding a good penetrator, you should work hard to stay with the dribbler by going under the screen. The decision to go under the screen is also based on the distance from the basket that the screen is set. If the screen is set outside of the dribbler's shooting range, you would obviously go under the screen. When the screen is set closer to the basket, you should work hard to fight over the top of the screen if the dribbler is a good shooter.

As shown in figure 12.11, player 4 sets a screen for player 1. Defender X4 shows soft by dropping back off the screener to give teammate X1, who goes under the screen (goes third), help against penetration (covering the turn). Defender X4 is also in a better position to defend the roll of the screener, player 4, or rotate back to player 5 when teammate X5 rotates to pick up player 4. Weak-side defenders help and recover to the players they were originally guarding.

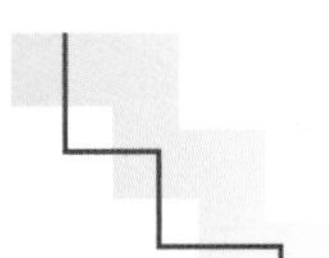

MISSTEP

Your teammate is not alert to being screened by your opponent.

CORRECTION

As your opponent moves to set a screen on your teammate, you must call out the screen and its direction.

Trap

Trapping the ball handler is a more aggressive coverage for defending the pick-and-roll, and it involves more risk. In addition to the actions of the two primary defenders (one defending the ball and one defending the screener), the other three defenders must be alert to give help and rotate. Two methods are used for trapping. The method involving the most risk is for you to trap the dribbler before the screen is set. The method used more often is for you to trap the dribbler when the ball handler is just coming off the screen. With either method, the risk is that the ball handler will be able to make a quick pass to the screener on a roll to the basket or a pop for an outside shot. This is why another teammate—in most cases, one near the basket—must rotate to the screener.

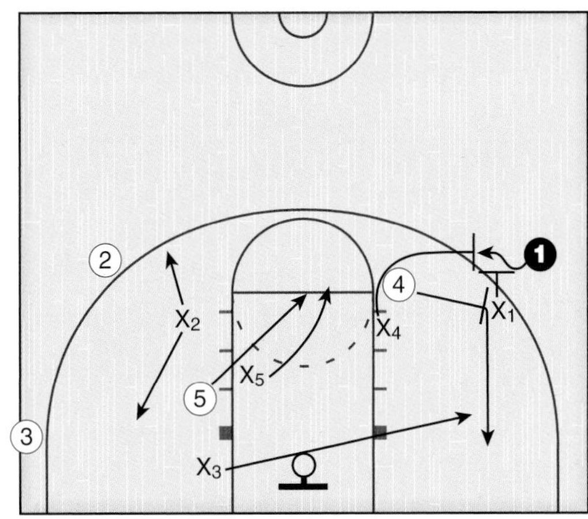

Figure 12.12 Trap.

As shown in figure 12.12, player 4 sets a screen for the ball handler, player 1. Defenders X1 and X4 trap player 1. When player 5 flashes to receive a possible pass out of the trap from player 1, defender X5 must deny the pass. When a pass is being attempted (the ball must be in the air) to screener 4 popping to the corner, weak-side defender X3 rotates to defend player 4. Weak-side defender X2 must be in position to rotate to either player 2 or 3.

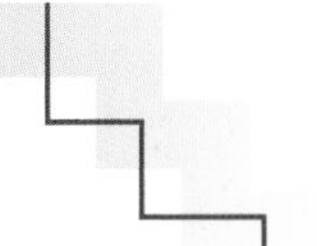

MISSTEP

On a defensive trap, the defender near the basket rotates to the screener popping out to the corner, but the pass is made to the offensive player whom the defender left, and this player gets an open shot.

CORRECTION

The defender near the basket must not rotate to the screener until the ball is in the air.

Squeeze

Occasionally, when the ball handler is a good penetrator and the screener is a good shooter and likes to pop out to shoot after screening, you should squeeze up on the screener. This helps your teammate who is defending the dribbler to go under both you and the screener (go fourth) to defend against the dribbler penetrating to the basket, and it allows you to stay with the screener. Call out the screen and yell "Squeeze!" Stay close to the screener, allowing your teammate to go under both of you to get to the dribbler.

As shown in figure 12.13, player 4 sets a screen for player 1. Defender X4 calls out the screen and squeezes up on the screener, player 4, allowing teammate X1 to move under both screener 4 and defender X4 (going fourth) to the dribbler to defend against penetration. Defender X4 stays with screener 4, who is popping out to the corner. Defender X5 is alert to help defender X1 or to rebound. Weak-side defenders X2 and X3 give help and then recover to the players they were originally guarding.

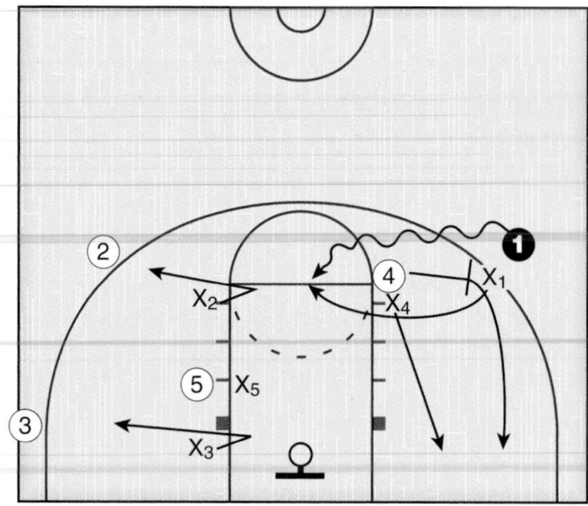

Figure 12.13 Squeeze.

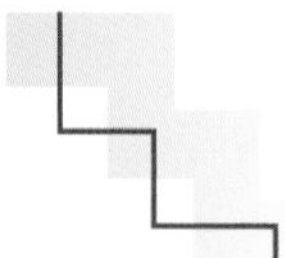

MISSTEP

Your teammate attempts to go under but bumps into you.

CORRECTION

Call out the screen and yell "Squeeze!" Stay close to the screener, allowing room for your teammate to go under both of you to get to the cutter.

Force Down Sideline or Baseline

When your opponent sets a screen on a teammate who is guarding a player at the wing or corner, you can use a defensive tactic called *force down toward sideline or baseline.* As the defender on the screener, you must call out this coverage with the signal "Down!" and drop back two or three steps toward the basket. On the call "Down!" your teammate guarding the ball handler must take a position on the high side of the ball handler and force the ball handler to dribble down toward the sideline or baseline and in your direction. If the screener is a good shooter and pops out for a jump shot, another teammate must rotate from the weak side to defend the screener, and you must rotate toward the weak side, looking for an open player. If the screener rolls to the basket, the weak-side inside defender must rotate and prevent the screener from making a front cut to the basket, and another weak-side defender must rotate back to get inside rebound position.

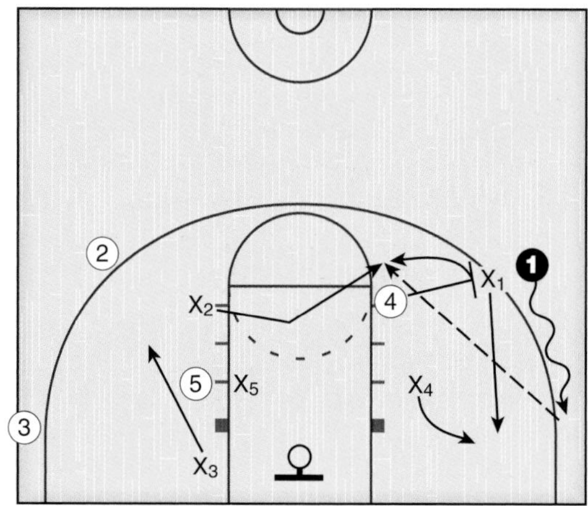

Figure 12.14 Force down sideline.

As shown in figure 12.14, player 4 sets a screen for player 1. Defender X4 signals to teammate X1 to take a position on the high side of the ball handler to force the ball handler toward the sideline. As X1 takes a position on the high side, defender X4 drops back two or three steps toward the basket to corral a drive and is prepared to trap the ball handler at the midpoint of the baseline. Defender X2 rotates to player 4, who is popping out above the strong-side elbow. Weak-side defender X3 is ready to rotate on a possible pass to player 2 or back to player 3. Defender X5 stays with player 5 but is alert to give help against penetration.

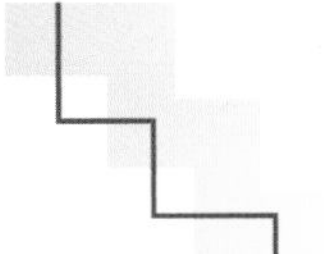

MISSTEP

Your teammate covering a ball handler at the wing or corner is not alert to being screened by your opponent and does not know what defensive coverage to use.

CORRECTION

When your opponent moves to set a screen on your teammate, you need to call out "Down!" This signals your teammate to take a high position and force the ball handler sideline or baseline and in your direction.

Switch

When you and your teammate are of equal size and defensive ability, you should switch opponents. If your size and defensive ability differ, switching should be the last option, because it allows the offense to take advantage of the mismatch. However, mismatches are not as dangerous as giving up open shots. On a mismatch in the post with a small defending a big, the nearest big defender can trap. If you switch, first call out the screen by yelling "Switch!" As you switch, aggressively get into position to stop the drive. The screener will roll to the basket or pop out for an outside shot.

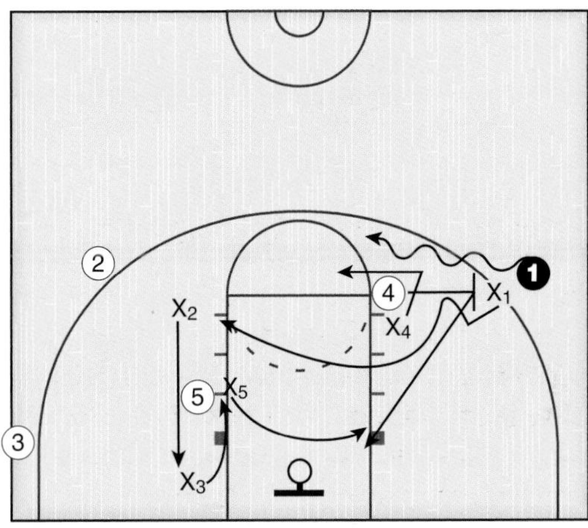

Figure 12.15 Switch.

When you are the player being screened and you hear the key word *switch,* work to get defensive position on the ball side of the screener.

As shown in figure 12.15, player 4 sets a screen for the dribbler, player 1. Defender X4 switches to player 1. Defender X1 works to get defensive position on the ball side of screener 4 and denies the pass back to her. As screener 4 rolls to the basket, weak-side defender X5 rotates to screener 4, and defender X3 rotates to player 5. Defender X1, who originally defended the dribbler, moves to the weak side to pick up the open opponent.

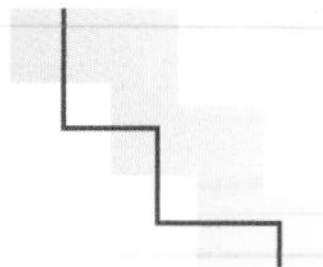

MISSTEP

On a defensive switch, the screener gets open on a roll to the basket or a pop-out for an outside shot.

CORRECTION

If you are the player being screened and you hear the key word *switch,* you must work to get defensive position on the ball side of the screener and deny a pass back to her.

Pick-and-Roll Defensive Drills. Two-on-Two Drills

Many two-on-two drills are useful for working on defending the pick-and-roll, including help-and-recover defense (two-on-two) (page 280), two-on-two (stretch the trap, page 282), open and slide under defense (two-on-two) (page 278), and switching defense (two-on-two) (page 276). These drills are included in step 10, two- and three-man plays.

DEFENDING A DOWN SCREEN

To defend screens that are set off the ball, you and your teammates must be able to communicate and help each other. The defender on the screener and the defender on the player being screened for should communicate with each other on how they will defend the screen.

Four players are directly involved in the screen, two offensive players (the screener and the cutter) and their two defenders. To make it easier to understand the methods for defending a down screen, we always refer to the cutter as the first player. If the screener's defender steps out to slow the cutter and help the cutter's defender stay close to the cutter's body as the cutter uses the screen, this means that the cutter's defender is going second. If the screener's defender opens up to allow the cutter's defender to slide between the screener's defender and the screen, this means that the cutter's defender is going through or going third. If the screener's defender squeezes close to the screener in order to allow the cutter's defender to go behind both the screener and the screener's defender, this means that the cutter's defender is taking a shortcut or going fourth.

Four basic methods are used to defend a screen off the ball: show and trail cutter, open and through, squeeze and shortcut, and switch.

Show and Trail Cutter

When your opponent sets a screen on a teammate who is guarding a good shooter within shooting range, you should help your teammate stay with the cutter. Call out the screen and show by stepping out into the cutter's path. This showing action will delay the cut or force the cutter to veer wide, giving your teammate time to follow the cutter (go second). When you show, you should keep a hand on the screener so you can stay with the screener if the screener releases early or slips to the basket.

When you are the defensive player being screened, you should keep close contact with the screener and trail the cutter's body as the cutter cuts off the screen. You will be more difficult to screen when you are directly behind the cutter. Work to get past the screen by first getting a foot past the screen and then the remainder of your body.

As shown in figure 12.16, player 4 sets a screen for player 2. Defender X4 shows by stepping into player 2's path, giving teammate X2 time to trail the cutter's body (go second).

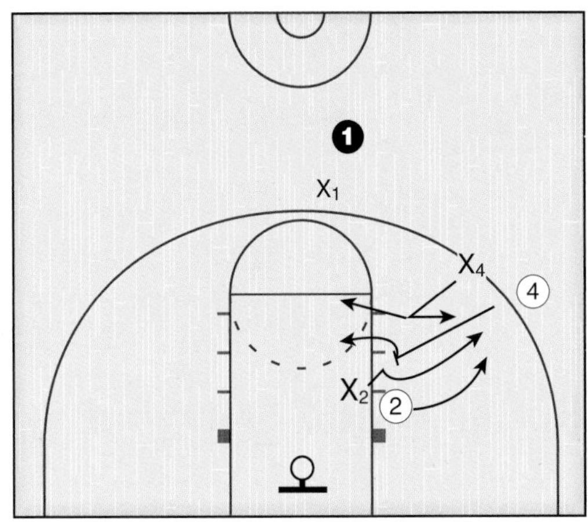

Figure 12.16 Show and trail cutter.

MISSTEP

Your teammate attempts to trail the cutter but gets beat on a quick cut.

CORRECTION

Show by stepping out into the path of the cutter to delay the cut or force the cutter to veer wide, giving your teammate time to trail the cutter's body. When you are the defensive player being screened, get directly behind the cutter's body and follow the cutter. Work to get over the screen by getting a foot over the screen and then the remainder of your body.

Open and Through

When your opponent sets a screen on a teammate who is guarding a quick driver or when your opponent sets a screen outside your opponent's shooting range, you should help your teammate slide through the screen between you and the screener (go third). Call out the screen and yell *Open and through!* Drop back and open space for your teammate to move between you and the screen so your teammate can get to the cutter.

As shown in figure 12.17, player 4 sets a screen for player 2. Defender X4 drops back (opens), making room for teammate X2 to move under or slide through the screen (go third).

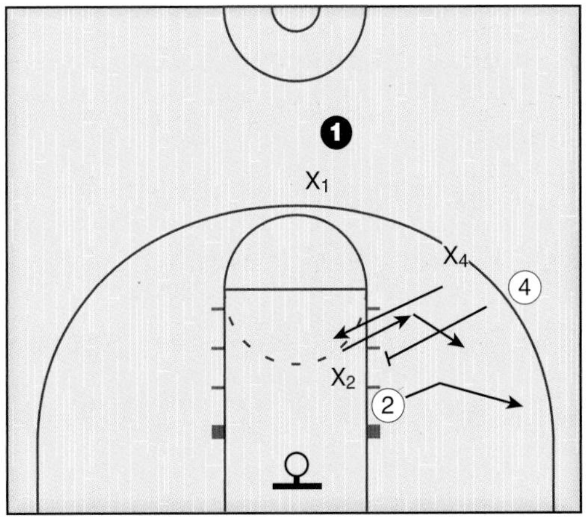

Figure 12.17 Open and through.

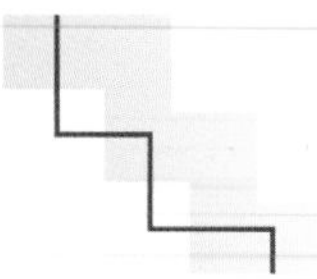

MISSTEP

Your teammate is not alert to being screened by your opponent.

CORRECTION

As your opponent moves to set a screen on your teammate, you should call out the screen and its direction.

Squeeze and Shortcut

Occasionally, when the cutter is a good driver or likes to curl or cut inside, and the screener is a good shooter and likes to pop out to shoot after screening, you should squeeze on the screener. This helps your teammate take a shortcut route under both you and the screener (go fourth). Call out the screen and yell "Squeeze!" Stay close to the screener, allowing room for your teammate to go under both of you to get to the cutter.

As shown in figure 12.18, player 4 sets a screen for player 2. Defender X4 squeezes on the screener, allowing room for teammate X2 to make a shortcut move over both the screener 4 and defender X4 (go fourth).

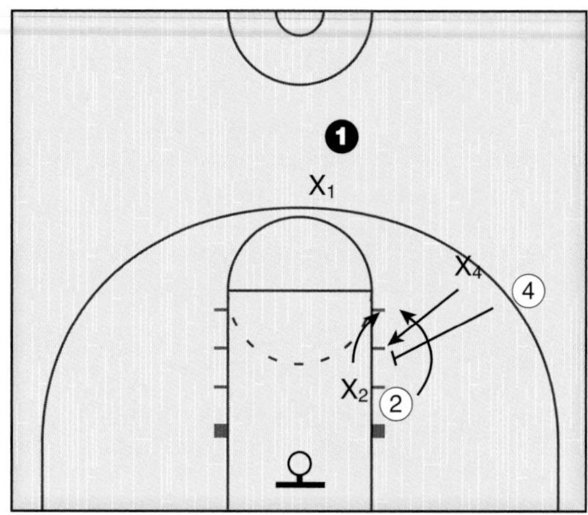

Figure 12.18 Squeeze and shortcut.

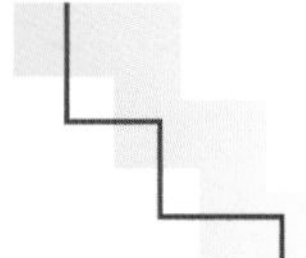

MISSTEP

Your teammate attempts to go under but bumps into you.

CORRECTION

Call out the screen and yell "Squeeze!" Stay close to the screener, allowing room for your teammate to go over both of you to get to the cutter.

Switch

When you and your teammate are of equal size and defensive ability, you can switch opponents. If your size and defensive ability differ, switching should be the last option, because it allows the offense to take advantage of the mismatch. If you switch, you should first call out the screen by yelling "Switch!" As you switch, aggressively get into position to deny a pass to the cutter (switch and deny). The screener will roll to the basket or pop out for an outside shot. When you are the player being screened and you hear the key word *switch*, you should work to get defensive position on the ball side of the screener.

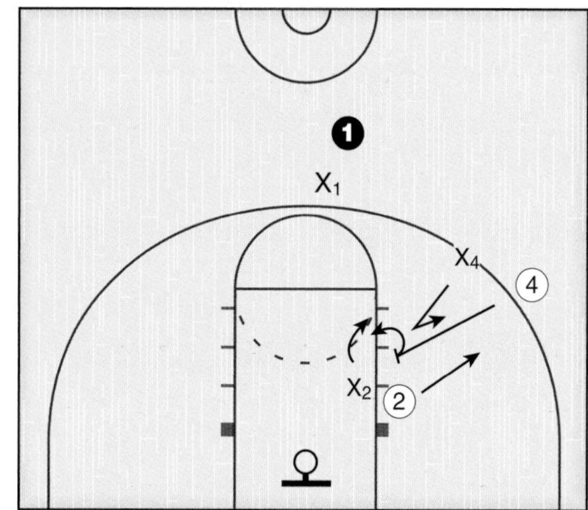

Figure 12.19 Switch.

As shown in figure 12.19, player 4 sets a screen for player 2. Defender X4 switches and denies a pass to player 2. Defender X2 works to get defensive position on the ball side of screener 4, who is rolling to the basket.

MISSTEP

On a defensive switch, the screener gets open on a roll to the basket or a pop-out for an outside shot.

CORRECTION

As the player being screened, if you hear the key word *switch*, you must work to get defensive position on the ball side of the screener.

DEFENDING A BACK PICK

To defend a back pick set off the ball, you and your teammates must be able to communicate and help each other. Four players are directly involved in the screen, two offensive players (the player setting the back pick and the cutter) and their two defenders. When you are the defender on the opponent who is setting the back pick, you should alert the defender being screened as soon as possible by calling out "Back pick!" To prevent the picker from setting a good pick, body up to him and force him away from the player cutting off the pick. You may be able to bump the cutter if he cuts over the pick and then recover quickly to prevent a catch and shoot play by the picker. When you are defending the cutter, get up on the cutter's body on the ball side and try to force the cutter away from the post and over the pick. If you run into the back pick, you should be physical and keep going to get your body to the ball side of the cutter between the ball and the cutter. Your teammate defending the passer must pressure the passer to prevent a lob pass.

As shown in figure 12.20, offensive player 2 sets a back pick for player 4. Defender X2 calls out "Back pick!", bodies up on player 2, and then recovers to prevent a catch and shot by picker 2. Defender X4 gets up on cutter 4's body and forces cutter 4 over the screen and away from the post. Teammate X1 pressures the passer to prevent a lob pass to cutter 4 and an easy reverse pass back to picker 2 on a pop-out.

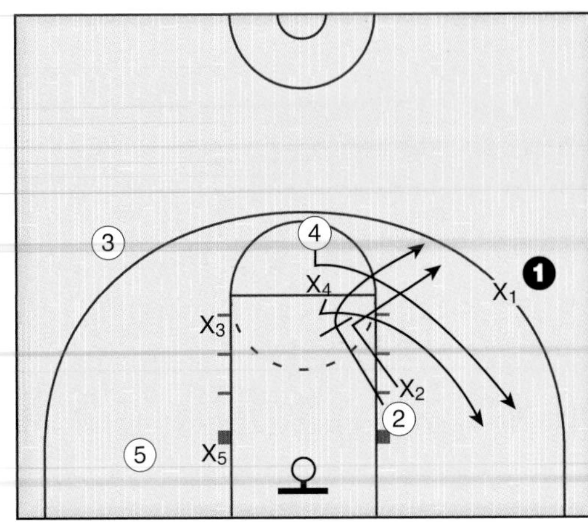

Figure 12.20 Defending a back pick.

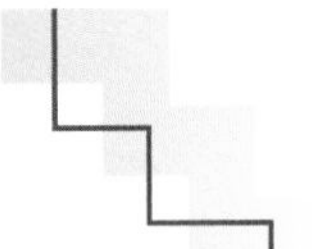

MISSTEP

Your teammate gets nailed by a back pick, you step out to help, and the picker you are guarding pops out for a quick catch and shoot play.

CORRECTION

Alert your teammate who is being screened as soon as possible by calling out "Back pick!" Body up on the picker and then recover quickly to prevent a catch and shoot play by the picker. Your teammate guarding the passer must pressure the passer to prevent a lob to the cutter and an easy reverse pass back to the picker on a pop-out.

DEFENDING A CROSS SCREEN

To defend a cross screen in the low-post area of the lane, you and your teammates must be able to communicate and help each other. Four players are directly involved in the screen, two offensive players (the player setting the cross screen and the cutter) and their two defenders. When players of equal size are involved, the defender on the screener calls "Switch!" Both defenders should stay on the high side of their opponents, and they should switch and deny. When players are not the same size, a basic high-high technique is a good method to use. When you are the defender on the opponent who is setting the cross screen, you should alert the defender being screened by calling out "Screen!" Get on the high side of the screener, be in position to help your teammate defending the cut (by bumping the cutter), and then recover quickly to prevent a quick pass to the screener stepping up in the lane.

When you are defending the cutter, get up on the high side of the cutter's body on the ball side and stay with the cutter as the cutter goes over or under the pick. When you get screened, you must be physical and keep going to get your body to the ball side of the cutter between the ball and your player. Your teammate defending the passer must pressure the passer to prevent a pass to the cutter or the screener. The cross screen can be defended in other ways, but you should master this basic high-high technique first before learning other methods.

As shown in figure 12.21, offensive player 2 sets a cross screen for player 5. Defender X2 calls "Screen!" and then gets on the high side of the screener, helping the teammate defending the cut by bumping the cutter; defender X2 then recovers to prevent a quick pass to the screener. Defender X5 gets up on the ball side of cutter 5's body and stays with her on the cut by the screen. Teammate X1 pressures the passer to prevent a pass to cutter 5 and an easy pass to screener 2 stepping up in the lane.

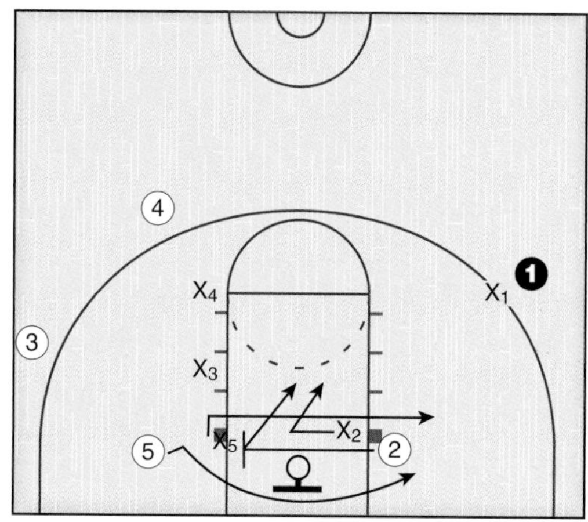

Figure 12.21 Defending a cross screen.

MISSTEP

Your teammate gets picked off with a cross screen set by the player you are guarding.

CORRECTION

Alert your teammate who is being screened as soon as possible by calling out "Screen!" Get to the high side of the screener and give help to your teammate defending the cut by bumping the cutter; then recover quickly to prevent a step-up catch in the lane by the screener. Your teammate guarding the passer must pressure the passer to prevent a pass to the cutter or screener.

DEFENSIVE ROTATIONS

Defensive rotation means that when a team member leaves an assigned opponent to defend another player, teammates must rotate defensive positions to cover the player left open. Rotations may involve all five defenders. All defensive players must play as a team and communicate well. Communication is helped by calling out key words or phrases such as *Switch!, I've got the ball!, I've got the post!, I'm back!,* and *I'm up!*

Imagine that your team traps the ball either away from the basket or in the low post. One of your teammates gets beat on a penetrating drive or a cut to an open area. When your team traps the ball, the defenders off the ball should rotate toward the ball to cover the immediate receivers. As the defenders rotate, the defender farthest from the ball should split the distance and guard the two offensive players farthest from the ball. As shown in figure 12.22 on page 344, defender X2 leaves player 2 to trap player 1. The weak-side defender (X4) rotates up to deny the pass to the weak-side guard (2). The farthest defender (X5) covers the two farthest offensive players (4 and 5).

When one of your teammates gets beat by a driver or backdoor cutter, your teammates should rotate defensive positions closer to the ball. The nearest defender, either on the low post or weak-side wing, rotates to the player with the ball. The defender on the weak-side guard drops back to cover the basket, and the defenders on the high

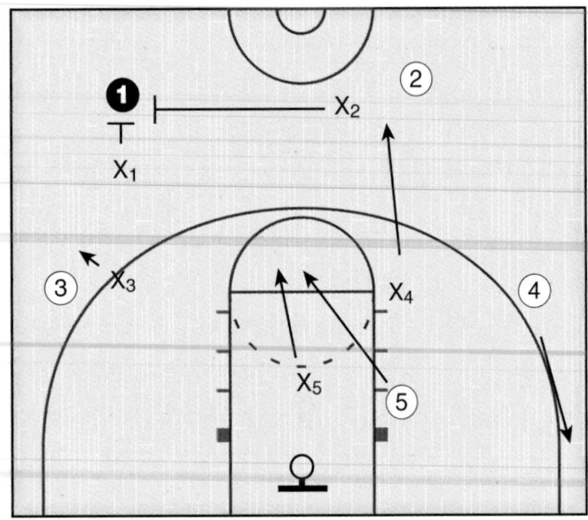

Figure 12.22 Rotating up on a guard-to-guard trap.

Figure 12.23 Rotating back to cover a baseline drive.

post and ball-side guard drop into the lane. As shown in figure 12.23, wing 3 beats defender X3 on a baseline drive. Defender X4 rotates to help and switches to wing 3, and X2 rotates down to cover for teammate X4. Defender X3 can trap with X4 or rotate to the weak side, looking to pick up first player 4, then player 2. X1 and X5 drop back into the lane.

MISSTEP

When you leave an assigned opponent to defend another player, your teammates, unaware of what you are doing, fail to rotate defensive positions to cover the player you left open.

CORRECTION

You must communicate to your teammates what you are doing. Reacting to any defensive situation, particularly one involving a defensive rotation, requires that all defensive players work as a team and communicate by using key phrases.

MISSTEP

You leave an assigned opponent near the basket to defend another player, but your teammates do not have time to rotate defensive positions to cover the player you left open, resulting in a pass to your opponent for an easy basket.

CORRECTION

Use judgment and a defensive fake (i.e., a fake toward the opponent you will be rotating to) before leaving an opponent near the basket to pick up an open player. This will give your teammates time to rotate to the player you are leaving.

Defensive Shell Drill. **Defensive Positioning**

This drill gives you practice in defensive positioning on the ball as well as defensive help-and-recover positioning for defending the ball-side and weak-side guard and forward. The drill requires eight players, four on offense and four on defense.

The four offensive players start with two guards at the top of the circle and two forwards at the wing positions. Each defender takes the correct defensive position. One of the offensive players is selected as the point guard or leader who will give commands. On the "In!" command, the guard passes the ball to the ball-side wing. On the "Out!" command, the ball is passed back out from the wing to the ball-side guard. On the "Over!" command, the ball is passed from guard to guard. In this drill, the players pass the ball around the perimeter (shell) for six passes: in, out, over, in, out, over. Check defensive positioning after each pass.

Each defender moves on each pass, adjusting defensive positioning. If the opponent you are guarding passes the ball, you must move off in the direction of the pass. The call for this move is "Jump to the ball!" By jumping to the ball, you get in position to defend a cut by your opponent and to give help on the ball.

Allow each defensive player to play for six passes at each of the four defensive positions. The defense then goes to offense, and the offense goes to defense.

Success Check

- On defense, try to make a correct change of defensive positioning on each of the 24 passes.
- Jump to the ball if the player you are defending passes the ball.

Score Your Success

20 to 24 correct defensive positioning changes = 5 points

15 to 19 correct defensive positioning changes = 3 points

10 to 14 correct defensive positioning changes = 1 point

Fewer than 10 correct defensive positioning changes = 0 points

Your score ___

Defensive Shell Drill. **Help and Recover**

This drill is similar to the defensive positioning drill except that each offensive player with the ball is allowed one penetrating dribble. Defenders get practice in defensive help and recover. This is also a good offensive drill. Offensive players work on establishing triple-threat position and being able to penetrate and pass (draw and kick). Eight players form two teams of four players each. One team is on offense, and the other is on defense.

The four offensive players start with two guards at the top of the circle and two forwards at the wing positions. Each defender takes the correct defensive position. Any offensive player with the ball is allowed one penetrating dribble. The defender nearest the ball moves to help stop penetration. Once the penetrating dribble is stopped, the penetrator passes the ball out to whichever player the help defender has left. After giving help to stop penetration, the defender recovers to his original opponent. The offensive player receiving the pass should be a triple threat to shoot, pass, or drive.

The offensive team gets 1 point each time it scores. If the defense commits a foul, the offense gets the ball and starts again. If an offensive player misses a shot and a teammate gets an offensive rebound, play continues. The defense gets a point when it gets the ball on a steal or rebound or when it forces the offense into a violation. Play to 5 points, and then switch roles.

Success Check

- On the dribble, move to stop penetration.
- After stopping the penetration, recover to your original assigned player.
- On offense, be a triple threat to shoot, pass, or drive.

Score Your Success

This is a competitive drill. As a team, try to score more points than your opponent, playing each game to 5 points. The goal is to win more games than your opponent. Give yourself 5 points if your team wins the most games.

Your score ___

Defensive Shell Drill. **Defend the Cutter**

This drill is similar to the other shell drills except that the offensive players are allowed unlimited dribbling and may make cuts to the basket. In this drill, the offensive players get practice in making a front cut, backdoor cut, or flash cut. Start with two teams of four players each, one team on offense and the other on defense. For the offensive team, two guards are at the top of the circle, and two forwards are at the wing positions.

Cutting will be allowed from only one position. Start the drill allowing cuts by only the ball-side guard. Next allow cuts by only the weak-side guard. Next allow cuts by only the strong-side wing, and then allow cuts by only the weak-side wing. After cutting to the basket, the cutter moves to an open weak-side position. Each of the offensive players may rotate to the designated position for cutting, so you will have practice in defending a cut by the ball-side guard, weak-side guard, strong-side wing, and weak-side wing.

To defend a cutter, you should be in position off the cutter and toward the ball. Do not allow the cutter to move between you and the ball. Be ready to withstand any contact that may occur as you prevent the cutter from going between you and the ball. If the cutter approaches the lane area, you should bump the cutter using the bump-and-release technique, staying between the cutter and the ball. If your opponent makes a backdoor cut to the basket, maintain a closed stance as you move on the ball side of the cutter, opening to the ball as the pass is thrown. Use your lead hand to knock away a pass.

The offensive team gets 1 point each time it scores. If the defense commits a foul, the offense gets the ball and starts again. If an offensive player misses a shot and a teammate gets an offensive rebound, play continues. The defense gets 1 point when it gets the ball on a steal or rebound or when it forces the offense into a violation. Play to 5 points, and then switch roles (the defensive team moves to offense and vice versa).

Success Check

- Do not allow the cutter to go between you and the ball.
- Be ready for contact.

Score Your Success

This is a competitive drill. As a team, try to score more points than your opponent, playing each game to 5 points. The goal is to win more games than your opponent. Give yourself 5 points if your team wins the most games.

Your score ___

Defensive Shell Drill. **Defensive Rotation**

Start with two teams of four players each, with one team on offense and the other on defense. For the offensive team, two guards are at the top of the circle, and two forwards are at the wing positions. Start the drill with a baseline drive or backdoor cut by an offensive wing, giving the defensive team practice in rotating positions. After allowing one of the defensive wings to get beat by a drive or backdoor cut, the drill becomes live. The offense attempts to score, and the defense tries to prevent a score by attacking the player with the ball and rotating defensive positions. The defender on the weak-side wing yells "Switch!" before attacking the player with the ball, who is driving or cutting. The defender on the weak-side guard drops back to cover the weak-side wing, and the defender on the ball-side guard drops back into the lane and covers the weak-side guard. The wing who gets beat retreats to the basket, looking to recover to the originally guarded player. Seeing a good rotation, the wing will pick up the open player, the ball-side guard.

When defensive players rotate, they must all play as a team and communicate well, calling out key words or phrases such as *Switch!, I've got the ball!, I've got the post!, I'm back!,* and *I'm up!* The offensive team gets 1 point each time it scores. If the defense commits a foul, the offense gets the ball and starts again. If an offensive player misses a shot and a teammate gets an offensive rebound, play continues. The defense gets 1 point when it gets the ball on a steal or rebound or when it forces the offense into a violation. Play to 5 points, and then switch roles (the defensive team moves to offense and vice versa).

Success Check

- On defense, communicate verbally with teammates by using key words and phrases.
- React to the offense as a team.

Score Your Success

This is a competitive drill. As a team, try to score more points than your opponent, playing each game to 5 points. The goal is to win more games than your opponent. Give yourself 5 points if your team wins the most games.

Your score ___

ZONE DEFENSE

When you play zone defense, you are assigned to a designated area of the court, or zone, rather than to an individual opponent. Your zone position changes with each move of the ball. Zones may be adjusted from sagging inside to pressuring outside shots, overplaying passing lanes, and trapping the ball. Zone defenses are named according to the alignment of players from the top toward the basket. These defenses include the 3-2, 2-3, 2-1-2, 1-2-2, and 1-3-1 zones.

Each zone defense has strengths and weaknesses. The 3-2 and 1-2-2 zones are strong against outside shooting but are vulnerable inside and in the corners. The 2-1-2 and 2-3 zones are strong inside and in the corners but are susceptible on the top and wings. The 1-3-1 protects the high post and the wing areas, but it can leave openings at the blocks and corners and is also susceptible to good offensive rebounding.

Here are some good reasons for using a zone defense:

- A zone defense protects the inside against a team with good drivers and post-up players and poor outside shooters.
- A zone defense is more effective against screening and cutting.
- Defenders can be positioned in areas according to size and defensive skill. Taller players can be assigned to inside areas for shot blocking and rebounding, whereas smaller, quicker players can be assigned to outside areas for pressuring the ball and covering passing lanes.
- Players are in a better position to start the fast break.
- Zone defenses are easier to learn and may overcome weaknesses in individual defensive fundamentals.
- A zone defense protects players who are in foul trouble.
- Changing to a zone may disrupt an opponent's rhythm.

Zone defenses also have some weaknesses:

- Zone defenses are vulnerable to good outside shooting, especially three-point shooting, which can stretch the zone, creating openings inside.
- A fast break can beat the zone downcourt before the defenders get set up, because it takes time for players to get in their assigned zones.
- Quick passing can move the ball quicker than zone defenders can shift.
- A zone defense is weak against penetration (draw-and-kick).
- The opposing team may stall more easily against a zone, causing you to change to individual defense if you are behind late in a game.
- Playing zone defense does not develop individual defensive skills.

3-2 Zone Defense

Let's start with the 3-2 zone defense. The names of the defenders in a 3-2 zone, their starting alignments, and their responsibilities follow.

Ball at Top

When the ball is at the top of the key (figure 12.24), the point is positioned inside the top of the circle, covering the area from elbow to elbow. Two wings, each with her inside foot on the elbow, cover the area from the elbow to the foul line extended. Finally, the deeps straddle the lane lines above the blocks, covering the area from inside the foul line to the corner.

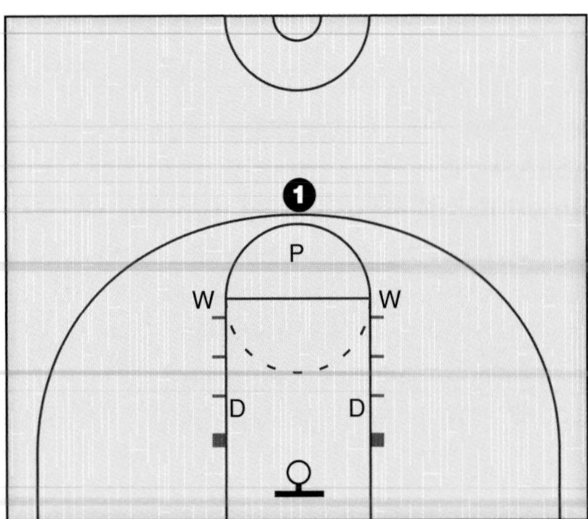

Figure 12.24 The 3-2 zone: ball at top.

Ball on Wing

The responsibilities for the defenders change with each move of the ball. When the ball is on the wing (figure 12.25), the strong-side (ball-side) wing defends the player with the ball. The point drops back to the strong-side elbow and places the hand closest to the basket in front of the high post. The strong-side deep player plays halfway between the low-post player and the corner player. The weak-side wing drops back below the level of the ball and directs the defense. The weak-side deep player slides to the middle and denies the pass to the low-post player with a hand in front of the player.

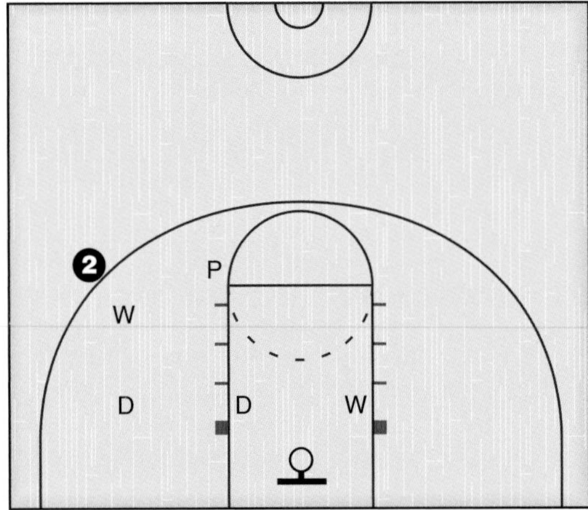

Figure 12.25 The 3-2 zone: ball on wing.

Ball in Corner

When the ball is in the corner (figure 12.26), the strong-side deep player defends the player with the ball. The weak-side deep player fronts and denies the pass to the low-post player. The point fronts and denies the pass to the high post and blocks out the high-post player on a shot. The strong-side wing plays the passing lane to the wing, forcing a lob pass to the wing, and helps on a drive to the middle. The weak-side wing drops back to the weak-side block and is responsible for a weak-side rebound.

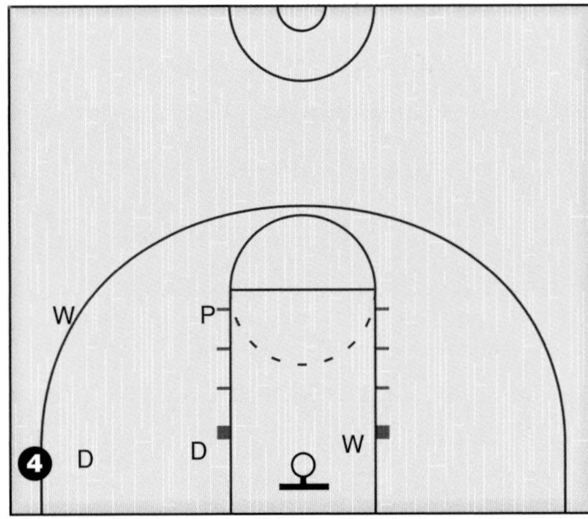

Figure 12.26 The 3-2 zone: ball in corner.

Ball at High Post

When the ball is at the high post (figure 12.27), the weak-side deep player yells "Up!" and defends the player with the ball. The strong-side deep player slides to the basket area, getting in position to cover a pass to the low post. The wings drop back to cover passes to the baseline area and are responsible for rebounds in the block area. The point traps the high post.

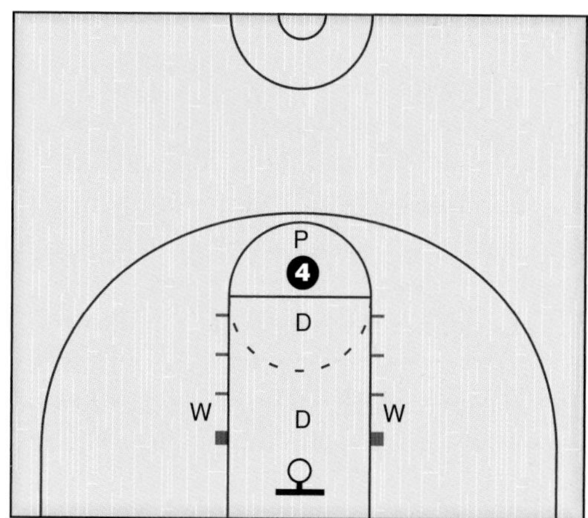

Figure 12.27 The 3-2 zone: ball at high post.

Ball in Low Post

When the ball is in the low post (figure 12.28), the weak-side deep player defends the low-post player with the ball. The strong-side deep player drops back and covers a pass to the baseline area. The strong-side wing drops to the level of the ball and covers the first pass out to the strong side. The weak-side wing drops back to the weak-side block and is responsible for any weak-side cutters. The point covers a pass to the opposite elbow area.

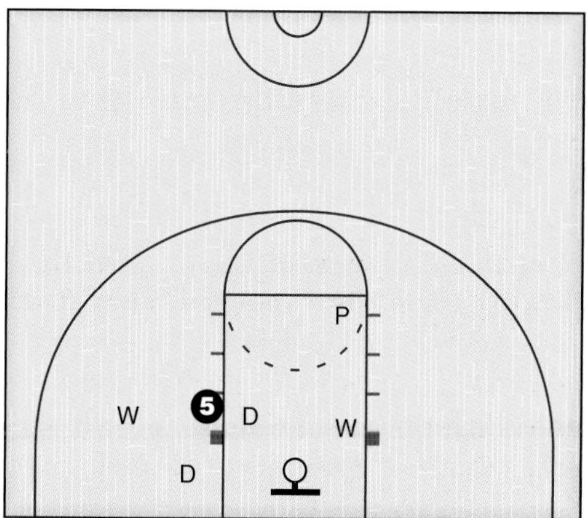

Figure 12.28 The 3-2 zone: ball in low post.

2-3 Zone Defense

The names of the defenders in a 2-3 zone, their starting alignments, and their responsibilities are as follows:

Ball at Top

When the ball is at the top of the key (figure 12.29), one guard takes the ball, and the other guard drops to a position just above the middle of the foul line, covering the area from the middle to the wing area.

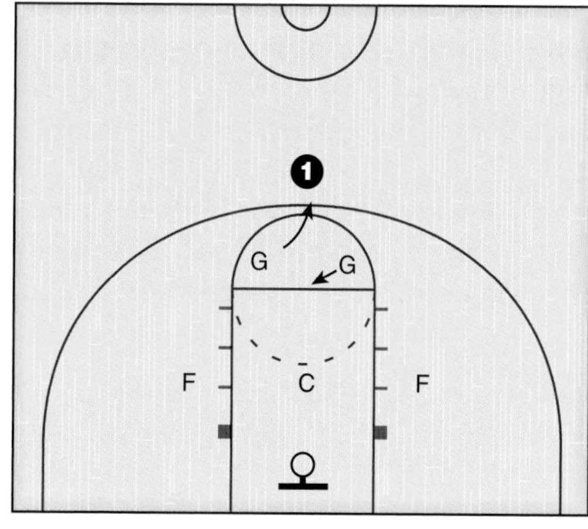

Figure 12.29 The 2-3 zone: ball at top.

Ball on Wing

The responsibilities for the defenders change with each move of the ball. When the ball is on the wing (figure 12.30), the strong-side (ball-side) guard at the elbow pauses there before defending the wing player. The guard at the top drops back to the middle of the foul line. The strong-side forward uses a bump move (fakes at the wing until the strong-side guard gets to the wing), then drops back between the low-post player and the corner player. The center covers the strong-side low-post area. The weak-side forward slides toward the middle of the lane and directs the defense.

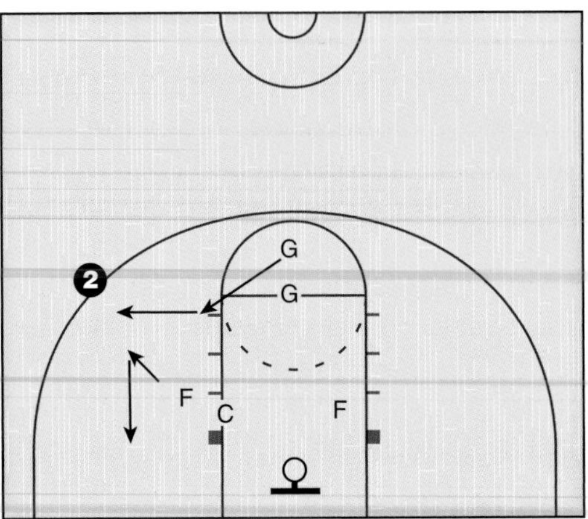

Figure 12.30 The 2-3 zone: ball on wing, bump move.

Ball in Corner

When the ball is in the corner (figure 12.31), the strong-side forward defends the player with the ball. The center fronts and denies the pass to the low-post player. The weak-side forward drops back to the weak-side low-post area—but must be alert to cover a pass to the high post—and blocks out the high-post player on a shot. The strong-side guard drops back and helps on a pass to the low post. The weak-side guard moves inside the foul line and covers a diagonal pass out of the corner.

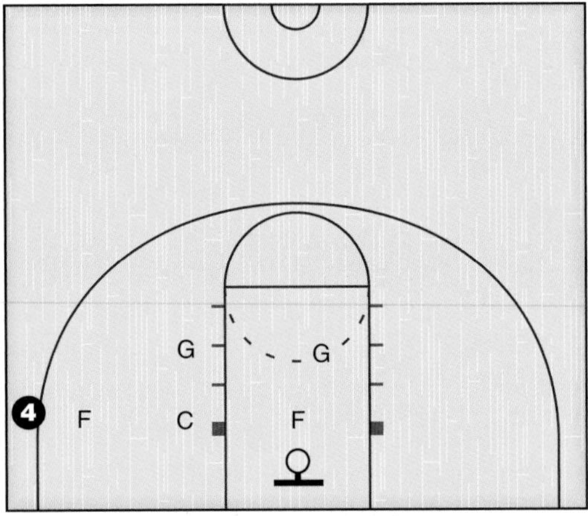

Figure 12.31 The 2-3 zone: ball in corner.

Ball at High Post

When the ball is at the high post (figure 12.32), the center defends the high-post player with the ball. The forwards cover the block areas on their sides. The guards cover the elbow areas on their sides.

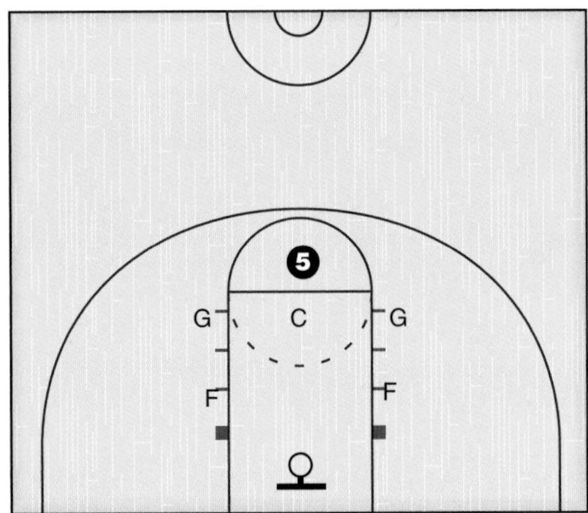

Figure 12.32 The 2-3 zone: ball at high post.

Ball in Low Post

When the ball is in the low post (figure 12.33), the center defends the low-post player with the ball. The strong-side forward drops back and covers a pass to the baseline area. The weak-side forward covers a pass to the middle of the lane and is responsible for a weak-side rebound. The strong-side guard drops back to halfway between the low post and the strong-side wing. The weak-side guard moves inside the foul line and covers a diagonal pass.

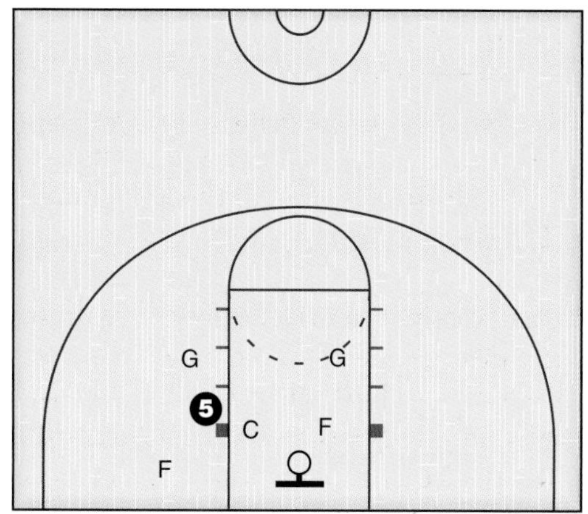

Figure 12.33 The 2-3 zone: ball in low post.

Matchup Zone

Any of the zone defenses can be adjusted to a matchup zone. A matchup zone enables you to match up and defend an individual opponent in your zone area. If no one is in your area, you should drop back toward the basket and middle, looking for someone flashing into your area from behind. The matchup zone is particularly effective against an offense that does not use much movement.

COMBINATION DEFENSE

In a combination defense, one or two players are assigned to specific individual opponents—for example, an outstanding shooter or ball handler—and the other players are deployed in zone areas. Combination defenses are special-situation defenses, not primary defenses. Among the most common combination defenses are the box-and-one, diamond-and-one, and triangle-and-two.

In the box-and-one, one player is assigned to deny the ball to the opponent's best scorer, shooter, or ball handler while the other four players set up in a 2-2 zone or box formation.

The diamond-and-one is similar to the box-and-one in that one player is assigned to deny the ball to the opponent's best scorer, shooter, or ball handler; however, the other four players are set up in a 1-2-1 zone or diamond alignment.

In the triangle-and-two, two players are assigned to individually defend two specific opponents while three defenders are set up in a 1-2 zone or triangle inside the free-throw line.

RATE YOUR SUCCESS

Working as a team on defense is vital if your team is to stop the opponent and regain control of the ball. Remember, only the team in possession of the ball can score. Thus, regaining possession from the offense is crucial to your team's scoring success.

For this final step, look back at how you performed the drills. For each of the drills presented in this step, enter the points you earned, then add up your scores to rate your total success.

Defense off the Ball Drills

1. Wing Denial ____ out of 5
2. Weak-Side Help and Recover ____ out of 5

Defending the Low Post Drill

1. Low-Post Denial ____ out of 5

Defending the Flash Drills

1. Deny the Flash and Deny the Backdoor Cut ____ out of 5
2. Six Points ____ out of 6

Defensive Shell Drills

1. Defensive Positioning ____ out of 5
2. Help and Recover ____ out of 5
3. Defend the Cutter ____ out of 5
4. Defensive Rotation ____ out of 5

Total ____ out of 46

If you scored 25 or more points, congratulations! You have mastered the basics of this step. If you scored fewer than 25 points, you may want to spend more time on the fundamentals covered in this step. Practice the drills again to develop mastery of the techniques and increase your scores.

About the Author

Dr. Hal Wissel has a wealth of experience in the National Basketball Association (NBA) as an assistant coach with the Atlanta Hawks, Golden State Warriors, Memphis Grizzlies, and New Jersey Nets. Hal was also director of player personnel with the Nets and scout and special assignment coach with the Milwaukee Bucks.

As a collegiate head coach, Wissel compiled more than 300 wins. He turned losing programs at Trenton State College and Lafayette College into conference and division champions respectively. Wissel led Florida Southern College to four straight trips to the NCAA Division II tournament and three straight trips to the Division II final four ('80, '81, and '82), winning the Division II national championship in 1981. Wissel coached Fordham University into the 1972 NIT tournament and also coached the Dominican Republic national team in 1975.

Wissel founded Basketball World and CoachWissel.com, instructional ventures featuring basketball camps, clinics, books, and DVDs. Basketball World's highly successful Shoot It Better Mini Camps are conducted worldwide for players from youth level to NBA and WNBA level.

Wissel received a bachelor's degree from Springfield College, a master's degree from Indiana University, and a doctorate in physical education from Springfield College. Wissel's best-selling book *Basketball: Steps to Success* has been translated into 11 languages. Wissel is also the author of *Becoming a Basketball Player: Individual Drills,* which has been made into a DVD. Wissel has also produced five basketball shooting DVDs.

Wissel's honors include being named *Coach & Athlete* magazine's Eastern Coach of the Year in 1972; Sunshine State Conference Coach of the Year ('79, '80, and '81); and Division II National Coach of the Year by the National Association of Basketball Coaches in 1980. Wissel has been inducted into the Florida Southern College Athletic Hall of Fame, the Sunshine State Conference Hall of Fame, and the New England Basketball Hall of Fame.

Hal and his wife, Trudy, reside in Suffield, Connecticut, and have five grown children and one granddaughter.

STEPS TO SUCCESS SPORTS SERIES

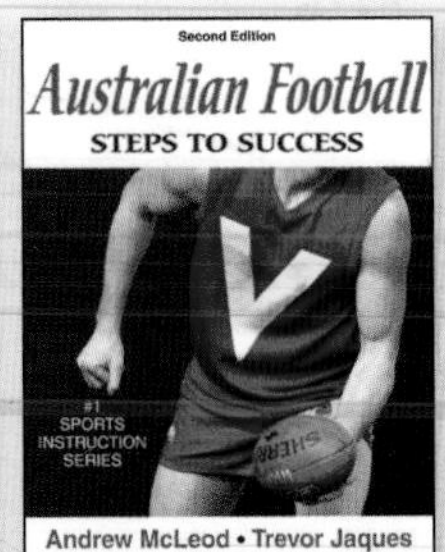

The *Steps to Success Sports Series* is the most extensively researched and carefully developed set of books ever published for teaching and learning sports skills.

Each of the books offers a complete progression of skills, concepts, and strategies that are carefully sequenced to optimize learning for students, teaching for sport-specific instructors, and instructional program design techniques for future teachers.

The *Steps to Success Sports Series* includes:

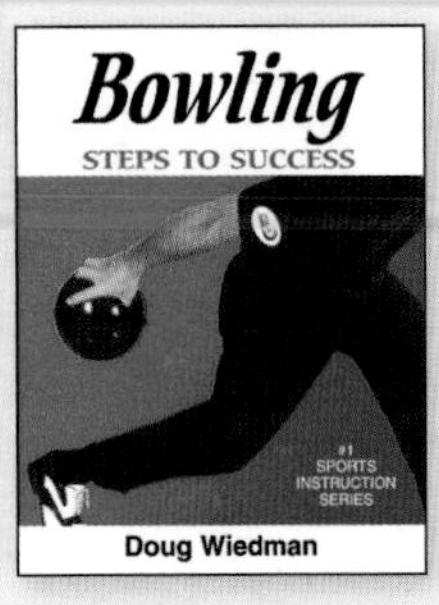

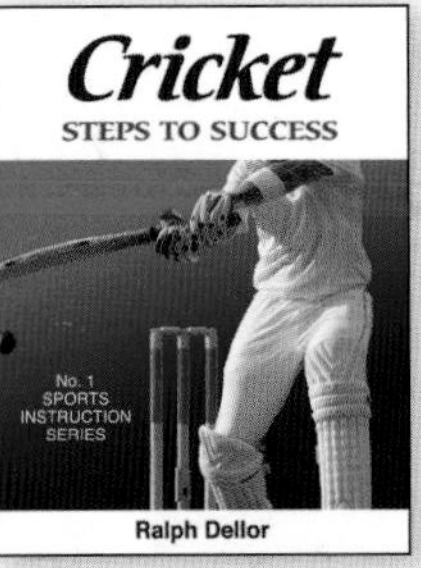

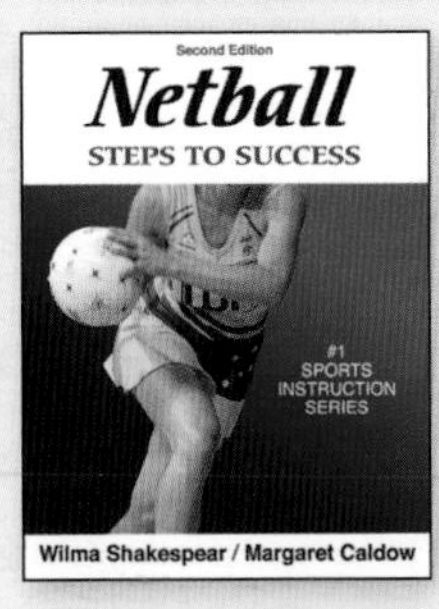

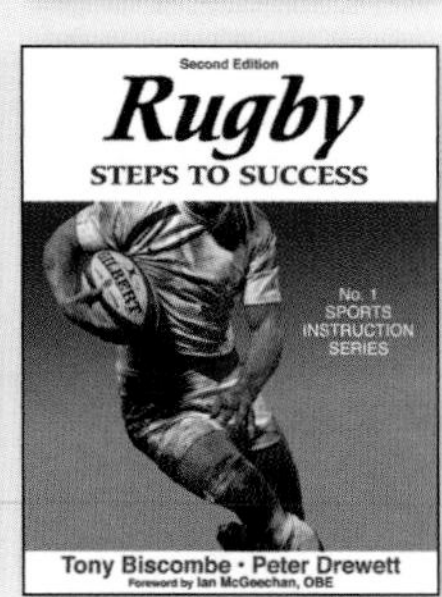

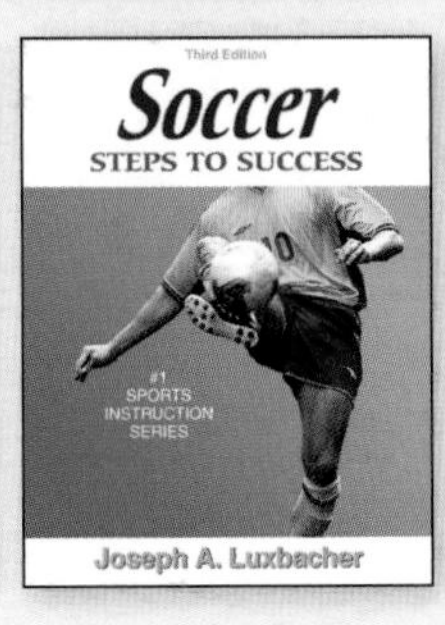

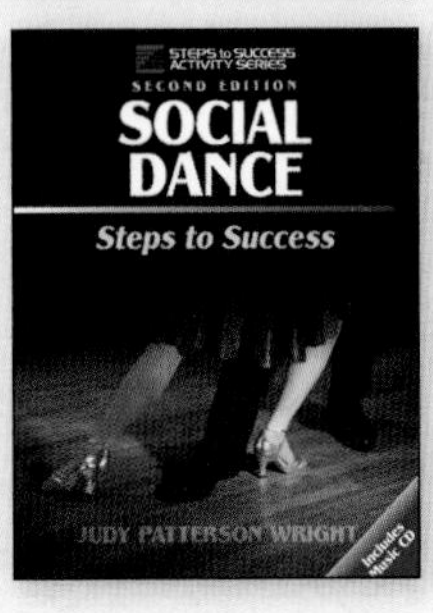

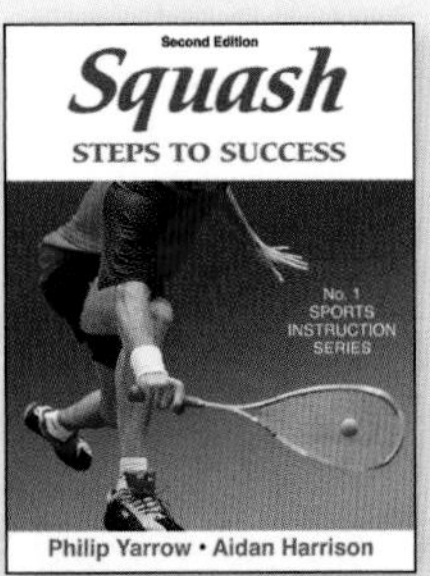

Table Tennis
STEPS TO SUCCESS
Richard McAfee

To place your order, U.S. customers call
TOLL FREE **1-800-747-4457**
In Canada call 1-800-465-7301
In Australia call 08 8372 0999
In Europe call +44 (0) 113 255 5665
In New Zealand call 0800 222 062
or visit **www.HumanKinetics.com/StepstoSuccess**

Volleyball
STEPS TO SUCCESS
Cindy Gregory

HUMAN KINETICS
The Premier Publisher for Sports & Fitness
P.O. Box 5076, Champaign, IL 61825-5076